Aging and The Human Spirit

A Reader in Religion and Gerontology

The Last of Life
For Which the First Was Promise

GRACIOUSNESS
>> freely inbreathing
>>> the liberty of Spirit

LIFE'S MATURING
>> rhythm-
>>> rhyming

LOVELINESS - WITHOUT - FALTER
>> space - walking
>>> with Truth.

>>>>> Ross Snyder

Aging and The Human Spirit

A Reader in Religion and Gerontology

Edited by

Carol LeFevre

and

Perry LeFevre

Exploration Press, Chicago

Dedicated to Faye LeFevre
in her 91st year of spirited aging

Exploration Press
Chicago Theological Seminary
5757 University Avenue
Chicago, Illinois 60637

ISBN: Cloth: 0-913552 -16-X-
      Paper: 0-913552 -17-8-

Library of Congress Catalog Card Number: 80-70859

Contents

Introduction

The rising interest in the study of aging and in the practical problems associated with the increasing number of elderly in American society have focused the attention both inside and outside the churches and synagogues on the relationship between religion and gerontology. Many within the religious institutions have been concerned to explore the intellectual and practical resources available in the faith communities for addressing issues related to aging. Publications have increased, local and national religious groups have organized meetings, conferences, and workshops. A National Interfaith Coalition on Aging has been formed. Efforts to expand training opportunities for the religious professional have taken root.

While the interest in gerontological issues has been rising in the religious community, the interest in religion among gerontologists appears to be declining. Though earlier social scientists gave some attention to the relation of religion to the aging process, much of the contemporary literature neglects the topic. The 1961 and 1971 White House Conferences on Aging gave significant recognition in their structure and organization to religion, but the legislation authorizing the 1981 conference made no provision for the inclusion of religious concerns. Yet the picture is not one of total neglect. There is in the gerontological literature material which takes the religious participation and the religious beliefs of the elderly as an important topic for exploration. More recently, Sheldon Tobin and some of his colleagues at the University of Chicago's School of Social Service Administration have begun a project studying the church as a service provider for the elderly.

The editors of this reader believe that the time has come to focus new attention on the relation of religion to gerontology and of gerontology to the concerns of religious institutions and religious professionals. There are resources in the gerontological literature and the social scientific perspective that can help those in religious institutions to think more critically and to serve more creatively in their work with the elderly. It may be too that the gerontologists have something to gain through broadening and deepening their own perspectives. Perhaps their understandings of religion have been too narrow or too superficial, or their fundamental images of the aging process too constricted.

Thus we think the time has come to retrieve some of the best writing on religion and gerontology and make it available to clergy, laity and other students of aging. Some of this material is unknown or not easily accessible to the clergy on the one hand or to the gerontological community on the other. We hope also to stimulate the thinking of both groups about the resources available in religion and religious institutions for responding to the needs of the elderly. It is our desire to deepen and arouse concern for creative thinking and action in the field of aging at both the levels of practice and of theoretical understanding. Finally it is our hope that we can focus the attention of both gerontologists and religious leaders on the need for new kinds of research and experiment in the field of aging.

It is our conviction that the churches and the synagogues are a major social resource for meeting certain of the needs of the aging in American society. The underlying testimony of our religious traditions that aging itself need not be experienced only as diminution and loss, but that it can be a time for the positive actualization of human spirit can contribute a needed corrective to both popular understanding and to some of the guiding images used in gerontology.

1

Bearing in mind the multiple purposes of this collection of papers, we have selected materials of various kinds. Some are academic papers, others are relatively popular accounts of institutional programming. There are social scientific studies, theological reflections on issues of meaning and value, and papers on the professional concerns of ministry.

Running through the whole text are two basic concerns. First we hope that gerontological studies might come to include issues of meaning and value and that gerontology might increasingly be informed by an image of the aging process which is both humanistic and humane. Second, we wish that the religiously and ethically motivated concerns for the elderly might be continually strengthened and made more critical and effective by bringing disciplined scientific study to the service of the religious communities. It is our desire to foster creative communication between the fields of religion and of gerontology.

I

Aging in the Western Religious Tradition

Historians have given little attention to the relation of religion and aging in western culture. Until recently they have given little attention to aging in any of its aspects. There is as yet no work comparable to Philippe Aries ' classic *Centuries of Childhood*. Recent works such as W. Andrew Achenbaum's *Old Age in the New Land*, D. H. Fischer's *Growing Old in America*, and Peter N. Stearn's *Old Age in European Society* are beginning to fill in the gap. These works, however, offer few clues about the relation of religion and aging. Much more needs to be done if we are to understand the way in which religious ideas and institutions have affected social attitudes toward aging, or the self-understanding of the aged, or the actual treatment of the old.

The two papers with which this reader begins offer sketches of the traditions of Judaism and Christianity in relation to the aged. In both the biblical sources and in post-biblical traditions there is an ambivalence about aging. There are, however, clear grounds for honoring, respecting and caring for the elderly. In the emphases on family values and the worth and dignity of the individual person as well as on the shared responsibility for social justice there are resources for thinking constructively about the responsibility of religious institutions and about society's accountability for the well-being of the increasing numbers of older citizens.

As the papers by Rabbi Blech and Father Knapp make clear, the religious response to the phenomenon of aging is deeply conditioned by existing cultural attitudes in every period of history. How much our contemporary concern for the aging in our midst is simply a response to changing conditions such as the changing family structure and the increasing number of aged in the population, and how much it is the result of an increased sensitivity to issues of care and justice derived from our religious and ethical traditions, cannot be finally assessed. In any case new occasions teach new duties and we will see in the material which follows in this reader that some important beginnings have been made in relating the religious tradition in the west to the problems of the aging in contemporary society.

Benjamin Blech

Rabbi Blech is the Spiritual Leader of the Young
Israel of Oceanside and teaches at the James Striar
School of Jewish Studies at Yeshiva University. This
essay was presented at the Interdisciplinary Confer-
ence on Gerontology held at Stern College in
November, 1975.

JUDAISM AND GERONTOLOGY

I

A personal experience clearly conveyed to me the tremendous
difference in attitude to the aged between Biblical ideal and contemporary reality. A former congregant, now confined to a
nursing home, turned to me with what he said was a deeply
perplexing religious question. "Rabbi," he wondered, "Why does
the Torah state a curse as the reward for fulfilling a *Mitzvah?*"
When he realized from my puzzled look that I had failed to
grasp his meaning, he sighed and rephrased his paradoxical question: "Why does God punish those who keep His commandments
by promising to make them old?"

What the Bible believed to be a blessing has indeed, for all
too many, turned into a curse. A tragic paradox of progress is
that as we succeed in lengthening the life span, society simultaneously alters its attitudes toward the elderly to such a degree
that death is often a preferable alternative. How poignant is the
title of a recent book on gerontology: *Why Survive?* It is a question posed by millions of elderly people who are kept alive by
miracle drugs while daily suffering from callous mistreatment
and indifference.

When the Bible summarizes the definitive trait of a barbaric
culture, it describes "A nation of fierce countenance, that shall
not regard the person of the old" (Deuteronomy 28:46). It is
by this standard, too, that we must engage in self-judgment—
and unfortunately we find ourselves wanting. Saul Bellow may
have overstated the case somewhat when he equated modern

treatment of the old with "a kind of totalitarian cruelty like Hitler's attitude towards Jews." But there is undeniable truth in his recognition of societal prejudice against those we have, with verbal camouflage, cast out of our concern via the euphemism "senior citizens."

Sociologists have coined a new name for our phenomenon: "ageism." It is a far broader and more contemporary concept than gerontophobia,[1] the classic fear of old age. "Gerontophobia," as Palmore points out, refers to "an unreasonable fear and/or irrational hatred of older people," whereas ageism has reference to a "deep and profound prejudice against the elderly which is found to some degree in all of us."[2]

"Ageism" is rapidly being recognized as a problem as serious as racism with one major difference: While we will never change color, all of us will hopefully grow old and become a part of the aged. How ironic, and to our sages not without significance, that the source text which promises length of days as reward is the Fifth Commandment:

> Honor Thy Father and Thy Mother, that thy days may be long upon the land which the Lord thy God giveth thee.

The second clause depends on the first not only for its fulfillment but its very definition. A society which honors its aged will, measure for measure, enjoy the blessing of longevity. Conversely, as my congregant so clearly understood, a culture which practices "ageism" finds that it in turn becomes the victim of its own ideology, suffering the curse of an undesirable life extension.

To be concerned with gerontology is to be pragmatically selfish. It is to insure our own future against the hostility of the generation which follows. It is to protect ourselves from the kind of reality which Edith Stern movingly describes:[3]

> Unlike some primitive tribes, we do not kill off our aged and infirm. We bury them alive in institutions. To save our face, we call the institutions homes — a travesty on the word. I have seen dozens of such homes in the last six months — desolate places peopled with blanked faced men and women, one home so like the other that each visit seemed a recurrent nightmare.

We have not come too far, after all, from the compassionless barbarians who dragged their unproductive old to their death on the mountain tops.

From the Biblical approach to gerontology, we may discover principles which make meaningful our religious striving for life; perspectives to ease our transition from middle age to senescence and to cushion the pain of physical decline and infirmity; precepts and prescriptions to give meaning to Browning's hope-filled lines in "Rabbi ben Ezra":

> Grow old along with me, the best is yet to be, the last of life for which the first was made.

II

Leviticus (19:32), in a text dealing with our special responsibility to the elderly, states:

> Thou shalt rise up before the hoary head, and honor the face of the old man, and thou shalt fear thy God: I am the Lord.

For one Talmudic teacher, the command is synonymous with respect for wisdom:

> You shall rise before the gray head. I might think that this includes even an old man who is an ignoramus. This is not so, for the verse continues with the words, "And ye shall honor the presence of the *zaken*, elder," and elder refers *exclusively* to a wise man as it is written "Gather unto me seventy men from among the elders of Israel" (*Kiddushin* 32b).

Age is thus deemed worthy of respect when it is accompanied by signs of wisdom. The simple, in view of this verse, have no Biblical claim to deferential treatment; the senile do not deserve special consideration.

A second Talmudic opinion (*Kiddushin* 32b) takes a different approach:

> Rabbi Yossi, the Galilean, said "Elder" (*zaken*) is only one who has acquired wisdom (independent of whether he has, in addition, years

as well) as it is written, "The Lord make me (*kanani*) as the beginning of His way" (Proverbs 8:22 — a play on the word *kanani,* similar to *zaken*).

In what way does Rabbi Yossi differ from the previous interpretation? Both views take the position that age alone has no claim on our "respect responsibility." The first, however, recognizes the validity of chronology insofar as it must be added to wisdom. Both the aged fool and the young scholar are sufficiently deficient to make them unworthy of this verse's favor. The opinion of the second sage, however, is that intellect *alone* is the sole Biblical criterion of *zaken.* One may be young in years, yet have an "old head on his shoulders"—thereby deserving special respect.

Neither of these Biblical interpretations has been adopted as normative Jewish law. The opinion which the codifiers have unanimously accepted as law is:

> Issi ben Yehudah said, "You shall rise before the gray head" (includes anyone who has attained advanced age—including even an ignoramus).

The criterion is not how much one has learned but simply how long one has lived. The reason is stated succinctly:

> Rabbi Yohanan would rise even before non-Jewish elders because he said, "How many adventures have befallen them"—that is to say how much have they experienced.

Judaism took the legal position that there is a form of wisdom implicit in simple survival; what the school of life teaches is as worthy of respect as books of learning.

III

How do we define our responsibility to the elderly? The first, and perhaps broadest principle, derives from the last phrase of the Biblical source-text concerning the aged quoted earlier. Why, the rabbinic commentators ask, does the verse conclude "I am the Lord?" Because God's greatest fear is that in dealing with the helpless elder, "One may shut his eyes as though he has

7

not seen him" (*Kiddushin* 32b). Therefore man is reminded, "I am the Lord" — who knows not only the deed of the hand but also the neglect of the heart.

One need not search far to recognize the contemporary relevance of this concept. An imaginative Rand Corporation study, entitled "The Post Attack Population of the United States,"[4] suggested methods the United States should initiate for old people, chronic invalids, and the insane in the event of nuclear war. The author, Ira S. Lowry, stated that after a nuclear war policy makers would be presented with a difficult problem because

> The working members of the society would insist on transferring some part of their personal advantages to members of their families who are not directly contributing to output.

The report continues by saying,

> The easiest way to implement a morally repugnant but socially beneficial policy is by *inaction*. Under stress, the managers of post attack society would most likely resolve their problems by failing to make any special provision for the special needs of the elderly, the insane, and the chronically ill. Instead of medicare for persons under sixty-five for example, we might have medicare for persons under fifteen. Instead of pensions, we might have family allowances. To be sure, the government would not be able—nor would it be likely to try—to prevent the relatives and friends of old people from helping them; but overall the share of the elderly in the national product would certainly drop.

"Benign neglect," it seems, also has a non-racial application. The easiest method of dealing with the problem of an unwanted, non-productive segment of society is to disregard it; the simplest way to treat expendables is—not to treat them at all. That is why the Jewish tradition recalls: I am the Lord—who will hold you responsible for what you *do not* do; indifference, from religious perspective, is comparable to inhumane behavior.

What does Judaism demand we do for our elders? The specifics have their source in two other Biblical verses given in context of primary responsibility. The direction of obligations in Jewish law moves from immediate family to successive levels of kin and then geographic proximity. For this reason the major texts defining the nature of responsibility refer to one's own parents.

The fifth of the Ten Commandments reads: "Honor Thy Father and Thy Mother" (Exodus 20:12). *Kabed* is the key word in this commandment. In Leviticus this commandment reads: "Ye shall *revere* every man his mother and his father." *Tira-u* is used instead of *kabed*. Why are different words used? The commentaries answer that each word connotes different legal obligations. The first, *kabed,* honor, requires a child to provide his parents with physical needs: "to give food and drink to clothe and to cover" (*Kiddushin* 31b). *Tira-u,* however, requires a child "not to stand or sit in their place nor to contradict them (*Kiddushin* 31a). The first therefore designates what we today place under the broad heading of "Social Security"; the second is a yet to be realized ideal we might call "Personal Security."

Jewish law is firm in specifying which of these concepts is more important. In a painfully relevant illustration, one rabbi tells us that providing for parents may at times be perverted from *mitzvah* to sin — if performed in such a way that "Social Security" is fulfilled while "Personal Security" is forfeited.

> Abimi, son of Rabbi Abbauhu recited: One may give his father pheasants as food, yet this drives him from the world; whereas another may make him grind in a mill and this brings him to the world to come (*Kiddushin* 31a-b). The son who fed his father expensive pheasants on being asked by his father how he can afford them, answered, "What business is it of yours, old man: Grind and eat."

He metaphorically sent a check to his "old man," paid his bills at the home — but made clear his contempt and lack of regard. The other son was engaged in grinding in a mill when his father was summoned for royal service. The son pleaded,

> Grind please for me, and I will go in your stead. Service is too demeaning and difficult for you.

What the second man's father lacked in cuisine was more than compensated for in self-respect.

This explains the peculiar choice of term for financial obligation of support to parents. *Kabed* does mean honor. When it is used to teach responsibility—to "feed, clothe and cover,"—it is to convey that these acts of physical concern only have meaning when they are performed via "honorable" methods.

How significant in this light is the text already quoted concerning treatment of aged beyond one's family. Support and respect were the two pegs upon which were built Biblical responsibility to parents. Of these two, one was singled out for special emphasis *vis-a-vis* the aged of the world: "Thou shalt rise up before the hoary head, and honor the face of the old man." Ask the sages: What constitutes honor? And the answer is: "One shall not sit in his place nor speak before him nor contradict his words."[5] Not medicare or medicaid but care rooted in concern for sensitivity and personal status is the Torah's major geriatric slogan. Food may keep the aged alive; only respect will make their lives meaningful.

To grasp this fundamental truth is to recognize the basic error underlying most programs and projects for the aged. While agencies speak of care for bodies, the soul goes unheeded, misunderstood and anguished.

To be old is to be heir to the disabilities of age. The author of the Book of Ecclesiastes (Chapter 12) draws a vivid picture of those days

> When the keepers of the house shall tremble, and the strong men shall bow themselves, and the grinders cease because they are few, and those that look out shall be darkened in the windows . . . Before the silver cord is snapped asunder, and the golden bowl is shattered . . . And the dust returneth to the earth as it was and the spirit returneth unto God who gave it.

Even as Judaism took note of age's disabilities, however, it emphasized that there were positive dimensions to life's final stage which might well prove to be far more significant. To identify these is to have a different perspective on a number of problem areas in the field of gerontology.

The Midrash gives a fascinating account of the way in which old age was first introduced into this world. The Bible describing the life of Abraham says, "And Abraham was old, well stricken in age" (Genesis 24:1). Previous to this, no one had been spoken of in this manner. The rabbinic commentators remark:

> Abraham introduced old age to the world. He came before the Lord with a plea. Master of the Universe, a man and his son walk together and no one knows unto whom to give honor. I beg of you, make a distinction between us.[6]

In the traditional view, old age was not a curse but a positive response from God to a human request. It answered a need. How else would people know whom to honor? It is God's gift of a visible badge of identification to those who deserve the honor age ought to inspire.

A parallel to this Midrashic tale is the famous story of Rabbi Eliezer ben Azaryah mentioned in the Passover Hagaddah. "Behold I am as a man of seventy years old" — the rabbi did not say he was seventy, only that he was like a man of those years. According to the Talmud, the rabbi was really a lad of eighteen. At that tender age he was appointed, in recognition of his brilliance, to head the academy. He feared to accept because of his youth. A miracle occurred, and overnight he grew a full beard. Now he was like a man of seventy — and capable of inspiring the necessary reverence in order to serve in his newly designated capacity (*Berakhot* 28a).

In both instances, the manifestations of turning old, rather than presenting a problem, were indicators of increased worth and status. Gray hair was meant not to be camouflaged but to be flaunted as a "crown of glory." Wrinkles were to be viewed as the rewards of experience; the disappearance of youthful visage, the mark of growth and maturity.

That is the way Abraham had hoped it would be. But our modern culture perverted this idea into a mockery. As Lin Yutang, in *The Importance of Living,* points out perceptively:

I have found no differences that are absolute between Eastern and Western life except in the attitude toward age. In China, the first question a person asks the other on an official call is: "What is your glorious age?" If he replies apologetically that he is twenty-three or twenty-eight, the other generally comforts him by saying that he still has a glorious future, and that one day he may become old. Enthusiasm grows in proportion as the gentleman is able to report a higher and higher age, and if he is anywhere over fifty, the enquirer drops his voice in humility and respect. People actually look forward to the celebration of their fifty-first birthday.

We, however, have in Hechinger's phrase, become a nation of "youth worshippers." Grandmothers in their eighties persist in calling each other "girls" and try to dress accordingly. Elderly men refer to themselves by the self-demeaning descriptive "boys" and in self-negating behavior which ignores reality in order to better fulfill contemporary ideal.

This is the "Peter Pan" "Syndrome" described by Taves and Hansen.[7] In a study of 1700 elderly persons, one-sixth thought of themselves as old between the ages of 54 and 69, one-third between the ages of 70 and 79, and only forty percent by age eighty and over. About one person in seven said they never thought of themselves as old. They refuse to accept what Abraham prayed for and so they affect the modes and behavior patterns of the young, pretending like Peter Pan, that they have never grown up. And, parallel to the racial counterpart which Negro civil rights spokesmen so correctly recognized, the real tragedy of mature individuals being referred to as "boys" is when the individual internalizes that designation, with all of its ramifications and begins to believe it himself.

Judaism deals with the problem of age by granting it status. Our culture copes with it by denying its existence. In the implicit absurdity of this approach lies the reason for our inevitable failure. Peter Pan is a fairy tale; respect for age from others, leading to self-respect, is the only viable possibility.

Negative feelings to the aged express themselves in our culture not only as an attitude *defining* interreaction but even further as cause for *preventing* interreaction from taking place. It has become common practice to keep the old out of sight in their homes, in institutions, or in retirement communities. It is a segregation which seeks almost total separation. And its ultimate evil is that the victimizers are quite possibly more harmed than the victims.

Urie Bronfenbrenner, in his insightful comparison between the United States and Russia in *Two Worlds of Children*, states:

> It is our view that the phenomenon of segregation by age and its consequences for human behavior and development pose problems of the greatest magnitude for the Western world in general and for American society in particular . . . We cannot escape the conclusion that if the current trend persists, if the institutions of our society continue to remove parents, other adults, and older youth from active participation in the lives of children, and if the resulting vacuum is filled by the age segregated peer groups we can anticipate increased alienation, indifference, antagonism, violence on the part of the younger generation in all segments of our society — middle class children as well as the disadvantaged.[8]

For the Bible, the old had a special role assigned to them:

> Ask thy father, and he will declare unto thee, thine elders, and they will tell thee (Deuteronomy 32:7).

Opportunities to learn from those who have accumulated the wisdom of life should be treasured. It is not simply an act of cruelty to dismiss the old from our sphere of communication; it is stupidity for which we as a society pay a price.

Moses, in his attempt to bring about the deliverance of his people, sought out the elders first. When leadership was required, God said to Moses:

> Gather unto me seventy men of the elders of Israel, whom thou knowest to be the elders of the people, and officers over them; and bring them unto the tent of meeting that they may stand there with thee (Numbers 11:16).

The Hebrew word for old, *zaken,* is possibly an acronym for the words *Ze She'kanah Hokhmah* — he who has acquired wisdom.

To disregard our most important living natural resource is to deprive ourselves of innumerable benefits. We do not learn from those most fit to teach us the nature of the entire life experience, of survival to old age. We miss a sense of ancestry, history and roots, and so lose a valuable understanding of ourselves. We fear the natural process within ourselves of growing and maturing to old age because late life is unfamiliar and forbidding territory. We are strangers to the accumulated wisdom of personal experience because we chose to make strangers of those who could enlighten us.

How much better to reflect upon the wisdom of Ethics of the Fathers:

> He who learns from the young, to what is he like? To one who eats unripe grapes, or drinks new wine from his vat. He who learns from the old, to what is he like? To one who eats ripe grapes, or drinks old wine.

Segregation deprives the young and harms the old. Senility, it now appears, is often an expression of what one assumes is an expected norm of behavior. Robert Butler describes surviving in America:

> The elderly's part in eliciting the kind of response which they receive from the young and from society at large is often a subtle but powerful factor in the public's general disparaging view of them. They collaborate with their ostracizers. Some individuals act senile: others may deny their true feelings in an attempt to "age graciously" and obtain the approval which is otherwise denied them.[9]

We have created self-fulfilling prophesies by telling the old what we expect of them—or, better put, why we expect nothing of them. It should not come as a surprise that they live up to our expectations. Psychologist Margaret F. Singer observed similarities between the Rorschach test findings of aged volunteers who are resigned in the face of aging and those of American G.I. prisoners of war who collaborated with their captors in Korea.[10]

The psychological impact of age segregation is an area that must be discussed. Self-image is often the key to self-actualization. Biblical concern for honor of the aged may intend primarily to enable the old to honor themselves. This would be in line with the sequence of the significant verse in Leviticus (19:18), "Love thy neighbor as thyself." For one can only love others if he is able first to feel positively about himself.

Our culture casts the old into a preconceived mold of decay and decline, cheerlessness and childishness. In response, many have assumed characteristics deemed appropriate for them:

> Regarding the elderly, some of the phenomena we have observed include pseudo-senility, a "Peter Pan" syndrome (refusal to grow up), and leadership pre-empted by the middle-aged, with neglect or "mascoting" of elderly and young (necessitating therapeutic intervention.[11]

To believe the Biblical proverb that "The hoary head is a crown of glory" may well prove to be the first step in making it a reality.

V

Closely related to the negative self-image of the aged is the popularly fostered misconception that advanced age and creativity are mutually exclusive. Forced retirement is seen not only as a function of economics but of ability. The late Rabbi Abraham J. Heschel, at the 1961 White House Conference on aging, put it well:

> Our work for the advanced in years is handicapped by our clinging to the dogmatic belief in the *immutability* of man. We conceive of his inner life as a closed system, as an automatic, unilinear, irreversible process which cannot be altered, and of old age as a *stage of stagnation* into which a person enters with his habits, follies, prejudices. To be good to the old is to cater to their prejudices and eccentricities.

> May I suggest that man's potential for change and growth is much greater than we are willing to admit and that old age be regarded not as the age of stagnation but as the *age of opportunities* for inner growth?

> The years of old age may enable us to attain the high values we fail to sense, the insights we have missed, the wisdom we have ignored. They are indeed formative years, rich in possibilities to unlearn the follies of a lifetime, to see through inbred self-deceptions, to deepen understanding and compassion, to widen the horizon of honesty, to refine the sense of fairness.

Heschel aptly summed up both the traditional Judaic view

as well as the fruit of contemporary research. Psychologist Harvey C. Lehman, in his classic work on the subject, *Age and Achievement,* conclusively demonstrates that "evidence of any stereotyped conception of later maturity is quite untenable" and, in a chapter entitled "Older Thinkers and Great Achievements," briefly describes an appreciable number of individuals who did notable creative work late in life, in some instances their most important.[12] Lehman's thesis has ancient antecedents. The Bible is a chronicle of achievements by those well-advanced in years. "And Moses was four score years old and Aaron four score and three years old, when they spoke unto Pharaoh" (Exodus 7:7). Two old men fostered a dream of redemption and brought it to fruition. Abraham, Isaac, Jacob as well as dozens of other Biblical heroes personified man's ability to turn age to advantage as they progressively rose to greater heights with increased years.

Human dignity has many dimensions. For Jewish law, the manner in which someone is addressed is an area of special concern. Neither one's parents, scholars nor the aged should be called by their first names. Significantly, this simple courtesy is usually one of the first to be disregarded by those dealing with the aged. As Pryor points out, patients, no matter what their past profession, are routinely and patronizingly called by their first names by nursing home personnel.[13] What is often difficult to bear for the old is to be stripped of their social standing. Slave owners understood this well when they deprived their charges of family names and titles. The Nazi system which sought to dehumanize victims replaced names with numbers. For this reason, Jewish law forbids counting individuals by number, since to do so is to negate the uniqueness of every person, to turn soul into cipher.

The old deserve the right to maintain their full names as well as whatever titles they achieved during their lifetimes. Former professionals and people of prominence, although well past their prime, dare not be treated with disregard. Beautiful is the Talmudic dictum:

> Both the Tablets and the broken Tablets rested in the Ark together (*Berakhot* 8b).

The holiness of what is intact and what once was whole ought to be treated with equal reverence.

VI

William Schofield has popularized what he described as the "YAVIS" syndrome — the tendency for psycho-therapists to treat only the *Y*oung, *A*ttractive, *V*erbal, *I*ntelligent and *S*uccessful (that is to say well-paying) clientele.[14] The elderly are not treated, and so their "sickness" is considered untreatable. Those deemed not worthy of therapy become therapeutically "unreachable."

Self-fulfilling prophecy here too explains why the old never seem to be able to get any better. One wonders whether those who comprise the fortunate YAVIS group would fare more favorably than the aged if they were given similar "care."

The Talmud believes that the old are not beyond help, they are still capable of personal growth. "As the wise grow older so too is wisdom added to them" (*Shabbat* 125a). Sholom Aleichem put it in the form of a Yiddish folk-saying. In the ghetto, he said, there was an unusual phenomenon: The young were old and the old were young. The young were old — because they absorbed so much study from youth. And the old were young because, ever thirsting for more knowledge, they were dynamic, vibrant, and capable of constantly "becoming."

Mental health professionals often choose to ignore this capacity. Psychiatrists and social workers are impatient and irritable with their older patients for not responding swiftly to their ministrations while it would not occur to them to push for similar rapid improvement in younger patients. They fear that there will not be enough time in which to achieve their goal. Paradoxically, the truth of the matter is that the old are very often able to change more rapidly because they know there is so little time left to them.[15]

In a Talmudic parallel to the Rip Van Winkle story, we are told of Honi the Circle Drawer who went to sleep and awoke seventy years later. He searched for his contemporaries but could not find them. In despair he prayed for death and was granted his wish. At the conclusion of the tale are the words of Raba: "Hence is derived the saying, either companionship or death" (*Taanit* 23a).

To deprive the old of their friends is to deprive them of their reason for living. Companionship for those yet engrossed in a full schedule of daily activities is a bonus. For the retired, it spells the difference between unbearable boredom and possible happiness.

Judaism not only recommends but in at least one instance demands companionship in fulfillment of Biblical commandments. The obligation to marry remains in force even for the aged who can no longer procreate because aside from the injunction to be fruitful and multiply, God indicated that "It is not good for man to dwell alone" (*Yebamot* 62b). To discourage marriage between the aged, as Social Security laws do, is Biblically sinful. To separate those already joined in wedlock, as some nursing homes do, is to deprive them of a basic right rooted in God's plan of creation in Genesis.

Sex, too, is viewed by Jewish law as a basic "pleasure need" independent of childbearing factor. Sexual relations are not only permitted but required, even in situations where no possibility exists for conception. *Onah,* regular intercourse, is in addition to food and shelter, one of the three basic requirements of marriage which may not be voided though it be mutually agreeable to both partners. Those already pregnant, for whom sex is obviously non-procreative, can engage in sex, provided there is no potential harm to the fetus. The aged similarly ought not to be made to feel that sexual stirrings are out of place for them. On the contrary, the Jerusalem Talmud tells us that after death one of the things every person will be asked to give an accounting for is any legally permissible pleasures on earth of which one did not take advantage. The "dirty old man" is not a Jewish descriptive just as sex itself is never demeaned by the use of that adjective.

Highly significant, too, in this regard is the Bible's attitude to remarriage of the old after loss of spouse. Few people remember that after the matriarch Sarah passed away, Abraham took another wife by whom he bore a number of children (Genesis

25:1-2). Commentators consider this a great accolade that Abraham paid to his good marriage — by being anxious to repeat the experience. Families who try to prevent their old parents from "being foolish" and "not acting in accord with their years" are expressing prejudices unacceptable to traditional Jewish practice.

These are but some of the major ideas implicit in the Biblical verse: "Thou shalt rise up before the hoary head, and honor the face of the old man, and thou shalt fear thy God: I am the Lord." They all emphasize the emotional-psychological aspects rather than those of physical-material support. The final phrase, "I am the Lord," is given two additional interpretations by the rabbis which serve as fitting summary: I am the Lord — I am the one who first fulfilled the *mitzvah* of standing for an elder, when I visited Abraham following his circumcision. So too, I expect you to be scrupulous in observing this commandment. Further, I am the Lord — oldest of all in the universe. Therefore I am anxious about the way you treat those who share this Divine quality — for attitude to the aged ultimately reflects upon attitude to the Eternal.

NOTES

1. Erdman Palmore, "Gerontophobia vs. Ageism," *The Gerontologist,* 12 (1972), p. 213.

2. Robert N. Butler, *Why Survive Being Old in America,* Harper & Row, (1975), p. 11.

3. Edith M. Stern, "Buried Alive," Women's Home Companion, June 1947.

4. Memorandum RN 5115 — TAB, prepared for Technical Analysis Branch United States Atomic Energy Commission, The Rand Corporation, Santa Monica, California, December 1966.

5. *Torat Kohanim,* Leviticus 19:32.

6. *Bereshit Rabba* 65.

7. Marvin J. Taves & G. O. Hansen, "One Thousand Seven Hundred Elderly Citizens," in Arnold M. Rose (ed.), *Aging in Minnesota* (Minneapolis: University of Minnesota Press, 1963) pp. 73-181.

8. Urie Bronfenbrenner, *Two Worlds of Children: U.S. & U.S.S.R.* (New York: Russel Sage Foundation, 1970), pp. 116-17.

9. Robert N. Butler, *op. cit.*, p. 14.

10. *Ibid.*

11. Robert N. Butler & Myrna I. Lewis, *Aging & Mental Health*: *Positive Psycho-Social Approaches* (St. Louis: C. V. Mosby, 1973).

12. Harvey C. Lehman, *Age and Achievement,* Princeton University Press 1953, pp. 200-201.

13. Robert N. Butler, *op. cit.*, p. 263.

14. William Schofield, *Psycho-Therapy*: *Purchase of Friendship* (Englewood Cliffs, N. J.: Prentice-Hall, 1964-1974).

15. Robert W. Gibson, "Medicare and the Psychiatric Patient," Psychiatric Opinion 7 (1970), pp. 17-22.

Respect for Age in Christianity: The Base of Our Concern in Scripture and Tradition

2

by
Kenneth R. Knapp, A.C.S.W., M.S.

When one begins to consider the question of age, one soon discovers that the concept of aging varies from society to society and institution to institution. It is difficult to state precisely at what age old age begins. The Social Security system places it at 65. The Church, which has long discussed the need for retirement within its ranks because of old age, has finally settled on an arbitrary figure of 75 for members of the hierarchy. Others place the beginning of old age at 60, while some say that Senior Citizens' rights begin at 50.

Concern about aging is not new to our society. As far back as the early sixteenth century there was discussion as to when a man grew old. The concept of old age, at that time, was tied very closely to productivity. Thus, we find the beginning of old age identified as being somewhere around the age of 35, or in the case of a professional or extremely skilled person around 50.[1] Many persons, at that time, died in their early 40's.

In many cultures where the idea of old age is not connected with chronological age but with productivity, the fate of the old is determined according to the interest and the potentialities of the community. In situations where the community as a whole is stable and wishes to maintain its traditions by means of tapping the resources of its old, their fate is good. Where this interest does not exist in the community, where a particular culture is not firmly established or is in a period of uncertainty and change, the old do not fare well.[2] Their wisdom as the fount of tradition is not valued.

Most information concerning old age found in history relates to men. "The societies that have a history are ruled by the men: the women, both young and old, may perfectly well lay claim to authority in private, but in public life their status is always the

Rev. Kenneth Knapp is Director of Catholic Charities Diocese of Evansville, Evansville, Indiana. He has two Masters' degrees, one in Social Work from the Catholic University of America, the other in Counseling from Indiana State University (Terre Haute).

same—that of perpetual minors. The masculine state, on the contrary, changes with the passage of time: the young man becomes an adult, a citizen, and the adult an old man. The men form age-groups whose natural limits are vague, though society may set precise bounds to them, as it does today by laying down the age for retirement."[3]

Historically, then, conditions of a society have determined the fate of its older citizens. In a well-organized, stable, and peace-filled society, respect for old age is apt to be more prominent than in a society in turmoil or war, where youth will take over.

Standing out among all the societies in terms of respect for old age are the Eastern cultures, especially the Chinese. Such great respect is not found in the Western culture nor is it overly evident in the writings and precepts of Christianity. This article reports the results of a searching out of some of the sources of respect for old age found in Christianity. First of all, let us turn to Scripture, then give attention to tradition and early writings influencing Christianity. Although a study of secondary sources is extremely important, time and space permit only the study of primary sources.

The theme of respect for age in Scripture is seen almost exclusively in terms of respect for parents. It has its origin in the Pentateuch, in Exodus: "Honor your father and your mother so that you may have a long life and the land that Yahweh your God has given to you."[4] The commandment to show respect to those who are older, again in the person of parents, is found in Leviticus, "Each of you must respect his father and mother."[5] And again in the Book of Deuteronomy is found a repetition of the Exodus citation: "Honor your father and your mother as Yahweh your God has commanded you so that you may have long life and may prosper in the land that Yahweh your God gives to you."[6] Related closely to these three texts is the admonition to wisdom in the Book of Proverbs: "Keep your father's principle my son, do not spurn your mother's teaching."[7] This section in Proverbs, relating to the other sections cited, is perhaps the closest that the early writings come to indicating some sort of respect for age. The wisdom of age appears here for the first time.

Respect for parents as a command appears again in the New Testament, first of all in the Synoptic Gospels. The Gospel according to Matthew states: "For God said, 'Do your duty to your father and mother'."[8]

In a similar passage in the Gospel of St. Mark, this commandment from the Pentateuch is repeated. However, a new element is added, an element which is also hinted at in the Matthew passage in Verses 5 and 6. The commandment carries with it some threat of punishment. "Anyone who curses_father and mother must be put to death. But you say if a man says to his father or mother, 'Anything I have that I might have used to help you is corban (that is, dedicated to God), then he is forbidden from that moment to do anything for his father or mother.' In this way, you make God's word null and void for the sake of your tradition which you have handed down and you do many other things like this."[9] Mark seems to indicate here the importance of the commandment in that the Jews were wrong in trying to make it subservient; yet it is not a clear indication of simple respect for age or for some tradition connected with age but for the role of fatherhood and motherhood.

The theme continues in the Pastoral Letters. In Ephesians, there is seen some promise of reward connected with this commandment of respect for parents, again almost exclusively in connection with the role of parenting. "Honor your father and mother," and the promise is: "And you will prosper and have a long life in the land."[10] In Colossians, even though the exhortation is clearly that from the Old Testament, much more stress is placed on the role of parenting and respect for parenting: "Children, be obedient to your parents always because that is what will please the Lord."[11] The presumption in these cases is that when one is speaking of parents, one is speaking of those who are older. There are also, especially in these Pastoral Letters, exhortations for parents toward their children and for roles of husband and wife toward one another, as is to be seen in this same place in Colossians. There is definitely, however, a carry-through of the Old Testament respect for age in the New Testament's admonitions on the role of parenting.

Again, in the Pentateuch, a series develops on this same theme in the person of parents, stressing however the seriousness of the command and the consequent threat of punishment. This is found first in Leviticus: "Anyone who curses father or mother must die. Since he has cursed his father or mother, his blood shall be on his head."[12] This is a very strong threat of punishment, the threat connected with life itself. Following in that same vein is the line in Exodus: "Anyone who curses father or mother must die."[13] Deuteronomy continues this same theme in a long list in Chapter 27 concerning the writings of the Law and punishments and sanctions connected with the writings. The age theme is found in Verse 16, "A curse on him who treats his father or mother dishonorably. And all the people shall say: Amen." The indication here is not only that one is speaking of care and concern for aging, but also about a certain respect due to aging —again, however, with almost exclusive reference to parents.

Again, in the Pastoral Letters of the New Testament, the theme appears in a somewhat more developed way. It extends now beyond parents, but it is not clear that it belongs only to those who are elderly. However, that assumption seems fairly safe from the context and wording of the letter. The seeming indication is that there is some need for care: "Anyone who does not look after his own relations, especially if they are living with him, has rejected the Faith and is worse than an unbeliever."[14] The sanction of the Old Testament is not quite so clear but the indication that it is a strong duty, a duty which now belongs to an expression of the Faith, becomes very clear in this section.

In the Wisdom books of the Old Testament, there is a clearer indication of this duty toward parents as well as the necessary respect connected with age. This is perhaps the union of some of the Law passages from Pentateuch and some of the promise and reward passages seen in Psalms or Proverbs. In Ecclesiasticus, Chapter 3, Verses 1 to 16, there is a very clear indication of duty toward parents: "Whoever respects his father is atoning for his sins, he who honors his mother is like someone amassing a fortune. Whoever respects his father will be happy with children of his own, he shall be heard on the day when he prays."[15] And then quite clearly following in Verse 6, "Long life comes to him who honors his father, he who sets his mother at ease is showing obedience to the Lord."

For the first time now in the Old Testament readings this passage from Ecclesiasticus makes some distinction about the age of the person: "My son, support your father in his old age, do not grieve him during his life."[16] There seems to be here an indication of a respect along with an extra kind of care which is needed by a father in more advancing years. Support here seems to carry a different meaning from the "respect" or "honor" passages seen prior to this. And the author continues in Verse 13, "Even if his mind should fail, show him sympathy, do not despise him in your health and strength; for kindness to a father shall not be forgotten but will serve as a reparation for your sins." The last phrase of that section is tying sympathy and kindness to a reward, to amassing some kind of fortune, to building up the idea of receiving the same kind of respect as one advances in years. And finally, toward the end of that section from Ecclesiasticus, the sanction is seen: "The man who deserts his father is no better than a blasphemer, and whoever angers his mother is accused of the Lord."[17] Some of the ideas in the Pastoral Letters most certainly relate to this section.

As Ecclesiasticus continues, there is a very clear indication of the duty which is imposed upon children. We see here, however, that the duty seems to be a repayment of what has been given on the part of parents, "With all your heart honor your father and never forget the birth pains of your mother. Remember that you owe your birth to them; how can you repay them for what they have done for you?"[18] The strong indication, again, is that the respect due to them is not necessarily connected with age, even though we presume that parents are of greater age than children, but the respect due to them seems to be connected with role, with parenting, with a just return for that which they have given to children.

Again in the Wisdom books of the Old Testament, this time in Proverbs, old age is seen as a reward, something which is to be sought after. Wisdom and Fear of the Lord are seen as the guarantors of old age. Old age here is lauded and upheld. Since nothing is said of the living condition or the actual everyday life of the older person, it is more a philosophical lauding of old age than a personification or an actual understanding of the situations connected with old age.

The theme runs consistently through the Book of Proverbs beginning in Chapter 3, Verse 2, "For these will give you lengthier days, longer years of life, and greater happiness." It is clear that it is Wisdom's reward: "In her right hand is length of days; in her left hand, riches and honor,"[19] which she will bestow with joy: "Listen my son, take my words to heart, and the years of your life shall be multiplied."[20]

The one connection with parenting in the Book of Proverbs seems to be in the form of advice in imitating the wisdom of parenting figures: "Keep your father's principle, my son, do not spurn your mother's teaching."[21] In Chapter 9, Wisdom again promises this reward in the personification of the Lord: "For days are multiplied by me and years of life increased."[22] The implication again is that long days are to be sought after; that multiplication of years of life is a reward. An upright life is also a guarantor of length of years; "The fear of Yahweh adds length to life, the years of the wicked will be cut short."[23] This same theme, this fear of the Lord as a guarantor of old age, appears again: "The fear of Yahweh is a life-giving spring, for eluding the snares of death."[24] And, finally, life and length of days are a reward to be sought after: "The reward of humility is the fear of Yahweh, riches, honor and life."[25] Notice again that in all of these situations the conditions of life are not related. There is, however, some indication that the conditions of life will be provided for by the Lord.

This idea that long life provided for by the Lord is to be seen as a reward appears again very clearly in Psalm 91: "I give them life, long and full, and show them how I can save."[26] This guarantee of long life as a reward is strengthened in Psalm 55, where short life is seen as a punishment: "As for these murderous, these treacherous men, You, God, will punish them down to the deepest pit before half their days are out."[27]

Thus, there are in Scripture two basic themes running throughout. The first, respect for age, is seen almost exclusively in connection with respect for parents. This is especially true when it is personified. However, ideally, advanced age is to be sought as a reward. It is guaranteed by wisdom, it is guaranteed by fear of the Lord, it is seen as a gift of God. Shortness of life, life-span being cut in half, is seen as a punishment, something to be feared.

In either case, however, little is seen in connection with the actual quality of care given to older persons. The implication is that when one speaks of respect in connection with the elderly, it becomes the duty of children to provide for, to care for, to honor, and to give that which is necessary to provide not only length of days but length of days which are happy and peaceful, which are a blessing of the Lord.

Of societies with a recorded history, the Eastern societies stand out above the Western in granting privilege to age. Of the Eastern societies, the Chinese is perhaps best-known because of the uniquely privileged position that it provided for its old men. China, however, among all known civilizations, remained static for many hundreds of years and maintained a strongly structured hierarchical state almost unknown in any other history. These comments, however, will be limited to Western societies, and most especially to Christianity and the cultures affected by it.

The study of moral theology as well as the early legal Church documents provide no evidence of privilege being granted to age. One might think that legal documents would turn up some evidence of concern for the aged, or that perhaps some areas of moral theology would indicate some practice of care and concern for those who are dependent because of age. No such evidence is available, at least in the early documents. The Burgundian Code promulgated around the fifth century, and other legal documents of that time, provide no evidence of special concern for the aged.

As was evidenced in Scripture, there was concern for love of others. The Acts of the Apostles provides a very idealistic picture of the early Christian society. It seems, however, that the triumph of Christianity over the Greek or Roman cultures or the earlier Barbarian cultures did not provide for a continued triumph of this ideology. For the first several centuries there was a strong clinging to the ideology. Evidence indicates, however, that there was gradual abandonment of the original idea of brotherhood and mutual aid, and adoption of some of the worldly customs of the peoples of the time. Often, the spread of Christianity into various cultures was accomplished by adopting the customs of those cultures in turn. And so it seems that even in Christianity the respect for age and the ideal of aiding those in need of help did not flourish. Certainly, in the Greek or Roman culture we find that the concept of age was often tied to misery and to limitation as a condition that was not to be desired. In order to establish some understanding that the ideal did not flourish it is necessary to cite some of the examples of the concepts of old age in the milieu of Christian thought.

Short life-spans, on the average, tended to keep the number of elderly relatively small. There was a fair amount of dispute as to the average life-span of individuals. Concern was evidenced for men especially since they were seen as the productive persons in society.

Other factors also added to the relatively small amount of information concerning care for the elderly. The strong family ties of the predominantly agricultural pre-eighteenth century society precluded, on the whole, the consideration of the elderly as a distinct class. Certain burdens were attributed to the elderly in this society, especially when they became non-productive. In feudal society, owners saw themselves as responsible for the care of their serfs in their later years.

Occasionally, one will find an idealization of old age. One evidence of this is Dante's *Convivio*, circa 1306. Examples such as this, however, are rare. More often than not, old age is lamented as a time of misery, a time of dependency, a time of non-productivity. Boethius laments his growing old, the loss of his pride from his bright-lived days, the unhappiness of age coming upon him without warning and the grief that has set in because of old age.[28]

Chaucer, in *The Reeve's Prologue*, laments the misery of growing old, the slow movements, the shame of gray hair, and how one is derided because of it, the many problems of aging.[29] Other such evidences exist in writings such as those of Erasmus of Rotterdam[30] and Montaigne, who saw old age as very gloomy:

> Let us but observe in the ordinary changes in the declinations we daily suffer, how nature deprives us of the light and sense of our bodily decay. What remains to an old man of the vigor of his youth and better days?[31]

Or, again, in the same place,

> An insensible pace step by step conducts us to that miserable state, and by that means makes it familiar to us, so that we are insensible of the stroke when our youth dies in us, though it be really a harder death than the final dissolution of a languishing body, the death of old age; for as much as the fall is not so great from an uneasy being to none at all, as it is from a spritely and flourishing being to the one that is troublesome and painful.[32]

Shakespeare, too, gave much evidence of the problems of old age in *Henry IV, Henry VI* and *As You Like It*. All carry evidence of the problems of aging, the difficulty of being non-productive and a burden on society.

And Milton laments:

> This is old age; but then thou must how to live thy youth, thy strength, thy beauty, which will change to wither'd, weak, and gray; thy senses then optruse, all taste of pleasure must forego to what thou hast, and the air of youth hopeful and cheerful in thy blood will reign a melancholy damp of cold and dry to weigh thy spirits down and last consume the balm of life.[33]

These and other such indications from the literature of the times give overwhelming indication that old age is lamented as a time of misery, is seen as a time of non-productivity, and is a time to be dreaded.

One point of positive contributions made by the Church was that from the fourth century onward it built asylums and hospitals in Rome and Alexandria. It sought the maintenance of orphanages and asylums for the sick. It looked upon alms-giving as a duty and continually stressed the importance of such. There is, however, little evidence that special treatment was given to the elderly as a class. Care for the aged generally was considered to be the natural responsibility of family members. The best source of such thinking along this line seems to be the many commentaries on the Fourth Commandment. A good example is Luther's *Larger Catechism*. This seems only natural, following from the strong stress in Scripture about this responsibility falling to children.

However, there is much evidence that family members did not always care for their older members as a matter of course, as would be suggested by the Fourth Commandment, or by the commentaries on the Fourth Commandment. At least during the Renaissance, there is evidence that contracts were made whereby older persons made over their property to their children in return for a guarantee of support—a support in sickness, in health, and for as long as their lives should last. There is evidence, too, that earlier, such support was bought from a landlord in promise for a lifetime of work. Here, again, in both instances, great stress is placed on the productivity of the person and little evidence is given concerning dignity of special position being offered him when elderly.

Not too infrequently one finds the elderly associated with the poor and the infirm, and often the care of these poor and infirm was somewhat neglected. There is evidence that as the Church grew in society, Church and State began to share the responsibility for them. This followed from the Church's establishment of asylums and hospitals and also from the State's dawning realization that some care of this type should also be provided through civil rule. The Monastic orders played a considerable role in this regard, especially Monastic rules such as that of St. Benedict which revealed something of a special concern for the elderly. There was a great surge of institutionalization of those needing such care in the twelfth and thirteenth centuries. This was not limited to the elderly alone but extended also to the infirm and the handicapped. In the thirteenth century, the British scientist and philosopher, Roger Bacon, was one of the first to advocate State Institutions designed specifically for the care of the elderly.

Some examples can be found of Utopian writings following somewhat the ideals set out in the Acts of the Apostles and the early Christian ideal of communal living and brotherhood. Cicero's *De Senectute* as well as Plato's *Republic* were early writings which were very influential on the development of Christian thought. A later example is Thomas More's *Utopia*, especially Book II. These Utopian writings provided some thinking as to the place of the elderly in society, at least ideally. But there is little evidence that these writings, expressing an ideal, had great impact upon Christian thought, at least in terms of transferring this thought into action.

A rather good modern source of a history of the elderly referred to earlier in this paper is *The Coming of Age* by Simone de Beauvoir. There is strong indication here that Christianity did not reach far down into the depths of people's way of thought and often kept the pagan roots of the people who embraced this new religion. There is some evidence in the essence of German folklore that the aged man is seen as one who ie full of experience and one who knows secrets of great value, thus maintaining some sort of position in society.

Even though this survey is brief, it provides some indication that the condition of the aged person depends very much upon the social context. In the context of Christianity, the ideals of concern for other persons indicated in the Acts of the Apostles, and the strong mandate of the Commandments to care for age in the personification of parents, as seen in Scripture, were tempered by contemporary mores. The older person, sooner or later, in most instances, is subject to a biological fate that has one inevitable economic consequence: he becomes unproductive. The effect of this upon his fate as a person in society depends very much on the community's resources. If a society is comparatively well-to-do, it is able to make various choices, and in such a society within Christianity, the older person has been pretty well provided for. Also, in societies, if he were in the landowner class, and not a serf, he often owned and controlled the family's source of maintenance and prosperity. In such a case, his fate was good. If, however, there was a pinch on productivity; if it were a time of war; if it were a time of extreme emphasis on youth, as was seen at times during the Middle Ages; then the evidence of care for the elderly is not so great.

It appears, then, that concern for the elderly and the dignity provided to the elderly is somewhat recent in strong Christian teaching. It would seem that through the development of philosophies, and a subsequent development of Christian thinking concerning the importance of the individual apart from productivity, a new awareness has been created for the elderly as a class. This awareness is heightened by the availability of longer life-spans through a highly developed technology. These elements have forced a rethinking.

To make other absolute conclusions without a further search of some of the other sources, such as the Theodocian and the Justinianian Codes and perhaps some of the volumes of Papal documents, would hardly be fair. There is great need for further work to search out all the secondary sources dealing with the treatment of the elderly in early Christian centuries. Such a study would be a major undertaking, difficult and lengthy. Since the subject of the elderly has received such little attention on its own, most of the material would have to be culled piecemeal from countless theological treatises, chronicles, legal documents and such.

However, since little emphasis was given the subject of aging on its own, and since great emphasis was placed on parenting roles and on productivity of the person, little basis has been found in Scripture or tradition for a theology on aging and for the social responsibility for providing the means for the elder to have a comfortable and rewarding place in the society. Granting respect to the elderly as a class, and valuing the wisdom and experience which exists within the class of elderly persons is seen as the task of this generation. An essential element in carrying out this task is formulating and acting upon the theological base of our responsibility and concern.

Footnotes

[1]Creighton Gilbert, "When Did A Man in the Renaissance Grow Old?" *Studies in the Renaissance,* XIV, (1967), pp. 7-32.

[2]Simone de Beauvoir, *The Coming of Age,* (New York: G.P. Putnam's Sons, 1972), p. 86.

[3]*Ibid.,* p. 90.

[4]Chapter 20, Verse 12.

[5]Chapter 19, Verse 3.

[6]Chapter 5, Verse 16.

[7]Chapter 6, Verse 20.

[8]Chapter 15, Verses 4-6.

[9]Chapter 7, Verses 10-13.

[10]Chapter 6, Verses 2-3.

[11]Chapter 3, Verse 20.

[12]Chapter 20, Verse 9.

[13]Chapter 21, Verse 17.

[14]I Timothy 5:8.

[15]Chapter 3, Verses 3-5.

[16]Chapter 3, Verse 12.

[17]Chapter 3, Verse 16.

[18]Chapter 7, Verses 27-28.

[19]Chapter 3, Verse 16.

[20]Chapter 4, Verse 10.

[21]Chapter 6, Verse 20.

[22]Verse 11.

[23]Chapter 10, Verse 27.

[24]Chapter 14, Verse 27.

[25]Chapter 22, Verse 4.

[26]Verse 16.

[27]Verse 23.

[28]Boethius, *The Consolation of Philosophy*, (New York: The Modern Library, 1943), p. 3.

[29]Geoffrey Chaucer, *The Canterbury Tales*, (Baltimore: Penguin Books, 1952), p. 129.

[30]D. Erasmus, "Poem on Old Age," *The Poems of D. Erasmus*, (Leiden, 1956).

[31]W. Carew Hazlitt, ed., *The Essays of Michel de Montaigne*, (New York: A. L. Burt Company, Publishers, 1892), Vol. I, 19, p. 72.

[32]*Ibid.*, p. 73.

[33]John Milton, *Paradise Lost*, (Chicago: The Great Books Foundation, 1956), p. 285.

Bibliography

Books

Beauvoir, Simone de. *The Coming of Age.* New York: G. P. Putnam's Sons, 1972.

Boethius. *The Consolation of Philosophy.* New York: The Modern Library, 1943.

Chaucer, Geoffrey. *The Canterbury Tales.* Baltimore: Penguin Books, 1952.

Choron, Jacques. *Death and Western Thought.* New York: Collier Books, 1963.

Cotton, Charles, trans. *The Essays of Michel de Montaigne.* New York: A. L. Burt Co., 1892.

Eliot, Charles W., ed. *The Harvard Classics*, Volume 9 and Volume 20. New York: P. F. Collier and Son, 1909.

Kittredge, George Lyman, ed. *The Complete Works of Shakespeare.* Boston: Ginn and Company, 1936.

Milton, John. *Paradise Lost.* Chicago: Great Books Foundation, 1956.

More, Thomas. Nelson, William, ed. *Utopia.* Englewood Cliffs, New Jersey: Prentice-Hall, Inc., 1968.

Modern Man and Mortality. New York: The Macmillan Company, 1964.

The Jerusalem Bible. New York: Doubleday & Company, Inc., 1966.

Articles

Gilbert, Creighton. "When Did A Man in the Renaissance Grow Old?". *Studies in the Renaissance*, XIV, (1967), pp. 7-32.

Malino, Jerome R. "Coping with Death in Western Religious Civilizations." *Zygon—Journal of Religion and Science*, Volume I, Number 4, (December, 1966), pp. 354-365.

Osborne, Richard L., Rev. and Pucci, Joseph J., Rev. "A Philosophy of Aging." *Hospital Progress*, The Catholic Hospital Association, St. Louis, Missouri.

Simmons, Leo W. "Aging in Primitive Societies: A Comparative Survey of Family Life and Relationships." *Law and Contemporary Problems*, (Duke University School of Law), Volume 27, Number 1, (Winter, 1962).

Warhasse, James Peter. "On Life and Death and Immortality." *Zygon —Journal of Religion and Science*, Volume I, Number 4, (December, 1966), pp. 366-372.

_____. "Attitudes Toward Aging and the Aged: Primitive Societies." *Journal of Gerontology*, Volume I, Number 1, (January, 1946), pp. 72-95.

II

Religion and Aging in Contemporary Theology

However neglected the theme of religion and aging may be by historians, the practical concern for the well-being of the elderly shared by the culture and churches and synagogues has turned contemporary theological reflection to a consideration of the meaning of aging. Drawing upon a vision of a transcendent source of human meaning and a religiously grounded understanding of human being and becoming, Jewish and Christian theologians have looked critically at contemporary images of aging shared by the culture and by many of the aging themselves. Countering reductionist views as well as those which avoid questions of ultimate meaning, the theologians offer alternative images in which aging is not simply loss and negation but may become a time of fulfillment and completion.

Rabbi Heschel's address to the White House Conference on Aging in 1961 has become a classic statement of both the criticism and of the constructive religious vision. Old age need not be "defeat," "punishment," "a disease," "stagnation," "irreversible decline." Growing older is an opportunity for achieving *significant being.* Aging can mean change, growth, celebration, the sanctification of time, an opportunity for experiencing a "comprehension which embraces us," for experiencing the Presence which makes us truly human. Seward Hiltner's paper points to the need for facing the real losses of aging together with the genuine possibilities of pursuing depth rather than breadth in fulfillment and of developing a sense of vocation and responsibility involving real service to real people in the aging years. Evelyn Eaton Whitehead, surveying a broad literature in the theology of aging, lifts up the images which establish a basis for self-worth less dependent upon economic productivity or social role, or for interpreting the significance of one's own life and death, or for coming to terms with the changes and losses of aging. Father Charles Curran counters the traditional metaphor of aging as a curving downward with the vision of an upward curve involving growing self-encounter, a deepening and expansion of one's relations to others, and a growing encounter with God. From within a Roman Catholic perspective he affirms a transformationist view of death and sees all of life through the image of pilgrimage. The human cannot be reduced to the physical, the biological, or the technological. To be human is to dwell in the dimension of meaning. Life has an upward curve as well as a downward one. All of these writers hold the conviction that our metaphors for aging shape our experience. The time has come to renew and enlarge our image of what truly human aging is. In his testimony to Spirit in the aging years, Ross Snyder offers a personal vision of what that image might be.

The Older Person and the Family in the Perspective of Jewish Tradition

3

By RABBI ABRAHAM J. HESCHEL

I see the sick and the despised, the defeated and the bitter, the rejected and the lonely. I see them clustered together and alone. I hear them pray for the release that comes with death or clinging to a hope for somebody's affection that does not come to pass. I see them deprived and forgotten, masters yesterday, outcasts today.

What we owe the old is reverence, but all they ask for is consideration, attention, not to be discarded, forgotten. What they deserve is preference, yet we do not even grant them equality. One father finds it possible to sustain a dozen children, yet a dozen children find it impossible to sustain one father.

Perhaps this is the most embarrassing aspect of the situation. The care for the old is regarded as an act of charity rather than as the highest privilege.

In the never dying utterance of the Ten Commandments, the God of Israel did not proclaim: Honor Me, Revere Me. He proclaimed instead: Revere your father and your mother. There is no reverence for God without reverence for father and mother.

Father and mother are always older, more advanced in years. But is being advanced in years to be considered an advance or a retreat?

Images of the Aged and Old Age

Ours is a twin-problem: The attitude of society to the old and old age as well as the attitude of the old to being old. According to Jewish tradition, reverence for the old takes precedence over reverence for God. And reverence is a matter of the heart as well as endeavor and action; a matter that calls upon our sensitivity, imagination, and initiative as well as conscience and compassion.

The typical attitude to old age is characterized by fear, confusion, absurdity, self-deception, and dishonesty. It is painful and bizarre. Old age is something we are all anxious to attain. However, once attained we consider it a defeat, a form of capital punishment. Enabling us to reach old age, medical science may think, it gave us a blessing; however, we continue to act as if it were a disease. More money and time are spent on the art of concealing the signs of old age than on the art of dealing with heart disease and cancer. You find more patients in the beauty parlors than in the hospitals. We would rather be bald than grey. A white hair is an abomination. Being old is a defeat, something to be ashamed of. Authenticity and honesty of existence are readily exchanged for false luster, for camouflage, sham, and deception.

A grey hair may destroy the chance for promotion, may cost a salesman his job, and inwardly alienate a son from his father. The fear of being considered old has become a traumatic obsession. Only very few people are endowed with the rare and supreme courage to admit their true age without embarrassment. With the rest of us, courage and honesty go underground when the question of age is discussed. The most delightful resolution this Conference could pass would be to eliminate from now on any mention of the date of birth from the birth certificate.

A vast amount of human misery, as well as enormous cultural and spiritual damage, are due to these twin phenomena of our civilization: The contempt for the old and the traumatic fear of getting old. Monotheism has acquired a new meaning: The one and only thing that counts is being young. Youth is our god, and being young is divine. To be sure, youth is a very marvelous thing. However, the cult of youth is idolatry. Abraham is the grand old man, but the legend of Faust is pagan.

What is necessary is a revision of attitudes and conceptions. Old age is not a defeat but a victory, not a punishment, but a privilege. In education we stress the importance of the adjustment of the young to society. Our task is to call for the adjustment of society to the old.

By what standards do we measure culture? It is customary to evaluate a nation by the magnitude of its scientific contributions or the quality of its artistic achievements. Yet the true standard is the extent to which reverence, compassion, justice are to be found in the daily lives of a whole people, not only in the acts of isolated individuals.

Culture is a style of living compatible with the grandeur of being human.

Responsibility of All the People: The Nation

The test of a people is how it behaves toward the old. It is easy to love children. Even tyrants and dictators make a point of being fond of children. But the affection and care for the old, the incurable, the helpless, are the true gold mines of a people.

In our own days, a new type of fear has evolved in the hearts of men; the fear of medical bills. In the spirit of the principle that reverence for the old takes precedence over reverence for God, we are compelled to confess that a Nation should be ready to sell, if necessary, the treasures from its art-collections and the sacred objects from its houses of worship in order to help one sick man. Is there anything as holy, as urgent, as noble, as the effort of the whole Nation to provide medical care for the old?

This is one of the great Biblical insights: The needs of the suffering humanity are a matter of personal as well as public responsibility. The representatives of the community are held responsible for the neglect of human life, if they have failed to provide properly for those in need. The ancient sages realized that it was not enough to trust to individual benevolence, and that care for the sick was a responsibility of the community.

It is in accord with this tradition that leading representatives of all major religious organizations have endorsed the principle of Government responsibility and the use of the Social Security mechanism as the most effective medium for dealing with the problem of medical care for the aged.

It is marvelous indeed that for the first time in history, our society is ready and able to provide for the material needs of its senior citizens. Yet in addition to the problem of material security we must face the problem of psychological and spiritual security.

How to save the old from despondency, despair? How to lend beauty to being old? How to regain the authenticity of old age?

The Responsibility of the Individual

Old age is a major challenge to the individual; it takes both wisdom and strength not to succumb to it. According to all the standards we employ socially as well as privately, the aged person is condemned as inferior. In terms of manpower he is a liability, a burden, a drain on our resources. Conditioned to operate as a machine for making and spending money, with all other relationships dependent upon its efficiency, the moment the machine is out of order and beyond repair, one begins to feel like a ghost without a sense of reality. The aged may be described as a person who does not dream anymore, devoid of ambition, living in fear of losing his status. Regarding himself as a person who has outlived his usefulness, he feels as if he had to apologize for being alive.

The tragedy is that old age comes upon us as a shock for which we are unprepared. If life is defined exclusively in terms of functions and activities, is it still worth living when these functions and activities are sharply curtailed?

The tragedy, I repeat, is that most of us are unprepared for old age. We know a great deal about what to do with things, even what to do with people; we hardly know what to do with ourselves. We know how to act in public; we do not know what to do in privacy. Old age involves the problem of what to do with privacy.

Sources of Strength

While we do not officially define old age as a second childhood, some of the programs we devise are highly effective in helping the aged to become children. The preoccupation with games and hobbies, the overemphasis upon recreation, while certainly conducive to eliminating boredom temporarily, hardly contribute to inner strength. The effect is rather a pickled existence, preserved in brine with spices.

What is the role of recreation in the life of the aged? Is it merely to serve as a substitute for work one has done in earlier years? It seems to me that recreation is serving a different purpose, and that an over-indulgence in recreational activities aggravates rather than ameliorates a condition it is trying to deal with, namely, the trivialization of existence. In the past it was ritual and prayer that staved off that danger. For thousands of years human existence was not simply confined to the satisfaction of trivial needs. Through prayer and ritual man was able to remain open to the wonder and mystery of existence, to lend a tinge of glory to daily needs.

Modern man has discarded ritual, failed to learn the art of prayer, but found a substitute for both in occupational routine. He severed all relations to God, to the cosmos, or even to his people, but became engrossed in the search for success and the excitement of success took the place of inspiration. Upon his retirement from labor or business, hobbies and the country club or golf take the place of church, synagogue, ritual, and prayer. This, then, is the fact: games and hobbies have become a substitute for ritual, not only for work. Should we not clearly distinguish between recreation as a substitution and recreation as a solution?

What are the basic spiritual ills of old age? The sense of inner emptiness and boredom, the sense of being useless to, and rejected by, family and society, loneliness and the fear of time. Let us analyze the root as well as the cure of these ills.

Old age is an age of anguish. The only answer to the age of anguish is a sense of significant being. The sense of significant being is a thing of the spirit. Stunts, buffers, games, hobbies, slogans are all evasions. What is necessary is an approach, a getting close to the sources of the spirit. Not the suppression of the sense of futility, but its solution; not reading material to while away one's time, but learning to exalt one's faculties; not entertainment but celebration.

To attain a sense of significant being we must learn to be involved in thoughts that are ahead of what we already comprehend, to be involved in deeds that will generate higher motivations.

There is a level of existence where one cannot think anymore in terms of self-centered needs and satisfactions; where the problem that cannot be silenced is—who needs me? Who needs mankind? How does one relate himself to a source of ultimate meaning? The cry for such relatedness which gains intensity with old age is a cry for a referent that transcends personal existence. It is not experienced as a need from within but as a situation of being exposed to a demand from without.

Significant being is not measured by the amount of needs that agitate a person but by the intensity and depth of the response to a wisdom in relation to which our minds are an afterthought, by the discovery that the moment to come is an anticipation, and expectation, waiting to receive our existence. Significant being means experiencing moments of time as a comprehension which embraces us.

What a person lives by is not only a sense of belonging but also a sense of indebtedness. The need to be needed corresponds to a fact: Something is asked of man, of every man. Getting older must not be taken to mean a process of suspending the requirements and commitments under which a person lives. To be is to obey. A person must never cease to be.

Age Can Be Growth

Our work for the aged is handicapped by our clinging to the dogmatic belief in the immutability of man. We conceive of his inner life as a closed system, as an automatic, unilinear, irreversible process which cannot be altered, and of old age as a stage of stagnation into which a person enters with his habits, follies, and prejudices. To be "good" to the old is to cater to their prejudices and shortcomings.

May I suggest that man's potential for change and growth is much greater than we are willing to admit and that old age is regarded not as the age of stagnation but as the age of opportunities for inner growth?

The years of old age may enable us to attain the high values we failed to sense, the insights we have missed, the wisdom we ignored. They are indeed formative years, rich in possibilities to unlearn the follies of a lifetime, to see through inbred self-deceptions, to deepen understanding and compassion, to widen horizon of honesty, to refine the sense of fairness.

One ought to enter old age the way one enters the senior year at a university, in exciting anticipation of consummation, of the summing-up and consummation. Rich in prospective and experienced in failure, the old person is capable of shedding prejudices and the fever of vested interests. He does not see anymore in every fellow man a person who stands in his way, and competitiveness may cease to be his way of thinking.

What the nation needs is senior universities, universities for the aged where men should teach the potentially wise, where the purpose of learning is not a career, but where the purpose of learning is learning itself.

The goal is not to keep the old man busy but to remind him that every moment is an opportunity for greatness. Inner purification is at least as important as hobbies and recreation. The elimination of resentments, of residues of bitterness, of jealousies and wrangling, is certainly a goal for which one must strive.

Just as many homes for the aging now have a Director of Recreation or a Director of Activities, so they should have a Director of Intellectual Activities or a Director of Learning.

The Importance of Anticipation

I am conscious of speaking to scholars and experts in the field, to people who carry out work of the highest quality day by day. It is with your permission that I ask you to consider not only the present-day situation but also the problems that will emerge in the decades to come. These problems arise at an early age. Only very few people realize that it is in the days of our youth that we prepare ourselves for old age.

This is an imperative we must be conscious of even in youth. Prepare spiritually for old age and learn how to cultivate it. It is an age of great spiritual opportunities, the age of completion rather than decay. The ancient equation of old age and wisdom is far from being a misconception. However, age is no guarantee for wisdom. A Hebrew proverb maintains: "A wise old man—the older he gets the wiser he becomes, a vulgar old man—the older he gets the less wise he becomes." People are anxious to save up financial means for old age; they should also be anxious to prepare a spiritual income for old age. That ancient principle—listen to the voice of the old—becomes meaningless when the old have nothing meaningful to say. Wisdom, maturity, tranquillity do not come all of a sudden when we retire from business. Lectures ought to be offered in public schools about the virtues that come to fruition, about the wisdom and peace that arrive in old age.

The Waste and the Sanctity of Time

One of the major ills of old age as well as one of the roots of the general fear of old age is the fear of time. It is like living on a craggy ridge over a wide abyss. Time is the only aspect of existence which is completely beyond man's control. He may succeed in conquering space, in sending satellites around the moon, but time remains immune to his power; no man can bring back a moment gone by. Being used to dealing with things he can manage, the encounter with time is the most stunning shock that comes to man. In his younger years, he is too busy to react to it; it is in old age that time may become a nightmare. We are all infatuated with the splendor of space, with the grandeur of things of space. "Thing" is a category that lies heavy on our minds, tyrannizing all our thoughts. Our imagination tends to mold all concepts in its image. In our daily lives we attend primarily to that which the senses are spelling out for us; to what the eyes perceive, to what the fingers touch. Reality to us is thinghood, consisting of substances that occupy space; even God is conceived by most of us as a thing.

The result of our thingness is our blindness to all reality that fails to identify itself as a thing, as a matter of fact. This is obvious in our understanding of time, which, being thingless and insubstantial, appears to us as if it has no reality.

Indeed, we know what to do with space but do not know what to do about time, except to make it subservient to space, or to while it away; to kill time. However, time is life, and to kill time is to murder. Most of us seem to labor for the sake of things of space. As a result we suffer from a deeply rooted dread of time and stand aghast when compelled to look into its face. Time to us is sarcasm, a slick, treacherous monster with a jaw like a furnace incinerating every moment of our lives. Shrinking, therefore, from facing time, we escape for shelter to things of space. The intentions we are unable to carry out we deposit in space; possessions become symbols of our repressions, jubilees of frustrations. But things of space are not fireproof; they only add fuel to the flames. Is the joy of possession an antidote to the terror of time which grows to be a dread of inevitable death? Things, when magnified, are forgeries of happiness, they are a threat to our very lives; we are more harassed than supported by the Frankensteins of spatial things.

Most of us do not live in time but run away from it; we do not see its face, but its makeup. The past is either forgotten or preserved as a cliche, and the present moment is either bartered for a silly trinket or beclouded by false anticipations. The present moment is a zero, and so is the next moment, and a vast stretch of life turns out to be a series of zeros, with no real number in front.

Blind to the marvel of the present moment, we live with memories of moments misled, and in anxiety about an emptiness that lies ahead. We are totally unprepared when the problem strikes us in its unmitigated form. It is impossible for man to shirk the problem of time. The more we think the more we realize; we cannot conduct time through space. We can only master time in time.

Time is man's most important frontier, the advance region of our age, a region where man's true freedom lies. Space divides us, time unites us. We wage wars over things of space; the treasures of time lie open to every man.

Time has independent ultimate significance; it is of more majesty and more provocative of awe that even a sky studded with stars. Gliding gently in the most ancient of all splendors, it tells so much more than space can say in its broken language of things, playing symphonies upon the instruments of isolated beings, unlocking the earth and making it happen.

Time is the process of creation, and things of space are results of creation. When looking at space we see the products of creation; when intuiting time we hear the process of creation. Things of space exhibit a deceptive independence. They show off a veneer of limited permanence. Things created conceal the Creator. It is the dimension of time wherein man meets God, wherein man becomes aware that every instant is an act of creation, a Beginning, opening up new roads for ultimate realizations. Time is the presence of God in the world of space, and it is within time that we are able to sense the unity of all beings.

Time is perpetual, perpetual novelty. Every moment is a new arrival, a new bestowal. Just to be is a blessing, just to live is holy. The moment is the marvel; it is in evading it that boredom begins that ends in despair.

Old age has the vicious tendency of depriving a person of the present. The aged thinks of himself as belonging to the past. But it is precisely the openness to the present that he must strive for.

He who lives with a sense for the Presence knows that to get older does not mean to lose time but rather to gain time. And, he also knows that in all his deeds, the chief task of man is to sanctify time. All it takes to sanctify time is God, a soul, and a moment. And the three are always here.

The Role of the Family

It is still considered proper to expect that the first responsibility in planning for the senior citizen rests with the family. Such expectation presupposes the concept of a family which is not only an economic unit but also an interplay of profoundly personal relations. It thinks of the family not only as a process of living together but also of a series of decisive acts and events in which all members are involved and by which they are inwardly affected.

What is characteristic of the modern family is that on the level of profound personal experience parents and children live apart. The experiences shared at home are perfunctory rather than creative. In the past, it was the role of the father to lead the children through moments of exaltation. Whatever stood out as venerable and lofty was associated with the father. Now we are entering a social structure in which the father is becoming obsolete, and in which there are only three ages; childhood, adolescence and old age. The husband of the mother is not a father, he is a regular guy, a playmate for the boys, engaged in the same foibles and subject to similar impulses. Since he neither represents the legacy of the past nor is capable of keeping pace with the boys in the pursuit of the future, his status is rather precarious.

Children today experience their highest moments of exaltation in a children's world, in which there is no room for parents. But unless a fellowship of spiritual experience is re-established the parent will remain an outsider to the child's soul. This is one of the beauties of the human spirit: We appreciate what we share, we do not appreciate what we receive. Friendship, affection is not acquired by giving presents. Friendship, affection comes about by two people sharing a significant moment, by having an experience in common. You do not attain the affection of your teen-age son by giving him an expensive car.

It is not necessary for man to submit to the constant corrosion of his finest sensibilities and to accept as inevitable the liquidation of the inner man. It is within the power of man to save the secret substance that holds the world of man together.

The real bond between two generations is the insights they share, the appreciation they have in common, the moments of inner experience in which they meet. A parent is not only an economic provider, playmate, shelter and affection. A human being is in need of security, but he is also in need of inspiration, of exaltation and a transcendent meaning of existence. And to a child, the parent represents the inspiration, the exaltation, and the meaning. To my child I am either the embodiment or the distortion of the spirit. No book, no image, no symbol can replace my role in the imagination and the recesses of my child's soul.

It is easy to speak about the things we are committed to; it is hard to communicate the commitment itself. It is easy to convey the resentments we harbor; it is hard to communicate the praise, the worship, the sense of the ineffable.

We have nearly lost the art of conveying to our children our ability to cherish the things that cannot be quantified.

This, then, is a most urgent problem: How to convey the inexpressible legacy, the moments of insight, how to invoke unconditional commitment to justice and compassion, a sensitivity to the stillness of the holy, an attachment to sacred words?

There is no human being who does not carry a treasure in his soul; a moment of insight, a memory of love, a dream of excellence, a call to worship.

We must seek ways to overcome the traumatic fear of being old, prejudice, discrimination against those advanced in years. All men are created equal, including those advanced in years. Being old is not necessarily the same as being stale. The effort to restore the dignity of old age will depend upon our ability to revive the equation of old age and wisdom. Wisdom is the substance upon which the inner security of the old will forever depend. But the attainment of wisdom is the work of a lifetime.

Old men need a vision, not only recreation.

Old men need a dream, not only a memory.

It takes three things to attain a sense of significant being.

God

A Soul

A Moment

The three are always here.

Just to be is a blessing, just to live is holy.

4

A Theology of Aging

by SEWARD HILTNER

THE THEME of this conference is "Organized Religion and the Older Person." In subsequent sessions we shall be considering what religion means to older people, what the churches and synagogues may do in relation to older people, and how the potential resources of religion and religious institutions may serve and be served by more older people. Plainly our over-all aim is to contribute all that we can to the genuine fulfillment of more older persons.

It has seemed to me wise that we look first at the deeper dimension of our problem before coming to the indispensable specifics. It is for that reason that my remarks are entitled "A Theology of Aging." By "theology" is meant the attempt to understand, state, and clarify the meaning of the faith. Some basic aspects of this can be considered without our having to deal with the differences that may exist between Christians and Jews or between Protestants and Roman Catholics, and it is my intention to speak of faith and of theology only in the sense that rises above such differences.

Every religious faith group will assert, and rightly so,

that faith is relevant to persons at all ages and stages of life. The essence of the faith is equally relevant to children and to adults, as well as to poor and rich, to men and women. Nevertheless, the resources of the total faith tend to be drawn upon selectively according to particular conditions such as age and stage of development. This fact is not only desirable but is also necessary if the faith, and the theology that expresses understanding of the faith, is to become relevant to all sorts and conditions of men. No one objects to it so long as we do not assert that the aspects selected are the faith as a whole.

One of the most winsome and convincing illustrations of this procedure may be found in Reuel L. Howe's book, *Man's Need and God's Action*.[1] This is an examination of the theology of parent-child relationships. Howe is thoroughly familiar with the work on child development, on education, and even on child therapy; and all these are valued positively. But he is impressed, finally, that no parent does or can do all the right things in relation to his child. Were it not for the fact of forgiveness, coming sometimes in surprising ways through child to parent, the rearing of children would be intolerable. Howe's delineation of the meaning of forgiveness in the parent-child situation is precise. It is something moving in both directions that makes possible fresh starts. It is the possibility of the fresh start that enables a parent to acknowledge his error without being ridden by guilt in a paralyzing sense. Howe would not assert that this fact of forgiveness, rightly understood, is the faith in its entirety. But it is the aspect or dimension of faith that is all-important at this age and in this kind of relationship. It is selected from the total faith, but experience with it leads one back to a better understanding of the meaning of the total faith. So understood, such a theology of parent-child relationships is not something peculiar standing off by itself. It is a focusing of the most relevant dimensions of faith in relation to a specific type of situation. Thus the relevance of the faith to this

1. Greenwich, Conn.: Seabury Press, Inc., 1953.

type of need is increased, and in turn there is deepened understanding of the faith as a whole.

In a similar fashion it would be possible to discuss a theology of other major developmental stages in life. Faith calls the late teen-ager to a kind of initiative and independence he has not had to exercise before, to decision about vocation and perhaps about marriage. For this there must be a sense of identity, a struggle with the relation between occupational realities and the ideal meanings of life, between the faith as received and the faith as wrought out on the anvil of painfully exercised adulthood. When we move on to young adults, the problem is to find reflective meaning within the busy round of a very activistic existence. Father is getting established and hopes to get ahead; mother is preoccupied with the demands of child care. Faith is properly activistic, even though it does require an undercurrent of reflectiveness unless the subsequent stage is to become disillusioning.

When we come to the middle years, a selectively relevant theology will appear rather different from that most meaningful to the young and busy married adults. As Carl Jung noted a generation ago, there is a revolution in the movement into middle years, but it is a quiet and internal revolution that many people fail even to acknowledge.[2] On the negative side, there comes a time when the flexibility on which one had always counted, if he wanted to change his job or his wife, is no longer with him. On the positive side, the time arrives when one either takes thought to plan his life in a new way or it automatically finds him in an unproductive rut regardless of external circumstances.

A theology for the middle years will be focused around the need for a spiritual rebirth that is initiated inwardly. The revolution of these years is not forced by outer circumstance in the same way puberty compels changes in the movement from childhood to adolescence. And it is unlike the kind of compulsion we sometimes see in later years

2. *Modern Man in Search of a Soul* (New York: Harcourt, Brace & Co., 1933).

when employment is denied, or there is a radical change in level of income or social status. This leads us directly to our own subject: a theology of aging.

There seems no good reason to begin elsewhere than with the most obvious fact, that the older years involve some loss in some kinds of powers that have previously been taken for granted. Set aside for the moment the question of whether these powers are important or not. The fact remains that something hitherto taken for granted begins to wane if not to disappear. In that sense there is loss. So the first question for a theology of aging is: How does it deal with the fact of loss?

If we ask how individual persons deal with loss we find a great variety of answers. At one extreme some persons accept and exaggerate the loss, and then give up to submissive resignation. At the other extreme some people deny there is any loss at all and undertake to prove it to themselves as well as others by compulsive activity twenty-four hours a day. Between the extremes come the vast majority, partly accepting, partly resigned, partly denying, partly overcoming.

The fact is that we have recently learned something about superior and inferior ways of dealing with loss. This knowledge has come chiefly through study of that most ultimate and poignant of all losses, bereavement. But there is every indication that its basic principles are equally relevant to the confrontation of less drastic losses than grief. Erich Lindemann[3] believes that grief cannot be understood without the notion of "grief work," or the work of mourning. This involves the painful mental confrontation with the image of the deceased person in relation to oneself— so painful that it can be tolerated only for brief periods. Eventually this grief work becomes less painful; and the bereaved person finally is able to invest himself in new relationships and activities. But during the acute phase the idea that he will some day be able to do this would itself

3. "Symptomatology and Management of Acute Grief," *American Journal of Psychiatry*, CI (Sept. 1944), 141-148.

be unacceptable. Eventually, one is able to live with the image of the dead person. Lindemann noted that some persons failed in varying degrees to carry out the work of mourning by, for instance, becoming cynical as a defense against accepting the full pain of the loss, or by completely suppressing their negative feelings, or by trying to deny that death is a loss at all. Let us note carefully that no condemnation of the persons unable to mourn rightly is implied. If they could, they would do so.

What do faith and theology have to say to the fact of grief and bereavement? There comes at once to mind the beatitude of Jesus, "Blessed are they that mourn for they shall be comforted." If we take seriously the processes indicated by Lindemann, then we can paraphrase the beatitude to read as follows, "Those who are able to mourn shall be comforted through their mourning." To this we may add the reminder that comfort does not mean "easy" or "without effort" but rather "with fortitude" or "with courage." It is a good thing to mourn when there has been loss. It is the strong, not the weak, who are able to do so. Those who are unable to mourn when there is loss should be helped to do so. They should not, with misplaced sympathy, be aided to deny the loss or to evade the pain brought by its realization.

The losses of aging, it may be contended, are seldom either so acute or so drastic as the bereavement analogy implies. That is correct. But the basic principle remains. The ability to face the loss as loss is very positive. Fortunate is he who has it. For facing the loss, with whatever pain goes along with it, is to free him for investment in things that transcend the loss. In contrast, if he is under inner pressure to deny the loss or the potential pain it would bring, he ties himself unproductively to it regardless of superficial appearances.

The first point in our theology of aging, then, counsels as follows. At the time you first begin to realize some kind of real loss of powers, then confront, if you can, the fact of loss itself. If you find that so painful that you cannot do so at all, then get special help. Do not try to turn to a

merely rational assessment of loss, so it can be made unimportant, until you have dealt with the fact of loss itself.
After that, assessment will be constructive. Before that, it
will prevent you from being released from the loss. None
of our high religious traditions, beginning with Job, has
professed to have a final answer to pain and suffering. But
all have asserted that our course is to seek the aid we need
to confront and come through it. We apply this general
principle to the specific situation.

My emphasis on what could be called the "work of
loss-facing" is not because the specific nature of the loss is
the most important long-term fact confronting the person
who is aging. Most such losses demand a husbanding of
resources but not a cessation of activity even in the physical
realm. They tend to narrow the range of what one can do,
but this is not necessarily negative since it may lead to a
deepening and intensifying of that which is selectively
chosen. Thanks especially to modern medicine and public
health, an increasing proportion of older people maintains
for many years a capacity to move and act in ways that are
potentially satisfying. If this be within some limits not
previously necessary, it may lead to a desirable kind of
depth from which one was separated in the earlier years
of unhusbanded energy. In other words, there is no reason
why the joy of inner fulfillment in older years has to be set
forth as a concession. My argument is that we can see and
experience the real potentiality of older years only if we
have first faced and dealt directly with the fact of loss in
older years. If we avoid the one, we shall be ambiguous
about the other. If he has not faced loss, the older person
may speak ecstatically of the compensations of age—and
that is what they will remain in his internal life, compensations, readjustments, something second best, when in fact
his life may mean new and deeper dimensions of living.

Our first point in a theology of aging dealt with the
facing of loss, with attendant suffering. Our second point
deals with the nature of joy and of fulfillment. Here we
encounter, in addition to what has already been said, a

surpassingly important fact about our culture. For the most part, the values of our culture are associated with youth. Beauty means the unlined feature. If lines and years bring out character and compassion, apparently beauty has fled. We seemingly want for ourselves, as well as for our automobiles, far more power than we can possibly use to any good end. There are many ways in which the culture derogates the very values that promise most to bring fulfillment in older years. If they accept this cultural judgment, older people fail to invest themselves in accord with their powers.

It is often said that younger people possess many rejecting attitudes toward older people, and there is much plain truth in this. A great deal of what appears to be negative feeling toward older people is, however, a symbolic attempt to deal with something about one's self. Older people are not seen in their own terms but as reminders of one's own earthly destiny. Unless older people can make some distinctions between person-directed injustice and projective distortion, they are likely to accept the youthful values of the general culture and thus fail to cultivate the deeper order of fulfillment that is open to them.

The first point in our theology of aging, then, deals with confrontation of loss despite suffering. The second is about the free and spontaneous cultivation of fulfillment in its depth dimension, without secretly crabbed thoughts about second best. "The best is yet to be" can be stated honestly only by one who has first faced the fact of loss of powers, and has then altered the youthful values of the general culture away from mere expansion and in the direction of depth and intensity.

We come now to a third point, the meaning of vocation and of responsibility in older years. All our Western religious traditions link vocation and responsibility closely. A "vocation" means a calling, a calling by God about one's work and also His service in all realms of life. So understood, every man is called by God. In following his calling, he fulfills the primary responsibility of his life. Sometimes this is interpreted with a grisly literalness. A man may possess no basis of self-respect if he is unable to work, nor a woman if she has not the care of children. Such views are distortions. Nevertheless, the larger truth is correct: that every man and woman is to have a calling, from birth until death. It may alter its character as life proceeds. But there is finally a threat to fulfillment unless one finds and exercises the calling and responsibility appropriate to him at every stage of his existence.

As earlier conferences in this series have made clear, our society is still far from having made possible a basic economic floor for all older people, from accepting them and their potentialities in all dimensions of life, and from planning sensibly with them in terms of housing, recreation, education, continued employment, and in other ways. But the fact remains that no amount of such necessary steps to help older people can do the whole job unless they can at the same time be aided to exercise a vocation and a responsibility that are inherently meaningful. Is this really part of our thinking? Or do we regard it actually as made-work? With the demand now high, a retired university teacher can usually get a job somewhere of part-time teaching on a year-to-year contract. Do we have equivalents for this for the people whose calling is no less genuine but a bit less specific? Or, when the earned income question is put aside, what can the older person do that fulfills his social responsibility and enables him to continue to exercise a religious vocation?

The plain implication is that we must think and plan to help him find this vocation and responsibility. But he has some obligation of his own to this end. Very often he thinks of retirement from a remunerative job as the cessation of his vocation and of his social responsibility. We know that such an illusion will catch up with him. But he can, from his religious faith, come to see that he still has a vocation, although it may well be necessary for him to reconsider its nature. It may not be a remunerative position. But unless it involves real service to real people in the real world, it will prevent deeper dimensions of his fulfillment in older years.

These three, then, appear to be the cardinal points in a theology for older people: confrontation of loss as loss, pursuit of depth rather than mere breadth in fulfillment, and adaptation of vocation and responsibility. They are not a complete theology. They are, rather, selections from the total faith of Judaism or of Christianity of peculiar relevance to older people. Understanding of these points can, I believe, help older people to help themselves, and can also help the rest of us to help them more effectively.

As addenda to the three main points, we may note briefly two facts that have a vital bearing upon a theology of aging. The first is the sheer massive fact of increased longevity. Every year added to the span of life makes it more imperative that the theology of aging be absorbed. Uncreative attitudes toward loss, compensatory attitudes toward fulfillment, and defeated attitudes toward vocation —all these become more dangerous as longevity increases. Hence these points are of much more importance than at any previous time in history.

The second fact is that women, on the average, are outliving men by about five years. This implies that, on a sheer statistical basis, there is need for helping the majority of women to anticipate not only the shock of bereavement of their husbands but also to prepare to live without them for an average period of five years. In a way this means that it is even more important for women to come to terms with a theology of aging than it is for men. The churches are at times accused of being more female than male institutions. At least in older years it is time we recognized that there is a good sociological reason for being just that.

Most of the present discussion has been about a theology of aging in the sense of the relevance of theology to older people themselves. But there is, plainly, a second sense in which we may speak of a theology of aging, namely, in understanding the aging process as beginning long before the older years have come. It has become a truism that those who have prepared their attitudes for older years before they come are much better off than those who postpone the shift. It is my contention that the basic principles enunciated here are as relevant to the preparation for older years as they are for the actual fact when it arrives. That is, our theology of aging is both a theology for older people and a theology for those preparing to be older.

Consider why this is so. Our first point deals with the confrontation of loss. This may come initially not on retirement, or when the last child leaves home, but perhaps with the first gray hair, or with the first child's going away to school. To the extent that this is met appropriately at the time, attitudes are set for the older years when the losses may be greater. The same is true of fulfillment. If there is some small voluntary shift in middle years, accompanied by a growing conviction that depth may be even more important than breadth, then one comes to older years prepared to accept fulfillment as genuine and not merely compensatory. The same is true for vocation and responsibility. If there is the beginning of adaptation, under one's own steam, then one comes to older years with a great advantage. We hold, then, that these basic principles for a theology of aging apply both to the fact of older years and to the preparation for it.

To all our high religious traditions of the West, man is made in the image of God, and yet he is a limited and finite creature. He has real freedom so that he can plan, imagine, and create. And yet he is limited and forgets this fact only on pain of complete defeat. There is a sense, therefore, in which a theology of aging is basic to all theology as the understanding and statement of the faith within our respective traditions. For every man must deal with the fact of limitation as well as with that of creativity, with the contracting as well as with the expanding dimensions of life, with loss as well as with gain, with frustration as well as with fulfillment. Perhaps our theology of aging can bring some illumination back to theology in general.

We offer a final word about the churches. In helping

older people the churches and synagogues may be able to do many things on many fronts, of which we shall hear in this conference.[4] But it is my judgment that nothing they can do is as important as helping a theology of aging to become imbedded in our thought and feeling, whether we are 35 or 60. To the degree that we can do this, we have a solid foundation for other activities. To the extent that we fail to do it, our activities, however good in themselves, are built on a house of sand. The material must build on the spiritual or it builds in vain.

4. See also Paul B. Maves and J. Lennart Cedarleaf, *Older People and the Church* (New York: Abingdon-Cokesbury Press, 1949).

Evelyn Eaton Whitehead

RELIGIOUS IMAGES OF AGING: AN EXAMINATION OF THEMES IN CONTEMPORARY CHRISTIAN THOUGHT

In the conference which signaled the start of this interdisciplinary discussion of aging, economist Juanita Kreps spoke to the question of the value of human aging.[1] Within the evaluative framework of contemporary American economics which stresses the relationship of expenditure to production, she noted, the aged person can be viewed only as a liability. Physician Robert Kohn, whose research has contributed to our understanding of the biology of aging, sounded a similar note.[2] In terms of the dominant values of medicine, he observed, the process of human aging can be viewed solely as negative. Certainly the negative evaluation of aging is not limited to such sophisticated sources. Many involved in the experience of growing older—and of being old—can document the multiple depreciations of aging. Loss of income, loss of role, loss of status, loss of affection, loss of competency, loss of power—these are but a few of the negative elements which characterize for many their experience of growing older.

Is this the whole story? Is loss the unqualified experience of aging? Is depreciation the only realistic evaluation possible of this universal human phenomenon?

We know this is not the case. Human life as well as literature attest to other characteristics of aging—maturity of the personality, a broadening of sensibilities, the ripening of genius, the testing of the spirit. Neither the positive nor the negative characterization of human aging alone are complete. Maturity and loss are common companions in adult experience.

The humanities—those disciplines devoted to the human traditions of thought, art, religion, literature—are rich repositories within which the variegated patterns of human maturity and loss are stored. The humanist's challenge today is to mine these resources of human culture. The goal of this effort will be to explore alternate evaluations of human aging which are not based simply on the diminishment of productive output or of biological functioning. Can the humanities, with their unique access to the cumulative resources of the spirit, provide the human community with a perspective within which the full ambiguity of the process of human aging can be seen as the basis for a more balanced evaluation of aging and the aged? If the answer is yes, the contribution of the humanities to both public policy discussion and to the critical internal dialogue of personal integration will be of real significance.

One of the veins of the cultural deposit to which humanists are heir is the religious heritage of western Christianity. This vein, to be sure, has produced its share of alloy. That ambiguous lot it shares with art, literature, science and other of humankind's attempts to transcend the limits of the obvious in the effort toward more enduring meaning. The ongoing Christian tradition is a complex system of image and belief, doctrine and symbol. The Bible is of central, even definitive, importance in Christianity, and through the centuries its texts have been subject to a wide range of diverse interpretations. Literal meaning, allegorical significance, congruence with philosophy, verification by history—each of these has been espoused as the basis of the orthodox interpretation of the texts. The heritage of western Christianity includes the checkered history of its efforts to be in the world but not of it, and its often less than successful attempts to stand as a sign of justice and mercy. Christian history documents recurring scandals of internal dissension and institutional arrogance; but it stands, as an ongoing witness of the transforming power of religious belief in people's lives.

Recently aging has become an issue of explicit religious and pastoral concern. Since 1960 we find in contemporary theological writing, as in the literature of the biological and human sciences, a rapid increase in the number and quality of publications considering human aging in its several dimensions. Early on, articles dealing with the practical problems of the aged-in-need began to appear in several ministry journals.[3] Gradually essays emerged dealing more directly with theological and religious themes.

Several contributions to this religious discussion of human aging from the mid-seventies are of particular note. In 1974 Henri Nouwen, an influential religious psychologist, and his colleague Walter Gaffney published *Aging: The Fulfillment of Life.*[4] That same year an issue of *Soundings,* the journal of the Society for Religion in Higher Education, addressed the theme of "Leisure, Retirement and Aging." The next year, under the impetus and editorship of Seward Hiltner, dean of American pastoral theologians, a group of prominent university-based theologians published *Toward a Theology of Aging.*[5] And in its 1976 issue devoted to "Adulthood," as prestigous a journal as *Daedalus* included substantive pieces concerned with human maturity and aging from the perspective of several religious-cultural traditions. William Bouwsma's important article on "Christian Adulthood" appears in this compilation.

If the test of the hardiness of any cultural tradition is its capacity to draw from the resources of its own symbol system those images which can provide meaning for the new, as yet unacculturated, experiences of the next generation, then one way to examine the usefulness of the Christian religious tradition as a basis for the positive evaluation of human aging is to explore how such contemporary religious writers are themselves drawing upon the resources of the Christian tradition in their considerations of aging. Clearly, the Christian tradition is not the only source to which these religious writers turn in their effort to illumine the human experience of growing older. The philosophic orientations of both phenomenology and linguistic analysis are in evidence; use is made of the psychological categories of Freud, Jung, Erikson. But it is upon the various uses made of the Christian heritage itself that I wish to focus. My concern here is neither to mount an apologetic for religious belief nor to discuss the merits of Christianity in relation to other systems for the interpretation of reality. Rather it is to ask: Which images do these thinkers retrieve from the repository of Christian history and tradition? How do they bring them to bear upon contemporary issues of human aging? And ultimately, of what relevance are these images to the humanist's self-appointed task? Therefore I will focus in this essay only upon a portion of the diverse and ambiguous heritage of Christianity. Following the lead of the French phenomenologist and gerontologist Michel Philibert, I shall use the term "images" in a very general sense. As he writes, "People hold opinions, beliefs, or mental attitudes toward aging which are more or less coherent and which carry images and memories together with the beginnings or outlines of knowledge. We shall call these *multi-form constructions* 'images.' They constitute orientations or perspectives . . . . "[6] In particular, I will consider, in turn, the use made of central images and religious themes in treating three challenges central to the personal experience of aging:

I. establishing a basis for self-worth less dependent upon economic productivity or social role.

II. interpreting the significance of one's own life, and

III. coming to terms with the changes and losses of aging.

1. Establishing a Basis for Self-Worth Less Dependent Upon Economic Productivity or Social Role

The realization that a person is more than what he does is a critical insight of human maturity. With this awareness can come—even if only fleetingly—a sense of liberation from many of the sources to which one ordinarily turns to bolster self-esteem. Reputation, accomplishment, beauty, influence, wealth—these evanescent advantages seem never fully achieved, finally and securely. In so far as a person's appreciation of himself and his worth is limited to these factors, he senses his vulnerability. In so far as one is able to find within oneself and one's own experience of life other sources of positive self-evaluation, sources less dependent upon the exigencies of chance or external control, one is more likely to experience the self as autonomous.

There are many vocabularies appropriate to a discussion of this struggle of the individual to come to a mature sense of personal worth. Psychology has much to say, as do poetry, drama, biography. Religion, too, has considered the question of the basis of personal value.

The major religious traditions of humankind have rebelled against the identification of the person with his or her usefulness to society. In Buddhism and Taoism as well as in Christianity, uselessness has appeared as a central religious category. As we see in the early chapters of the influential *Vimalakirti Sutra,* the ultimate uselessness of all worldly things is a basic ienet of Buddhism. In Taoism the most memorable celebration of uselessness occurs in Book Four of *Chuang Tzu,* in the story of the massive, ancient tree which at first sight appears attractive to the woodsman. Upon closer examination, however, it is seen to be gnarled and therefore useless to his purposes. Indeed, it is this uselessness, we are told, that guarantees the tree its transcendent longevity. These examples reflect the conviction deep in each of these traditions that a person does not *earn* his or her way into a relationship with that which is ultimate.

The Christian image of God's unfailing love, both unmerited and unmeritable, can be interpreted as a symbol suggesting that the real basis of one's worth is beyond "good works"—beyond one's productivity, vigor, or wealth. This conviction of God's unconditional love for humankind is rooted in the Old Testament accounts of Yahweh's relationship with the people of Israel. *Genesis* relates the story of Yahweh's gratuitous covenant with Abraham, which constituted him father of the chosen people. The subsequent books of the Old Testament recount God's continuing faithfulness to this people, in spite of their frequent disobedience and obstinacy. The Lord's love of the Israelites is unconditional, neither limited by their worthiness nor dependent upon their response. In the New Testament, Jesus reminds his followers that the Father's care for the birds of the air and the flowers of the field is unrelated to their productivity (*Luke* 12). This belief finds expression in Paul's conviction that we are not saved (in more humanistic terms, that we do not achieve self-realization) by our own individual effort (*Romans* 4). Such self-realization is experienced ultimately as a surprising gift, a gracious occurrence in our life beyond our own best efforts at self-instigated growth.

Nouwen and Gaffney turn to this Biblical tradition of unconditional love in an evocative discussion of the "painful suffering of many old people which makes their aging into a way to the darkness." Noting that the painful lot of many among the aged is more a reflection on the evils of our society than upon limitations inherent among the elderly, they go on: "Yet for those who suffer, the rejection by their society can lead to the recognition of an acceptance we ourselves have not been able to give. Out of the recognition that life is determined neither by what one did, had, or achieved, nor by one's friends or relatives, nor even by one's own self-understanding, the way might be found to Him whose heart is greater than ours and who says through His own son, the broken servant of Yahweh: 'You are accepted.' "[7]

William Bouwsma suggests another image in the tradition of western Christianity as a resource to the critical issue of self-esteem in mature age. "The biblical idea of time," Bouwsma asserts, "is the foundation for the conception of the worth of the individual personality."[8] In Christian mythology, he argues, creation is a true beginning. The temporal dimensions of process and change are real (not illusory) and good (not imperfect manifestations of unchanging ideal forms). The biblical God has underscored the positive significance of time, process, and change through His continuing presence and intervention within the unique and unrepeatable events of human history. Thus, the pattern of the life experience of each individual is unique. The individual's past, as a history of his or her personal encounter with life—and with God—is holy as well. "The past demonstrates God's care and will for men and therefore cannot be ignored or repudiated," writes Bouwsma; "The significance of the past also points to the indelible importance of all human experience. It gives meaning to the particular temporal experiences that have shaped each individual during the whole course of his life." [9]

For Bouwsma, then, the Christian meaning system can provide an interpretation of time, history, and individuality that permits a positive evaluation of one's life based not simply upon what has been done or what can be done. Beyond the record of these "doings," the history of one's life is also an account of God's continuing care and of His saving action in the world. Appreciation of life, therefore, need not be limited to criteria of productivity or social usefulness. One's life is of value—a person is of value—beyond such partial considerations.

These two Christian images—God's unconditional love and the religious significance of personal life history—suggest that there are bases of self-worth independent of economic productivity and social role. Noting this claim, or hope, implicit in this religious language, the humanist may find here a potential resource. The underlying insight—that personal worth does not depend simply on one's usefulness to others—transcends the limits of the various vocabularies in which it is expressed. Its salience for the humanist need not be diminished, indeed, it can be enhanced by a consideration of the particular nuances of meaning that these Christian categories add to the basic human insight.

II. Interpreting the Significance of One's Own Life

As a person grows older the question of the significance of his own life must be faced. Of what use has it been to oneself? To others? Will the values which one has attempted to realize end with death? Are they of meaning in any larger context? Will anything come of one's efforts, often felt to have been less than successful, to find value, to extend value, to preserve value in the world beyond the self?

Erik Erikson designates this central crisis of late adulthood as the challenge of integrity, "the acceptance of one's one and only life cycle and of the people who have become significant to it as something that had to be and that, by necessity, permitted no substitutions." [10] Successfully resolved, this struggle for integrity results in an "accrued assurance" of the meaning of an individual's life, as well as of the larger flow of generations. Recently Erikson has described this struggle in powerful detail in his analysis of Dr. Borg, the central character in Ingmar Bergman's classic film *Wild Strawberries*. "I found this screenplay an incomparable representation of the wholeness of the human life cycle," Erikson states, "which I now feel I should spell out for this new generation of adults who (after all we have learned about childhood and youth) feel impelled to comprehend, not without some reluctance and distaste, what adulthood and old age are really all about."[11] The film records the day's journey of an elderly Swedish physician from his retirement home in the countryside to the University in Lund, where he is to be honored for fifty years of service in his profession. "But this journey by car on marked roads through familiar territory," Erikson maintains, "also becomes a symbolic pilgrimage back into his childhood and deep into his unknown self."[12] Over the course of the day's events we witness Dr. Borg's struggle to reach a sense of personal meaning that can overcome the threats of despair and disgust. The vital strength of the human spirit which is evoked and tested in this struggle is, according to Erikson, wisdom. *"Wisdom, in whatever systematic or implicit, eloquent or quiet way it may be expressed, is the detached and yet active concern with life itself in the face of death itself, . . . it maintains and conveys the integrity of experience, in spite of the decline of bodily and mental functions."*[13] Such wisdom is the final fruition of hope, which is "the first and most basic human strength."[14] And like hope, wisdom "must rely on the power of unconscious processes as well as on some confirmation by fate—and by faith."[15]

Don Browning, a theologian whose work has been influenced significantly by Erikson,[16] turns to the religious images of salvation and hope in his appraisal of the potential of Christian symbols to illumine this crisis of integrity and the accompanying emergence of wisdom. Characteristic of the earliest narratives and stories of Jesus, notes Browning, is an insistence on the relationship between the present and the future. Jesus calls his followers to participate by their present actions in God's saving action of ushering in the Kingdom. As Browning puts it, "participation of early Christians, both individually and corporately, in God's saving and redeeming work gave them a sense that their own finite efforts were caught up in the activity of God and therefore had an objective significance to them that would transcend their own suffering and eventual death."[17] Through subsequent centuries this understanding of one's own life and actions as participating in God's saving plan for humankind has provided for many believing Christians a sense of ultimate personal significance, and Browning suggests that it might be possible to retrieve this religious image of individual significance as a means of confronting the contemporary crisis of meaning in old age. One's own limited and often apparently fruitless efforts gain potency when understood as part of God's plan for the world.

Within such a context the task of coming to accept the particularity and peculiarity of one's own life can be undertaken with an added measure of hope. One can be confident that the good work which God has begun in the self (and, through one's efforts, in the world) will be brought to completion (even beyond one's efforts). The active and responsible involvement in the world which appropriately characterizes early and middle adulthood can be transmuted—as one's ability to control and contribute gradually diminish—into a more disengaged concern. Browning suggests that this desire for some sense of the lasting significance of one's life can find its ground in the Christian concept of personal salvation. Quoting psychologist and theologian James Lapsley, he argues that salvation "must refer primarily to the preservation in the life of God of the values realized in the world, especially in the lives of men."[18]

"What does this understanding of hope and salvation in these crucial New Testament sources suggest for the problem of aging?" asks Browning. These images function, he responds, as "symbolic representation(s) of an objective activity on the part of God that transforms the world and preserves the values of those who participate in His work." In addition, they provide "ideological reinforcement to our efforts to make generativity and care victorious over stagnation and self-absorption."[19]

Here again the humanist may look to the deeper human hope for personal significance implicit in this religious language of hope and salvation. It is possible that an image of personal significance, drawn from religious sources or from elsewhere among the traditions of western humanism, could speak powerfully in the contemporary discussion of human aging.

III. Coming to Terms with the Changes and Losses of Aging

For Americans today, growing older is most often accompanied by changes in income, residence, patterns of social interaction and the personal use of time. For many, there is also the experience of loss—of one's spouse, of cherished friends and companions, of status and established social roles, of physical vigor and health. Not all these changes need be, or are, experienced as negative. And many of the debilitating effects of the losses of aging can be mitigated by personal planning and effective social policy. But the alterations of change and loss are endemic to the human experience of growing older. One's ability to in some way come to terms with these inevitable losses of old age is a critical test of human maturity.

The religious authors we are considering make use of several images in their attempts to suggest a religious perspective appropriate to the experience of change and loss in mature age. In the context of our earlier discussion of self-worth, we noted Bouwsma's reference to a Christian understanding of time. Here we will consider his explication of a Christian understanding of adulthood. The essential note of the Christian biblical understanding of human maturity, for Bouwsma, is its emphasis on the dynamic processes of continuing change and growth. This focus on continual development distinguishes the biblical view from a more classical notion of adult maturity as a state which—once achieved—is to be sustained without deviation. In the

Christian conception of human life, according to Bouwsma, the goal of human development is total conformity to the manhood of Christ. But since this is a transcendent goal, the practical emphasis in Christian adulthood is on the process rather than its end. Since it is impossible to achieve perfect maturity in this life, the duty of the Christian is simply to develop constantly toward it. The essential element in the Christian idea of adulthood is, accordingly, the capacity for growth, which is assumed to be a potentiality of any age of life." [20] For the Christian, then, the changes of late adulthood, like those of adolescence and middle age, can be interpreted as continuing opportunities to grow into the full stature of Christ.

Bouwsma does not take up explicitly the issues of old age; his focus is adulthood, not aging. But his discussion of human maturity offers a religious symbol that can be relevant to the individual involved in the significant personal changes of aging—the Christian as pilgrim. "The Christian is not to evade the challenges, the struggles, the difficulties and dangers of life, but to accept, make his way through, and grow in them," remarks Bouwsma. He continues: "This understanding of life finds expression in the figure of the Christian as wayfarer (*viator*) or pilgrim; Christian conversion is thus not, as in the mystery religions, an immediate entrance into a safe harbor but rather, though its direction has been established, the beginning of a voyage into the unknown. . . . From this standpoint, just as the essential condition of Christian adulthood is the capacity for growth, . . . its opposite—what might be called the Christian conception of immaturity—is the refusal to grow, the inability to cope with an open and indeterminate future (that is, the future itself), in effect the rejection of life as a process." [21] The acceptance of life as a process, the appreciation of the open-endedness of both personal and social development, the identification of oneself as a pilgrim-on-the-way—these realizations suggest that one's experience of *change* in aging can be interpreted as an invitation from God to continue the process of growth toward full human maturity.

Among religious writers today there are also attempts to provide a religious perspective upon the *losses* experienced in aging. Of particular interest is the appeal to the images of an ascetical spirituality of "emptying" and "letting go," a tradition found in Christianity as well as in Eastern religious thought. In Christianity, this spirituality of emptying, or *kenosis,* finds its most forceful expression in the Pauline description of Jesus as one who "emptied himself, taking the form of a servant" (*Philippians* 2:7). [22] Eastern religious thought provides even more powerful elaborations of this theme. The development of the notion of *sunyata* in Madhyamika Buddhism, [23] as well as the paradoxical role of emptiness (*hsü*) in Taoism, [24] attest to the central importance of this symbol.

In each of these religious traditions, the ascetical challenge is similar—to let go one's own determinations regarding the self as the prerequisite discipline for undertaking the spiritual quest; to empty oneself of the distracting ambitions and false criteria of value that stand as obstacles to one's realization of the transcendent. In such a perspective, the losses of aging need not be experienced solely as negative. Physical, social, and financial loss can be interpreted as part of a spiritually significant process of "emptying" and "letting go." The individual is invited to recognize the religious possibilities hidden within even those aspects of human aging which are obviously deleterious.

In this context my colleague James Whitehead writes, "the social event of retirement performs a religiously ironic function: it empties out of a person's life perhaps the most sturdy crutch of self-worth, one's social role and usefulness. In this moment of stripping away, of death to a former style of life, the Church's ministry must not be that of substituting ersatz identities, but of celebrating this emptying process which leads to God."[25] Stripped of these partial sources of identity, the religious person can grow to recognize, even celebrate, a deeper truth—that no one ever "earns" his way, that life's meaning is more a gift than a reward.

Sidney Callahan and Drew Christianson, writing in the interdisciplinary journal *Soundings,* suggest the Christian mystical tradition as another point of reference in uncovering a significance to the losses of old age that goes beyond an exclusively negative appraisal of their impact. "Mystics in every tradition," they note, "have pointed to the need for living fully *now,* making 'a sacrament of the present moment' with a concentration on the immediate experience. In obtaining this fullness in the present, a discipline is imposed, as in old age: one must be removed from power, be divested of external social roles, and turn away from the world's claims. So too the remembrance of death and finitude has always been considered an essential means to living fully now. The 'letting go' required of death creates an appreciation of each present hour."[26]

The losses of age can be viewed, in other words, as vivid reminders of the finitude and contingency of all human life. This insight into human contingency is understood as central in religious traditions of both East and West. In facing and accepting the real diminishments of one's own aging, the older person is led to see things as they really are. Thus the quest for spiritual awareness is continued, even brought to maturity, in the challenge of the acceptance of one's old age.

These images of acceptance of aging are potentially powerful vehicles of religious awareness. Care must be taken, however, that they do not deteriorate at the political level into catch-phrases used to sanction individual resignation or communal passivity in the face of society's less-than-adequate response to its aging members. Many of the negative aspects of growing old in America can be changed. Retirement, financial security in mature age, preventive medicine and health care delivery, continuing participation of older Americans in civic life—these issues must be addressed with more creativity than American public policy has shown to date. Religious images, used to delay or divert this public discussion, are misused.

Conclusion

In this paper we have considered six religious images, examining the manner in which they are currently being interpreted in relation to the human experience of aging. These images are:

a. *personal salvation*	The values and achievements of a person's life will be taken up and endure in the continuing life of God.
b. *hope*	Confidence that one's life is a part of God's plan; the efforts toward good that one has begun will not end with one's life; they will be brought to completion beyond the self.
c. *religious sense of time and personal history*	God acts in and through the lives of individuals; there is religious significance in the unique, cumulative experience of the individual's life.
d. *God's unconditional love for the individual*	God's love is not dependent upon one's works; there is thus a basis for self-esteem independent of productivity, social role, physical vigor or beauty; a person is more than what he does.
e. *spiritual discipline of "emptiness" and "letting go"*	The deprivations and losses of advancing age are opportunities to divest oneself of the illusory ambitions and false securities of life which often serve as distractions from the life of the spirit; letting go of these distractions, one is able to live more fully in the present, to see life as it is.
f. *image of the Christian as pilgrim-on-the-way*	It is in the continuing experience of change throughout life that the person develops more fully into the "full measure of Christ," thus the Christian need not fear aging, for the future and its demands for personal change can be interpreted as the invitation of God.

It is likely that for some in American society today the religious quality of these images will enhance their power and efficacy as interpretive devices. Others will find the religious origin of the images irrelevant, or even distracting. Even for this latter company, I suggest, these images may serve as examples of ways in which the imagination of western civilization has attempted to give expression to its awareness of the potentially positive dimensions of aging.

Each of these images resonates with a basic realization or hope of the human spirit. That ones life has significance, that ones worth transcends accomplishments, that apparent "losses" may, in fact, be gains—these intuitions, which often give rise to the religious sense, are not limited to religious expression. The humanist can trace expressions of these intuitions elsewhere in literature and art, in history and biography. These intuitions, expressed in religious language or in other symbol systems, can lead to an understanding of aging which permits the appreciation of its positive, self-enhancing, developmental aspects. By recalling from our collective cultural memory some of the positive images and models of aging, by attempting to express and to interpret these in contemporary culture, the humanist can expand the range of attitudes toward aging available in American society today.

Michel Philibert reminds us that "our attitude toward aging shapes our experience."[27] Our evaluation of mature age—as "good" or "bad," as a phase of life to be welcomed or to be avoided—will be conditioned by the opinions, beliefs, and images we carry within us regarding the human experience of growing older and being old. If our basic perspective toward aging is developed from largely negative images, it is likely that we shall find in our experience of aging only its negative aspects. If our orientation toward aging can be broadened beyond simply negative categories, it is possible that more positive aspects of the ambiguous human experience of aging may be experienced and savored.

Included among the products of the western imagination collected in our humanistic heritage is a wide range of both positive and negative images of aging. The religious themes we have examined above can be interpreted as positive images of aging. As such these symbols may enable us to contribute to the expansion of the perspective through which the phenomena of human aging can be evaluated and appreciated within contemporary society.

Notes

[1] "Human Values, Economic Values and the Elderly," paper delivered at the "Human Values and Aging" project, Case Western Reserve University, Cleveland, Ohio, October 10, 1975.

[2] "Biomedical Aspects of Aging," address delivered at the "Human Values and Aging" project, Case Western Reserve University, Cleveland, Ohio, October 11, 1975.

[3] The following journals are rich sources of such articles: *Christian Century, Christianity Today, Journal of Pastoral Care, Religion and Mental Health, Review of Religious Research, Pastoral Psychology.*

[4] *Aging: The Fulfillment of Life* (New York: Doubleday, 1974).

[5] *Toward a Theology of Aging* (New York: Human Sciences Press, 1975).

[6] "The Phenomenological Approach to Images of Aging," *Soundings,* 57, No. 1 (Spring 1974), 34.

[7] *Aging: The Fulfillment of Life,* p. 131.

[8] "Christian Adulthood," *Daedalus,* 105, No. 2 (Spring 1976), 83.

[9] Ibid.

[10] *Identity, Youth and Crisis* (New York: Norton, 1968), p. 139.

[11] "Dr. Borg's Life Cycle," *Daedalus,* 105, No. 2 (Spring 1976), 3.

[12] Ibid., p. 1.

[13] Ibid., p. 23.

[14] Ibid.

[15] Ibid.

[16] See his *Generative Man: Psychoanalytic Perspectives* (Philadelphia: Westminster, 1973).

[17] "Preface to a Practical Theology of Aging," in *Toward a Theology of Aging.* p. 162.

[18] Ibid., quoted in James Lapsley, *Salvation and Health* (Philadelphia: Westminster, 1972), p. 53.

[19] Browning, *Generative Man,* p. 162.

[20] Bouwsma, "Christian Adulthood," p. 83.

[21] Ibid.

[22] Herbert G. May and Bruce M. Metzger, eds., *The Oxford Annotated Bible* (New York: Oxford Univ. Press, 1962), p. 1422.

[23] See T.R.V. Murti, *The Central Philosophy of Busshim* (London: Allen and Unwin, 1955) and Frederick Streng, *Emptiness: A Study in Religious Meaning* (Nashville, Tenn.: Abingdon Press, 1967).

[24] See especially chapters 3, 4, 5, 15, 16 in *Lao Tse,* trans. D.C. Lau (Baltimore: Penguin Books, 1963).

[25] "The Parish and Sacraments of Adulthood: Access to an Educational Future," *Listening: Journal of Religion and Culture,* 12, No. 2 (Spring 1977), 80.

[26] "Ideal Old Age," *Soundings,* 57, No. 1 (Spring 1974), 11-12.

[27] Philibert, p. 33.

Aging: A
Theological Perspective 6

by Rev. Charles E. Curran, S.T.D.

This paper attempts to give a theological perspective on aging and the elderly. A few preliminary clarifications are in order.

Theology can be described as systematic reflection on human life and experience in the light of faith. Theological reflection does not pretend to have all the answers or to solve all the problems confronting humanity. Theology, in fact, must be in intimate contact and dialogue with human experience and with all that science and reason can tell us about the human. I theologize out of the Roman Catholic tradition which has constantly emphasized that theological reflection involves both faith and reason and has even gone so far as to assert that there cannot be a contradiction between faith and reason. Theology, therefore, cannot dispense with biology, sociology, psychology, gerontology, medicine, and all the other sciences which tell us about the human. Theology is constantly learning from the human, and the experience of the human, in all its various dimensions.

The title avoids any pretension of giving a complete theology of the aging. Our goal is much more modest,—a theological perspective on aging and the elderly. This perspective will deal primarily with the question of the meaning and understanding of aging and not with programmatic or policy approaches to the aging. Theology itself should have something to contribute to the ongoing dialogue about programmatic and policy questions concerning the aging and elderly in our country, but still the primary function of theology should be in terms of the more ultimate questions of meaning. Even here in the question of the meaning and significance of aging, a theological perspective recognizes the important contributions made to the meaning of aging by the other human sciences and must be in constant dialogue with them.

Father Curran is Professor of Moral Theology at the Catholic University of America; former president of the Catholic Theological Society of America; and author of *New Perspectives in Moral Theology* and *Catholic Moral Theology in Dialogue*. The above paper was delivered on April 27, 1979 at the Colloquium on Aging that was part of the Sixtieth Anniversary celebration of the National Catholic School of Social Service.

Social Thought, Summer 1979
© *1979 National Conference of Catholic Charities*
Washington, D.C.

In many contemporary discussions about aging and the elderly, the meaning and significance of aging in the light of faith-filled reflection are often not discussed. One can readily understand the reason for such a gap. In our pluralistic society, there are many different faith perspectives as well as many different positions which claim to exclude all faith presuppositions. The easiest way to solve such a pluralism is to leave these ultimate questions of faith and meaning to the individual and to the private sphere, whereas the scientific, programmatic, and policy aspects of these questions can be dealt with in public dialogue. Unfortunately, a dichotomy is thus set up, and the questions of ultimate meaning tend to be ignored, both in themselves, and in their important relationship to what should be involved in the programmatic and policy approaches to the aging.

Recently, I viewed a proposed series of TV shows on questions of bioethics. It was interesting to note the tendency to stay away from questions of ultimate meaning, because these questions obviously involve a faith perspective on which many people in our society differ. Both theoretically and practically, there are problems in not addressing these questions of meaning as interpreted by faith. Theoretical considerations remain incomplete and even distorted when some important questions of meaning are not discussed. From the practical perspective, I think most people in our society would admit that faith, or even lack of faith, is a very significant aspect of their understanding of human existence, and especially of human death. To pretend that this important aspect does not exist or does not color the way in which people actually think about death seems to distort the reality itself. On this particular series of television programs, all other aspects of the question were mentioned and discussed—the biological, the sociological, the psychological, and, in addition, various programmatic and public policy issues were raised. The ultimate question of meaning was studiously avoided.[1]

One must appreciate the opposite danger. Religious pluralism is a fact of life in our society. In many ways we have suffered as a nation when one group has tried to impose its religious convictions upon others in public life. The problem requires a balancing of our faith understanding and our respect for the consciences of others and their different faiths. The easiest solution to the problem seems to be the path of least resistance which is most often taken—all such questions of ultimate meaning involving faith are excluded from the public forum and public debate. However, it is precisely such a solution which is inadequate, both on theoretical and on practical grounds.

The National Catholic School of Social Service of the Catholic University of America, as part of the celebration of its Sixtieth Anniversary, addresses the question of the aging and elderly in our society. In my judgment, precisely such a school and such a forum should be the place in which, in a public manner, the question about the ultimate meaning and significance of aging, life, and death can and should be raised.[2] In the context of this symposium, my considerations are based on a Roman Catholic theological understanding. Obviously, many people in our society will bring to their consideration a different understanding of aging and of life and death. Even those who do not share this same faith vision might actually come to some of the same conclusions which I will reach in this paper. However, I make no apologies for my approach, except to note that it would only be fully accepted by those people who share the same basic vision.

In discussions about the aging and the elderly, there always lurks the danger of hubris, or pride, on the part of those involved in the discussions. Too often, the question is explicitly or implicitly posed in terms of what society can and should do for the aging and the elderly. The presupposition is that the aging and the elderly have nothing to say about us or about the worldview of our society. In these days, we recognize the danger that a majority group in society might very readily impose its self-understanding on others. One can think, for example, of the role of women in a male-dominated society. A Christian perspective reminds all of us of the need for conversion and the recognition of our own sinfulness so that we can be self-critical and enter into dialogue with others. There are important things that the aging and the elderly can say to the rest of us in our society.[3]

Aging and Death in the Light of Paschal Mystery

One very common view of old age sees it in the light of a slope, or peak, view of human existence. There is a sharp upward movement representing childhood, youth, and adolescence, which then continues to develop at a lesser rate to a peak, which is followed by a gradual decline, after which there is a sharp downward thrust of the curve in old age towards death. Such a vision of human existence tends to see the productive work which most adults do in our society as the most meaningful aspect of human existence. Childhood and adolescence are a preparation for work, and then retirement and old age indicate withdrawal from work and a downward curve in the meaning of human existence. In this paper, such a view of the meaning of human existence will be challenged. Not only should we disagree with such an understanding of old age and the elderly, but we should also challenge its presuppositions about what is the meaning and dignity of human life.

The finality of death, and its relationship to birth, at the opposite end of the scale, give credence to the slope view of human existence described above. To overturn such a view, this paper will propose a different understanding of death.[4] The Christian concept of the Paschal Mystery sheds light on the meaning of death, as well as the meaning of life for the Christian. The central mystery of Christianity is the dying and rising of the Lord, and, through Baptism, Christians are initiated into the new life of the risen Lord and share and participate in that Paschal Mystery.

Death in the Christian understanding has a number of different aspects.[5] In general, I propose a stance or perspective for Christian ethics which sees all reality in terms of the fivefold mysteries of creation, sin, incarnation, redemption, and resurrection destiny. In the light of this perspective, three different aspects of death must be considered. First, biological death is the lot of all that has organic life. Death is inherently connected with our created human existence and is something belonging to our very biological existence. In this sense, death is a natural event. Second, death, in the Christian understanding, is intimately connected with sin. According to St. Paul's understanding, death came into the world through sin (Romans 5:12). In the book of Genesis, with its poignant meditation on the problem of evil, sin and death are closely related. Sin separates us from the giver of life. The natural consequence of sin is death. This is the ultimate explanation of the fact that those who sinned were no longer able to live with Yahweh in the peaceful relationship in the garden. If God did not intervene to save his people through Noah (which has become a symbol of salvation through the waters of Baptism in the Christian tradition), sin would have come to its logical conclusion in the death and destruction of all that lives.[6] The New Testament sees the death of Jesus in terms of the power and even the triumph of sin and of the forces of darkness.

Thirdly, death is also seen in the light of the resurrection and of the fullness of resurrection destiny. For Jesus, death and sin were not the end. Through the resurrection which the Scriptures attribute to the power of the Spirit (the one who gives life), Jesus triumphed over death itself. The resurrection transformed death into a saving mystery. One and the same reality, which seemed to be the end and the triumph of sin, was ultimately transformed into the victory of life itself. Thus, there are three aspects of the meaning of death in the Christian understanding—death as natural and biological event; death as affected by sin; and death as transformed by the resurrection into the fullness of life.

The failure to consider all these aspects of death often results in a distortion. In the last few years, the liturgical emphasis in Roman Catholicism has focused on the aspect of death as transformation through the power of the resurrection. The vestments, the joyful songs, and the hopeful refrains of the Mass of the Resurrection testify to such an approach. While agreeing with the primacy of the resurrection motif, I am fearful that present Catholic celebration and articulation do not give enough emphasis to the aspect of death as affected by sin. Death is rightly associated with loneliness, isolation, and ultimately loss. Death is something over which we have no ultimate control. Especially in the death of the young, or death by accident, the brutal and harsh reality of death becomes even more evident. The full reality of death, as affected by sin, should not be too easily glossed over in the light of the cheap grace of the resurrection. Yes, the resurrection transforms the reality of death, but one must always experience the sin-related aspect of death and all that is connected with it.[7]

Our understanding of death, as seen in the light of a natural event infected by sin and transformed by the resurrection, raises further questions about the exact relationship between life in this world and life after death. The Christian belief calls for life after death, but what is its relationship to life in this world? Is this relationship one of continuity or discontinuity between this world and the next? In more technical terms, is the Paschal Mystery of death and resurrection to be interpreted in paradoxical or in transformationalist terms? Arguments for discontinuity and a paradoxical understanding are based on the apparent opposition between the symbols and explanations used to describe the Paschal Mystery in Jesus—life in the midst of death, light in the midst of darkness, joy in sorrow, and power in weakness. Death thus appears as a complete break, separating two different aspects of existence—earthly life, which ends in death, and the heavenly life, which begins anew. Pushed to its logical conclusions, this view understands our present world and existence primarily as a vale of tears, marked, above all, by the presence of sin, suffering, and death, from which the Christian is mercifully saved by the gracious intervention of God, who after death, brings the individual to the new life. Life in the world and the future life appear to be in a paradoxical or discontinuous relationship.

However, I would argue for more continuity between this world and the next, between life before death and life after death. In this view, death for the Christian is seen more in transformational terms and with some continuity between this life and the next, although, obviously, there is not total continuity.[8]

An older, scholastic Catholic theology stressed more the aspect of continuity rather than total discontinuity. This theology viewed eternal life primarily in terms of immortality rather than in the more Biblical concept of resurrection. Immortality is ultimately grounded in the spiritual nature of the human soul created by God, which, even now, is the form of our existence. Such a perspective emphasized continuity, but, when it was exaggerated, downplayed the importance of the material, the bodily, the worldly, and the social aspects of human existence and did not give enough importance to the concept of resurrection. Traditional scholastic theorizing about eternal life described it in terms of the beatific vision. The two highest faculties or powers of the human soul are intellect and will. The whole dynamism of human existence is grounded in the fact that our intellect and will are striving for the true and the good. Heaven or eternal life must involve the fulfillment of the intellect and the will, which alone can give perfect rest and peace—the intellect knows truth itself and the will loves the perfect good. Again, criticisms of this understanding are in order, but the basic thrust of the understanding argues for some continuity between this life and the next.[9]

The very words "death" and "life" seem to argue for discontinuity and a totally paradoxical relationship between this world and the next. However, our Christian understanding sees the Paschal Mystery of Jesus as paradigmatic of the whole of the Christian life and not only of Christian death. Through baptism, the Christian first enters into the Paschal Mystery. Through baptism, we die to sin and rise in the newness of the life of the risen Lord. The Christian, even now, in life, shares in the first fruits of the resurrection. Thus, after death, we share in the fullness of that which is now ours in its first fruits as the gift of the resurrected Lord to all who believe. Death for the Christian does not mark a total break with what has gone before, because one has already been sharing in the life of the risen Lord. Theology in the 1960's became too optimistic and saw too much continuity between this world and the next, between human progress and the coming of the Kingdom. However, death for the individual Christian should not be seen as the ending of our life and the beginning of an entirely different reality but, rather, as a transformation of our earthly existence into the fullness of the life of the risen Lord.

How does such an understanding jibe with human experience? As mentioned earlier, theology must always be in touch with human experience. Is there anything in human experience which would support (not prove) the transformationist understanding of death and the recognition of some continuity between this world and the next? A phenomenological view of human existence has been proposed which is in harmony with such a transformationist view.[10]

In human existence, one can readily see two different curves— an upward curve and a downward curve. At first sight, it might seem that such an understanding of these two curves would support the slope or peak theory—a curve which, in the very beginning, goes upward, until it reaches a peak, and then gradually descends, until it suddenly cascades to its finality in old age and death.

There is no doubt that a downward curve is more evident and pronounced in older life, and death appears to be the ultimate fulfillment of this downward curve. Aging and old age bring with it a diminishment often accompanied by pain, suffering, loneliness, and isolation. The biological and physical aspects of human existence slow up and begin to diminish. The deterioration which started with glasses for the eyes, dentures for lost teeth, and hearing aids for deaf ears quickly seems to spread throughout the physical organism. Limbs shrivel, bones stiffen, arthritis inflames the joints. How sad it is at times to see old people who were so vibrant and full of energy now reduced to a wheelchair or totally confined to a bed. Those who, during life, ranged far and wide are now confined, often within the limits of a room, a bed, or a chair. People who had social and professional responsibilities of great magnitude are now reduced to almost total dependence on others for anything they might want to do or even to fulfill their own basic needs. At times, deterioration also affects the mental powers—memory goes, intellectual stimuli are lessened, and thought becomes confused. Advancing old age is often characterized by greater and greater passivity and dependence.

However, there is an upward curve about human existence that speaks of growth and development and is characterized by a growing self-encounter, a greater and deeper expansion of our relationships with other persons and the growing encounter with our God. This upward curve can be seen in many aspects of our human existence. From earliest years, the upward thrust entails a movement from dependence on others in a narrow environment to a greater independence and an overcoming of the limitations of time and space. Childhood and adolescence obviously mark such a growth toward a true independence (note that this is not to be understood in a selfish way) and at the same time to a greater widening of our horizons and relationships. This upward thrust continues through maturity, for, here, the individual both strives to become more and more the creative center of his or her own existence and more deeply related to others in ever-widening horizons and relationships. Through graceful maturity, the individual comes to an ever deepening self-encounter whereby he or she is less perturbed by the immediate happenings of existence and is able to be much less influenced by the changing circumstances of life. This is the ideal picture of the wise old person who, through years of experience and accumulated wisdom, having seen the beauty of human existence and its degradations, having experienced the love of other human beings and known, as well, hatred and vengeance, now serenely and peacefully views human existence and strives for meaning and intelligibility. Now, less dependent than ever on the vicissitudes of time and space, and purified in the struggle of human existence, the aging person comes to grips with him/herself in an ever-deepening encounter and acceptance of who he/she is and how life should be lived. The upward curve also indicates growing and deeper relationships with others, as, through the direct experience of life and manifold vicarious experiences, the aging person overcomes the narrowness and confines of his or her own historicity and tends to broaden and deepen relationships and horizons. In this process, the believer also sees a growth in his or her relationship with God. Thus, the ideal picture of the upward curve of human existence involves a richer encounter with ourselves, an ever broadening and widening of our horizons and relationships with others, and a strengthening of our relationship with the source of all life itself.

How can old age and death be interpreted in the light of these theological and phenomenological considerations? The believing Christian does not see death as the end but as a way to the fullness of life. Death at first seems to be the triumph of the downward curve of existence, but the believer sees through death the ultimate triumph of the upward curve. Eternal life can be interpreted as the upward curve of human existence coming to the fullness of self-encounter, to the fullness of our relationships with others in the world, and to the most intimate of relationships with our God. Thus, death remains the ambivalent reality par excellence— apparently the end, but, for those who believe, the entry into the fullness of life whereby the present is transformed and ultimately brought to its fullness.

Applications of the Theory

In the light of this understanding of the paradigm of the Paschal

Mystery, and of a transformationist interpretation of death, a number of significant applications can be made to our understanding of life in general and of old age in particular.

First, death is understood in the perspective of a crisis situation in which destructive and threatening forces are ultimately transformed. The crisis situation of death has great similarities with other growth and crisis situations in human existence in which the believer sees again the Paschal Mystery at work. In the crisis of early life the paradigm described above is quite evident. Take the child's first day in school. It is usually a traumatic experience—something new and threatening replacing the security and comfort of a former situation. No wonder that tears and tantrums so often mark that day. Growth demands a dying to the past so that one can go beyond it—but it is always a painful process. The essential ambiguity is that the type of existence which gave comfort and security now becomes narrow, confining, and limited. Growth calls for us to pass beyond this stage so that we might enter into a deeper experience of life. But the pain of dying to the past and rising in the newness of life will always be there.

Christian marriage serves as another illustration. Marriage calls for the wife and husband to die to the past and to enter into the newness of life. We are reminded in the Scriptures that for this reason they shall leave father and mother, brothers and sisters, and cling to each other as two in one flesh. Although joy and happiness abound at the celebration of marriage, there also remain fears, insecurities, and even a sense of pain, loss, and separation. Death and the crisis of old age preceding it should be seen in the same light. Here, too, it is necessary to pass beyond the limits of old age that prevent further self-development. Ultimately the crisis of death involves dying in order that the fullness of life might come. We see only one side of the crisis of death with our eyes, but our hearts through faith and hope rely on a deeper meaning of transformation that will take place and even now is at work. The crisis of death involving dying and rising is thus related to other crises in our lives.

Such a view of human existence and growth in human existence coheres with an understanding of life as a pilgrimage. Christian anthropology today often refers to our human existence as a pilgrimage in which we are called to continual conversion.[11] As pilgrims, we are constantly on the road—change and growth always characterize our lives, and the challenge is to make these changes into true growth. Growth and development are not just physical and biological. Too often, we tend to think of growth only in these very visible and quantifiable ways. The peak model of human development shares this basic narrowness of perspective. Growth calls above all for a greater encounter with one's self, with others, with all of creation, and with God. Too often, we fail to realize what constitutes true growth and thereby falsify our understanding of life, of old age, and of dying itself. A world that has begun to listen to the message that small is beautiful should also be ready to abandon our more quantifiable and less personal criteria of what truly constitutes human growth and development.

A second corollary, based on the importance of the Paschal Mystery as an interpretation of Christian death, old age, and life, concerns the active aspect of death and of old age. The literature generally describes old age and death in terms of passivity. Death readily fits into the category. We have no control over our death. In a sense it comes from outside and thrusts itself upon us. Infirmity and death are seldom willed or intended by ourselves but come despite our best efforts. The same can be said of old age. But such a judgment of death and of old age is distorted. Death and old age also involve a very active aspect which must be more recognized and acknowledged if we are to come to a better understanding of their meaning.

Look again at the death and resurrection of Jesus. Death is forced on Jesus from the outside. He is led to death as a sheep to the slaughter. The enemies of Jesus described under the theological symbols of death and sin are the active elements in the drama of the crucifixion. Jesus is passively dragged from here to there and finally nailed to the cross on which He died. But Jesus, through the loving gift of Himself, and the loving acceptance of His death, has actively transformed death into a saving mystery. Death has been changed through the power of his love into the resurrection and the fullness of life.

Many contemporary theologians likewise maintain that, for the Christian, death involves a very decisive and creative act and is not just something one passively endures from the outside. In the moment of death, the Christian affirms his or her deepest self-encounter, and at the same time his or her relationship with God and with all others. Once the restrictions and confining realities of our aging earthly existence are dissolved, the Christian can then fully affirm him/herself in loving relationship with God, others, and self. In death the limitations of the present fade away, and the person can now fully affirm him/herself in terms of these multiple relationships.[12] Even from the psychological perspective, Kübler-Ross points out that the final reaction to death is acceptance—but here, too, there is an active element present and not a mere receptivity.[13] For the Christian, it is a hope-filled acceptance in the light of seeing death as a way to eternal life through transformation.

In the same sense, old age calls for activity—but activity properly understood. Too often, activity is described in terms of external goods and technological productivity. Obviously, old age in this sense is less productive and less active. However, look at the works of art, music, and literature that have been done by people in old age. At the very least, such a consideration reminds us that activity and productivity should not be confined merely to material things or a technological understanding of human existence.

The challenge of old age is to be truly active—in the sense of accepting old age, appropriating it, giving it meaning, and integrating it into oneself as a person. Some philosophers characterize the human person as a meaning-giver. This is the active aspect of personal development for all of us—to give meaning to our existence and to incorporate all the realities of life into the integrated whole of the person. Yes, in a technological sense we produce less in old age; we do less in the terms of the material and the physical; but we are called upon to be active, to give meaning and intelligibility to our lives. The old and the old-old should truly be active in the most personal sense of being active—giving meaning and intelligibility to their lives. For the Christian, the meaning comes in terms of the living out of the Pachal Mystery by which we come to know and experience the Lord in the fellowship of his suffering and in the power of his resurrection.[14]

Our human experience seems to support the above analysis. Look at those who, in our judgment, have aged successfully—and not just those who are in good physical shape but even those who have suffered handicaps and debilities. These are the people who have actively given meaning to their life and integrated all aspects of their existence into their persons. We all admire the truly beautiful person who cheerfully bears witness to what it means to be human. A recognition of the true activity of all life and of old age belies the often accepted notion of old age as passive. The old face the crisis and challenge of giving meaning to their existence. A more scientific rendering of the psychology of human existence also seems to corroborate the active aspects of old age.[15] Erikson has proposed a theory of ego development in which the stage of aging is characterized by what he called integrity. Integrity involves an acceptance of one's own and only life and a detached and yet active concern with life itself.[16]

As a third corollary, the ways in which this understanding of old age calls into question some common assumptions in our society can be discussed. Too often, society attributes value and dignity to persons in terms of what they do, make, or accomplish.

The person becomes identified with his/her job. However, the Christian vision sees dignity and worth primarily in terms of the fact that life is a gift of the gracious God. Such an understanding of the value of human life not only calls into question many of the assumptions of our society but also furnishes a very solid basis for defending the basic equality of all human lives. A false quietism would deny any value to human actions and efforts, but the ultimate reason for human dignity does not rest on our works or our accomplishments. The Biblical emphasis on the importance of the needs of the neighbor underscores the danger of judging others and ranking them on the basis of what they do.

Throughout this study, a technological view of human meaning and existence has been challenged. There is a place for technology in human development, but the human can never be reduced merely to the technological.[17] Too often our society is in danger of making that reductionism. Intimately connected with such a view is the insistence on technologically productive work as the ultimate meaning of human existence. As a result, we might re-examine our whole understanding of work and how it fits into the meaning of the human. Already, some older patterns are changing because education is proposed as a lifelong process and not just as a preparation for one's productive years. True, some of the need for continuing education is to keep abreast of modern technological developments, but there is also a recognition that there is more to life than material productivity.

The insistence on the fact that old age is characterized not by passivity but by truly human action also serves to correct many of our notions about what human activity is. The cult of youth and emphasis on consumption in our society are also called into question by the understanding of old age and human activity proposed here.

The mutual relationship between the aging and others in society also stresses the social fabric of our existence and goes against the individualism which so often characterizes our society. Yes, in many ways the aging are in need of the help of others in society, but the relationship with the aging is more than a one-way street. This recognition of our mutual dependence and relationship should mean that the aging remain an integral part of society. Often, the aging and the elderly have been segregated from society and isolated from others.

In conclusion, the limited aspect of this study must be recognized. The purpose has been narrowed to the question of the meaning of aging and old age for the Christian believer in the Catholic tradition. Any such presentation, by its very nature, tends to be abstract and idealistic. However, an attempt was made not to pass over the sufferings, diminishments, and problems that some people will encounter in old age. Realism recognizes that many people fail to give a meaning to their aging and do not age gracefully. These failures, together with all the sufferings of old age, as well as the failures and suffering of all life, are also seen in the light of the Paschal Mystery.

What has been proposed here remains abstract and general. Every person must give meaning to his/her life and aging in the context of the unique individuality that is the human person. Aging will have different effects on different people. Think of the differences in terms of health, wealth, familial and social relationships. Nevertheless, all must appropriate and give meaning to their own aging. The understanding of aging and death proposed here should have some influence on the way in which Christian individuals appropriate and give meaning to their aging.

There is a danger that faith will be seen as an easy solution to the hard problems of life, aging, and dying. Here, it is necessary to point out that faith in the Paschal Mystery does not protect one from the sorrows and sufferings of the Cross, nor does such faith provide a cheap or easy victory. The pilgrim character of Christian existence, together with the recognition of our apprehension of both the presence and the absence of God, has occasioned much writing in recent years about the crisis of faith, both in general, and in various times of development, especially in youth. Undoubtedly there also exists a crisis of faith for many in old age. The Church itself is now recognizing more the importance of its role in ministering to the aging and the elderly.[18] As a result, we hopefully will see some interdisciplinary studies about faith and even the problems and crisis of faith in the aging and the elderly.

Footnotes

[1]For a negative critique of theological bioethics for failing to bring out the explicit faith dimensions of reality, see James M. Gustafson, "Theology Confronts Technology and the Life Sciences," Commonweal 105 (June 16, 1978), 386–392.

[2]Mention should be made of other symposia which have tried to give importance to faith and theological perspectives. One of a continual series of Pastoral Psychology Institutes at Fordham University discussed the question of aging, and its proceedings have been published: Aging: Its Challenge to the Individual and to Society, ed. William C. Bier (New York: Fordham University Press, 1974). The National Retired Teachers Association and the American Association of Retired Persons sponsored a Conference on the Theology of Aging in the spring of 1974 which was published in Pastoral Psychology 24 (Winter 1975), 93–176.

³For a provocative statement of such an attitude, although the development of the main idea is somewhat disappointing, see Peter Naus, "The Elderly as Prophets," *Hospital Progress* 59 (May 1978), 66–68.

⁴Other approaches have been employed by theologians to dispute the peak or slope view of human existence. Paul W. Preyser, "Aging: Downward, Upward or Forward?" *Pastoral Psychology* 24 (1975), 102–118, explicitly rejects "the peak-slope illusion." Henri J. M. Nouwen and Walter J. Gaffney, *Aging* (Garden City, New York: Doubleday, 1974), employ the "wagon wheel" model. David Tracy, "Eschatological Perspectives on Aging," *Pastoral Psychology* 24 (1975), 119–134, interprets aging in the light of the eschatological perspective calling for the acceptance of past, present, and future modalities of time.

⁵My discussion on death is heavily influenced by the following three books: Ladislaus Boros, *The Mystery of Death* (New York: Herder and Herder, 1965); Karl Rahner, *On the Theology of Death* (New York: Herder and Herder, 1961); Roger Troisfontaine *I Do Not Die* (New York: Desclee, 1963).

⁶This concept of the Noachic covenant restraining the destructive power of sin is well developed in Lutheran theology. See Helmut Thielicke, *Theological Ethics I: Foundations* (Philadelphia: Fortress Press, 1966), pp. 439ff and passim.

⁷Leo J. O'Donovan, "The Prospect of Death," in *Aging: Its Challenge to the Individual and to Society*, ed. William C. Bier, pp. 212–224. O'Donovan insists on not oversimplifying death by recognizing the aspects of fear, loneliness, and suffering as well as trust, communion. and redemption.

⁸For a more complete development of a transformational understanding of the Paschal Mystery, contrasting it both in theory and in practice with a paradoxical understanding, see my "Crisis of Spirituality in Priestly Ministry," *American Ecclesiastical Review* 166 (1972), 94–111; 157–173.

⁹For a contemporary insistence on immortality and its importance for Christian ethics in this present world, see Marjorie Reiley Maguire, "Ethics and Immortality," *The American Society of Christian Ethics 1978: Selected Papers from the Nineteenth Annual Meeting*, ed. Max L. Stackhouse (Waterloo, Ontario, Canada: Council on the Study of Religion, 1978), pp. 42–61.

¹⁰The authors mentioned in note 5 propose such a phenomenological view.

¹¹Conversion has become an important theme in contemporary theology. See *Conversion: Perspectives on Personal and Social Transformation*, ed. Walter E. Conn (Staten Island, New York: Alba House, 1978).

¹²Some theologians are fearful of the concept of a final option at the moment of death, because it gives decisive importance to an act which does not take place in this world. See Gisbert Greshake. "Tod und Auferstehung: Alte Probleme neu überdacht, *Bibel und Kirche* 32 (1977), 2–11. However, one can avoid this problem by insisting on the continuity between that act and the whole life of the person in this world.

¹³Elizabeth Kübler-Ross, *On Death and Dying* (New York: Macmillan, 1970).

¹⁴Edward Fischer has attempted to give meaning to old age by seeing it in terms of worhsip. See Edward Fischer, "Aging as Worship," *Worship* 52 (March 1978), 98–108.

¹⁵For an explanation of a parish program for the aging based on a developmental theory of aging with a truly active role for the aging, see M. Vincentia Joseph, "The Parish and Ministry to the Aging," *The Living Light* 14 (1977), 69–83.

¹⁶For an exposition and application of Erikson's theory of development to the aging, see Don S. Browning, "Preface to a Practical Theology of

Aging," *Pastoral Psychology* 24 (1975), 151–167.

[17]Drew Christiansen makes an interesting distinction between neo-naturalism and technological humanism. I agree with the basic idea, but the distinction should never become a total dichotomy. Drew Christiansen, "Ethical Implications in Aging," *Encyclopedia of Bioethics I*, ed. Warren T. Reich (New York: The Free Press, 1978), 63,64

[18]Alfons Deeken, *Growing Old, and How to Cope With It* (New York: Paulist Press, 1972); Leonard J. Rizzo, "Participatory Catechesis and the Elderly," *The Living Light* 12 (1975), 100–103; Sara and Richard Reichert, *In Wisdom and the Spirit: A Religious Education Program for Those Over Sixty-Five* (New York: Paulist Press, 1976). In 1976 the Roman Catholic Bishops of the United States issued a statement entitled "Society and the Aged: Towards Reconciliation." The text is found in *Origins*: N.C. Documentary Service (May 20, 1976), 758–761.

In the Aging Years: Spirit 7

"Come hell or high water
    Hang on to the basics of being human!!"

1.

Shrink as it will . . .
With all the disconnectings going on . . .
Still to be a worlded self.
    Still collect events and persons
        that I care about
    Have enterprises in motion
        with many things to talk about.

2.

With life crowded more and more
    with
        frustrations
        diminishings
        defeats
Nevertheless
    keep recovering my feeling for a God
    whom to serve is freedom.

3.

With attention more clamored
by my own needs and hurts
    Still make persons present to me
        Understand their struggle to make a home place
        in a precarious world.

4.

Despite failing nerve synapses
And cortex power to mobilize all the consciousness I once was
    Still continue
        to turn lived moments
        into meanings which are me
    Continue
        to believe in possibilities.

5.

Even though it hurts
And adds haunting burdens . . .
    To care about what happens to me and
        to those I care about
    To feelingly think.

6.

I shall listen
To what the highest and best said in their heart
    as they fought their way thru
I shall yet be membered
    In an ecology of Spirit
        that nourishes me and to which I contribute.
Still to be an Inner-Personal region!

7.

I am Awesome Mystery
    which I will not profane or trivialize
Nor is anyone else
    to profane or trivialize.

8

Still to be Spirit!
    though dimly, and at times murky
Still to be *lived* moments
    which light up with significances!
       even though I am in process of disappearing.

9.

Still to be a meaningful story
    since soon that will be all.

10.

I have a story
    and I have a song
And the song will be sung
    till my day is done.

Ross Snyder

III

Facts and Myths of Aging

The Bible and religious tradition have provided us with a two-sided image of aging. On one side of the coin is the danger of neglect, disrespect, and abandonment of the old; on the other side is the call to sensitivity, respect, and care toward the aging. Many of the authors in this volume assume that Americans have been particularly guilty of the former and careless of the latter. Many also assume that most people view aging only as loss, deficit, a continuous downward curve toward death, and call upon us to recognize the possibilities for wisdom and continuing personal growth and meaning in the later years. In this section we present several articles which attempt to assess the accuracy of these assumptions and images, to compare the cultural image with the facts of contemporary American life.

In the first article LeFevre presents some demographic data concerning the population aged sixty-five and over which may assist the reader in evaluating statements concerning the situation of the older population. An important historical perspective is provided by Kastenbaum, who challenges the common assumption that the old were necessarily better off in earlier generations. He analyzes recent shifting attitudes toward old age and offers a provocative "alternative scenario" for the future. Harris reports on the largest nationwide survey to date of attitudes toward older people by both the under and over sixty-five age groups, and of the attitudes of persons over sixty-five toward their own lives and situation. The results confirm the generally negative image persons of all ages have toward older people in general. Yet when people over sixty-five report on their own lives their answers are not significantly different from those of younger persons.

Why, then, is the negative stereotype of aging so pervasive in our culture? Kalish suggests that the professional advocates of the aging, with their focus on those members of the older population who have the most problems, have inadvertently contributed to the distortion. In the last article Shanas refutes another common assumption, that American families shun, neglect, and readily institutionalize their elderly members. Reviewing a substantial body of research she concludes that, on the contrary, most families go to great lengths to care for their old and to avoid institutionalization.

A DEMOGRAPHIC PROFILE
OF THE OVER-65 POPULATION

Carol LeFevre

A great many generalizations are made about older people in the United States. How accurate are these views? This paper presents a brief summary of facts about the over-65 population. Some of the information confirms widely held views of the aging; some may seem surprising. These facts may provide some background for evaluating arguments and considering issues raised in this book.

Population Trends

There have been a number of important changes in the composition of the older population in this country. First, the *number* of persons over age 65 has increased from three million in 1900 to 22.4 million in 1975.[1] Second, several factors—high immigration and birth rates in the late nineteenth and early twentieth century and increased life expectancy—have contributed to an increase in the *proportion* of the population in the older age group. In 1900 only 4.1 per cent of the population had reached the age of 65 or above; by 1980 11 per cent of the population was in the older age group. Third, there has been an increase in the number of people attaining very old age. Only one person in 500 lived to the age of 85 or above in 1900, but by 1975 one in 100 survived to become that old. Fourth, because life expectancy has increased significantly more for women than for men the sex ratio within the older population has shifted. At the turn of the century there were 102 men to 100 women in the 65-plus age bracket; now there are 69 men to 100 women, and at 75 the ratio drops to 58 men to 100 women. Thus we now have an "aging" national population, a growing number of old people, more "old-old" who are likely to require special care, and especially more very old women.

Employment

At the same time that the old are increasing in numbers and in percentage of the population there has been a steady trend toward earlier retirement, voluntary and involuntary. In 1900 two-thirds of the men over the age of 65 were still working. Sixty-five as the official age of retirement had not yet been invented; that occurred with the passage of the Social Security Act in 1935. By 1975 three-fourths of the men and one-half of the women age 55-64 were employed and one-fifth of the men and under one-tenth of the women 65 and over. Many workers retired by choice. A large segment of the labor force does not find work rewarding and looks forward to leaving arduous or routine jobs as soon as possible. Leisure, freedom to engage in expressive activities, and more time with their families are attractive. Others leave the labor force because of prolonged unemployment, poor health, or mandatory retirement policies. While the retirement age in many occupations has now been raised to 70, predictions of the number of people who will actually remain on the job vary widely. Professionals and other high level workers who gain important satisfactions from their vocations, persons without families who enjoy the social contacts at work, and those who face inadequate retirement incomes frequently want to continue working as long as possible.

Income

On the average the retired population has about one-half the income that the employed population has. While more older than younger people have been poor all their lives and others experience sharply reduced income upon widowhood or retirement, the contemporary generation of old people is considerably better off economically than their parents were in old age. Most persons over 65 have adequate or good incomes. About 15 per cent (compared to 12 per cent of the general population) are living at the poverty level, with another 10 per cent near that level. However, in 1959 30 per cent of older families and 66 per cent of older individuals were living at the poverty level. Social Security benefits tied to the cost of living, government and private health programs, hot lunches and food stamp programs, and reduced taxes, fares, and other benefits based on eligibility by age have significantly increased the actual resources of the old. In the decade from 1967 to 1976 the mean income of the old actually rose at a faster rate than that of the general population. More persons over 65 (70 per cent) than of the general population (64 per cent) own their own homes, and 61 per cent own one or more automobiles. Thus although the high rate of inflation in the last few years has undoubtedly eroded the fixed incomes of the old, they also have income and assets which have risen in value. Serious economic problems clearly exist for a substantial minority, but most older people are able to live, many quite comfortably, on their total available resources.

The New Old

The present population of old people include the poor, and poorly educated, immigrants who came to this country around the turn of the century. With each succeeding year those who reach the age of 65 have had more education and have enjoyed a higher standard of living. The proportion who have graduated from high school has risen from 23 per cent in 1965 to 35 per cent in 1975 and by 1990 will be nearly 50 per cent. Greatly improved health care and nutrition in this century and less arduous conditions of work mean that many people are considerably "younger" at 65 now than their parents and grandparents were at the same age. Families have often been completed earlier and, as we have noted, employment ends sooner. Thus Neurgarten speaks of a new group, the "young-old," persons in the 55 to 70 age range who "are relatively free from traditional social responsibilities of work and family, . . . are relatively healthy, relatively well-off, and . . . are politically active."[2] The election of Ronald Reagan to the presidency at the age of 69 not only exemplifies this group but reminds us that there is a larger number than ever before of affluent, vital older people who retain command over many resources and options. There is tremendous variation in the older population, as much or more than in the younger.

Family Status and Residential Distribution

Most older people live in families. Most older men are married, while one-half of older women are widowed. The largest group of older people are married couples living together in a household. About one woman in five lives with another family member, usually a child. Only three percent of older persons are in three generation households, and only five percent are institutionalized—although Palmore estimates that perhaps as many as 25 percent will enter an institution at some time before death.[3] Two-thirds live in metropolitan areas, one-half of those in the central cities, as many as live in all non-metropolitan areas.

Health

The great majority (68 per cent) of persons over 65 consider themselves in "good" or "excellent" health compared to others their own age and report that they are able to carry out their daily activities without any serious impairment. Eighty-five to 90 percent are able to manage independent living in the community, and another 2.4 million are healthy enough to remain semi-independent—if supportive services and appropriate housing are available. Older people have fewer acute illnesses but most (86 per cent) have one to several chronic health conditions or disabilities such as hearing loss. For the first time in our history medical care is available to the great majority of the elderly and they average more visits to the doctor per year than younger persons. On the average internists spend 60 percent of their time treating the 40 percent of their patients who are 65 and over. In contrast the old receive only two percent of the time of private psychiatrists and 2.3 per cent of psychiatric outpatient services, although old people must adjust to more life changes and crises than most younger persons. Lack of geriatric training and pessimism about the possibility of helping the old result in the failure to treat many conditions which could be alleviated or reversed.

Sex Differences

There are a number of very important differences between the situation of older men and of older women. Because women not only live longer but also marry older men who die younger, they are far less likely than men to have living spouses (39 per cent of women, 79 per cent of men aged 65 and over) or to live in a family setting (58 per cent of women, 81 per cent of men). Women are more likely to live alone (40 per cent of women, 18 per cent of men in the 75 and over age group) and, largely as a consequence of living alone, are more vulnerable to institutionalization (10 per cent of women, 7.4 per cent of men in the 75-plus age group—more than twice the *number* of women). Because so many older women are widowed housewives, and those who were employed usually received far less income than men, women have a median income about one-half that of men ($2,642 vs. $4,961 in 1975) and are more likely to be poor (26.4 per cent of female-headed households, 9.8 per cent of male-headed). Indeed, most of the elderly poor are women. Men, on the other hand, have a shorter life expectancy but are more likely to have a (younger) spouse to care for them if they become ill. They make a poorer adjustment to living alone when widowed but are more likely to remarry, and have a sharply rising suicide rate in the later years.

Race

Race also significantly influences both whether one will live to reach old age and the kind of situation in which one is likely to find oneself in the later years. Higher mortality rates in the earlier years of life, shorter life expectancy even at older ages, and higher birth rates all contribute to the greater proportion of youth and smaller number of old persons in the black and Hispanic populations. Whereas persons over age 65 constitute 11 percent of the white population, they make up only 7.4 per cent of blacks and 3.6 per cent of Hispanics. The median income of blacks age 65 and over is about two-thirds that of whites, and only 40 per cent own their own homes compared to 70 per cent of the total population. Poorest of all are black females; 78 per cent have incomes near or below the poverty level. In 1974 the median income of older white families was $7,519, of black families

$4,909; for unrelated individuals white men had a median income of $3,731, white women $2,959, black men $2,152 and black women $1,998. Blacks are less likely to be covered by Social Security or, if covered, are more likely to receive minimal benefits. However, in minority groups as well as in the total population there is tremendous variety, including significant numbers of middle class and even affluent persons.

Conclusions

All in all, the facts give a mixed picture of the situation of the aging. Most older people live in families and the vast majority live in the community. Only a small minority at any time are the frail, institutionalized, impaired elderly we hear so much about, but about one in four will be in this situation at some time. Although older people are worse off economically than the general population, they are considerably better off than their parents or grandparents were. Women make up the great majority of elderly poor, and black women are in double jeopardy. There are many important problems which need to be addressed, some specific to the older age group but others a function of general economic trends and social conditions or of discrimination throughout life based on race or sex or, from middle age on, on age. One resource older citizens retain and have used well to improve their lot is the power of their vote.

Shifting the perspective from the national to the world scene, we live in a time when the whole world, including the United States, is recognizing that progress and resources are not unlimited. Nonetheless Palmore reminds us that, compared to many areas of the world, "it is probable that the retired in the United States enjoy one of the highest standards of living of retired period *(sic)* in the world . . . Furthermore, it appears that elders receive a share of the national personal income that is about equal to their proportion in the population . . ."[4] Whether this statement continues to be true probably depends upon how wisely choices are made in relation to human needs.

References

1. *Fact Book on Aging: A Profile of America's Older Population,* (Charles S. Harris, Research coordinator). Washington, D.C.: The National Council on the Aging, Inc., 1978. Most of the statistics in this paper are from this source.
2. Palmore, Erdman. United States of America. In Erdman Palmore (Ed.), *International Handbook on Aging: Contemporary Developments and Research.* Westport, Connecticut: Greenwood Press, 1980, p. 442.
3. Neugarten, Bernice L. The Future and the Young-Old. *The Gerontologist,* 1975, *15*, p. 8.
4. Palmore, Erdman. *Op. cit.,* p. 437-438.

ROBERT KASTENBAUM 9

EXIT AND EXISTENCE:
SOCIETY'S UNWRITTEN SCRIPT FOR
OLD AGE AND DEATH

The timekeeper mentality of our society does not permit us either to enter or to exit without proper registration. It is not enough simply to have a certificate of birth: this document must also specify the day and the hour of our coming forth. Similarly, the death certificate records our passing from society with a nice, if often arbitrary, concern for time. Custom also dictates that of all the available information about our lives, it is the dates of birth and of death that must adorn our grave markers.

Fascination with temporality may seem misplaced when the topic is death or aging. These are among the universals of human experience. What does it matter if the calendar registers A.D. 948, 1894, or 1984? Old is old and dead is dead.

And yet the historical time frame may be critical to our understanding of what aging and death mean, perhaps even what aging and death *are*. The universal may be mutable as well. This paper explores some continuities and changes in society's relation to aging and death. Nevertheless, it presents the view not of a historian with a definite notion of the situation that existed in the past, but of a psychologist who is attempting to look ahead and understand how things may be in the future. It is entirely possible that our future relation to aging and death will be strongly influenced by what we do with the options that remain in our hands today.

In the portrait gallery of the mind, our society often envisions an elder of distinguished countenance. Certain characteristics are invariant: the elder is male, venerated by his society, and prepared to answer the summons of death out of the ripeness and wisdom of a long life well lived. Women, shifty-eyed used-camel dealers, and senile wrecks need not apply for the job. The past must be as reassuring to us as the present is not.

Given stringent conditions, we can, in fact, retain this portrait. Select a person who in youth had strength, intelligence, and a knack for survival. Place him in a traditional, relatively static society. Make sure that neither unkind fate nor ruthless competition does him out of his steadily increasing share of the power base. Pray that he keeps his faculties. Bless him with progeny who in turn successfully reproduce their kind. Such a man may indeed be ready to sit for the noble portrait. He is wise, functional, valued, important.

The history of aging and death, however, cannot be limited to so fine a focus. A sick, confused, penniless, childless old woman shunted into a third-class nursing home also has legitimate claim upon our sympathy. It is extremely doubtful, however, that she would have fared much better in the same society that yielded our grand old sage.

Here, then, are a few generalizations about death and aging in the past that appear consistent with the current state of knowledge in gerontology and related fields.

1. *There has been a definite bias in favor of males in most of the cultural traditions that flow into our own.*[1] A schoolchild with a retentive mind can recite the lifespans of Methuselah and a dozen other biblical patriarchs. What *learned* person can do the same for matriarchs? The Scriptures also tell us that King David took the young virgin Abishag to bed, presumably to inhale her breath and thus restore something of his own lost youth. This strategy continued to find advocates down through the centuries. But where do we find old women encouraged by society to take virgin males into their beds? Rabelais conjures up such scenes in his generous imagination, but historically documented instances of such encouragement are difficult to find.[2]

Alongside the portrait of the dignified patriarch, social history is inclined to display the crone, the hag, the witch. The "weird sisters" who forecast Macbeth's rise and fall and the frightful female who flies a broomstick through the dark Halloween skies had many less dramatic counterparts in real life. An aging woman without secure social connections had almost everything to fear, especially neglect. But as Slater has observed, the older woman's actual lack of power frequently promoted other people's fantasies of her mysterious and destructive propensities.[3] She might even accept the imputation of great malevolent powers in preference to seeing herself as completely helpless, vulnerable, and uninteresting. A person might prefer being in league with the devil to being in no league at all. The old woman as witch is but an extreme point on a cultural continuum of dysvalue for the aging female.

There have been important exceptions to this generalization. However, as we shall see, the development of conditions favorable to the aging woman still requires a special advocacy beyond a basic commitment to gerontology and geriatrics.

2. *Respect and solicitude for the aged have been selectively, not universally, bestowed.* It is true that some cultures have been especially eloquent in their advocacy of affection and concern for the aged. Social gerontologists today, however, question some of the implications that have been drawn from this expression of concern. Lipman, for example, distinguishes between true respect for the aged and the kind of "ritualistic deference" that maintains courtesy in superficial transactions but does not preclude neglect or ridicule behind the elder's back.[4] Generally, it has been the healthy, well-connected, well-liked person whose status has remained intact or even been enhanced through advanced age. The lifelong derelict, the unpopular individual, the person seriously debilitated in body or mind, could not expect much from his culture simply because he had grown old. Even societies apparently committed to care of the aged made distinctions according to merit.

Furthermore, the fact that a particular culture has had to reiterate its affection and concern could itself be taken to mean that care of the aged was an ideal, rather than a common practice. In the Scriptures, the child is taught to honor father and mother; the righteous person is rewarded with long life. Yet a plea reaches out across the centuries: "Cast me not off in the time of old age; forsake me not when my strength faileth."[5] Are we to believe the good intentions and teachings of a culture, or the anxiety of its elders? We should probably look at both.

Specific characteristics of the culture also operated either to promote or to discourage solicitude toward the aged. Simmons has found that the elderly most often retained status and power in slowly changing, authoritarian cultures.[6] In these, the elders often controlled much of the property and had other vested sources of power that reinforced their importance. Rosow has added that these also tended to be cultures in which most transactions between individual persons took place face to face, among people who had clearly determined relationships to each other and who saw each other regularly.[7] The position of the aged has generally been more precarious when these conditions have not existed. Societies with limited specialization in jobs also tended to favor old people. There was usually some constructive activity for their hands to perform, freeing more vigorous people for tasks appropriate to the young.

Furthermore, the society's general value system affected the well-being of the aged. For example, the highly developed family life and social organization of the Egyptians, combined with their discoveries in health care and their religious values, provided a favorable environment for the elderly. It was not so much that the elderly were singled out for special attention as that the family and community network embodied a total-care system.[8] On the other hand, the Hellenic Greeks have left us magnificent reminders of their cultural achievements; yet they embraced a value system which regarded old age as "the most evil of things."[9]

It is, then, far from accurate to maintain that the attainment of old age ensured respect and solicitude in cultures prior to our own. The past was not necessarily simpler or less varied than the present.

3. *Dying at an early age was common; living to a ripe old age was not.* Reaching the status of an elder was a rarity in most societies prior to our own. Dublin has estimated the average life expectancy in various periods in history.[10] His figures indicate that our ancestors in the prehistoric period usually were in their graves by age eighteen, with only rare survivors into the third

decade and beyond. Even in the great civilizations of Greece and Rome, life expectancy had increased only three or four years beyond that of prehistory, if statistical estimates are accurate. By this time, however, a scattering of true elders had appeared on the scene. Longevity seems to have increased approximately 50 percent between Roman times and the Middle Ages. Yet, as Hendrik and Hendrik point out, the available information is strongly biased toward the more fortunate members of society, the aristocracy and the upper class.[11] The average life expectancy in the Western world still remained near thirty-five years at the time of the American Revolution.

Perhaps a double perspective is needed here. A person born into an affluent family who had already survived the hazards of the first two decades of life had at least a fair chance to live for several decades more, perhaps into advanced old age. But the infant born into a peasant or lower-class household was in immediate jeopardy from infectious disease, malnutrition, and accident. The infant-mortality rate was so high that census takers rarely bothered to tally children under two years of age. Warfare and other forms of violence also took a large toll on the young. The prospects for reaching maturity, then, were uncertain for most infants, while socially favored individuals who had successfully navigated the hazards of childhood and young adulthood did have an opportunity to experience a full lifespan. We sometimes forget, however, that it was not only the very young who were vulnerable to the epidemic and endemic diseases that have afflicted human beings throughout history. As the adult moved into the later decades, he or she again became exceptionally vulnerable. In the preindustrial era, it was not uncommon for an infant and an elder to be on their deathbeds at the same time—and, of course, in the same household.

Although mortality rates were especially high for the young and the old, we should not forget that by current standards the risk of death was high at every age. This meant that one did not automatically associate death with old age, although one might, in a particular society, associate the old with the *dead*, and the old ones of the society might have a special link or a special "in" with the ancestors and, on this basis, enjoy special status.

At least two other points are worth considering in this connection. First, we should differentiate between chronological age and functional status. A person who was not "old" by modern standards might take on elder status in his or her community because of *relative* seniority. He was an "old-timer" because almost everyone else was so young. In addition, he had been given elder status because the community *needed* a certain minimal number of people in that role. If we hear, then, that elders "had it made" in a particular society, we might be carried away with images of doddering nonagenarians receiving tender loving care, when in reality many of the "elders" had counted only forty or fifty birthdays.

There is a further implication in this regard: how well could a person function at a particular chronological age? We do not have dependable answers to this question for various times and places; only in recent years has strong evidence begun to emerge in our own society. Yet it is likely that two conflicting forces have been at work in many cultures. On the one hand, the rigors and hazards of life may have caused much wear and tear on the individual, so that by age fifty, for example, accumulated injuries and impairments had resulted in a degree of debilitation greater than that experienced by a relatively pampered seventy-five-year-old in the United States today. On the other hand, greater selectivity in survival would mean that those who did reach an advanced age were the hardy, resourceful people, better able to avoid or overcome adversity. On this view, the fifty-year-old serf or tribesman may have enjoyed better functional status in some important respects than a like-aged civil-service employee today who lives a sedentary existence, propped up by a wide variety of medical services within a relatively protective environment. Without trying to answer here a question that requires much further study, I would simply suggest that functional aging—in both individual and socially relative senses—probably has varied much in past cultures, and may distinguish many past cultures from our own. And should we care to define age in terms of distance from death instead of distance from birth, further differences between the past and the present must be acknowledged.

The second point concerns the older generation's investment in the future. Religious faith might comfort the elder as he contemplates the inevitable exit from this existence. But needs, motives, and responsibilities continue to strive for expression. An aging father reminds his vigorous son that we may "attain to a kind of immortality, and in the course of this transitory life perpetuate our name and seed, which is done by a progeny issued from us in the lawful bonds of matrimony." The elder presses his command forward: "I shall not account myself wholly to die, but to pass from one place to another, considering that, in and by thee, I continue in my visible image living in the world." It is clearly the grown son's responsibility to seed future generations, guaranteeing an unbroken sequence stretching back to Adam and ahead to the Last Judgment. The elder already has taken pleasure in seeing "my bald old age reflourish in thy youth," but the real test is in the future.[12] Junior must maintain his own reputation and do his part to bridge the chasm of death with another birth.

This letter from Gargantua to Pantagruel expresses something of the bond between father and son and, as the letter shows, between the father and *his* progenitor. But it also conveys the significance of what might be called the family soul, or perhaps the name soul. The waning generation seeks to preserve something of supreme value. It can do this only in the person of the generation it has seeded. The body dies, but before it does the proud and fond father should be assured that the name soul has transcended the death of the individual and will also bridge the next chasm that awaits son as well as father. (We see again the masculine bias here: the name soul most often is propagated by the male succession, with females as the necessary auxiliary agency.) After countless generations, the treasured name soul will be gathered up into deity, the safe homecoming. With such a philosophy and kinship network flourishing, the old man was more likely to be able to look squarely at his own death without flinching.

4. *We have always had mixed feelings about aging and death.* In a particular culture, one pole of the ambivalence or the other might be the more evident. The Greeks, as we have noted, raged at old age and death, while the Chinese and some other Asian peoples have worshiped ancestors and honored the dead. Yet ambivalence existed in both of these societies, and in all others that we know anything about. What are the general sources of this ambivalence? The following seem especially important.

First, we must credit our ancestors with astute powers of observation. There is no doubt that miseries and infirmities associated with advanced age were clearly noted by past societies. Descriptions in vivid clinical detail exist. Although a particular society may have found a place in its value and caring systems for old people, this did not mean that anyone sought a condition of progressive decrepitude, or preferred to interact closely with those so afflicted.

Second, in addition to being physically distressed, the aged have often been seen as unpleasant, undesirable characters. The ridiculous old person has long been a stock theatrical figure. Pope Innocent III carried on Aristotle's and Horace's earlier blasts against the aged when he labeled them "easily provoked, stingy . . . sullen and quarrelsome, quick to talk, slow to hear, but not slow in wrath, praising former times, despising the moderns, censuring the present, commending the past."[13] Shakespeare and other Elizabethans continued the catalogue of the personal and social failings of old people. When Swift introduced the infinitely miserable and misery-inducing Struldbrugs, we had perhaps the most compelling image of people condemned to perpetual aging. There was no love, glory, majesty, or satisfaction for these people whom fate had denied the ultimate release of death. This recalled the ancient myth of Tithonus, a goddess's mortal lover who, by her intercession, was granted eternal life—but regrettably not eternal youth.

Third, these sometimes unpleasant and unproductive old people have been competing with all other members of society for resources for survival. Who should be given that last bowl of rice, the child or the ancient? This dilemma was not invented in modern times. No matter how the problem was resolved, we must suspect that the tension and emotional pressures were there. Balancing one life against another cannot have been an easy matter, even when relatively clear cultural guidelines were available. The mother might consent to infanticide in order to preserve an elder—but are we to imagine that this decision was made without pangs of sorrow? The elderly person might take the initiative to self-destruct when this was expected by society—but are we to suppose that this was invariably an action unmarked by fear, anger, or regret?

We, as cultural outsiders, tend to assume that those on the inside of such alien cultures actually experience no more or less than their guidelines seem to advertise. We have been quick to assume that people in cultures different from our own possess simpler, less sensitive emotions, or can take decisive actions without being troubled by alternatives. I personally find this attitude questionable and self-serving. The fact that old people often have had to compete for scarce resources with other members of society can only have heightened tension and increased ambivalence. The notion of the old man slipping off gently into that good night appears to make it that much easier to withhold the affection, and thus the material and social resources, that could have helped him to remain a while longer.

Finally, the most obvious point of all: in the opinion of many people over the centuries, there was not really much choice between old age and death. Aging itself has been seen at times as part of the process of dying.[14] Gruman has shown that the revolt of the spirit against both aging and death has led indirectly to many advances in science, in hygiene, and even in the exploration of the planet Earth.[15] While reaching a good old age has been a common hope, being old has rarely been anyone's ambition. "I'd rather be young," said the greybeard of ancient Egypt as he studied "The Book for Transforming an Old Man into a Youth of Twenty."[16] There seems to have been no market for "The Book for Transforming a Youth of Twenty into an Old Man."

Best of all is youth. A good old age runs a distant second, historically, in the affections of humankind. I suspect, however, that a universal retrospective survey of attitudes toward the choice between death and a bad old age would result in a preference for an honorable demise. The young or middle-aged person obviously cannot know what kind of old age lies in his or her future—or even *whether* he or she will reach old age. It is the uncertainty itself that must be reckoned with. Under conditions of subjective uncertainty, a person may assume either the better or the worse, or may suffer so much from the uncertainty itself that a premature closure of the issue is forced. A life hurled about recklessly can sometimes be traced to a person's insecurity about what may happen in the future.

A further word about the other (that is, positive) side of the ambivalence is in order. If *all* aged people suffered or were insufferable, then the choice of death would be an easier one for most people in most situations. Yet the nomad of biblical times could see as well as we can today that there are appreciable individual differences in what old people are like and how well they fare. With luck, he or she might have a good old age.

Furthermore, death itself has also been painted in various shades of hope and dread. Death is release, or it is reward. It is unrelenting horror, or it is nothing at all. Perhaps death is just not very different from the life one has already known.[17] So a person is ambivalent, not only toward advanced age, but also toward death. The conflicting movements of the spirit in a particular historical epoch have depended greatly upon the interrelated ambivalences toward old age and death, which are part of a larger constellation of approach-avoidance maneuvers for which I have elsewhere proposed the concept of *omnivalence.*[18]

Not So Very Long Ago

Average life expectancy increased impressively throughout the 1800s but took a truly spectacular leap ahead during the early decades of the twentieth century. In technologically advanced nations like our own, approximately two full decades were added to the average life expectancy; it has already been noted that this was the length of the *entire* life expectancy in Greek and Roman times.

Recent increases in life expectancy have been less spectacular. However, the resulting shifts in population structure and in the phenomena we associate with death are still with us. There are more old people alive at this moment—whether we calculate in absolute numbers or in proportion of population—than ever before. Furthermore, the experts predict that this trend will extend into the next few decades at least. About a hundred years ago, this nation included an estimated 1.2 million people aged sixty-five and older, or less than 3 percent of the total population. By the turn of the century, there were 3.1 million Americans in this age range, accounting for 4.1 percent of the population. Today there are more than 20 million elders, who represent about 10.3

percent of the population. It is estimated that by the end of this century there will be approximately 29 million elders in the United States.[19] The *percentage* of elders in our population at that time will depend upon the interaction of various trends, but it appears that approximately one person in five living in the year 2000 will have passed his or her sixty-fifth birthday.

We can easily identify some of the corollaries and consequences of this shift, although in doing so we will be forced to neglect many other changes in life style that have influenced our current attitudes toward old age and death.

1. *More adults have living parents and grandparents than ever before in history.* This means, for example, that a sixty-year-old is not necessarily the family's ranking elder. It also means that the emotional bonds between parent and child may persist through each one's later decades. The sixty-year-old retains certain expectations and conflicts involving Momma and Poppa and at the same time represents the parent and grandparent to younger generations. Both phenomenological and intergenerational life have the potential for becoming extraordinarily complex. It has been found that a person in the postreproductive phase of life is less likely to dream of or imagine a dead parent than were earlier generations; instead, such persons' visitations and interactions remain a part of the tissue of everyday life.

2. *Although more elders are surviving longer than ever before, the association between old age and death has become stronger.* This is a paradoxical development in one sense: the fact that more people live to an advanced age might be thought to further weaken the association between old age and mortality. But it is also evident that *fewer* people are dying at an *early* age. We hear a parent explaining a death to a young child on the basis that Granny was "very old." By implication, Mommy and Daddy and the child will not die until they are also "very old," an incredibly long time from now. This is just one manifestation of the strong link between aging and death which has seized our thinking. Death? See Old Age. Old Age? See Death.

3. *We have become enthusiastic about preventive care and acute-treatment techniques; however, most deaths actually result from long-term deterioration and invasive processes.* Breakthroughs in public health and medicine in the past have helped

many people to survive into old age. But our society's priorities remain fixed on the dramatic cure, the wondrous elixir, and the surgeon's astonishing virtuosity. Continuous, systematic care for the person who is old today and will be one day older tomorrow has not captured our imagination. In this way, we tend to abandon those who have reached a state of need and peril just *because* our models of preventive care and acute treatment have proved effective. Convert this octogenarian into a child again, and we will inoculate him against life-threatening disease and stand ready to hurl every weapon in our medical arsenal against any prospect of his untimely death. But careers are not made, nor are programs funded, on the premise of converting an old man of eighty into an old man of eighty-one.

4. *Emphasis is shifting from acute to anticipatory grief.* The trajectory from life to death seems to be extending into a longer, perhaps more gentle, slope. While it is true that sudden, unexpected deaths still occur, it is increasingly common for a long life to fade off into death, providing much opportunity in advance for the family to adjust to the impending loss. I do not intend to minimize the impact of the actual death itself or to assert that all people do in fact anticipate bereavement even when the elderly person has been ill for a long time. However, when a person dies in his seventies or eighties today, there is probably less acute grief on the part of society than was the case for a modal death in past generations. And if the elder previously has been "disengaged"—removed from the mainstream of family and community life—the social significance of the death is likely to be even further reduced.[20]

5. *Being old is not special anymore.* It is not only that the novelty of having many elderly people around is starting to wear off; it is also that more and different kinds of people are surviving into advanced years. If the phenomenon of "survival of the fittest" ever existed in this regard, it was more likely to have been found in the past than in the present. In the past, a person had to be especially strong, able, and fortunate to survive past life's first prime; now a person has to be unusually vulnerable and unfortunate to perish young. There is probably still a tendency for the more competent to survive longer, but not to such a striking degree as in the past.[21] Yesterday's old person, then, had a higher

probability of earning respect both on his or her own distinctive merits and as an exemplar of a rare resource. Today's old person has a greater probability of being just about the same as everybody else in society, adding or subtracting differences attributable to life styles characteristic of a particular generation.

6. *Demands upon social resources are shifting from young to old dependents.* In general, young and middle-aged adults carry the burden of supporting not only themselves but also those who cannot function successfully on their own. Until recently, our society clearly owed most of its obligations to the young and immature. Public-health and educational programs and much of our national life style reflect this orientation. The dollar we do not spend on ourselves is likely to be spent on our children.

The balance is now shifting. The "postmature" make up an increasingly large proportion of economically- and physically-dependent people in our society. It seems we have not yet recognized the scope and significance that this shifting balance will have, especially if zero population growth prevails. Shanas and Hauser warn that "a rugged individualism philosophy [with regard to] the aged will be increasingly inapplicable in the face of their increased numbers and their continuing needs. Zero population growth will make a welfare society for the elderly inevitable. . . . ['Welfare society'] is not a pejorative phrase nor a form of undesirable socialism. It appears to be a rational response to changes in population structure and to technological advances." Whether or not one cares to accept this view completely, the facts suggest that traditional attitudes toward care of the young and the old will soon be called into question as it is perceived that these attitudes no longer reflect social reality.

How It Will Be From Now on: A Scenario

Although the background sketched in here is selective and simplified, enough salient features have been described for us to be able to construct a scenario for the future. This projection is organized with reference to the way society has been answering the following question: what value is there in being an old, dying, or dead person?

It is useful to introduce one further concept: "the death system." This term refers to the functional network through which a society comes to terms with death, including people, places, objects, and symbols.[23] Some of these components are identified primarily, and permanently, by their role in the death system—for example, the funeral director, cemetery, death certificate; other components may be recruited into the system as the occasion demands. The death system performs several vital functions: predictions and warnings of the possibility of death and actions intended to prevent it; care of the dying or otherwise doomed person; physical disposition of the corpse; consolation and re-integration of survivors and the establishment of an orientation toward or relationship with the dead. Explanations and rationalizations of death are part of the system. Those actions which have the effect of bringing about death are as much a part of the system as the components of prediction and prevention. Certain aspects of the society's economic function and structure are, of course, part of the death system. How much money do you suppose changes hands in our society each year for death-related reasons? The answer to this question would include much if not all of the national defense budget; "life" insurance premiums, payments, and commissions; floral offerings; the pet-food industry; newspaper income from death notices; and so on.

These functions can be discerned in all societies; relative emphasis varies, however, from one society to another, or within the same society in different periods. The relative proportions of children, adults, and elderly adults at a given time will be a factor; but so will the prevailing system of religious beliefs and practices or a cycle of good or poor harvests.

The scenario for the future that suggests itself for our own society is based on the assumption that certain current trends will become dominant while other already entrenched attitudes and practices will continue. It is important to emphasize that this present-tense description represents one view of the way things *might* be. One approach to this scenario can be obtained by working backward from death itself.

1. There is no point in being dead. This view has now been made palpable by the systematic conversion of burial grounds to other, more utilitarian, purposes. Except for those relatively few

cemeteries now designated as historical sites, the burial ground has virtually disappeared from the landscape. Again, with few exceptions, the recently deceased are not commemorated by conspicuous, space-wasting monuments. This practice had been losing much of its vitality for decades, anyway, as suggested by the increasing standardization of tombstone inscriptions. Other kinds of memorial practices have also been reduced to a minimum that a previous generation might not have thought possible. Traffic is no longer held up by the slow-moving cortege of limousines and mourners. Busy people no longer miss a day's work to stand in the wind or rain while a deceased colleague is lowered into the earth. Efficiency and common sense have at last prevailed. Our death system's gradually lessened interest in relating to or utilizing the dead, a phenomenon observed by a few in previous years, has moved from the mental-emotional sphere to the physical and official change of visible practices associated with disposal of the dead and with remembrance.[24] Naturally, services are available for those deviant and troubled individuals whose functioning is impaired by unresolved feelings about a dead person. According to the latest clinical and scientific reports, systematic desensitization to bereavement as a routine activity of the behavior modifiers has had reasonably consistent success.

2. There is little point in dying. In fact, as compared with the previous generation or two, there is relatively little "dying" per se. One reason for the diminished significance of dying, of course, has been the perfection of an integrated, computerized system for (1) determining a person's level of viability; (2) evaluating availability and cost of alternative treatment and maintenance procedures; and (3) resolving the problems of terminal care and body disposal. The United States Public Health Service operates the Super-Euthanasiac Computer, into which all relevant data are constantly programmed. When the computer detects and validates a critical configuration of disability, prognosis, and cost estimate, a quick and painless termination is accomplished— including selection of the appropriate body-disposal route. It is no wonder that the president of the American Medical Association has expressed unstinting approval of this technique. The need to make life-and-death decisions that began to weigh so heavily upon medical personnel in the 1960s and 1970s has now been

almost entirely eliminated. Moreover, the unacceptable expense of maintaining incurable and unproductive citizens has been sharply reduced (although it must be admitted that the cost of the new computer system has been considerably higher than anticipated). Some observers were surprised, however, when the Pope herself expressed strong approval. Few could quarrel, however, with her assertion that the new system would promote favorable reallocation of scarce resources for safeguarding the lives of those who still had a chance. The development of the Church's own Vaticaniac Computer Program to guide determinations of viability of Catholic patients based on applicable tenets of their religion no doubt had something to do with the acceptability of the system as a whole.

Another reason for the reduced significance of dying and of being a dying person is more psychosocial than technological. Dying retained some importance as long as there was any point at all in being dead. Now that the status of the dead has become so attenuated, little significance need be attributed to the preparatory phase. The "exit" phase of existence has become relatively unimportant and vestigial. It is not a critical part of the transition from one social status to another; there is little significance that dying can borrow from its destination. "I am not going to be anything to anybody when I am dead; therefore, as I approach dead-status through the process of dying, my value progressively diminishes." Much of the individual's social value is depleted, then, before the moment of death arrives.

3. There is no point in being old. This is in part a function of the reverse sequence we have been describing. Society has no use for the dead, and therefore little use for the dying. For many years, being old has meant a general reduction in social value for reasons not directly associated with death. However, with the shift in mortality peaks from early to late in the lifespan, and with other socioeconomic and attitudinal changes, a more specific association has also been strengthened between *advanced* age and death. Now when a person is recognized as "old," this status initiates a trajectory of dysvalue that moves inevitably through dying- and dead-status. "I am an old person, which means that before long I will be a dying person; therefore, as I approach dying-status through the aging process, my value progressively

diminishes." Old, dying, and dead are stations of life still differentiated by our society, but collectively they represent an essentially trivial postscript to authentic existence as a person in society.

This situation was anticipated by the low priority which society gave for many years to the care of the aged. Moreover, the growing trend for the aged to die in an institutional setting, coupled with the usual way in which institutions responded to the dying and the dead, provided a firm model for progressive dysvaluation.[25] Aged residents were likely to observe that the dying were isolated, and the dead removed quickly. Implicit were the messages that "Nobody has died," and "Dying and being dead are nothing." These messages registered with the impact that "Nobody has been alive," and "I *will have been* nothing when I *become* nothing." So thoroughly were the aged dying and dead ejected from the scene that the fact that they had ever been alive (and perhaps valuable) seemed entirely inconsistent. With this sort of rehearsal for their own deaths, the institutionalized aged saw their present existence drained of value.

Today, the transitions from old to dying to dead are better managed. Much of the ambiguity has been eliminated, along with the accompanying tension and occasional guilt on the part of caregivers and family as well as the aged themselves. Only a few of the factors contributing to this change can be cited here.

One important development was the change in official recognition of the start of old age, from sixty-five to seventy.[26] Although gerontologists argued, with good evidence, that even seventy is "too young to be old" for many people today, a compromise at seventy prevailed. In retrospect, the identification of official old age with the biblical specification of "threescore and ten" seems to have proved fortuitous. People in their sixties now receive a full share of benefits and privileges. The slide of value-into-dysvalue throughout the seventh decade of life has been sharply reduced. Other factors in the change include the development of more flexible retirement plans, the cultivation of multiple careers, and the increased prominence of women in the work force.

Perhaps the single most important factor, however, has been the great success of the voluntary-termination plan. Once surrounded by prohibitions and negative emotions, suicide has become, under certain circumstances, an action with great positive value. This trend was anticipated some years ago. It was shown that the implicit preferences of most Americans regarding the "ideal" way to die included the following characteristics: (1) an identifiable and rational cause; (2) some element of control; (3) an acceptable physical setting; (4) occurrence at the right time; (5) little or no suffering or experiencing; (6) rapid onset; (7) consistency with the individual's distinctive or most valued style of life. It was predicted that all of these characteristics could most dependably be invoked by suicide.[27] The suicide would, of course, have to meet certain pragmatic and moral criteria, which were also discussed in some detail.

Apparently, two major factors in the success of the voluntary-termination plan were the decades-long subjection of the aged to low-priority status and the rapid diminution of the value of the dying and the dead in our death system. People simply incorporated these cultural orientations into their own attitude structures, and when they had themselves grown old, they began to act upon the implicit commands.

The well-achieved suicide (to use the old-fashioned expression) bestows upon the old person's exit a value that it can attain in no other way. Instead of fading into a prolonged phase of senescence and dysvalue, the man or woman on the brink of old age now can elect a self-termination mode that consolidates and validates his or her existence up to that point. A good citizen, having lived a good life, no longer faces the prospect of a retroactively spoiled identity because of unnecessary aging and dying.

An Alternative Scenario

It is possible to accept the background facts and trends that generated the above scenario and yet arrive at a different one. This requires the recognition of several other trends and options that have not yet been mentioned.

"THE ROAD DOESN'T END HERE ANYMORE" The county historical society almost lost in its campaign to preserve the street in its old form as a designated reminder of how things used to be. Little could be said in favor of the structures themselves. The aesthetic appeal was virtually nil, and somehow the "bad vibrations" seemed to cling to the walls. Yet enough people appreciated the moral and educational value of preserving the row of "nursing homes" and "funeral homes" to allow the historical society to keep this relic of the not-so-distant past before contemporary eyes.

Surprisingly, the street has proved to be a popular if sobering attraction. "So this was the end of the road," a visitor may say, shaking his head as though to clear away disbelief. "You have to wonder how people felt when they turned down this street. It must have been like leaving life behind, entering a kind of slaughterhouse district, but with most of the bleeding *inside*, in the heart. How could people let the road end that way?"

The street of nursing homes and funeral homes—peculiar remnants of the past—certainly is out of place now. Old age and death once were considered the end of the road, almost functionally equivalent in many people's minds. This inaccurate assumption no longer burdens society. Advances in scientific knowledge have contributed to the change: increasingly, it has been recognized that many of the so-called inevitable changes "caused" by the aging process can in fact be attributed more accurately to a variety of specific factors. Each new rank of chronologically old men and women reaches a particular age checkpoint in better health and with greater functional capacity than the preceding one. There was no single "breakthrough"; instead, health maintenance throughout the lifespan has steadily improved. The physical impairment and vulnerability to chronic disease that were fostered by sedentary, careless, and unmonitored life styles have been sharply reduced. Sixty-five-year-olds are more physically active today than many forty-year-olds of a few generations back. Good nutritional habits carefully cultivated in the early years of life are now paying good dividends in the later decades. Specific changes, such as the enrichment of beer with vitamins, have helped to preserve the functioning of memory and the overall integrity of personality among people who in the past might have suffered deterioration not much past midlife.

The overall change, however, has occurred in the minds both

of the elders themselves and of the allied health professionals. Suffering, impairment, and disease are no longer considered especially "natural" in old age. More can be done to prevent problems and to correct or compensate for them when they do occur.

Gerontologists from a variety of disciplines have helped to clarify the distinction between growing old and becoming ill. A core of processes remains that could be characterized as "normal aging," although even this core is still subject to continuing review and experimentation.

In similar fashion, a clearer distinction has been recognized between growing old and "getting stale." As developmental psychologists finally enlarged their horizons to encompass the whole lifespan and to establish appropriate ways of assessing behavior and experience from infancy through old age, it became evident that individual patterns are at least as significant as age-related changes. There was no escaping the conclusion that some men and women have "staled out" by their forties or fifties––or even their twenties or thirties—while others show few, if any, of the stereotypical age changes after they have passed their seventieth, eightieth, or ninetieth birthday. Circumstantial evidence has long suggested the importance of individual patterns; now, abundant research supports this view in detail.

In both biomedical and psychosocial terms, then, the assumption of a close link between old age and deterioration—and therefore between old age and death—has been shown to be faulty. While it is still true that some chronologically old people are physically ill and impaired, and some very limited in their ability to experience and adapt to their environments (not necessarily the same persons in both cases) such difficulties and illnesses no longer *define* old age. In addition to the greater national commitment to the maintenance of physical health throughout life, there is now more encouragement of continuing personal growth. Recreation, for example, has become more re-creational for many people; education is now a lifelong process for a greater number; and self-development groups have survived the fad stage to become an effective and respected part of the cultural milieu. While, of course, some people continue to reach the end of the road early in life; this is no longer the expected pattern. Chronological age simply does not have much to do with the quality of one's life. As old age (in the once-traditional chronological sense of the term) has been liberated from its association with the end of health and mental vigor, so the association with dying and death has been reduced to more realistic dimensions. People still die old if they do not die young, but they are not surrounded by clouds of gloom and dysvalue while they still walk the earth.

Many other changes have contributed to the revised image and reality of old age. Reaching a particular age (and remember when that was as young as sixty-five!) once meant a virtually complete exit from the social scene. The individual stepped (or was pushed) across a single threshold and from that point on was little more than an occasional offstage voice. Now, of course, fewer of the exits are controlled by chronology. Mandatory retirement did not tremble and fall with an overwhelming crash after a fierce struggle; it just gradually passed away.

More flexible ideas of what constitutes a working life have made the single-career pattern just one among several. The framework of young adult to elderly retiree has altered just as the nine-to-five workday has given way to more flexible arrangements. Now, people move into and out of occupations in a variety of patterns, taking a year out here for re-education, six months there for community service, and so on. The availability of a large number of vigorous, skilled elders who are interested in part-time or temporary employment has proved extremely helpful to many industries and government agencies. The "average" person now may have, in effect, "retired" several times before reaching age sixty-five and yet, in another sense, not have retired at all. The ever-changing flow of workers of various ages and degrees of development of their capacities has made age-based mandatory retirement anachronistic—and eliminated one of the main symbols of exit from social participation.

The great improvement in the status of women has also been very important. The woman of today must have an informed sense of history in order to recognize that once her life might have been considered over when the last child had left the "nest," or when she became a widow (as often happened to women in earlier generations before the longevity of males improved). Today's woman, fully competent in the management of her life outside as well as inside the home, brings many skills, achievements and interests to the later years of her life. She is seldom faced with a confusing and unfamiliar world of financial management for example, or frustrated by other problems that someone else would have looked after in the past. She is resourceful and successful throughout her life and has no reason to be otherwise as she reaches any particular chronological-age mark.

Both men and women, of course, have found the toppling of assumptions and prohibitions regarding sexual intimacy in later life to be a truly liberating development. In the past, physical death seemed almost an afterthought for some people when they had already exited (in society's view) from the life of labor and the life of love. Now, better general health has contributed to the general maintenance of sexual tone in elders; but the change in attitudes has also been very important. The overall maturation of public opinion in relation to many aspects of human development shows some of its most favorable results in relation to old age and intimacy. There was a period in which the existence of only two "kinds" of women was generally acknowledged: "good women," and those who enjoyed sex. Then, as women achieved sociopolitical equality with men, sexual liberation followed, sometimes accompanied by new problems for some men. It took some time for many men to adjust to women who were at least their equals in all spheres, and there *were* some "casualties" along the way. Now, however, adults share sexual intimacy at all points of the life span.

In general, men and women, now able to function well physically, maintain and develop personality strengths, participate fully in the work and productivity of society according to their individual interests, and remain sexually active, seldom regard any chronological age as the end of the kind of lives they have made for themselves. Those who choose, or are forced, to leave a particular domain in which they have functioned successfully can open other doors to a rewarding life. The humanization and individualization of technology has provided many more possibilities for maintaining control after such functions as muscular strength, mobility, reaction time, and sensory acuity have been impaired. In other words, a person is not necessarily rendered powerless and isolated just because a particular physical function has become less dependable. This ability to compensate for age-related deficits has, in turn, greatly reduced passive yearning for death, as well as active suicide, among older adults.

In essence, society has come to realize that within its power is the ability to develop alternative "scripts" for the whole human lifespan. The *programmed impetus* given to each person as birth-right may run its course around mid-life, if not before: the "job specifications" written into the genes have completed their schedules.[28] For many centuries there was no concerted effort on the part of society to augment this partial script for a human life; few people survived long enough to require it. Now, however, a variety of alternative paths exists for the second half of life, and the variety is constantly increasing. Development through old age is almost as enthusiastically demanded and expected—and applauded and enjoyed—as development through the childhood years.

Society places greater value on the *completed person.*[29] Although a child of ten may be, in one sense, all that he or she can be, true fulfillment of human possibilities is now seen as requiring a long life in which knowledge increases and is enriched over the years. The young are fresh and daring; middle-aged people (the term now applies to a much longer space of life) would please Aristotle with their balancing of the novel and the familiar, the necessary and the possible; elders integrate all the qualities of previous years with a cultivated sense of perspective.

THE EXIT FROM EXISTENCE   *Being old* has shifted to a positive value. Yet dying and death have not been banished from the human condition, nor have they continued to operate secretly and to bizarre effect under the lugubrious apparatus of massive denial. Compared with the situation in the past, in fact, dying and death are much more out in the open today. This is due, in part, to the increased value placed upon *life* in old age. As a number of keen observers have remarked over the centuries, the person who has lived well and fully does appear more at ease with mortality.

But part of the new attitude is a result of a greater appreciation of dying, death, *and the dead* per se. When the old death system was functioning at its peak, the elderly progressed on a sort of assembly line from old age through dying to death and oblivion.[30] It is perhaps easier to understand this progression in reverse. For a time, honoring and memorializing the dead became a greatly attenuated process. Funeral processions, the use of cemetery space, and most forms of integrating the dead psychologically into the lives of individual survivors and the culture were under attack and erosion. In effect, the dead seemed to have no role in the symbolic life of society, with a few notable exceptions.

The nonutility of the dead was a phenomenon which then worked ahead in time. It made the dying person more of a threat, annoyance, or burden than a gathering place for social values and concern. There was no point in "being dead," hence little point in being a person who would soon be forgotten. This part of the process often was exemplified in congregate facilities for the care of the aged. The nonutility of the dying person worked forward in time to strip value from the old person. The elder would die, and the dead would blow away like the wind with its debris. Little wonder that many aging men and women, taking their cues from mandatory retirement, the death of a spouse, or some other major change in their lives, would disassociate from themselves just as society was pulling away from them.

Today, the aged have been liberated in both directions. In life, there is no longer an age-determined exitus from full participation and status. On the side of death, society has regained its sense of history and continuity. We no longer feel so lost, shift our feet, and avoid eye contact at leave-taking rituals. Death is not seen as a failure by the individual or the health professions. Thoughts and feelings toward the dead are accepted as a vital thread of continuity that symbolizes our existence as members of the human race rather than as solitary individuals. The neutral, objective-functional abandonment of the dead once in vogue has yielded to a more intuitive relationship, one that gives the present generation more in common with ancestors across the centuries than with those of just a few years ago. In caring about the dead and the dying, those who have barely started to approach their own elder years are already preparing the way for a personal sense of continued value throughout all the bright days and deep nights of life's seasons.

1. R. Kastenbaum and B. Ross, "Historical Perspectives on Care of the Aged," in *Modern Perspectives in the Psychiatry of Old Age*, ed. J. G. Howells (New York: Brunner/Mazel, 1975), pp. 421–48.

2. François Rabelais, *Gargantua and Pantagruel*, trans. Sir Thomas Urquhart and Peter Mottux, Great Books of the Western World, vol. 24 (Chicago: Encyclopaedia Britannica, 1952).

3. P. E. Slater, "Cross-cultural Views of the Aged," in *New Thoughts on Old Age*, ed. R. Kastenbaum (New York: Springer, 1964), pp. 229–36.

4. A. Lipman, "Prestige of the Aged in Portugal: Realistic Appraisal and Ritualistic Deference," *Aging and Human Development* 1 (1970): 127–36.

5. Psalm 71:9.

6. L. Simmons, "Aging in Preindustrial Societies," in *Handbook of Social Gerontology*, ed. C. Tibbitts (Chicago: University of Chicago Press, 1960), pp. 62–91.

7. I. Rosow, *Social Integration of the Aged* (New York: Free Press, 1967).

8. F. D. Zeman, "Old Age in Ancient Egypt: A Contribution to the History of Geriatrics," *Journal of Mount Sinai Hospital* 8 (1942): 1161–65.

9. B. E. Richardson, *Old Age among the Ancient Greeks* (Baltimore: Johns Hopkins Press, 1933).

10. L. I. Dublin, *Factbook on Man* (New York: Macmillan, 1965).

11. J. Hendrik and C. Hendrik, "The Good Old Days: What Was Old Age Really Like?" *International Journal of Aging and Human Development* 8 (1978): 139–150.

12. Rabelais, *Gargantua*, p. 81.

13. G. R. Coffman, "Old Age from Horace to Chaucer. Some Literary Affinities and Adventures of an Idea," *Speculum* 9 (1934): 249–77.

14. J. Taylor, *The Art of Holy Dying* (1651; reprint ed., New York: Arno Press, 1976).

15. G. R. Gruman, "A History of Ideas about the Prolongation of Life," *Transactions of the American Philosophical Society* 56 (1966): 1–97 (reprint ed., New York: Arno Press, 1976).

16. Ibid.

17. R. Kastenbaum, "Is Death a Life Crisis?" in *Lifespan Developmental Psychology: Normative Crises and Interventions*, ed. D. Natan and L. Ginsberg (New York: Academic Press, 1976), pp. 19–50.

18. R. Kastenbaum, "Should We Have Mixed Feelings about Our Ambivalences toward the Aged?" *Journal of Geriatric Psychiatry* 7 (1974): 94–107.

19. E. Shanas and P. M. Hauser, "Zero Population Growth and the Family Life of Old People," *Journal of Social Issues* 30 (1974) : 79–92.

20. E. Cumming and W. E. Henry, *Growing Old* (New York: Basic Books, 1961); B. G. Glaser, "The Social Loss of Dying Aged Patients," *Gerontologist* 6 (1966) : 77–80.

21. K. F. Reigel and R. M. Reigel, "Development, Drop, and Death," *Developmental Psychology* 6 (1972) : 306–19.

22. Shanas and Hauser, "Zero Population Growth," p. 91.

23. R. Kastenbaum and R. B. Aisenberg, *The Psychology of Death* (New York: Springer Publishing Company, 1972); R. Kastenbaum, *Death, Society, and Human Experience* (St. Louis: C. V. Mosby Company, 1977).

24. Kastenbaum and Aisenberg, *Psychology of Death*; R. Blauner, "Death and Social Structure," *Psychiatry* 29 (1966) : 378–94; R. Kastenbaum, "Two-way Traffic on the River Styx" (Paper presented at the annual meeting of American Psychological Association, 1969); R. Fulton, private communication.

25. E.g., R. Kastenbaum and S. E. Candy, "The 4% Fallacy: A Methodological and Empirical Critique of Use of Population Statistics in Gerontology," *Aging and Human Development* 4 (1973) : 15–22.

26. This was a futuristic proposition when presented at the conference; it is now becoming the law of the land.

27. R. Kastenbaum, "Suicide as the Preferred Way of Death," in *Progress in Suicidology*, ed. E. S. Schneidman (New York: Grune & Stratton, 1976), pp. 425–43.

28. R. Kastenbaum, "Theories of Human Aging—The Search for a Conceptual Framework," *Journal of Social Issues* 21 (1965) : 13–36.

29. R. Kastenbaum, "Time, Death, and Ritual in Old Age," in *The Study of Time*, ed. J. T. Fraser (New York, Heidelberg, Berlin: Springer-Verlag, 1975), 2: 20–38.

30. R. Kastenbaum, *Death, Society, and Human Experience*.

Who the Senior Citizens Really Are 10

By Louis Harris

For many years now, the stereotype of people 65 and over, according to the media, has been that of a relatively sedentary, inactive, increasingly lonely, growingly sick, and less useful citizens. The plight of the elderly as it is most commonly put, touches our conscience as a nation, leads to occasional outbursts of indignation, albeit at the very same time jobs are not available for senior citizens who want to work, an increasing number are conveniently tucked away into segregated older people communities, and they are just about the last people thought about in terms of the impact of inflation upon their meager and often fixed incomes. And let me add a caveat to President Ford right here and now: While people want trimming of Federal spending, do not start nor end by cutting the heart out of the life of senior citizens.

Under the sponsorship of the National Council on the Aging, with a substantial grant from the Edna McConnell-Clark Foundation and the Burden Foundation, our firm has just completed the most definitive study of people 65 and over, as well as the rest of the public 18-64. In this study, we have been able to assess not only how senior citizens perceive themselves, but also how they are viewed by the rest of the population. In all, we surveyed 4,254 adults in person in interviews which lasted well over an hour in length. The sample of the 65 and over group is undoubtedly the largest in any survey research project: 3,000 individuals in total - 1,033 who are 65-69 years of age, 1,295 who are 70-79 , and 469 who are 80 years of age and over. Taken together, the 65 and over group now represents 15% of the total U.S. adult population, a significant group of 21 million citizens.

The perception of people 65 and over by those who have not yet reached that age is both fascinating and revealing:

- — 16% feel a very serious problem for senior citizens is that they do not have enough clothing to wear,
- — 28% feel they do not have enough friends,
- — 35% think they have poor housing,
- — 38% feel they do not have enough to do to keep busy,
- — 45% think they do not have enough medical care,
- — 47% feel they do not have enough job opportunities,
- — 50% think they are in poor health,
- — 56% believe people 65 and over feel they are not needed,
- — 61% feel they suffer from loneliness,
- — 63% feel they do not have enough money to live on.

In addition, the non-65 and over group views the 65 and over group as basically inert. For example, only 5% feel that they are very sexually active; only 19% think they are very open-minded and adaptable, only 29% very bright and alert, 35% very good at getting things done, and 41% think most senior citizens are very physically active.

To put it bluntly, the portrait of senior citizens drawn by younger people is that of unalert, physically inert, narrow-minded, ineffective, sexually finished old people deteriorating in poor health and suffering the miseries of loneliness. Oh, to be sure, people 65 and over are credited with being very wise from experience in the judgment of 66% of those under 65 and 82% think they are friendly and warm.

Basically, the rest of society thinks that senior citizens are a growing body of ne'er do well, pitifully inadequate, unhappy oldsters who nonetheless smile bravely to the rest of the world, as they fade away in their final years and head for the grave. It is a sense of deep guilt and deep pity, not for other human beings who have a right to be respected for themselves, but rather for 15% of the adult population which somehow is tolerated, represents no threat to the rest of us, and won't be around long anyway.

Not only do people *under* 65 feel that senior citizens exist this way, but even more sadly, the net assessment of senior citizens when they are asked about their own age group is essentially the same. They also tend to think of their group as not open-minded and adaptable, not good at getting things done, not being bright and alert, not being physically active, not being sexually active. They think the elderly do not have enough money to live on, are in poor health, suffer from loneliness, have poor housing, not enough clothes, have not enough to do to keep busy, live in mortal fear of crime, don't have enough friends, do not feel needed, have not enough job opportunities, and not enough medical care. In other words, the long litany of the prevailing profile of senior citizens in this country for the *under* 65 age group is *also* held by only slightly smaller percentages by the 65 and over group.

I am therefore thoroughly delighted to report to you here and now today that the mind's picture of the 65 and over people in this country is a flat and unmitigated libel and downright lie, according to this most definitive, in-depth study we have just completed.

Let me run down the litany of those degenerating characteristics and plights I have just been discussing and which large numbers of all of the adult population think are accurate descriptions of senior citizens. We not only asked people what they thought of senior citizens, we asked the senior citizens in depth to tell us about themselves. And, lest there will be some who protest that people just don't want to admit to problems that really haunt them, let me point out that using precisely these same techniques, a majority of the American people are unafraid to tell us they are alienated and disenchanted with life in the country today, nor are 35% unafraid to tell us that someone in their family has a drinking problem. No the truth is that we had better take the word of the 65 and over group seriously in its testimony about its own status.

You recall that 16% of the total public thinks that senior citizens do not have enough clothes to wear. Well, only 3% of the senior citizens themselves say this is a very serious problem for them personally. A substantial 28% of the public feels that the elderly are suffering from not having enough friends, but only 5% of the 65 and over group report that is the case. An even 50% of the public feels that older people live in constant fear of crime, but the actual number is 23%, substantial but not nearly as high as is estimated. Again, 50% of the public think older people are in poor health but this compares with 21% of the senior citizens who report they are infirm—again, high but not nearly as bad as the public thinks. A substantial 37% of the public thinks older people have not enough to do to keep busy, but only 6% of those 65 and over say that is the case with their own lives. A high 54% of the public thinks the elderly have a sense of not being needed, but only 7% of the 65 and over group actually feels that way themselves. A substantial 60% of the public thinks that elderly people suffer from loneliness and that this is a very serious problem. But not more than 12% of the 65 and over group feels the same about themselves.

And on the even grosser libel that senior citizens are inert, why the senior citizens themselves say such charges are just patent nonsense as far as they personally are concerned. Only 29% of the public thinks that mature citizens are bright and alert, but 68% of the mature citizens themselves feel they are. Only a slightly higher 73% of the people under 65 feel they are bright and alert themselves, hardly any difference in self-perception. Only 35% of the entire public thinks that senior citizens are good at getting things done. But a much higher 55% of the senior citizens feel that way, compared with only a slightly higher 60% of the population under 65. Only 21% of the public thinks that older people are open minded and adaptable, but a much higher 63% of the mature citizen group feel they are, compared with 67% among those under 65. And, on that pat-on-the-head attribute widely credited to the elderly they that are "friendly and warm" believed by 82% of the under 65 group, well only 72% of the 65 and over group shares that feeling. Incidentally, a smaller 63% of the under 65 group feels they themselves are friendly and warm.

Does all of this mean that senior citizens have it much easier and indeed do not suffer from poor housing, inadequate incomes, fear of crime, not having enough medical care, not enough job facilities, not having enough money to live on? No, indeed. By objective standards, much needs to be done to meet the needs of older people. But on many of them, I might add, they are not necessarily indigenous problems for the 65 and over segment of the population. Many Americans, unfortunately, still suffer deprivation despite the growth of affluence and privilege in this post-industrial society. And recent runaway inflation has not made this situation better, to vastly understate the case.

The key fact is that people 65 and over are very much alive and well. They are decidedly not prepared to view themselves as individuals who are rotting away and will soon rid society of the added load they put upon the rest of us. They are not only alive and well, but they want to live better and they want to be more active and they want to contribute to society, above anything else.

When all of the results are added up, the single biggest and most substantial message from the one in six people 65 and over is this, "look, you are drowning us with pity and your bad conscience has convinced us as well that the plight and lot of older people is well nigh hopeless. Well, we want to tell you that we are in much better fettle, in much better command of our competence and capabilities, and much more willing to bear our share of societal responsibilities than you ever imagined."

So, concludes the 65 and over group, "give us less pity and give us more opportunity, give us the respect not simply for having lived so long, but respect born of what we are and still can be, much more than what we have been; do not count us out; do not put us on the ash heap, wringing your hands all the way to the graveyard about our aging miseries."

Allow me to cite some facts from this survey which ought to be made indelible on the consciousness of those under 65. If these facts were inscribed on the minds of the non-senior citizens, and were to replace the stereotypes of pitying that pervade today, maybe at last something positive could be done in this country to bring mature citizens into their own as they so desperately want.

Seventy-four percent of all senior citizens say they would prefer to spend most their time with people *not* of their own age, but with people of all ages. So the 65 and over group is saying to us in loud and clear terms: do *not* consign us to rot away in old age ghettoes, where our supposedly feeble minds and inert pace of life can find empathy with others who have feeble minds and inert lives. Out with such nonsense, they are literally shouting today. Not only do mature citizens want to be more interactive with all ages, but they report they do indeed perform a whole host of useful services: 34% run errands for their children or grandchildren, 3% give advice on how to deal with life's problems, 45% actually help out by giving their younger kin money, 54% take care of small children in the family, 68% help out when someone is ill, and 90% help out their offspring by giving them gifts.

In fact, the contribution of senior citizens extends far beyond the level of the family. In the area of gainful employment, their current and their potential contribution should not be underestimated. A substantial 18% of the 65 and over group is still part of the labor force: 3% employed full-time, 9% employed part-time, and 6% who are still looking for work but cannot find it and are unemployed. While 12% of all people 65 and over are employed, a much higher 18% in the 65-69 age group are working. And it should be added that 8 in every 10 mature citizens who are working have no intention whatsoever of retiring.

Sadly, among the majority who have retired, a substantial 37% said they did not stop working by choice—they were forced to retire, they were put on the shelf involuntarily or put in the vernacular, tossed on the dump heap. Among blacks 65 and over 49% said they were forced to retire and 46% of those in the under $3,000 a year income group said the same. So those who not only least wanted to retire, but who could also least afford to retire found themselves the most retired, but not out of their own choice.

When taken together, those 65 and over citizens who did not want to retire and would like to be employed gainfully came to 4.4 million. They are not counted as unemployed in official statistics. They are felt by society to be safely retired, beyond the reach and responsibility of society for allowing its citizens to work. If they were counted in the unemployment columns, and a case could be made for that, then we would have close to 10% unemployment in this country instead of the just over 5% today.

The fact is that retirement is rapidly becoming a dirty word to more and more senior citizens. Forced retirement is a very dirty word, for it means that the ability of a mature citizen to use his or her talents, energies, ambitions, drive is stripped away. The group which hasn't yet reached the age of 65 feels than an even lower fixed retirement age is a good and desirable thing. But the group 65 and over disagrees. Why? Simply because they feel that work in itself makes a person feel useful and keeps them from becoming old, that just because a person passes 65 in no way, shape, or fashion means that they are not qualified to work, work hard, and make a significant contribution to society. By a thumping and nearly unanimous 86-11%, a smashing majority of mature citizens say, and they wish the establishment would only hear it, that "nobody should be *forced* to retire because of age, if he wants to continue working and is still able to do a good job."

The fact is that discrimination in firing people when they reach 65 (the polite word is "mandatory retirement") is rife in this country, and, what is more, nearly everyone admits that is the case when pressed on the point. By 80-13%, a big majority of all the public believes that "most employers discriminate against older people and make it difficult for them to find work. Among those executives we surveyed who have direct hiring and firing responsibilities, an impressive 79% admitted to discrimination in retirement practices through the polite but brutal process of "mandatory retirement."

The senior citizens in our midst want so to participate in and to contribute to society that 22% today report they do volunteer work, for which they receive no pay. Interestingly enough, those who are employed also tend to do more volunteer work in addition to their jobs, than those who are not employed, thus proving out David Reisman's theory about "the more, the more." In addition to the 22% engaged in volunteer work, another 10% of the people 65 and over also would like to do volunteer work, but have trouble being accepted for such duty. Even when they want to work for nothing, they are still not welcomed. Thus, the bottom line on potential volunteers among the senior citizen group: an impressive 6.6 million people.

Thus, it is fair to conclude that senior citizens in the United States today feel that they are simply not used by society as they ought to be. As many as close to 4 in 10 of all people 65 and over would like to be actively engaged in work, either for pay or for free, which allows them to contribute to the mainstream of American society. Beyond this, the vast majority want to mingle with, help in many different ways, and be active with people of all ages.

The trouble with the way we deal with mature citizens in our midst is not nearly so much that we have relegated them to an inferior economic standard, although much, much needs to be done to improve their lot in these bread and butter areas, and especially in these times of cruel inflation. But the basic libel and the basic shame about the way senior citizens are treated is that they are not given the credit that even a modicum of human decency would require that they be allowed to contribute from their skills, their energies, their drive that has simply not left most of them. The basic libel is that people are declared dead and useless long before their time, and in a society which will be aging dramatically in the next decade, this can be a highly dangerous political fact.

So it is time indeed for the establishment in America and especially all people who have not yet reached 65 to wake up and realize there is a vast untapped potential of solid energy out there which does not want to be dumped on the scrap heap of inactivity to rot away in the protection of benign neglect, albeit the old are supposed to take it all with a smile. Behind that smile, I will tell you, is a scowl of frustration and simmering rage. It is not hard to predict that we shall see a wave of militance among senior citizens as their numbers rise. But it will not be to ask the rest of society to take pity on them and to give them bigger quantities of handouts. Rather, it will be to allow mature citizens to take their rightful place at work, in the work-endeavors, in the unfinished business of making the quality of life in America better. For the senior people among us know as well as anyone that quality has deteriorated in this country at nearly every hand. All they want is the chance to make it better, not just for themselves but for everyone. And that has to be the best tonic you can give people 65 and over today. So I say, take that promise . . . before it is too late. Shed that guilty conscience and do something. Stop pitying and start action to let them back in. Stop wringing your hands and open your minds to the mainstream. There is still a lot of sinew in those hands that might have a few wrinkles on them and there is still a lot of creativity in those hearts that want to help their fellow men. In short, the senior citizens want to relieve society of its so-called burden and want in. They are saying, open the gates, brother, for we are marching in, and it will be right here on earth. *St. Peter's gates can wait.*

The New Ageism and the Failure Models: A Polemic

11

Richard A. Kalish, PhD[1]

Social gerontologists and social geriatricians have made considerable use of the term *ageism* as a counterpart to the more familiar *racism* and *sexism*. The general assumption underlying the application of this term is that ageist individuals and ageist societies or communities or organizations exist.

Ageists, the assumption holds, express overt and covert dislike and discrimination regarding the elderly. This is, they avoid older persons on an individual level, they discriminate against older persons in terms of jobs, other forms of access to financial support, utilization of social institutions, and so forth. Further, the ageist individual derides the elderly through hostile humor, through accusations that the elderly are largely responsible for their own plight, and through complaints that they are consuming more than their share of some particular resource. They may also contend that older people deserve what they get, are in effect a drain on society, are functionally incapable of change or improvement (or, conversely, are capable of change and improvement and should be required to do so with their present resources), and do not contribute adequately to the society from which they are taking resources. Ageism involves stereotyping, prejudice, discrimination, segregation, hostility . . . the list can go on and on.

The New Ageism

I would like to propose that there is another form of ageism, that it is equally pervasive in our society, and that it is found in advocates of the elderly as often — and perhaps more so — than among their antagonists.

This form of ageism, which I will refer to as the New Ageism, although it is certainly not new, has the following characteristics:

(1) It stereotypes "the elderly" in terms of the

'California School of Professional Psychology, 1900 Addison St., Berkeley, CA 94704.

characteristics of the least capable, least healthy, and least alert of the elderly, although its rhetoric is punctuated by insistence that "all elderly are not alike."

(2) It perceives the older person as, in effect, a relatively helpless and dependent individual who requires the support services of agencies and other organizations.

(3) It encourages the development of services without adequate concern as to whether the outcome of these services contributes to reduction of freedom for the participants to make decisions controlling their own lives.

(4) It produces an unrelenting stream of criticism against society in general and certain individuals in society for their mistreatment of the elderly, emphasizing the unpleasant existence faced by the elderly.

The message of the New Ageism seems to be that "we" understand how badly you are being treated, that "we" have the tools to improve your treatment, and that if you adhere to our program, "we" will make your life considerably better. You are poor, lonely, weak, incompetent, ineffectual, and no longer terribly bright. You are sick, in need of better housing and transportation and nutrition, and we — the nonelderly and those elderly who align themselves with us and work with us — are finally going to turn our attention to you, the deserving elderly, and relieve your suffering from ageism.

The New Ageism obscures individual and group differences within the 23,000,000 or so persons in the country normally defined as elderly. In fact, the definition of "elderly" tends to slip and slide a bit, which permits the New Ageists to seem on more solid ground than they really are. The New Ageists begin by stating that there are 23,000,000 persons over age 65; they often ignore the immense diversity among these persons and they also tend to ignore that most of these persons are intact, functioning effectively on their own, and getting along adequately on what money they have. Then their definition of "the elderly" changes from one based on chronological age to one based on sickness and poverty, but the change is implicit, not explicit, and so the listener is still focused on the 23,000,000 elderly and makes the assumption, without realizing it, that the spotlighted elderly represent the totality of elderly.

The Failure Models

The New Ageism has another message, one which I believe is more subtle and more pervasive than the message described in the previous discussion: the Failure Models. The general message of the Failure Models is that this or that older person has failed or is going to fail. This is accomplished in two related but very different fashions: the Incompetence Model, an approach that constantly reminds older people how incompetent they are; and the Geriactivist Model, an approach that establishes a rigid set of standards for appropriate behavior and faults those who do not adhere to the standards.

The Incompetence Failure Model has been developed in part as a tactic to get funding from governmental and private agencies. In effect, it is the ability to say, "Those persons for whom I am advocate are greater failures than those persons for whom you are advocate. They are such great failures that the only solution to their failure is more money." The obvious difficulty with this model is that as soon as the failures become successes, the incompetents become competent and in need of fewer services, and the advocates will lose their jobs and, more than that, lose their status as serving the "Incompetent Failure of the Year."

This model is best represented by a superficial reading of the distressingly excellent Pulitzer Prize winning book, *Why Survive,* by Robert Butler. I describe this as "best" because it simultaneously is a masterful job of chronicling the ills that have befallen the elderly, basing this chronicle on thorough research and careful documentation, and includes a virtually prototypical example of the Incompetence Failure Model. This book has served effectively to rally the sympathetic and persuade the dubious that the plight of *the* elderly requires remediation. But what accumulative effect does this book, and its kindred media and political writings and speechs, have on older persons? Now that television and columnists have "discovered" the elderly, how has their discovery affected the persons discovered?

I certainly admit that I don't know these answers; indeed I don't think that anyone has a clear idea. There are no research data, and I cannot recall ever having read any analytical article. The very title of Butler's book suggests a possible reaction that an elderly reader or, even more likely, a reader approaching his or her later years, would have: Why Survive? Indeed, what can be gained by living?

One possible effect on older people of the Incompetence Failure Model is that they internalize what they read and hear and come to believe it of themselves as individuals. If this is the case, then the work of the advocates of the elderly becomes as damaging to the self-esteem of older persons as is the view of those who damn them with benign neglect or even those who express overt ageism.

A second possibility is that each older individual accepts the information literally, but excludes himself or herself and closer friends. This is the "those-old-people-over-there" position. A third alternative is that the rhetoric and polemic are seen as political in nature and have little or no effect at all. And a fourth is that the elderly individual is strengthened by recognizing the responsibility for his or her plight as emanating from a society that ignores him or her, thus requiring a redoubling of effort which will lead to the assuaging of discomfort.

I suspect that all of these operate, at different times and with different persons, although I believe that the second view prevails. Thus, the elderly person denies that the model applies to him or her, but acknowledges that it is descriptive of "those old folks."

I don't wish to make a scapegoat of *Why Survive?* It served a very important purpose, but unfortunately the valuable discussion of a better life for the elderly in the later part of the book did not receive the attention that the earlier Incompetence Failure Model received. Nor do I wish to present the position that the elderly need all kinds of protection. That notion has been exaggerated: the elderly are much tougher and more resilient than they are given credit for being.

The second message of failure is the Geriactivist Model. I coined this term about ten years ago to describe the older people who are themselves active in the causes of the elderly. They develop a symbiotic relationship with younger advocates, and together they maintain the call for an active and involved old age. The Geriactivist needs the younger associates who have jobs in the community and who can participate in making decisions; the younger advocates — social workers, recreation workers, agency staff, politicians — need the activist older person as both a source of inexpensive support labor and to legitimize the activist position. The activist position is established as the *only* appropriate way for older persons to function. Something is assumed to be wrong with older people who wish to sit around and talk with elderly friends, who wish to stay at home and read, who thoroughly enjoy television, who wish to pray or meditate or jog by themselves, who for whatever reasons prefer their world to be comfortable, comforting and manageable rather than stimulating, challenging, and risky, who prefer their inner worlds to the external world. One geri-activist — my model for this role — went so far as to tell me that any older person who would not participate actively, either socially or politically, was probably lacking in moral integrity or in emotional stability.

Older persons who respond to their inner worlds or who enjoy and desire passive entertainment are seen as challenges to be overcome, rather than as individuals who are adapting to a life-long (or recent) preference that could only be fully realized when retirement and the empty nest made it possible. Thus, once again the sense of failure is communicated. "Those who are not part of the solution are part of the problem; those who do not adhere to my rules of healthy old age are, by definition, failures." Diversity is not recognized, nor are inner life and intrinsic satisfactions seen as a proper definition for a healthy personality.

Overall the Failure Models probably generate anger among the elderly with society and simultaneously with themselves. The implication is that the older person is not only victimized, but also is impotent and powerless to have any significant impact on the society and/or individuals who perpetrate the victimization. The built-in assumption is that change is governed from without, a view guaranteed to intensify the sense of impotence. And since the older person is perceived by others through the lens of this model, the initial response many people have to the older person is that of helpless victim, a view made worse by the assumption that it actually favors the elderly.

The source of the victimization is often stated as being an impersonal bureaucracy and a depersonalizing society, run for the betterment of some vaguely labeled "establishment" or else for some other age or power group. All of this adds up to a perceived conspiracy to deprive the elderly of their entitlements, a situation guaranteed to increase frustration and anger. And made worse by the pity and sympathy that are often the result. Further, to the extent that it is perceived as accurate and authoritative, it will discourage older persons from attempts to gain their rights since this will be seen as a futile action.

Perpetrators or Innocent Bystanders?

Who is really responsible for the Failure Models? Is it the funding agencies that must compete with other funding agencies in their presentation to Congress of the dire need they represent? Perhaps, but only in part, since it is obviously political pressure, as well as extent of need, that produces results.

Are the media responsible? Yes and no. Certainly they exploit the Failure Models, but nonetheless they tend to respond primarily to what they perceive their audience as wanting to view.

Are the members of Congress the true villains? No, since they only respond to some combination of political demand and perceived need.

Is it we gerontologists and geriatricians? Again, yes and no. We are familiar with the successes, and we are familiar with the need to respect diversity, but we are also pressured by the importance of keeping our own programs going, and we can't do this without money and personal support. At the same time, many of us are both active and activists, and our natural inclination is to view these qualities in others in a positive light. Indeed, for some of us, our entire professional value system is predicated on the importance of activity and involvement. What is important to watch here is how we define involvement and that we do not place highly restrictive boundaries on what we consider mentally healthy aging.

So who has perpetrated the Failure Models? All of us, and with many valid reasons, but without adequate thought of consequences. There was a time in history when people who succeeded were considered to be chosen by God, when it was often assumed that those who were healthy or financially successful must be so because of God's will. Now the opposite view seems to prevail, and advocates focus on the weaknesses and victimization of those they represent in order to develop a viable position.

There are no villains, yet we are all responsible.

Some Existing Models and an Alternative

In the 15 or so years that I have been involved in gerontology, I have noted several models in our society that have been used to describe the nature of aging. I'm presenting them here, fully cognizant that they are highly impressionistic and far from being expressed in readily operational terms.

The first model I've termed the Pathology Model. Old age is seen as pathological, a time of sickness and strangeness and falling-apartness. It is also seen as a static period, without much chance for change in a positive direction. It just *is*.

Following that, both in severity and, in my experience, in chronology, is the Decrement Model. This model is based on cross-sectional studies that showed the substantial age-related differences that were initially interpreted as age-related changes. Decrements are not as bad as pathology, but they partake of the same kind of distress.

The third model, initiated when we became aware that longitudinal studies suggested a much smaller decrement than previously assumed, might be termed the Minimal Change Model. Herein older people were presumed to be continuations of what they were as younger people, but with a small degree of decrement. So we talked about biochemical and social and psychological and health impairments that could occur at any age, but occurred more frequently with old age and are sometimes accumulative so that they were, in any event, likely to take a heavier toll in the later years. In these ways, age per se was not the villain, but the age-related changes were.

The fourth model prevails among gerontologists today. It is the Normal Person Model. Older people are simply people, like all other individuals. They are highly diverse. They do resemble each other in some ways, because of when they were socialized to certain values or when they experienced certain events; they share increased likelihood of being grandparents, being retired, being diabetic, being widowed, but they differ in more ways than they are similar. Their behavior is understandable in terms of the situations they confront, so that any form of conservatism is explained in terms of their social and political values and the economic situation they face; reaction time changes are explained in terms of biochemical changes that the elderly learn to compensate for with considerable success; cognitive changes are

likely to arise from isolation as often as from physiological brain change, but in either event, it is a health problem, not an aging problem per se.

I would like to propose a fifth model, perhaps an outgrowth of the Normal Person Model: a Personal Growth model. The later years can be a period of optimum personal growth. Not for everyone: some are not in adequate health, some are too financially restricted, some have been socialized in their early years in ways of thinking and behaving that make later growth impossible. But the later years can be a time for growth. For one thing, many earlier responsibilities are no longer in evidence. Children no longer make significant demands; aged parents are often (but not always) dead; repetitive and unstimulating jobs no longer consume time and energy; stressful competitive needs no longer stir the ego.

Second, older persons no longer need to be constrained by what others think of them. No longer are they likely to be threatened with loss of jobs or the demands of dependent children if they step outside the fences that had previously circled their lives. Of course, they may not be able to do this, or they may not wish to do this, but the option is there.

Third, many elderly have worked through their fears of their own death, and they have therefore learned better than any others how to develop priorities that satisfy them. They have also learned to cope with their own health problems and with losing others. Obviously, death, health, and loss don't cease to be problems, but many older persons have a period of years — sometimes many years — when these are not inhibiting problems.

Fourth, there is tremendous discretionary time. One of the major difficulties of retirement is that of using time for one's own satisfaction. Those who fail to solve this problem probably do not lead enjoyable retirement lives; those who do solve the problem learn how to schedule themselves for optimum pleasure, whether the pleasure comes through physical labor, social relationships, or leisure.

Fifth, there is the motivation caused by knowing the future is finite. For some elderly, this knowledge is so destructive that enjoyment or satisfaction is virtually impossible. Others, however, not only cope more effectively, but respond to the pressure by a highly appropriate use of time. The time boundary justifies their ignoring the minutes of life, if they wish, and to concentrate on what matters to them. This might be gardening or painting or political action or earning money or seeking enlightenment or praying or talking with friends or reminiscing. They do not mark time; they use time for themselves. They learn to enjoy the passing minutes by becoming absorbed in those minutes.

The Personal Growth Model of aging is obviously not one I have created in this paper. The SAGE program, developed by Gay Luce, has been using this model for several years; many senior centers have encouraged personal growth; the rapidly increasing emphasis on facilitating the return of older people to formal and informal educational programs reflects the same intent. Nonetheless, there is too little awareness of the potential for continued growth and personal satisfaction among the elderly and, simultaneously, unduly narrow boundaries as to what constitutes growth and satisfaction.

Some Final Preaching

I am not Pollyanna. Normally I am Cassandra. I do not wish to take a Geriactivist position and place the burden of trying to attain a standard of personal growth on an elderly person who is fighting for life against physical or financial hardship. Rather, I am trying to emphasize the possibility of growth at any time in life and the recognition that the growth that does not occur in the later years is never going to occur.

I am also suggesting that we can develop a Personal Growth model, so that we approach older persons with the expectation that they have the potential for continued growth, that even sickness and financial restriction can be a source of growth, although not desirable, and that our task is to facilitate that growth.

There are programs, many programs, that are doing just that, and there are articles in the media and television programs that show what these programs are doing. Often, of course, the implication of the media is that these older people are unusual and that is why we must put them on display, but the other message can also be heard: you too can be like these people.

There is also something that each individual can do, rather than feeling helpless to fight the overpowering bureaucracy. We can communicate to older persons that we have faith in their abilities, that we recognize that they are capable of making decisions (even those decisions that we assume, perhaps correctly, will turn out wrong), that we respect their ownership of their own bodies and time and lives. In brief, we can communicate a Success Model instead of the Failure Models.

It is not my point that the elderly in the U.S. and Canada enjoy the best in the best of all possible countries. Many older people are certainly in need of better housing, better transportation systems, better nutrition, more recognition of needs for human relationships and for stimulation and challenge. Nor is this a call for reduced services. Needs and wants will always outrun resources.

The difficulty is that by describing the elderly as helpless individuals, beset by problems, incompetent in finding their own ways, and obligated to meet a set standard of activity, we are expressing the New Ageism. It influences our views of the elderly, their views of themselves, and — I can only assume — the behavior that both the elderly and nonelderly exhibit in regard to aging and older people. If we define older people as victims, we will approach them as victims and expect them to behave as victims. Even by defining something as A Problem, we are initiating a self-fulfilling prophecy.

I would like to see the definition of older people develop so that they are perceived as equally — perhaps more — capable of personal growth and life satisfaction and happiness. This means a Success Model instead of a Failure Model, without blinding us to the very real problems that some older people do face. We can then stop confusing the elderly with the least competent consumers of geriatric services, and begin to work toward the development of a community that recognizes the competent, autonomous, self-esteeming, generative older person as the norm. We can refocus our attention on the later years as opportunities for flexibility, joy, pleasure, growth, and sensuality.

The Robert W. Kleemeier Award Lecture 12
Social Myth as Hypothesis: The Case of the Family Relations of Old People[1]

Ethel Shanas, PhD[2]

Every society has its own social myths. Such myths are those collective beliefs which everyone within a given society knows to be "right," and which everyone accepts as "true." Because everyone, or almost everyone, believes in them, social myths act as a cohesive force within a society. They may be described as a glue which holds societies together. However, such myths or beliefs may also serve to obstruct both thought and action by encouraging people to accept as fact that which may really be fiction.

The Myth of Alienation

This paper deals with a social myth — the widely-held belief that in contemporary American society old people are alienated from their families, particularly from their children. All sorts of theories have been proposed to justify this myth, including those theories which stress the values of the nuclear family in industrial society. Proceeding from the assumption that this myth is "true" there has also been a special emphasis on programs to meet the needs of the alienated aged, who, in keeping with the myth, are assumed to be the majority of the aged.

Evidence to support the belief that the aged are alienated from their families, particularly children, is sparse, however. Much of it is comprised of illustrative case studies of individuals known to the adherent of the alienation myth. The strongest evidence that can be mustered to support the myth is the fact that many old people in the U.S. live apart from their children. Some old people, with or without children, even have the temerity to live alone. The assumption that old persons who live alone

or apart from their children are neglected by their children and relatives is implicit in the alienation myth. Why young persons who live alone are not regarded as alienated from their parents and relatives is an interesting if peripheral question.

The myth that old people are alienated from their families and children has guided much of social gerontological research about the elderly for the last 30 years. The myth and its multiple ramifications are reminiscent of the Hydra, the monster of Greek mythology slain by Hercules. The Hydra had nine heads. These heads were unique in that each time one was cut off, it was replaced by two others. In the same way, each time evidence has been presented that old people are not alienated from their families, new adherents of the myth rise up, not only among the mass media and the writers for the popular press, but also among research investigators and even among old people themselves. Many old people when describing their active involvement with their children and grandchildren will say "But, of course, my family is different." The extent to which old people have internalized the alienation myth may be further illustrated with a finding from a national survey. Those old people who were most likely to agree with the statement "Children don't care anything about their parents except for what they can get out of them" turned out to be the persons who had no children.

The theme of this paper is adopted from a statement of Thomas Huxley who described as the great tragedy of science "the slaying of a beautiful hypothesis by an ugly fact." The beautiful hypotheses to be discussed here are the various corollaries of the belief that old people are rejected by their families. The ugly facts are that these hypotheses have been demonstrated to be in error. In contemporary American society, old people are not rejected by their

[1]The 1957 survey of the elderly was supported by the Health Information Foundation; the 1962 survey by the NIMH and the Community Health Services Division of the Bureau of State Services of the USPHS; the 1975 survey by the AoA, Grant no. 90-A-369, and the Social Security Admin., Grant no. 10-P-57823. Presented at the Gerontological Society Annual Meeting, Dallas, TX, Nov. 1978.

[2]Prof. of Sociology, Univ. of Illinois at Chicago Circle, Box 4348, Chicago, IL 60680.

families nor are they alienated from their children. Further, where old people have no children, a principle of family substitution seems to operate and brothers, sisters, nephews and nieces often fulfill the roles and assume the obligations of children. The truly isolated old person, despite his or her prominence in the media, is a rarity in the United States.

Some Acknowledgements

I propose to present the evidence that I have collected over the last 25 years that destroys the "beautiful hypotheses." Before I do so, however, I should like to acknowledge those persons who influenced me in my search for "ugly facts." These include Robert J. Havighurst and the late Ernest W. Burgess with whom I began my career in aging research some 30 years ago; the late Clyde W. Hart, one-time director of the National Opinion Research Center at the University of Chicago and Selma F. Monsky of that center, now of the University of California, who urged me to investigate the spatial distribution of older parents and their adult children; Bernice L. Neugarten, my long-time colleague at the University of Chicago; and Wilma Donahue and Clark Tibbitts who for a quarter of a century gathered together at the University of Michigan persons interested in aging and the aged and encouraged each of us in our professional growth and enthusiasms. I have been influenced in my view of society and of how people, young or old, are incorporated into social groups and act together by the teacher in my first course in Sociology and subsequently, a life-long friend, Herbert Blumer, now Professor Emeritus of Sociology at the University of California at Berkeley.

Almost a score of years ago, I demonstrated, at least to my own satisfaction, that old people in the U.S. were not rejected by their families nor alienated from their children. Because the alienation of old people from their families was often considered to be a concomittant of industrialization, I sought verification of these U.S. findings in other industrialized societies. I wanted to know whether old people in the U.S. were unique in their involvement with family and kin helping networks, or whether similar phenomena were to be found in other industrialized countries. European colleagues in both the highly industrialized and less developed countries sharpened and clarified my thinking on these topics. I am particularly indebted to Peter Townsend, Dorothy Wedderburn and Amelia I. Harris in Britain, and to Henning Friis, Poul Milhøj and the late Jan Stehouwer in Denmark.

Most of all, in the search for facts I owe a debt to those thousands of older men and women and the members of their families who answered my questions and told me and my associates about their lives. It is from older people themselves, living both in the community and in institutions, that I learned what the family life of old people in the U.S. is really like.

Definitions

Old age, like other social phenomena, can only be studied by asking pertinent questions, testing observed reality against theoretical constructs, and by modifying or even discarding these constructs for others should they prove inadequate in explaining observed behavior. Before one can ask pertinent questions, however, one needs to define one's terms. I shall therefore begin this discussion of my empirical findings about old people and their families with a definition of the family and a discussion of the function of the family. In contemporary U.S. many definitions of the family are possible. Since World War II a variety of family forms and life styles have emerged which, as Marvin Sussman has said, "if not legitimized are at least tolerated" (1976). These variant family forms, however, have been more popular with the young than with the old, and seem to have been embraced by only a small proportion of older people in this country. For most older people, the family is that group of individuals to whom they are related by blood or marriage and this is the definition which I have adopted. This definition of the family implies that the family includes more than the individual's immediate family, that is, spouse, children, and perhaps siblings. The family may include those persons somewhat distantly related by blood or marriage, such as cousins of various degree or in-laws, all of whom may be perceived as family members. Further, for any one person the family network is not static. It may expand to include even more distant relatives as a need arises for information, services, or help from these relatives.

Nothing in this definition of the family as a kin network implies that a family must live under the same roof. Those living together under the same roof may or may not be a family as here defined. They comprise a household. While households of unrelated old people who act as though they were related family members are becoming more common, only a tiny fraction of the elderly live in such arrangements.

Peter Laslett in his work on family and household makes a strong case for distinguishing family, that is, perceived kin, from household, that is, co-residents (1972). Much of the rhetorical murkiness which surrounds discussions of old people and their children stems from a confusion of family as here defined, and household. In these discussions there also seems to be an underlying belief that somehow several generations living under the same roof makes for happiness for older household members, and that the separation of the generations into separate households makes for unhappiness on the part of the older generation. I forbear from further comment on this topic except to quote from a 23-year-old female respondent in a national survey whose parents and parents-in-law were all living. When asked about living arrangements for older people she said: "I don't approve of sharing a kitchen with anyone, old or young" (Shanas, 1962).

The Functions of Families Today

In our society, most families are no longer economic units. Further, human service systems, organized into powerful bureaucracies, provide education for family members, care for the sick and frail, and even offer professional emotional support to individuals if necessary (Shanas & Sussman, 1977). The 20th century indeed can be described as the age of the social worker. What then does the contemporary family do? It is still the family, that group of individuals related by blood or marriage, that is the first resource of both its older and younger members for emotional and social support, crisis intervention, and bureaucratic linkages.

Moreover, I would argue that the one place in contemporary life where the individual may be "himself" or "herself" is within the family. The complex nature of contemporary urbanized society results in individuals, whether children or adults, living segmented roles within different life sectors. The busy executive is quite different from the scout leader, the ardent sportsman from the community volunteer. Yet, these roles may all be facets of the life of the same person. It is in the family that the basic "persona," not the segmented social image, can

show itself. The family as a refuge and private place for its adult members may perhaps be more important now than earlier in its history.

Talcott Parsons, the American sociologist, is perhaps the best-known exponent of the theory that the nuclear family, husband, wife, and their offspring, is the most functional type of family in contemporary society. Social researchers, following Parsons, have stressed that the primary function of this nuclear family is the socialization of the child. Many scholars seem less acquainted with another Parsonian dictum, a response perhaps to those scores of anthropological and sociological studies which demonstrate the existence and operation of family kin networks. Professor Parsons has also stated: "The family can thus be seen to have two primary functions, not one. On the one hand it is the primary agent of socialization for the child, while on the other it is the primary basis of security for the normal adult" (1965).

The findings on family relationships given in this paper are a validation of Professor Parsons' belief that the family is the primary basis of security for adults in later life. The data come from nationwide probability surveys of non-institutionalized persons aged 65 and over, commonly defined as older people. These surveys made in 1957, 1962, and 1975 may be thought of as snapshots of the aged population in the community at three points in time and over a period of 20 years. In surveys such as these there are no volunteer subjects. Every eligible person has a predetermined chance of being selected. Not every eligible person is located, however, and some small proportion of those located cannot be interviewed. The probability design is such, however, that for practical purposes the chances are about 19 out of 20 that the true proportion of any variable will be within the range of estimate reported here, plus and minus one standard deviation.

The surveys report the situation of the non-institutionalized elderly living in the community. In 1975, at the time of the latest survey, about 94 to 95% of all persons over 65 were community residents (Siegel, 1976). That 5 or 6% of the elderly in institutions, whether in homes for the well or the sick aged, differ in demographic characteristics from the community elderly. On the average, institutional residents are older than persons living in the community. About one of every eight persons over 80 years of age now lives in an institution. Old people in institutions are three times as likely as the community elderly to have never married, and are twice as likely to be widowed. Those persons without close family, the never married and the very old widowed, are more likely than other persons to seek residence in a home for the aged or to be institutionalized when they are ill.

The Alienation Myth Revisited

To this stage I have given a definition of the family, discussed the functions of the family, and indicated the scope of the populations studied. I want now to return to the alienation myth, the belief that older people are alienated from their families, and to consider some of the hypotheses which derive from it. These are: (1) Because of the geographic mobility of the population of the U.S. most old people who have children live at great distances from their children; (2) Because of the alienation of old people from their children, most older parents rarely see their children; (3) Because of the predominance of the nuclear family in the U.S., most old people rarely see their siblings or other relatives; and (4) Because of the existence and availability of large human service bureaucracies, families are no longer important as a source of care for older people.

These hypotheses all seem reasonable. Everyone knows that Americans move all the time, everyone knows at least one old person whose children all live at the other end of the continent, and everyone knows of a sick old person whose adult children are trying to find a residence for him, or, more usually, her. Despite what everyone knows, each of the above hypotheses has been disproved. In the U.S. most old people with children live close to at least one of their children and see at least one child often. Most old people see their siblings and relatives often, and old people, when either bedfast or housebound because of ill health, are twice as likely to be living at home as to be resident in an institution.

About four of every five noninstitutionalized persons over 65 in the U.S. have living children. The proportion of old people with living children is unchanged over the last 20 years. The proportion of old people with children who live in the same household with one of these children has declined, however, from 36% in 1957 to 18% in 1975. At the same time that the proportion of parents and children living in the same household has declined, there has

been a rise in the proportion of old people living within ten minutes distance of a child. As a result, the proportion of old people with children who either live with one of their children or within ten minutes distance of a child has remained fairly constant over 20 years: 59% in 1957, 61% in 1962, and 52% in 1975. The findings indicate that while old people no longer live in the same household with a child, they now live next door, down the street, or a few blocks away. Older people and their children both place a value on separate households. Many old people say they want to be independent. Their children in turn stress a desire for privacy. As the economic situation of old people and their children has improved over the last 20 years, it has become possible to implement the desire for independence and privacy of both generations.

Old people who live alone are commonly considered a particularly isolated group among the elderly. Among all old people who live alone, however, half of those with children are within ten minutes distance of a child (Shanas, 1962; Shanas et al., 1968). Many of these persons stress that they and their children share "intimacy at a distance" (Rosenmayr & Köckeis, 1963). It is. the childless elderly living alone who are the vulnerable elderly but even they, as we shall see, call upon family resources.

Whether old people in the future increasingly will live at greater distances from their children cannot be answered from the data from the years 1957 to 1975. What these data do show is that despite the geographic mobility of the population of the U.S. older people who have children live close to at least one of these children. In 1975, three of every four persons with children either lived in the same household as a child or within a half hours' distance of a child. The first hypothesis, that because of the geographic mobility of the population of the U.S. most old people who have children live at great distances from their children, must therefore be rejected.

Living near adult children is no guarantee that the older parent will see his or her children. In 1975, however, 53% of persons with children, including those with a child in the same household, saw one of their children the day they were interviewed or the day before that. The proportion of older parents who saw at least one child during the week before they were interviewed has remained stable over roughly 20 years: 83% in 1957, 77% in 1975.

Perhaps even more important, the proportion of older parents who have not seen at least one of their children for a month or more has remained stable over the 20 year period, at about one in ten. What of old people with children who live alone? About half of these persons had seen at least one child the day they were interviewed or the day before that, and three of every four had seen at least one child during the week before they were interviewed. There has been no decrease in visiting between parents and at least one of their children from the first survey to the last.

Again, the data do not answer all the questions that might be raised about the relationships between older parents and their adult children. We do not know whether these meetings between parents and children are brief or lengthy, friendly and warm, or acrimonious and hostile. Every family is a separate constellation of interacting persons. The visits between some parents and their children may be unpleasant for both generations. On the other hand, some parents and their children may find joy and comfort in knowing that each generation is well and functioning. What the data do show is that older parents see adult children often. The second hypothesis, that because of the alienation of older parents from their children, most older parents rarely see their children, must also be rejected.

Even though most older people live close to and see at least one of their children often they still may have lost touch with their brothers and sisters or other relatives. The data show otherwise. David Schneider, the anthropologist, in discussing the family life of old people, speaks of the "hour glass effect" in the American kin system. Persons have many contacts with siblings and other relatives in their youth, these contacts shrink in young adulthood and middle life, and increase in later life.

Brothers and sisters, in particular, become important to the older person. The proportion of old persons with siblings was the same in both 1962 and 1975, about eight of every ten. Even when those persons over 75 years of age are considered separately from those under 75, seven of every ten still report surviving brothers and sisters. In 1975 one-third of all old persons with living brothers and sisters saw at least one of these during the week before they were interviewed, and more than half of old people with brothers and sisters saw at least one of these during the month before they were interviewed.

Widowed persons and old persons who have never married are especially dependent on their brothers and sisters. For many widowed persons, siblings assume some of the responsibilities of a now deceased husband or wife. Many persons who have never married live in the same household with a sibling. While about one-third of all persons with siblings had seen a brother or sister the previous week, three-fourths of these who had never married saw a brother or sister during that time.

Old people not only visit with and are visited by siblings, they also visit with other relatives who are not among their direct descendants. In 1975, about three of every ten older persons said that they had seen some relative, who was neither a brother nor a sister, a child nor a grandchild, during the previous week. For the childless elderly this relative often is a niece or nephew who assumes the responsibilities of a child.

The data confirm the findings of many other studies of family and kin in the U.S. The dominant family form for old people in the U.S. is the modified extended family. This family includes not only members of the old person's immediate family and relatives of his own generation such as siblings, it also includes nephews, nieces, and other relatives by blood or marriage. The hypothesis that because of the predominance of the nuclear family in the U.S. older people rarely see their siblings or other relatives is contradicted by the evidence and must be rejected.

Finally, what of that hypothesis that postulates that because of the existence of large human service bureaucracies, families are no longer important as a source of care for older people? Data from a variety of studies are available to test this hypothesis. Because the health system, of all contemporary bureaucracies, probably impinges most directly on the life of the elderly and their families, I shall discuss some relevant findings about families and the health care of the elderly.

In the 1962 national survey, 2% of the elderly in the community were reported as totally bedfast at home and 6% were reported as housebound. These persons were being taken care of by family members, with some minor assistance from public health nurses and other home aides. That 8% of the elderly bedfast and housebound at home was about twice the proportion of old people in institutions of all kinds whether these were institutions for the well or the sick aged.

132

Health insurance for the aged, Medicare, became operational in 1966. Medicare, Title XVIII of the Social Security Act, and a companion program of medical assistance, Medicaid, Title XIX, together provide payments for long-term care of the elderly in such health institutions as chronic disease hospitals, extended care facilities, and skilled nursing facilities. Many persons expected that the passage of this legislation would result in a great increase in the number and proportion of the elderly in long-term institutions. Indeed, one of the arguments used by opponents of this legislation was that it would destroy the will of the family to take care of its sick aged.

The 1975 survey, however, indicates no marked change from 1962 in the proportion of the elderly bedfast and housebound at home. Neither is there a marked change in the proportion of the elderly in institutions. In 1975, nine years after Medicare, about 3% of the elderly were bedfast at home and about 7% were housebound. That 10% of old people bedfast and housebound at home, just as in 1962, was almost twice the proportion of old people in institutions of all kinds. There is some indication in both these surveys, however, that the greatly impaired aged are more likely to be in institutions and the less impaired are more likely still to be at home.

Family help in providing long-term care for the elderly persists despite the alternative sources of care available in 1975 which were not available in 1962. Rosenmayr has made an interesting comment on why family help patterns may tend to continue despite the presence of such alternative help sources. "Public action to give support to the elderly has the innate danger to classify them as marginal. It is the dialectics of institutionally organized help to a certain group that this group becomes conscious of a certain bereavement; whereas individual and informal help and assistance based on intimacy may avoid this type of consequence . . ." (1975). It is the alienation of the elderly that the family wants to avoid by providing health care at home.

The circumstances that bring the elderly to institutions have been carefully studied. The United States General Accounting Office in a study in Cleveland, Ohio focusing on the costs of care concluded that "The importance of family and friends is evidenced by the fact that greatly or extremely impaired elderly who live with their spouses and children generally are not institutionalized, whereas those who live alone usually are" (Laurie, 1978). Incidentally, our own research indicates that ill health on the part of the parent is often a cause of older parents and adult children living together.

Elaine Brody, among others, has pointed out that clinical evidence reinforces gerontological research findings that adult children do not "dump" old parents into institutions. In this connection she says: "Studies of the paths leading to institutional care have shown that placing an elderly relative is the last, rather than the first, resort of families. In general, they have exhausted all other alternatives, endured severe personal, social and economic stress in the process, and made the final decision with the utmost reluctance" (1977).

The hypothesis that because of the existence of large human service bureaucracies families are no longer important as a source of care for the elderly, like the other hypotheses derived from the alienation myth, must also be rejected.

In this paper I have presented evidence to show that the belief that old people are alienated from their families, particularly their children, is a myth, not a truism. I now wish to comment on some of the kinds of research and the kind of social policy that should follow the abandonment of this myth.

Research and Policy in the Wake of the Slain Myth

We need more studies of those family forms in which some old people live which differ from the norm. While the number of persons in such arrangements is small now they will undoubtedly increase in the future. We especially need to know what services these pseudo-families can and cannot perform for their members and what supports they need to function effectively. We need research on the special situation of the childless elderly. If the birth rate continues to drop, some 35 years from now we will have a large proportion of old people who have no children or only one child. We should now investigate how childless old persons establish helping relationships with child substitutes among their available pool of kinfolk and among their friends. If we knew how these arrangements develop we would be able both to better assist the present elderly and to establish guidelines for the future.

I would also like to suggest a research topic that might be more difficult to implement. A question that concerns me is why we Americans who are interacting with our older relatives in a helping way persist in believing that we are neglecting our elderly. Why do we continue to berate ourselves while each of us is saying "But my family is different?"

In the area of social policy every effort should be made to assist families to maintain viable relationships with their older members. This means that services should be made available to old people irrespective of whether they live alone or with others. Sometimes, good family relationships are dependent on such services. Further, human service systems and their personnel must cease to behave as though the families of the elderly were enemies of the system. There is a need for an increased sensitivity to both older people and their families and for a willingness to listen on the part of such systems and their functionaries (Shanas & Sussman, 1977).

In conclusion, this paper has been designed to underscore one of my beliefs. My work has been a search for facts, for I believe that if social research and social policy in aging are to be more than exercises in futility they must be based on the facts about older people and their families, and not upon myths, however seductive.

References

Brody, E. Long-term care for older people. Human Sciences Press, New York, 1977.

Laslett, P. (Ed.). Household and family in past time. Cambridge Univ. Press, Cambridge, England, 1972.

Laurie, W. F. Employing the Duke OARS methodology in cost comparisons: Home services and institutionalization. Center reports on advances in research 2, Duke Univ. Ctr. for the Study of Aging and Human Development, Durham, NC, 1978.

Parsons, T. The normal American family. In S. Farber, P. Mustacchi & R. H. Wilson (Eds.), Man and civilization: The family's search for survival. New York, 1965.

Rosenmayr, L., & Köckeis, E. Propositions for a sociological theory of aging and the family, International Social Science Journal, 1963, 15, 410-426.

Rosenmayr, L. The many faces of the family. Paper presented at a meeting of the Int. Assoc. of Gerontology, Jerusalem, Israel, 1975.

Shanas, E. The health of older people: A social survey. Harvard Univ. Press, Cambridge, MA, 1962.

Shanas, E., & Sussman, M. B. Family and bureaucracy: Comparative analyses and problematics. In E. Shanas and M. B. Sussman (Eds.), Family, bureaucracy and the elderly. Duke Univ. Press, Durham, NC, 1977.

Shanas, E., Townsend, P., Wedderburn, D., Friis, H., Milhøj, P., & Stehouwer, J. Old people in three industrial societies. Atherton and Routledge Kegan Paul, New York and London, 1968.

Siegel, J. Demographic aspects of aging and the older population of the U.S. Current population reports: Special studies. USGPO, Series P-23, No. 59, Washington, DC, 1976.

Sussman, M. The family life of old people. In E. Shanas & R. H. Binstock (Eds.), Handbook of aging and the social sciences, Van Nostrand Reinhold, New York, 1976.

IV

Social Science Research

Social science research on religion and aging has largely consisted of surveys of religious behavior and attitudes and attempts to relate them to such variables as age, life satisfaction, and alienation. There has been little or no interest in exploring the meaning religious behavior, concerns, and questions may have for older people, or in how these might differ, if they do, from the religious issues which are of most import to younger people. Only rarely have the elderly been asked what they want from their churches, and evaluations of the degree to which church programs are meeting their needs are notably absent from the literature. The editors' purpose in presenting the articles in this section is to familiarize the reader with the kind of research which has been done and to point up the need for new modes of inquiry which might imaginatively and sensitively seek to understand the part religious issues play in the lives of the aging.

The first two papers in this section review the research on religion and aging up to 1971. E. F. Heenan provides an overview of the type and number of studies carried out. We have divided Hammond's article into two sections. The first, presented in this section, reviews the pre-1970 research on the "religiousness" of older people. (The remainder of the paper is presented under the title "Churches and Older People" in Section V.) In general the results of the studies agree that old people are more religious, as measured by expressed interest and religious activity, than younger groups in the population, but whether this is because people become more concerned with religion as they get older or whether it is a generational difference reflecting historical change is not clear. Hammond also suggests that with retirement people may shift from task-oriented to expressive interests; he explores the implications of this change for church programming.

In the third paper Philibert takes a critical view of much gerontological research based on scientific models derived from the physical sciences and suggests that, far from generating scientific principles governing aging, it may merely be describing one exceptional cultural-historical generation of old people. He proposes an alternative phenomenological approach focusing on symbols, images, and cultural meanings of aging.

The remaining papers in this section include reports on several of the better social science studies in the decade since Hammond's review. Longino and Kitson provide an answer from one clergy group to Hammond's question concerning clergy attitudes toward working with the old, finding them to be moderately positive. A rare longitudinal study of aging carried out by Blazer and Palmore at Duke University over an 18-year period includes data on religion and provides some support for the theory that religion may become an increasingly important factor in adjustment as persons move through old age. In a midwestern study a group of Missouri elderly interviewed by Mindel and Vaughan were low in church attendance but remained involved in home religious observances and practices, a finding which may come as no surprise to most clergy, yet previous researchers

135

rarely included questions about religious practices outside the church or synagogue. Kivett, studying a somewhat younger group (age 45-65), is one of the few researchers to look at the relation between certain personality factors and religious motivation.

The two final papers do not focus directly on religion but are included because they deal with issues—attitudes toward life and death, and alienation—which are considered by many writers to be central religious concerns especially salient for persons during the later years of life, and because they included older persons in their study population.

Sociology of Religion and the Aged: *13*
The Empirical Lacunae

EDWARD F. HEENAN

Department of Sociology
Bowling Green State University

This study presents a comprehensive bibliography on the relation between religion and aging. One hundred and forty social science journals were surveyed, 80 from their inception and 60 over the last 25 years. The results reveal four major areas of research effort: (1) church participation, (2) religion and the personal adjustment of the aged, (3) the meaning of religion to older persons, and (4) religion and death. The results also show that sociologists of religion are responsible for only a small part of the literature on religion and aging. This finding is surprising in view of the significance attributed to death by most sociological theories of religion.

Theoretically, one would expect a great deal of intellectual cross-fertilization between sociologists of religion and gerontologists. For instance, they both have a research interest in the phenomenon of death. Sociologists of religion should be interested in death since it is related to the genesis of religious ideologies and institutions (Berger, 1967), and gerontologists should be concerned with death since it is the major event to which their subjects must adjust (Feifel, 1959). In addition, it is generally believed that older persons are more religious than younger persons (Glock, Ringer, and Babbie, 1967: 46).

However, in spite of this theoretical link between the two fields, there is minimal cross-fertilization. The relative inattention of sociologists of religion to research among the aged is paradoxical in view of the great attention many of them give to the matter of death in their grand theories of religion. Gerontologists, on the other hand, are primarily concerned with the processes of physical, emotional, and institutional adjustment of the aged rather than their religious practices, beliefs, or even how these beliefs might assist in adjustment to senescence and death.

A survey of 140 social science journals reveals that there are approximately 55 articles or books researching the nexus between religion, death, and the aged.[1]

In addition, the survey shows there has been fairly low research productivity over the years, though there was a modest increase in research output in the decade following the 1961 White House Conference on Aging. Twenty-two of the 55 empirical studies were published before or during 1961 and 33 were published after that date. Spiritual well-

---

1. The survey included all of the major sociological, psychological, sociology of religion, and gerontological journals. Eighty journals were surveyed in their entirety and the remaining 60 were surveyed from 1945-1971.

being was one of the concerns of the 1971 White House Conference on Aging (White House Conference, 1971). Perhaps this concern will inspire greater research efforts in the next few years.[2]

Moreover, the authors of the 55 works include only four recognized sociologists of religion. Fichter's study was done in 1952, on one denomination (Roman Catholics), in a specific region of the country (the South), and with an inadequate sample of the aged (Fichter, 1952). Glock also gathered his data in 1952 for other purposes than studying the aged. In his study the oldest age cohort includes individuals as young as 50. Stark also gathered data for purposes other than studying the elderly, but Stark's data are more recent (1963), he does have a sufficient number of cases over 65 years of age, and he does include more dimensions of religiosity than did previous research (Stark, 1968).

Moberg is the only sociologist of religion who has consistently explored the relationship between religion and the aged. He is the only sociologist of religion who has drawn adequate samples of the aged, and he is the only sociologist of religion who has published his findings in the two major gerontological journals (Moberg, 1953a, 1953b, 1965b, 1965c). However, even Moberg has limited himself to empirically exploring one or two of the dimensions of religiosity among the aged.

In addition to general works and summaries of research findings (Caven, *et al.*, 1949; Maves and Cedarleaf, 1949; Hunter and Maurice, 1953; Scudder, 1958; Maves, 1960; White House Conference on Aging, 1961; Gray and Moberg, 1962; Moberg, 1965; Moberg, 1965c; Riley and Foner, 1968; White House Conference on Aging, 1971) and miscellaneous studies (Fichter, 1952; Gorer, 1955; Catholic Charities of St. Louis, 1955; McCann, 1955; Cauter and Downham, 1964; Heenan, 1968; Buxbaum, 1969; Weihl, 1970; Lawton, Kleban, and Singer, 1971), the research in the area of religion and the aged may be conveniently divided into four categories: (1) organizational participation, (2) the meaning of religion to the aged, (3) religion and personal adjustment for the aged, and (4) religion and death.

ORGANIZATIONAL PARTICIPATION

In the literature, organizational participation is generally restricted to the frequency with which the elderly attend church and belong to church groups. Of these areas, aging and church attendance is the largest. It contains 21 articles or books (Bultena, 1949; Waterman, 1949; Catholic Digest, 1953; O'Reilly, 1957; Lazerwitz, 1961; Orbach, 1961; Wilensky, 1961; Lazerwitz, 1962; Moberg, 1965a; Moberg and Taves, 1965; Catholic Digest, 1966; McGreevey, 1966; Stere, 1966; Glock, Ringer and Babbie, 1967; Riley and Foner, 1968; Stark, 1968; Beard, 1969; Hammond, 1969; Pihlblad and Rosencranz, 1969; Bahr, 1970; Wingrove and Alston, 1971). However, 14 of the 21 studies appeared after the White House Conference in 1961. Therefore, over half of the studies of church participation among the aged conducted since 1961 have been concerned primarily with one subdimension of religiosity—church attendance. Moreover, during the same period of

2. In addition to the studies mentioned here, there are a number of other works of geriatricians, which are mostly descriptive, and of churchmen, which are mostly prescriptive. Although these works have implications for the social scientific study of the relationships between religion, aging, and death, they are tangential to the nature of that relationship.

time, sociologists of religion were discovering the multidimensionality of the religious variable (Glock and Stark, 1965; Faulkner and DeJong, 1966; Faulkner and DeJong, 1969; Weigert and Thomas, 1969). For example, when Stark (1968) examines the relation between age and five dimensions of religious commitment, he concludes that the relationships between older age and piety are confined to private devotionalism, denominational differences, and belief in immortality. In contradistinction, most researchers who have focused on church attendance have considered neither the physical disabilities nor the private devotions of the aged.

THE MEANING OF RELIGION TO THE AGED

Although there are numerous scattered references to the relation of values and the meaning of religion to the aged, only four articles are directly focused on the subject (Albrecht, 1958; Barron, 1958; Covalt, 1960; Ludwig and Eichorn, 1967). Three of the articles appeared before 1961. This is clearly an oversight in research and it indicates an implicit assumption among researchers that no important religious changes occur from the time an individual is defined as elderly until he dies. Of course, that assumption is subject to empirical test, especially since geriatricians have observed that many older persons become interested in essentially religious questions concerning the meaning of life (Butler, 1964).

RELIGION AND PERSONAL ADJUSTMENT

A total of seven studies on religion and the personal adjustment of the aged have been conducted (Pan, 1950; Moberg, 1953a; Moberg, 1953b; Moberg, 1956; O'Reilly, 1957; Barron, 1958; Moberg and Taves, 1965). Of these, only one (Moberg and Taves, 1965) appears after 1961, and four were written by the same author. This body of literature is again open to the criticism of having limited the dimensionality of the religious variable. Unfortunately, the literature since 1961 on religious and personal adjustment in old age does not utilize the more recent refinements in the measurement of religiosity.

RELIGION AND DEATH

Most recently, the relation between religion and death has been explored (Martin and Wrightsman, 1964; Martin and Wrightsman, 1965; Williams and Cole, 1968; Templar and Dotson, 1970). These studies can be criticized with regard to their samples. In general, they do not study the elderly directly but extrapolate from data collected from younger segments of the population. Since death is more salient to older persons, these studies would have been greatly improved if they had used the aged as their target population.

DISCUSSION

Sociologists of religion have, for the most part, neglected the final stages of the life cycle. There is no coherent body of literature on the interrelationships between religion, death, and aging. Beyond that, the work that has been done is open to several criticisms. First, it is not cumulative; in most of the literature one finds little reference to the works of others. For example, the work of sociologists of religion has not been disseminated in gerontological journals. Second, most studies impose on their aged subjects a research design and questions created for younger cohorts. Third, the samples of the aged are small and regionally based, which makes generalizations risky. Fourth, sociologists of religion have overlooked the relation between denominationally affiliated institutions and care for the aged. Fifth, they have neglected the possibility that religiosity takes new forms among the elderly as they approach death. Finally, there is a total lack of cross-cultural research on religion and aging.

CONCLUSION

A question that cannot be answered from the survey of the literature is why sociologists of religion have not shown more interest in aging. Four reasons come readily to mind. First, gerontology as a subdiscipline of sociology is relatively young. Second, as a result of its age, and to some extent its subject matter, it is a low-status subdiscipline within the field. Perhaps the sociologist of religion, also a member of a low-status subdiscipline, does not receive sufficient academic prestige for researching this area and reporting his findings in gerontology journals. Third, the aged are not the most attractive subjects to study and they are not found in attractive settings. Nor do they offer the prospect of exciting or esoteric findings. Finally, we should not eliminate the possibility that sociologists of religion do not have the methodological techniques for researching this unique segment of the population.

The latter point leads us to conclude that sociologists of religion and gerontologists alike would profit from academic reciprocity. The goal of the gerontologists is a scientific one—to comprehend the phenomena and process of aging. To do this he must have more sophistication in researching the religious variable. That sophistication can be provided by the sociologist of religion. The goal of the sociologist of religion, on the other hand, is to understand the nature and dynamics of religion in whatever setting it manifests itself. He cannot afford to neglect a segment of the population that is closest to the ultimate crisis that plays such a large part in his theories about why people need religion. However, in order to do research on the aged he must depend upon the gerontologist for workable techniques of interviewing the elderly. If this reciprocity is not developed, an important segment of the religious life cycle might well continue to be neglected.

REFERENCES

Albrecht, R. E.
1958 "The meaning of religion to older people—the social aspect." Pp. 53-70 in D. L. Scudder (ed.), Organized Religion and the Older Person. Gainesville: University of Florida Press.

Bahr, H. M.
1970 "Aging and religious disaffiliation," Social Forces, 49 (September), 59-71.

Barron M. L.
1958 "The role of religion and religious institutions in treating the milieu of older people." Pp. 12-33 in D. L. Scudder (ed.), Organized Religion and the Older Person. Gainesville: University of Florida Press.
1961 The Aging Americans. New York: Crowell.

Beard, B. B.
1969 "Religion at 100," Modern Maturity, 12, 1-4.

Berger, P. L.
1967 The Sacred Canopy: Elements of a Sociological Theory of Religion Garden City, N. Y.: Doubleday.

Bultena, L.
1949 "Church membership and church attendance in Madison, Wisconsin," *American Sociological Review*, 14, 384-389.

Butler, R. N.
1964 "Viewpoint—An interview with Robert N. Butler," *Geriatrics*, 26, 65-75.

Buxbaum, S. T. M., R. E.
1969 "The use of religious resources in the care of the aged," *Journal of Religion and Health*, 8 (April), 143-162.

Catholic Charities of St. Louis
1955 *Older People in the Family, the Parish, and the Neighborhood*. St. Louis: Catholic Churches of St. Louis.

Catholic Digest
1953 "How important religion is to Americans," 17 (February), 7-12.
1966 "Do Americans go to church?" 30 (July), 24-32.

Cauter, T. and J. S. Downham
1964 *The Communication of Ideas*. London: Readers Digest and Chatto and Windus.

Cavan, R. S., E. W. Burgess, R. J. Havighurst, and H. Goldhammer
1949 *Personal Adjustment in Old Age*. Chicago: Science Research Associates.

Covalt, N. K.
1960 "The meaning of religion to older people," *Geriatrics* 15, 658-664.

Faulkner, J. E. and G. F. DeJong
1966 "Religiosity in 5-D: An empirical analysis," Social Forces, 45 (December), 246-254.

Feifel, H. (ed.)
1959 *The Meaning of Death*. New York: McGraw-Hill.

Fichter, J.
1952 "Profile of Catholic religious life," *American Journal of Sociology*, 58 (July), 145-149.

Glock, C. Y. and R. Stark
1965 *Religion and Society in Tension*. Chicago: Rand McNally.

Glock, C. Y., B. R. Ringer, and E. R. Babbie
1967 *To Comfort and to Challenge*. Berkeley: University of California Press.

Gorer, G.
1955 *Exploring English Character*. London: Cresset.

Gray, M. and D. O. Moberg
1962 *The Church and the Older Person*.

Grand Rapids, Michigan: William B. Eerdmans Publishing Co.

Hammond, P. E.
1969 "Aging and the ministry." Pp. 293-323 in M. W. Riley, J. W. Riley, Jr., and M. E. Johnson (eds.), *Aging and Society*, Volume two: *Aging and the Professions*. New York: Russell Sage Foundation.

Heenan, E. F.
1968 "Aging in religious life," *Review for Religious*, 27 (November), 1120-1127.

Hunter, M. W. and H. Maurice
1953 *Older People Tell Their Story*. Ann Arbor: Institute for Human Adjustment, Division of Gerontology, University of Michigan.

Lawton, M. P., H. H. Kleban and M. Singer
1971 "The aged Jewish person and the slum environment," *Journal of Gerontology*, 26 (April), 231-239.

Lazerwitz, B.
1961 "Some factors associated with variations in church attendance," *Social Forces*, 39, 301-309.
1962 "Membership in voluntary associations and frequency of church attendance," *Journal for the Scientific Study of Religion*, 2, 74-84.

Ludwig, E. C. and R. L. Eichorn
1967 "Age and disillusionment: A study of value changes associated with aging," *Journal of Gerontology*, 22 (January), 59-65.

Martin, D. and L. S. Wrightsman, Jr.
1964 "Religion and fears about death: A critical review of research," *Religious Education*, 59, 174-176.
1965 "The relationship between religious behavior and concern about death," *Journal of Social Psychology*, 65, 317-323.

Maves, P. B.
1960 "Aging, religion and the church." Pp. 698-749 in C. E. Tibbitts (ed.), *Handbook of Social Gerontology*. Chicago: University of Chicago Press.

Maves, P. B. and J. L. Cedarleaf
1949 *Older People and the Church*. New York: Abingdon-Cokesbury Press.

McGreevey, M. V.
1966 *The Aged Catholics in Two Cities: A Comparative Analysis of Social Factors and the Theory of Disengagement*. Dissertation Abstract, University of Notre Dame, 27 (4A), 1122.

Moberg, D. O.
    1953a "Church membership and personal adjustment in old age," *Journal of Gerontology*, 8 (April), 207-211.
    1953b "Religion and personal adjustment in old age: A study of some aspects of the Christian religion in relation to personal adjustment of the aged in institutions," *Religious Education*, 48 (May-June), 184-185.
    1956 "Religious activities and personal adjustment in old age," *Journal of Social Psychology*, 43, 261-268.
    1965a "The integration of older members in the church congregation." Chapter 8 in A. M. Rose and W. A. Peterson (eds.), *Older People and Their Social World: The Subculture of Aging*. Philadelphia: Davis.
    1965b "Religion in old age," *Geriatrics*, 20 (November), 977-982.
    1965c "Religiosity and old age," *Gerontologist*, 5, 78-87, 111-112.

Moberg, D. O. and M. J. Taves
    1965 "Church participation and adjustment in old age." Chapter 7 in A. M. Rose and W. A. Peterson (eds.), *Older People and Their Social World: The Subculture of the Aging*. Philadelphia: Davis.

Orbach, H. L.
    1961 "Aging and religion," *Geriatrics*, 16, 530-540.

O'Reilly, C. T.
    1957 "Religious practice and personal adjustments of older people," *Sociology and Social Research*, 43, 119-121.

Pan, J. S.
    1950 "Personal adjustments of old people: A study of old people in Protestant church homes for the aged," *Sociology and Social Research*, 34, 3-11.

Pilhblad, C. T. and H. A. Rosencranz
    1969 *Social Adjustments of Older Persons in the Small Town*, Volume IV, No. 1. Columbia: University of Missouri.

Riley, M. W. and A. Foner
    1968 *Aging and Society*, Volume I: *An Inventory of Research Findings*. New York: Russell Sage Foundation.

Scudder, D. L. (ed.)
    1958 *Organized Religion and the Older Person*. Gainesville: University of Florida Press.

Stark, R.
    1968 "Age and faith: A changing outlook or an old process?" *Sociological Analysis*, 29 (Spring), 1-10.

Stere, P. J.
    1966 *The Lutheran Church and the Needs of the Aged, A Survey of the Attitudes of Members of the Susquehanna Region, Central Pennsylvania, Synod*. Department of Sociology and Anthropology, Lycoming College, Williamsport, Pennsylvania.

Templar, D. I. and E. Dotson
    1970 "Religious correlates of death anxiety," *Psychological Reports*, 26 (June), 895-897.

Waterman, L.
    1949 "Religion and religious observance in old age." Pp. 99-112 in C. F. Tibbitts (ed.), *Living Through the Older Years*. Ann Arbor: University of Michigan Press.

Weigert, A. J. and D. T. Thomas
    1969 "Religiosity in 5-D: A critical note," *Social Forces*, 48 (December), 260-263.

Weihl, H.
    1970 "Jewish aged of different cultural origin in Israel," *Gerontologist*, 10 (Summer), 146-150.

White House Conference on Aging
    1961 *Religion and Aging*. Washington, D. C.: U.S. Government Printing Office.
    1971 *Spiritual Well-Being*. Washington, D. C.: U.S. Government Printing Office.

Wilensky, H. L.
    1961 "Life cycle, work situation, and participation in formal associations." Pp. 213-242 in R. W. Kleemeier (ed.), *Aging and Leisure*. New York: Oxford University Press.

Williams, R. L. and S. Cole
    1968 "Religiosity, generalized anxiety, and apprehension concerning death," *Journal of Social Psychology*, 75 (June), 111-118.

Wingrove, C. R. and J. P. Alston
    1971 "Age, aging, and church attendance," *Gerontologist*, 11 (Winter, Part 1), 356-358.

Aging and the ministry *14*

PHILLIP E. HAMMOND

> For gray hairs are a glorious crown, which
> is won by a righteous life.   *Proverbs 16:31*

But—

> Cast me not off in the time of old age; forsake me
> not when my strength faileth.   *Psalms 71:9*

Idealization of the past is not an uncommon tendency among men, regardless of the society or historical epoch in which they live. Despite speculation to the contrary, however, there is little evidence that the aged in traditional societies experienced fewer anxieties and insecurities than do old people in America today. As the line from Proverbs suggests, senior members of Biblical times were supposed to be venerated, but the plea of the writer of the quoted Psalm indicates that veneration was not always forthcoming. Old age was sometimes accompanied—as it is today—with fears and concerns.

It may be, though, that the basis of those fears and concerns has changed. The argument is sometimes advanced that the aged are of diminishing utility to modern, industrialized societies. As Leo Simmons claims, special possession of knowledge (especially of supernatural powers) has allowed old people in many primitive societies to occupy "key positions in a wide range of social activities. They are esteemed as experts in solving the problems of life."[1] By contrast, "problems of life" in modern society may have become increasingly technological in nature, and the old, relatively lacking in technical education, have no special competence. Written language and the spread of literacy, moreover, have allowed books, which may be read by all, to become the repositories of knowledge. Thus the act of becoming old may have lost much of its traditional functional basis for others in society.

Even if we grant validity to the argument of decreased utility, we still may question whether veneration, respect, or security must therefore automatically diminish. Just as infants are welcomed into different societies despite their uniform lack of immediate utility, so also may the elderly be viewed as worthy of respect despite their possibly decreasing utility in modern society. Moreover, from the standpoint of Western religion, the question of the social usefulness of the individual is in part irrelevant. For one of the most significant themes

---

[1] Leo Simmons, *The Role of the Aged in Primitive Society* (New Haven: Yale University Press, 1945), 175.

143

in the Judeo-Christian heritage is the *inherent* worth of the individual, irrespective of his familial, occupational, or social ties. Thus although his utility may wane, the elderly person is entitled to consideration of his needs and desires. Assuming continued persistence of this theme, then, the only question for religion is *how*, not whether, these needs should be met. Organizations of religion are publicly committed to meeting the needs of old people, and they do direct some of their resources to the aging. The issue to be confronted in this essay is how these resources can be allocated to achieve maximum benefit.

As a social scientific treatment of the issue, this essay is concerned more with strategy than with moral admonition. It must be recognized, however, that decisions of strategy, as choices between alternative courses of action, presuppose certain value positions. Although, as already pointed out, religious values are basically sympathetic to the aged, commitment of limited church resources requires specification of *priorities* in satisfying the needs of various age groups that are potentially in competition for the same resources. The establishment of such priorities is outside the province of this essay. Whether scarce resources should be made available to the aged in preference to the youthful, for example, is an issue to be decided within particular religious organizations. The purpose of this essay is not to provide a set of directives but to suggest a framework, a set of conceptual tools, by which religious organizations—and individual ministers—may assess their work with the aged.

In developing this framework for analysis, consideration must be given to a number of questions. How much is known about the "religious" needs of old people? What are churches and clergy doing now in their ministry to the elderly? What are the costs of following one path rather than another; that is, what are the values foregone? What is the likelihood of making an impact through various programs?

In the discussion to follow, we shall first examine the relation of older people to the church, paying special attention to a facet of aging —diminution of role playing—which may be of particular importance in planning church programs. Next, we focus on current church practices relating to the senior members of society. Finally, we draw together these elements into an analysis of ecclesiastical strategy and provide illustrations consonant with recommended strategy.

Throughout the essay we shall use such words as "church" and "minister" in their generic sense. We are concerned with all faiths, sects, and denominations that are within the Judeo-Christian tradition.

Older people and the church

What is the relationship of older people to religion? [*See Vol. 1, Chap. 20, pp. 483–500.*] As will become clear in this section, the answer is not at all easy to formulate for two reasons. First, the data—dealing as they do with a "religiosity" concept that is amenable to many definitions—are frequently contradictory and therefore difficult to interpret. And second, even when an answer is formulated, causal connections often remain unclear. Because cross-section researches are conducted at single moments in time, their results could reflect the *aging process*—but they could as well reflect *generational* (cohort) *differences*. If older persons are found to express more belief in God than do younger persons, for example, we may ask whether this difference tells us something meaningful about the way aging and religion interact, or whether it reflects merely a persisting contrast between younger generations and the generation who happens now to be old.

The voluminous research in the area of aging and religion is not worthless, however. At the least it helps present-day clergymen *define* their clients among the older generation, helps them know something of the relative rates of attendance, devotional practices, death concerns, and so on. In this section, therefore, we shall summarize a number of these findings, attempt to relate these to our developing conceptual framework, and then draw implications for church policy.

It is part of the forklore about aging that religious concerns increase with advancing years. Thus:

Because of the numerous problems older people experience in our society because of the gradual approach of death, because they have more time to think than they have had for decades previously, and for various other reasons, many older people turn to religion in old age with renewed fervor. . . . It is natural for older people to turn to the church.[2]

Is there basis in fact for such folk wisdom? Almost all older people regard themselves as having some religion. Only 3 per cent do not, and only 22 per cent do not report themselves as members of a church or synagogue. [*See Vol. 1, Chap. 20.1, pp. 484–485.*] Church and other religious organizations are second only to lodges and fraternal organizations as voluntary association affiliations for older persons (55+). [*See Vol. 1, Chap. 20.3.a, p. 490.*] Attendance in church, moreover, is maintained into old age, though after the decade of the 60's, special circumstances intervene, such as ill health (which diminishes attendance) and a preponderance of females in the elderly population (which, because females are more active than males in church, inflates attendance rates relative to younger age groups). [*See Vol. 1, Chap. 20.2, pp. 485–490.*]

Some studies report different findings if based on selected populations. Harold Orbach, for example, concludes after an analysis of several large-scale surveys: "The mixed trends observed between age and religious attendance when relevant sociologic variables are introduced, point to the absence of any simple relationship and suggest

[2] Robert M. Gray and David O. Moberg, *The Church and the Older Person* (Grand Rapids, Mich.: William Eerdmans, 1962), 38.

that the picture of an almost level plateau through the adult life span
. . . represents a merging of the various sociologic influences (such as
denomination, sex, race)."[3] A similar conclusion is reached by Ruth
Albrecht who, summarizing a number of attendance studies, remarks
that on the basis of them alone, "it is not possible to believe that
older people become more religious."[4]

Other conclusions are possible, however, when evidence other
than church attendance is used to define religiosity. For example,
older individuals are more likely than those younger to: (1) read the
Bible at home, (2) pray in private, (3) be able to name correctly selected books of the Bible, (4) believe in immortality, (5) report the
personal value of religion, (6) favor teaching religion in school, and
(7) feel the world needs religion more than economic security. [See
Vol. 1, Chaps. 20.4, 20.5, and 20.8.c, pp. 490–493, 498.] Joel
Smith, contrasting a sample of "well" older people (65 +) with a sample of adults 21 to 64, found that, though there was some decrease in
church attendance among the elderly, they were more involved in
"ecstatic religion" as indicated by their greater exposure to emotional
radio church services and more primacy given to afterlife than this
life.[5] Gray and Moberg conclude that religious beliefs, especially regarding death and afterlife, are more characteristic of the aged.[6] And
Milton Barron summarizes his analysis of the subject: ". . . religiosity
among older people is a surprisingly modest part of their overt lives.
. . . But in the inner or subjective lives of older people, religion . . .
does play a larger role and tends to intensify as people grow older."[7]

Such a conclusion is supported in what is perhaps the best syn-
thesis of research reports on religion and age. Using Glock's dimensions of religiosity,[8] as his scheme for classifying a number of studies,
Moberg states: "Research to date seems to indicate fairly conclusively
that ritualistic behavior outside the home tends to diminish with
increasing age, while religious attitudes and feelings apparently increase among people who have an acknowledged religion."[9] A similar
conclusion is drawn by R. G. Kuhlen: ". . . in all studies examined,

[3] Harold L. Orbach, "Aging and Religion," Geriatrics, 16 (1961), 539.

[4] Ruth E. Albrecht, "The Meaning of Religion to Older People—the Social Aspect,"
in D. L. Scudder (ed.), Organized Religion and the Older Person (Gainesville,
Fla.: University of Florida Press, 1958), 69.

[5] Joel Smith, "The Narrowing Social World of the Aged," in Ida Harper Simpson
and John C. McKinney (eds.), Social Aspects of Aging (Durham: Duke University Press, 1966), 233.

[6] Op. cit., 39–43.

[7] Milton L. Barron, The Aging American (New York: Crowell-Collier Press, 1961),
178.

[8] See Charles Y. Glock and Rodney Stark, Religion and Society in Tension
(Chicago: Rand McNally & Company, 1965), Chap. 2.

[9] David O. Moberg, "Religiosity in Old Age," The Gerontologist, 5 (1965), 86.

with the exception of those relating to church attendance, trends indicate an interest in and concern about religion as age increases, even into extreme old age."[10]

An occasional demurrer is found,[11] but the current consensus would appear to be that the elderly are, at least subjectively, more "religious." What is still very much at issue is whether this religiousness *results* from aging or is simply a *correlate* of generational differences. Although a final answer requires further research, the direct implications for church policy should be considered. If the religiosity of old people *results* from aging, then the church must be prepared for succeeding generations of "clients" roughly in proportion to the current older generation. If, on the other hand, the religiousness of the aged is in part a *correlate* of generational differences, then, given what appears to be the present association between religion and age, the church must be prepared for the possibility of relative decline in the size of its clientele with succeeding generations.

Whatever may be the case for the future, the religiosity of current generations of old people, whether measured by church attendance or by religious feeling and belief, indicates that the church confronts a sizable religious "market" in the elderly; the church is, potentially at least, of considerable significance in their lives. We may ask, then, whether religion appears to have a measurable effect; that is, what difference does it make in the lives of older persons?

One frequently cited kind of evidence comes from the "religion and adjustment" area. One study has found, for example, that the more religious (as measured by religious activity and by "fundamentalist" or "orthodox" Protestant or Catholic attitudes) among the aged "look forward to death" more than do others. "Fearful" or "evasive" attitudes were more characteristic of the latter.[12] [*See Vol. 1, Chap. 14.6, pp. 332–337.*] Another investigation found that one-half of an aged sample reported religion to be "more helpful" in old age than it had been earlier, while one-third proclaimed it less helpful. [*See Vol. 1, Chap. 20.6.c, pp. 495–496.*] Moberg and Taves, studying a random sample of aged, noninstitutionalized Minnesotans, discovered "church leaders" (very active members) to have better personal adjustment (that is, greater satisfaction with various aspects of

---

[10] R. G. Kuhlen, "Trends in Religious Behavior During the Adult Years," in L. C. Little (ed.), *Wider Horizons in Christian Adult Education* (Pittsburgh: University of Pittsburgh Press, 1962), 23. Quoted in Moberg, *op. cit.,* 86.

[11] For example, Nila Kirkpatrick Covalt, "The Meaning of Religion in Older People —the Medical Perspective," in D. L. Scudder (ed.), *Organized Religion and the Older Person* (Gainesville, Fla.: University of Florida Press, 1958), pp. 79 ff. Doctor Covalt claims that in twenty-five years of practice she can recall no patient who brought up religion as a subject, who asked for clergy help, or, when dying, who "called out to God or audibly prayed." Nor had her colleagues reported such experiences to her.

[12] Wendell M. Swenson, "Attitudes Toward Death in an Aged Population," *Journal of Gerontology,* 16 (1961), 51. This study is based on very few cases.

life) than did regular church members, and the latter were better adjusted than nonmembers.[13]

Such findings are not unusual; Gray and Moberg summarize numerous others.[14] But as they point out, the frequently observed relationship between religion and adjustment is very likely spurious.[15] It is probably not because such persons go to church or remain religiously active that they exhibit better adjustment. Rather, those who are better adjusted manifest that adjustment in the religious sphere as well as elsewhere. Thus, old people who are organizationally active are also more engaged in occupational and marital roles, informal visiting, Golden Age Clubs, and so forth. [See Vol. 1, Chap. 21, pp. 501–510.] Barron, therefore, concludes:

> Without doubt research exposes the shortcomings of religion as an effective geriatric force. Although . . . there are some indications of inner religiosity intensifying in later years, there is little change of interest in the church and synagogue with advancing age and *very little indication that organized religion has succeeded in helping most of the aged adjust to their personal and social situations.*[16]

Where does this state of affairs leave the church in the lives of old people? Shall we conclude that the church either has no special mission to old people or, more discouraging, has failed in that mission? One way of assessing such a question would be to ask what the elderly themselves expect of religion and the church and then to ask whether the "religious" needs of older people, as they themselves perceive them, are currently being satisfied. Research evidence on this point is almost totally lacking. Some suggestive clues are revealed, however, if we reason indirectly from certain aspects of the total situation of the aged in American society. We shall, therefore, in the next section discuss in some detail the nature of one aspect of aging—decline in levels of activity—which is of special relevance to church policy.

Aging and disengagement

Of critical importance to an assessment of the religious situation and needs of old people in American society is a proper interpretation of the constriction of role behavior which apparently accompanies aging. [See Vol. 1, Chap. 17, pp. 409–420.] Unfortunately, much needed evidence is not in hand. Not only the lack of research evidence but the difficulties—of varying definitions, of cross-section versus life-cycle

---

[13] David O. Moberg and M. J. Taves, "Church Participation and Personal Adjustment to Old Age" (Paper presented at the Gerontological Society, Inc., Miami Beach, Fla., 1962).

[14] *Op. cit.*, 43–49.

[15] *Ibid.*, 53.

[16] Barron, *op. cit.*, 181. Italics added.

effects, of controls for spurious relationships—encountered in attempting to evaluate existing research findings necessarily impart a high degree of tentativeness to the discussion. Although we shall present a number of interpretative ideas which would seem to be consistent with the available research findings, such ideas are more properly regarded as hypotheses for subsequent investigation than as direct inferences from adequate evidence.

There can be little doubt that old people are in the process of relinquishing significant portions of their prior social worlds. Loss of occupation, of spouse, of old friends who have died, coupled with the infirmities and ill health often associated with old age, imply that old people typically must reduce or radically modify past activities. There is, however, ample room for debate concerning the nature of the change that takes place, change that has a number of implications for church policy regarding the aged.

Research indicates that the older person plays, on the average, fewer social roles, has fewer interpersonal contacts and exhibits a generally lower level of activity than younger persons. Scattered clues suggest a concomitant withdrawal on the psychological level. [See Vol. 1, Chap. 12, pp. 275–287.] Although older individuals are no more likely to report worries and insecurities, they are less likely than younger persons to express positive satisfaction with life. They are less likely to report expectations that important events will happen to them. They are more introverted, exhibit generally less affect. It is as though the lives of the aging "flatten out," becoming less dramatic, more benign. Thus it has been suggested that older people might be involved chiefly in what has been labeled "disengagement"—withdrawal from specific roles and from life generally. [But see Vol. 1, Chap. 15, pp. 341–359.]

One theological writer refers to the final stage of life, therefore, as one of "achieving simplification of life in its physical, material, and spiritual aspects, so that the soul may, with less and less impediment, progress toward its chosen destiny."[17] Psychologist Erik Erikson claims that the "crisis" during the last "age" of man is one of "ego integrity" versus "despair." Successful resolution of the crisis brings "renunciation and wisdom."[18] And Bernice Neugarten refers to *psychological* disengagement as "increased interiority of the personality," wherein, "with the change from active to passive modes of mastering the environment, there is also a movement of energy away from an outer-world to an inner-world orientation."[19]

[17] Lewis Joseph Sherrill, *The Struggle of the Soul* (New York: The Macmillan Company, 1958), 9.

[18] Erik H. Erikson, *Childhood and Society* (New York: W. W. Norton and Company, Inc., 1963), 268–269, 274.

[19] Bernice L. Neugarten, "Adult Personality: Toward a Psychology of the Life-Cycle" (Paper presented to the American Psychological Association, New York City, 1966), 6.

Of crucial interest to those planning programs for the aged is whether disengagement is volitional; that is, do old people, given a choice, elect to abridge social ties? Does withdrawal result in greater happiness and adjustment? Or is disengagement an unwanted necessity, thrust upon the aged by the exigencies of their general situation?

Certainly the data in hand indicate that simple *inactivity* offers few psychological blessings. For example, general satisfaction is greater among those still working than among the retired. Although individuals vary greatly in activity styles and adjustment, those with low levels of activity tend to be less satisfied with life, have more feelings of loneliness, uselessness, and loss of affection. [*See Vol. 1, Chap. 15, pp. 341–359.*]

Construed simply as a general tendency to withdraw, moreover, the disengagement notion would seem not entirely consistent with some of the empirical findings. It is not clear whether the finding of role diminution in old people reflects change over the life cycle or simply the relatively lower socioeconomic and health status of old people today. Some exploratory findings indicate that given individuals, as they age, tend to maintain a level of activity similar to their younger years. If, despite retirement and the increasing likelihood of conjugal and friendship loss, the elderly manage to maintain given levels of activity, the implication is that relinquishment of some past ties is compensated by other relationships and other kinds of contact with the environment. Thus old people apparently do not decrease participation in religious and political activities. [*See Vol. 1, Chap. 19, pp. 463–482.*] The fact that they do not exhibit a tendency to withdraw from *all* social activities suggests there may be a meaningful pattern to those they give up and those they retain.

Given the American value pattern, the connection between low levels of activity and dissatisfaction with life is not unexpected. Nonetheless, some individuals, given a choice, do elect to withdraw from some social activities, and these are more satisfied than those whose withdrawal is forced. Retirement, for example, offers to some individuals a welcome release from a disliked occupation. [*See Vol. 1, Chap. 18, pp. 421–462.*] Reduction of activity is less closely related to dissatisfaction than whether such reduction is seen as externally imposed. Perhaps, then, successful aging is contingent on a pattern of *selective* disengagement, on the opportunity to relinquish some kinds of activities and to retain others.

Cumming and Henry, the originators of disengagement theory, describe what they regard as the typical pattern of change:

The reduction in interaction and the loss of central roles result in a shift in the quality of relationship in the remaining roles. . . . There is a wider choice of relational rewards, and a shift from vertical solidarities ("mutual dependence bonds") to horizontal ("bonds of similarity") ones.[20]

The shift from "vertical" to "horizontal" solidarities may be conceived more broadly as a change in emphasis from "instrumental" to "expressive" orientations. We propose that, given a choice, old people would tend to reduce activities that might be called instrumental—endeavors in which persons are expected to achieve, to produce, to withhold emotions, to restrict their range of obligations; but they would retain and seek out expressive relationships and activities—diffuse endeavors in which they can spontaneously "express" themselves, in which their actions are ends in themselves rather than instruments to the accomplishment of other ends. The roles of spouse, of grandparent, of neighbor, of friend are primarily expressive roles, and the aged wish to retain them. By contrast, the work role, the child-rearing role, many roles in voluntary organizations, are instrumental, and old people may be less reluctant to give up such roles.

Although the research evidence is scanty, scattered findings are highly suggestive of a desire on the part of the aged to turn from instrumental to expressive activities. [*See Vol. 1, Chap. 13, pp. 289–313; Chap. 14, pp. 315–339.*] For example, older individuals are less oriented to achievement, place less stress on capacity or performance, and give more emphasis to goodness and moral virtue than younger persons. Willingness to continue work beyond age 65 is more pronounced among individuals who stress the noneconomic meanings of their jobs. [*See Vol. 1, Chap. 18.B.3.f, p. 440.*] Among old men who continue voluntary association memberships, the retired are more likely than those still working to belong to sociable rather than occupationally oriented organizations. [*See Vol. 1, Chap. 21.3.c, p. 508.*] Those older individuals taking adult education courses are more likely than younger persons to say they enroll to become better informed rather than for job-related reasons. [*See Vol. 1, Chap. 22.5.b, pp. 526–527.*] And, given large amounts of leisure time, old people spend many hours visiting, watching television, reading, and gardening—all expressive activities for the most part. [*See Vol. 1, Chap. 22, pp. 511–535.*]

Such evidence is not decisive, especially since much of the research does not disentangle cross-section from life-cycle effects. A further difficulty of interpretation arises because most activities have *both* expressive and instrumental components, and it is not always easy to decide which aspects are sought out or stressed by partici-

[20] Elaine Cumming and William E. Henry, *Growing Old* (New York: Basic Books, Inc., 1961), 217. See also Elaine Cumming, "New Thoughts on the Theory of Disengagement," in Robert Kastenbaum (ed.), *New Thoughts on Old Age* (New York: Springer Publishing Co., 1964).

pants. On balance, however, the data would seem consistent with the thesis that older people willingly give up their segmented, specific, task-oriented activity *if* they can retain their diffuse, integrative, socio-emotional activity.

Thus the premise of our remaining discussion is that the aged in American society confront the church as people who (assuming their subsistence needs are met) are more concerned with "being" than with "doing," more interested in being wanted than being useful, more expressive than instrumental. As a surrogate family or point of community, the church remains a factor in their lives; as an agency of instrumental achievement, it declines in importance. To use the title of a recent monograph on parishioner attitudes, old people especially expect the church "to comfort" rather than "to challenge."[21]

In his Long Beach study of 606 elderly persons, for example, Charles McCann found that, when asked what more the church could be doing for them, they put home visitations at the top of the list.[22] A survey of a Catholic parish in St. Louis found exactly the same first choice among its aged.[23] A less prosaic and more poignant expression of this attitude is seen in the comments of a dying patient to a hospital psychiatrist:

I was dumbfounded to find that when I requested a chaplain in the middle of the night there was no night chaplain. I mean, this is just unbelievable to me. Because, when does a man need a chaplain? Only at night, believe me. That's the time when you get down with those boxing gloves and have it out with yourself. . . . When does a man need a minister? He needs him about three o'clock, ordinarily.[24]

It is being suggested, then, that in contrast to younger people, who may maintain a variety of orientations toward religion and the church, the aged tend to narrow their religious outlook. Disengaging not in the sense of withdrawing from church but in the sense of bringing simplified expectations to it, they seek from the church a feeling of anchorage, of community, of neighborhood and "location" in their religious activity. Older people, we are asserting, expect the church to be expressive, not instrumental.

Before we turn to a discussion of church practices in relation to such expectations, one more aspect of aging in society needs to be set in context. The secular trends in America of greater industrialization, urbanization, bureaucratization—what has been called increased differentiation—may operate with special impact on old people, who

[21] Charles Y. Glock, B. B. Ringer, and Earl R. Babbie, *To Comfort and to Challenge* (Berkeley: University of California Press, 1967).

[22] Charles W. McCann, *Long Beach Senior Citizens Survey* (Long Beach, Calif.: Long Beach Community Welfare Council, 1955), 53.

[23] Catholic Charities of St. Louis, *Older People in the Family, the Parish and the Neighborhood* (St. Louis: Catholic Churches of St. Louis, 1955), 10.

[24] Elizabeth Ross, "The Dying Patient as Teacher," *The Chicago Theological Seminary Register*, 57 (1966), 13.

face both increasing differentiation and role loss. Thus, old people in large cities are less likely than those in areas of smaller population to know many families, have most of their friends in the neighborhood, visit with younger neighbors, or have someone stop by regularly. [*See Vol. 1, Chap. 6.A.3, pp. 125–128.*] The exceptions occur where the elderly are concentrated, as where there are old people's homes or where neighborhoods are deserted by younger cohorts, leaving behind the oldsters. Aged persons in cities are increasingly differentiated *by age*, and their needs are increasingly met by *specialized* services— for example, old people's homes, geriatric hospital wings, retirement communities, Golden Age Clubs—rather than through social structures serving other age groups as well.

Highly differentiated structures, in which social interaction tends to be segmented and impersonal, present a number of barriers to the development and maintenance of expressive relationships. It may well be one of history's greater ironies that, at the same time society becomes more differentiated, it produces larger proportions of aged persons whose needs appear to be for less differentiation. As an institution in society, the church, too, is subject to trends of increasing differentiation. This fact may, on the one hand, greatly complicate its task of meeting the expressive needs of its parishioners; on the other, used strategically, increased differentiation may facilitate an enlightened ministry to the aged. We pursue that strategy, following a discussion of present church programs for the elderly.

THE PHENOMENOLOGICAL
APPROACH TO IMAGES OF AGING

15

MICHEL PHILIBERT

GERONTOLOGY: DEVELOPMENT AND STAGNATION

IN THE PERIOD after World War II, the study of aging (known as "gerontology" since 1929) has expanded considerably. It has not been clear, however, that quality has materialized from quantity—a fact that has led several observers to suggest that gerontology as a field has not yet reached its full fruition.[1] It has wanted to be scientific in its methods; but it has borrowed its models and methods predominantly from the experimental natural sciences. The result, according to some, is an impasse, from which phenomenological approaches might point a way out.

PHENOMENOLOGY AND SCIENCE

At first glance phenomenology seems to turn its back on science. It wants to describe things as they appear to consciousness instead of looking for a hidden structure behind the veil of appearances, for a deeper reality, or for necessary relationships. This conspicuous neglect of scientific concerns could serve gerontology, however, to the extent that the appearance of human aging is inseparable from its reality, and to the extent that our attitude toward aging shapes our experience. What, then, is a phenomenological approach to images of aging?

Michael Philibert is Professor of Philosophy, University of Grenoble, France. He is co-director of the Gerontology Center there, and has been an active participant in the development of humanistic gerontological studies in the United States. He has published extensively in this field. The present essay was translated by John Orr, Erika Georges, and Suzanne DeBenedittis, all of the University of Southern California.

IMAGE

This paper will use the term "image" in a very general sense. I do not intend to limit analysis either to scientific concepts and theories of aging, or to mental pictures, schemas, dynamic sequences, or mental films. People hold opinions, beliefs, or mental attitudes toward aging which are more or less coherent and which carry images and memories together with the beginnings or outlines of knowledge. We shall call these *multi-form constructions* "images." They constitute orientations or perspectives; or, to borrow Donald Evans' term, they are "onlooks" on aging.[2] As an analogy, my economic activity can be looked on as a way of earning a living or as a vocation: two perspectives. Likewise, one can look on aging as a threat or as an opportunity: two views, or two images.

AGING

The term "aging" is intended in the most neutral and most general sense. It is the advancing of age. Time passes in the movement from birth to death; we gain in age; we change irreversibly. I do not believe that the term aging should refer only to unfavorable changes which affect us proportionately with the passage of time, or to changes associated with being elderly. My bias, though, is not universally shared. For many persons, particularly in certain cultures, aging is viewed as a negative process, or a terminal one, or both of these simultaneously.

AGING AND RELATED CONCEPTS

Therefore we cannot limit our investigation to images of "aging"; we must extend it to associated images and concepts. We must examine what relations exist between *aging* as a process and *old age* as either a final period of life or as a social category. What is the relation between *aging* and *growth*? Are these distinct, successive, and antithetical phases, or are they two aspects of the same dynamic process? What continuity or discontinuity can be observed between *youth* and *old age*? Is *aging* an *illness*? Is it a victory over *death*, or is it the period when death is quickly approaching? Whether our image of aging is precise or hazy, sophisticated or naïve, coherent or contradictory, it includes an image of old age, of the old, of growing, of youth, of adulthood, of the age-rank ladder.

Data for the Investigation of Aging

Where should we look for the images of aging? The sources are extensive: (1) in popular literature and in more universally conceived forms of literature: texts, rituals, liturgies, magic formulae, poems, dramas, comedies, chronicles, essays, novels, stories, songs, hygienic and medical prescriptions; (2) in laws, customs, and the shape of institutions; (3) in the arts: in paintings, mime, dancing, music, movies; (4) in the sciences: biology, demography, psychiatry, psychology, sociology, anthropology, administrative science, economics, politics; (5) in the enormous and dispersed documentation of travelers, anthropologists, geographers, lawyers, and historians of institutions, law, religion, the arts, and literature.

With the exception of Leo Simmons, most gerontologists have neglected these data, in part because the quantity and heterogeneity of material make collection, classification, and analysis a long and difficult undertaking. More important, though, gerontologists have avoided these data because they resist classification within the scientific models which they habitually utilize. The statements and symbols which express the images of aging and which have been created by mankind in the course of its thousands of years of experience are not scientific statements or symbols. They express biases, opinions, beliefs, and fantasies, which are of interest only for the collector of folklore, the historian of ideas, and perhaps the psychologist who is interested in peculiarities of the human spirit. The gerontologist, on his part, "is not interested." He yearns to substitute a scientific language for one that is pre-scientific, because he is committed to discovering objective laws, not the subjective opinions that have surrounded the experience of aging.

The gerontologist will simply have to be persuaded that, as a scientist, he can be helped in understanding human aging through the examination of these images. It will not be an easy task to convince him that he needs the help of lawyers, geographers, historians, anthropologists, literary critics, and exegetes; but it is a task that humanistic scholars cannot avoid.

The Development and Decline of an Illusion

Instead of taking the long detour through anthropology, history, and the analysis of texts, for over a quarter of a century gerontologists have preferred the pathway of direct observation. Fascinated by the success of the experimental natural sciences, as Hume was with Newton, they have thrown their efforts into laboratory analyses and studies dominated by cross-sectional sampling techniques. Whether they have dealt with muscular power or memory, the activity of the heart or verbal fluidity, they have observed, measured, analyzed, and compared the performances or functions of old and young subjects. They have interpreted the *differences* they found as the expression of *changes* resulting from aging. They have believed that the multiplicity of observations would generate facts, then laws, and that, in turn, the laws would generate theories. They have believed that from the juxtaposition of genetic, biochemical, physiological, psychological, demographic, sociological, and economic studies, an interdisciplinary, synthetic, integrated knowledge of human aging would emerge.

Today we are becoming aware of the naïvete of this projection —even of the fragility of the hopes and convictions which nourished it. Still, for a growing number of people and institutions who are earning their living by working professionally in gerontology, the illusion of a scientific career in the field continues to retard their ability to adopt new methods.

A New Awareness

The differences between young and old subjects may represent, instead of the effects of aging, inborn differences between successive cohorts or generations, but they may also represent effects imposed by particular socio-cultural, historical environments. For example, the great majority of observations accumulated during the past twenty-five years refer to only a fraction of humanity (from European or Western cultures, or from industrialized countries), a unique generation whose historical destiny seems to be exceptional. In order to evaluate properly the characteristics of the aged, it would be necessary to relate these to the circumstances of adult life, of youth and childhood, and even to the circumstances of birth and conception. And, in order not to confuse the differences as of today between the young and the old with the changes that accompany aging, it would be necessary to observe the same generation during one hundred and ten years.

Of course no researcher, no team or research institution can undertake a study of such length; no method, hypothesis, or theory can be sure to survive for such a long period. And, even if it were possible, such a study would not enable us to distinguish among changes that result from the historical circumstances peculiar to the generation studied and those that relate to universal laws of aging. To distinguish such laws would require the comparison of styles of aging within different generations (by definition, successive generations). Thus, taken seriously, gerontology's method of direct observation, far from being a short-cut, requires at least *two hundred years* of research.

ANOTHER METHOD

A tentative comparison among the styles of aging associated with different generations is still possible if, without waiting for the results of future observations conducted according to current scientific canons, one turns to observations accumulated for thousands of years in the literature on customs, rituals, and religion, in which pre-scientific humanity had already formulated its experience of life and its experience of aging. When Molière has Sganarelle say (*Don Juan*, V, ii) that "the young must obey the old," and when Plato has Socrates say the same thing, we are given two choices. We can decide, on the one hand, that the assertion does not express a scientifically demonstrated or demonstrable truth; then we may exclude the assertion from the proper domain of gerontology, since it cannot teach us anything useful about the human experience of aging or about ways to formulate our approaches to aging today. On the other hand we may decide that the assertion has played an important role, historically, and we may want to ask literary critics and historians of philosophy (in short, the exegetes) to define this function in the context of the works where it is described. We may also want to ask historians and sociologists about how societies other than our own determine the allocation—verbal and real—of functions of authority among the young and the old. In that case we may begin to understand something about the *norms* (rather than the "laws") of human aging, and perhaps about which norms we should denounce, modify, restore, or promote in our political life.

TOWARD THE DEFINITION OF CRITERIA

One of the first tasks of a phenomenology of aging is the determination of criteria for a typology of images and concepts of aging. I am suggesting six points which, if examined, will allow us to characterize on a set of scales any image of aging, be it scientific or not, explicit or implicit, in behavior, gesture, or institution:

(1) What role does the image or concept attribute to physical aging within the process of human aging? An essential or a secondary role? First cause or a part of a whole, a link in a circular chain of causality, a moment in a dialectical process?

(2) Is aging regarded mainly as a decline, a process of destruction, of degradation, of deterioration, or as ambivalent and capable of furnishing man with an opportunity for an opening up, an improvement, a development of his being?

(3) Is "aging" considered to be coextensive with the entire course of life, or is it limited to its final portion (which may be shorter or longer)?

(4) Is aging viewed predominantly in its universality, or is its differential character stressed through an emphasis on functional, individual, and social differences?

(5) Is aging presented as a necessity, i.e., as a calamity one must suffer, or as a phenomenon that can be modified by individual or collective action?

(6) How is the relation between aging and death viewed? More precisely, how do the anticipation and the approach of death affect the image of old age? Do they diminish or augment the importance of old age?

Toward the Construction of a Typology

The application of these criteria to the analysis of images and concepts of aging and old age, whether they are scientific, prescientific, or non-scientific, leads to the identification of two ideal types which are opposed to each other, and in terms of which the multiple images of aging can more or less be identified. To be sure, particular images sometimes appear to be incomplete or inconsistent—a fact which in my opinion can be explained by the ambivalence of the advance in age. But, however related in their actual appearance, the two ideal types are at least logically separable: (1) images that emphasize the predominantly physical and largely negative, terminal, universal, necessary, and gruesome characteristics identified with aging; (2) images that emphasize the socio-cultural features, that view aging as coextensive with the entire length of life, that stress the differentiated and controllable dimensions of aging and look on it as offering opportunities for further growth.

LITERARY EXAMPLES: AGING AS SPIRITUAL GROWTH

At this point it will be helpful to examine some concise images of aging. For this purpose, we could easily draw from the sculptures of Vigeland (Oslo), which are dominated by a preoccupation with the course of life, or from such films as *The Shameless Old Lady* by René Allio or *Wild Strawberries* by Ingmar Bergman. To do so, however, would require too long a discussion, as well as an iconography that is difficult to assemble and reproduce. Therefore we will borrow our examples from literature.

In *Conversations with Confucius*, as reported by a disciple, we find a short autobiography of the Chinese master, which runs as follows:

> At fifteen, my mind was bent on learning. At thirty, I stood firm. At forty, I was free from delusions. At fifty, I understood the laws of Providence. At sixty, there was nothing left in the world that might shock me. At seventy, I could follow the promptings of my heart without trespassing moral law.

The conception of aging underlying this quotation considers aging as a spiritual rather than a biological process. Confucius looks on his own experience in aging as a lifelong growth in creativity and wisdom. Continued growth and final fulfillment are not seen as a universal feature of man's life, nor as a gift from Fortune to the happy few, but as a kind of achievement rewarding a lifelong dedication. Living is learning, aging is learning, for those who pay the price. Development through adult and mature years is linked to lifelong self-education. Aging as spiritual growth is an opportunity that may either be enjoyed or neglected. Aging is seen as a differential and manageable process.

The same pattern appears in the following quotation from Baudelaire's *Curiosités Esthetiqués:*

> At the end of his career, Goya's eyesight had weakened to such an extent that his pencils, so it was said, had to be sharpened for him. Yet even at this time he executed some big and most important lithographs, including a number of bullfights full of swarming crowds, admirable plates, enormous features in miniature—a further proof in support of that strange law governing the destiny of

great artists, according to which, since life and intelligence move in opposite directions, they make up on the savings what they lose on the roundabouts, and, following a progressive rejuvenation, they grow forever stronger, more jovial, bolder, to the very edge of the grave.[3]

Such a conception, however, remains the exception in recent Western tradition. Baudelaire is aware of referring to a "strange law." In effect, industrial society devaluates old age, and most often presents aging as a process having negative value. To grow old signifies decline—to move downhill.

LITERARY EXAMPLES: AGING AS PHYSICAL DECLINE AND AS SOCIAL DISGRACE

I put forward three passages in order to illustrate this image of growing old. The first two are borrowed from some recent French novels. Benoîte Groult relates in *La part des choses* the morose reflections of a fifty-year-old woman:

> The garish sun on this December morning does not leave a single one of these fifty years in the darkness, and her too fresh rose nylon robe is prejudicial to her dark complexion. She arrived at this distressing age at which one can topple over any time from the experience of being a woman who is still beautiful to that of being an old woman whose looks touch without ever exciting. Little by little the second definitively would occupy the stage, leaving to the first, for some time still, a few brief and heart-rending appearances.[4]

Paul Guimard, in *L'ironie du sort*, records the reflections of a person, born in 1916, who in 1949 gathers his thoughts beside the tomb of one of his friends and contemporaries, shot down by the Germans in 1943. He at least will not grow old.

> I am already catching a glimpse of the forty-year-old man waiting for me around the corner. He will appropriate all that you have known about me, all that I have been. He will make poor use of it. His hair is thinner, breath shorter, heart less lively, skin lusterless, his spirit less sure than mine. He will not make use of this heritage, which he has not deserved. He will disentangle himself from what is encumbering him, and I will not be able to help it. I am already his prisoner. Then will come the man of fifty, and the one of sixty, who will make me die a little at a time. They will take away my teeth; they will knit me with wrinkles. I hate these old men who lie in wait for me in order to beleaguer me and mutilate me.[5]

These two texts equally ascribe to older adults the inability to project themselves into old age and accept as their own the an-

161

ticipated image of the old persons they will become. For them there is no conceivable continuity between what they are and what they are going to be. They cannot imagine any progress in wisdom or authority that could compensate for the irremediable physical decline. The heroine of Benoîte Groult's novel at first sees her future like the passing of the same self from one state to another: from the state of being the still beautiful woman to that of being an old woman (beauty and age being mutually exclusive). Within the next phrase, however, her thoughts turn to a more radical formulation: it is no longer a question of successive stages, but of two distinct persons, one of whom is chasing the other—two different women who are not identical any more at all. The subject identifies herself with the present state and views her future state as another person, foreign and hostile, who will take her place and take her life away.

For the hero of Guimard's novel there is not only a dual personality but disintegration into a series of aggressive and detestable strangers. This image of age-related periods of the personality expresses, in his own self-consciousness, the extent to which society devalues old age and the power of the segregation it structures among age groups. The individual pathology of the schizoid type, which breaks the personal unity into pieces, reflects and reinforces the social pathology, which shatters the cycle of exchange and renewal among successive generations.

For the reader who is tempted to find the term "pathology" abusive in this context, I would like to cite a clinical case, recently filmed within a hospital at Ivry, under the supervision of Professor Vignalou. Among the subjects is a sick, senile woman, who has been hospitalized for several years. She expresses the wish to leave the hospital in order to go to a retirement home—to a place where she can retire from her occupation as a concierge, which, she says, is her real identity. Her feeling of personal identity has remained attached to a situation that she has lost and a phase of her life which is already over. The actual phase which is being lived—a strange and hostile one—is purely and simply denied.

An American example will illustrate a less severe form of the difficulty which many people experience in accepting their advancing age, frightened by the image of stagnation they associate with the adult life and by the image of decay they associate with old age. At the conclusion of a recent novel by Dan Greenburg,

162

Scoring, the difficulty is recognized and defined by the hero-novelist at the very moment when he overcomes it.

> My ghastly thirtieth birthday had finally descended upon me. I would never again, even in my most egomaniacal moments, be able to think of myself as a boy wonder. Boy wonders become at the age of thirty merely moderately successful or even very successful men, but they are no longer boy anythings. The great promise they saw in you has either been kept or broken. You are at thirty, willy-nilly, as close as you are ever likely to get to being a genuinely grown up person. I walked through Times Square one day, . . . and I figured All Right. I figured Why Not. I figured, You've already gotten your first lousy marriage out of the way and possibly even learned a couple of things not to do the next time. I figured, so one of the reasons you're scared of marriage is that it brings you one life process closer to death, so remaining a bachelor isn't going to keep you from aging or from dying either. I figured, So you're scared of the total commitment of marriage, so what, so everybody's scared of that, so big god-dam deal. I figured, You're thirty goddam years of age, which is nearly half your life, so what are you waiting for—let's get on with it already. Let's take the next step in life. Let's do it.[6]

To place at the age of thirty, the age when the promises of childhood have been either broken or fulfilled, the middle of life, is an opinion that hardly contains anything scientific. It is the reality of a man who has only recently entered into his thirties; who lives in a society where chronology is of great importance, where chronological age has a social and symbolic significance, where one uses a decimal number system, where youth is overvalued, and where old age is devalued. Still such non-scientific statements must not be neglected by the science of aging. Indeed, they constitute primary data for a science that purportedly is interested in the human experience of aging.

THE SCIENCES OF MAN ARE NOT NEUTRAL

How does this phenomenological analysis relate to the picture of gerontology as a scientific enterprise? It seems to me that it should help to correct gerontology in general, and social gerontology in particular, by doing away with its illusory pretensions to a kind of objectivity or neutrality which cannot be attained by the sciences of man. A science of man which pretends to reject all normative considerations, to eliminate any consideration of values, to treat man as a pure object of science, becomes indeed an accomplice to the social practices that devalue man in treating him like an insect, like a tool, like a thing. Every science of man declares itself for or against man, contributes to his liberation or his enslavement, his development or his deterioration, by the methodology it uses and the theoretical status it claims. In reintegrating, via phenomenological methods, the images of aging in either of the two families of images, the sciences that cooperate within the broad field of gerontology will illumine the unacknowledged non-scientific presuppositions of so-called scientific activity and will lay bare the methodological biases that direct scientific procedures and falsify scientific results.

FROM THE PHENOMENOLOGY OF AGING TO THE PHENOMENOLOGY OF GERONTOLOGY

A phenomenological approach to aging leads to the development of a phenomenological approach to, and then to a critique of, gerontology itself. An analysis of the methodological and theoretical literature of gerontology reveals, in fact, that far from presenting a homogeneous appearance and demanding uniform research practices, the field of gerontology includes contradictions and incoherences which already afflict each of the sciences involved.

There are a number of different gerontologies, coexisting in anthologies, in congresses and conventions, in the minds of funding authorities, of students, of scholars, who ignore their radical differences and entertain the fiction that gerontology as a science is homogeneous, coherent, and sure of its protocol and its results. These gerontologies are actually irreconcilable, and indeed the future of gerontology depends on lucid choices being made among the diverse images of the field.

TWO IMAGES OF GERONTOLOGY

I will content myself here with viewing two definitions of gerontology and its object, drawn from the work of two authorities on gerontology, Nathan Shock and James Birren. My comments will deal only with two passages, and their scope is consequently limited. I do not intend to examine the context within which the definitions are developed, even though that might help to add nuances and correct my understanding of the authors' points of view.

These passages, both of which were published in roughly the same period, are at least a dozen years old. Shock and Birren have subsequently published a large number of studies; their thinking has evolved, and they might no longer quite recognize themselves in the mirror with which I am attempting to reflect their images. I am not pretending, however, to evaluate their entire work, nor the quality of their spirit; gerontology owes much to both. Still, the definitions that I want to juxtapose are in the public domain, and they are contained in papers (one of which has been re-edited) that continue to be utilized widely in the education of gerontologists. It seems legitimate, therefore, to show that Shock and Birren are simply not speaking about the same gerontology.

James Birren's image of gerontology was expressed in "Principles of Research in Aging," published in the *Handbook of Aging and the Individual* (1959):[7]

> Broadly speaking, the purpose of research on aging is to be able to characterize the nature of the older person and to explain how the organism changes over time, that is, to be able to make succinct statements explaining increasingly large numbers of facts about aging individuals. The role of the scientist studying aging appears to be not different from that in other fields of investigation.

Shock's definition is taken from "Some of the Facts of Aging," published in 1960.[8] Shock concludes his article with a review of hypotheses which at that time merited examination:

> In my opinion, the impairments in performance associated with advancing age are due to (a) dropping out of functional units in key organ systems, (b) some impairments in the functional capacities of cells remaining in the body of the aged, and (c) breakdown of neural and endocrine integrative functions in the individual.
>
> Although advancing age is accompanied by biological impairments that offer fertile grounds for the development of disease and pathology, there are compensatory devices which can maintain effective behavior in the human into advanced old age. Investigation of these as yet unmeasured and little understood inner resources over the entire life-span of the individual is the goal of research in gerontology.

Both Shock and Birren are attempting to do the same things: (1) to specify the object or the project of gerontological research; (2) to link this definition with a suggestion concerning the method or style of research.

TWO IMAGES OF AGING

It is in relation to this shared double intention that the differences between Shock and Birren can be clearly delineated.

First oppostion: With reference to the third criterion that I suggested, Birren's explication of aging (how the organism changes over time) seems to limit the phenomenon of aging to the last years of life. He is interested in characterizing the older person. By contrast Shock is interested in investigating aging "over the entire life span."

Second opposition: Although Birren utilizes the concept of change, his attitude is much more static than Shock's (at least in the passages under consideration). Birren appears to be concerned with gerontology as a science whose objective is to account for "facts," and he assumes that aging is a tangible phenomenon that can be described and analyzed; such is the "nature" of the older person. According to Shock, however, aging should be viewed as development and process, to the point that even the concept of relative stability must be understood in terms of temporal processes that can maintain (or fail to maintain) effective behavior.

It is impossible to distinguish Birren's position from Shock's with reference to my first criterion. Birren alone speaks about the aging of the "organism"; Shock speaks about the "body." Birren uses the term "person" while Shock uses the term "human." Both discuss *individuals*. Thus, although both appear to be mainly sensitive to biological dimensions of aging, neither rigidly limits himself to biological aspects.

The *third opposition* between the perspectives of Birren and of Shock becomes apparent from the perspective of my fourth criterion. Birren's statement underlines the universal character of aging, since he is attempting to delineate the universally shared experience of aging, the nature of the older person, and he is attempting to discover the laws of that process. Shock, on the other hand, points to devices which can compensate for the process of decline and thus maintain certain levels of behavior. For him the process of aging is relative to individual differences.

Two Conceptions of Science

It is not only the images of aging that differ in the two essays. Birren and Shock differ also in their fundamental images of scientific activity. According to Birren, research begins with the discovery and collection of facts, then moves to a second phase, the formulation of judgments that subsume these facts. He thus describes a simple model of inductive empiricism. We are provided with a model of gerontological methodology in which a scientific method, such as it is—unversal, eternal—is applied to a new object, the nature of the aged person. Birren makes no allusion at all to applications (therapeutic, pedagogic, political, or other) which might be able to ameliorate the conditions of health or of life among aged persons, or to modify the manner in which persons grow old.

Admittedly it is a delicate task to interpret the silence of a text. Let us risk, however, saying that Birren's statement postulates a theory of science that not only distinguishes its task (to account for the world, or, in this case, man) from technics (to *change* the world, or man), but draws from this distinction (wrongly) the possibility and the obligation of science's constituting itself independently from its own application. To identify science with action (praxis) is to risk, according to this conception, the contamination or the falsification of scientific observation of facts. Once scientific truth has been attained, of course, non-scientists may want to utilize the knowledge of the connection of cause and effect in order to put some sure means in the service of desired ends. But responsibility for the utilization of science resides with the politician, the teacher, and the technician, while the scientist contents himself with objective observation and does not involve himself in the problems of application.

If it is not absolutely evident that the conception of science I have just outlined is implied in Birren's essay, at least there is no contradiction. Shock's essay, on the other hand, supposes a different conception of science.

RELATION OF THEORY AND PRAXIS

We cannot be certain whether Shock would disagree with Birren's formulation of the scientific enterprise, but his essay suggests another attitude. After enumerating "some of the facts of aging" and hypotheses concerning age-related impairments, Shock speaks about resources capable of compensating for and combating negative aspects of aging. This relation between theory and practice is not an expression of confusion. Indeed, it is an expression of the fact that gerontology is being subsidized by the public, foundations, and government not because of a love of truth but because they anticipate that gerontology will contribute to the quality of life and aging. This anticipation does not imply that the possibilities for applied knowledge should dictate the kind of conclusions sought by science. But in gerontology, as in the other sciences, progress in the development of theory will be linked to the analysis of practical difficulties and the reappraisal of current prejudices.

More precisely, we should not have to wait to care for the aged sick, to prepare for their retirement or aging, or to engage in the politics of aging, until pure gerontology has found the truth, in the meantime being forbidden any policy intervention. The conditions of aging change from year to year and from generation to generation in response to forces (some intended, others spontaneous) that affect our living conditions, our educational systems, our production of goods and services, and our social, economic, political, and cultural lives. The investigation of compensatory possibilities can result neither from pure observation nor from experimental laboratory activity alone. Compensatory actions are suggested by selective research in relation to individuals and groups—research that is informed by *norms* and that is directed toward making behavior more effective, aging more satisfying, and old age more fulfilling. The kind of research required is one in which gerontologists will engage in social experiments not under their control, pursuing it in accordance with ideological, political, or ethical norms, i.e., non-scientifically, in an "uncontrolled" way. This kind of research must often proceed tentatively, using resources whose effectiveness cannot be known until late in life, but which must be detected and cultivated in infancy and adulthood.

The Concept of Resource

The term "resource" implies in effect the idea of virtuality or potentiality; by definition it can be neither measured nor understood independently of the multiform biological, personal, and social life it attempts to affect.

We certainly want to move beyond Shock's position in not limiting gerontological investigations to "inner" resources. I believe that the quality of life and the positive or negative character of aging depend, much more broadly than Shock admits, upon the interaction of the person and his physical, social, and cultural environment. In broadening the concept of resource and consequently the objective of gerontological research, I want nevertheless to identify with Shock's inventive and evolutionary scientific attitude and with his suggestion that new scientific objectives, i.e., research on "as yet untested and little-understood resources," demand new scientific methods.

A NECESSARY CONVERSION

Gerontology as a science has everything to gain and nothing to lose by renouncing the *a priori* methodologies and doctrines that still dominate the greatest part of research and are leading this research to an illusory pursuit of the *nature* of the aged person and the *laws* of aging, to a definition of aging as biological decline or as a natural phenomenon, universal and necessary. Having discerned some images of old age and aging which shape the mentality of our contemporaries, our customs, and our institutions, we find that their pervasive influence extends to gerontology itself, thus impinging on its hopefully scientific attitude.

A *phenomenological* approach to gerontology could proceed fruitfully with recourse to hermeneutical and semiological methods. The sciences of man have long dreamed of attaining the rigor and fecundity of the experimental natural sciences by appropriating their methods and hypotheses. But the frustration of so many psychologies and sociologies should lead the science of man to look for some models and methods within disciplines that have accomplished the most fertile developments during the past few years: such are linguistics, exegesis, hermeneutics, semiology. Paul Ricoeur has shown that the social institutions, historical events, and human actions—through and through symbolic—should be studied as texts, by means of methods which have dramatically revitalized the analysis of texts.[9]

THE FUTURE OF GERONTOLOGY

Human aging is a complex process whose biological conditions are embedded in and modified by a social and cultural, which is to say symbolic, context. One cannot study aging independently of the images, naïve or sophisticated, in which it is expressed and constituted. These images require our investigation largely through the mediation of the disparate texts which express them, comment on them, or convey them. Gerontology was dominated in the first stage of its brief history by the doctors and the biologists. In a second stage a place was created for the psychologists and the sociologists, flanked by some economists and demographers. Now gerontology is at the threshold of a third stage, and a period of renewal, based upon the gathering of geographers, historians, linguists, exegetes, hermeneuticists, and semiologists around problems of aging. This new era obviously will not proceed without a period of combat.

The development is inevitable. But much depends on gerontologists. They can, of course, retard it, thus making gerontology into a rear guard discipline, breathlessly running behind physics, chemistry, and biology. Or they can hasten this new stage, opening the way for multidisciplinary approaches, and initiating and advancing a transformation of method and doctrine which psychology and sociology will recognize tomorrow.

NOTES

1. "The knowledge produced in universities is increasingly vulnerable to the accusation of irrelevance" (Birren, Woodruff, Bergman, "Issues and Methodology in Social Gerontology," *Gerontologist*, vol. 12, no. 2, part 2, Summer 1972).
2. Donald Evans, *The Logic of Self-Involvement* (London, 1963; New York, 1969).
3. Charles Baudelaire, *Curiosités Esthetiqués* (Chauvet trans. London, 1972).
4. Benoîte Groult, *La part des choses* (Paris, 1972).
5. Paul Guimard, *L'ironie du sort* (Paris, 1961).
6. Dan Greenburg, *Scoring* (New York, 1972).
7. James Birren's paper has been reproduced in Bernice L. Neugarten, ed., *Middle Age and Aging* (Chicago, 1968), p. 545.
8. Nathan W. Shock, *Aging: Some Social and Biological Aspects* (Washington, D.C., 1960).
9. Paul Ricoeur, "The Model of the Text: Meaningful Action Considered as a Text," *Social Research*, vol. 38, no. 3 (1971).

Parish Clergy and the Aged: Examining Stereotypes[1]

16

Charles F. Longino, Jr., PhD,[2] and
Gay C. Kitson, PhD[3]

Hypotheses concerning clergymen's enjoyment of their pastoral contacts with older parishioners are examined using data from a national probability sample of 654 American Baptist parish ministers. The hypotheses test the ideas that ministers do not enjoy pastoral contacts with the elderly and that these contacts reflect the clergymen's ageist preferences and concern with instrumental over expressive values. The findings suggest that: (1) the majority of the clergy studied do not seem to have an aversion to ministering to older people; while not among the most enjoyable of their activities "ministering to the aged" clearly is not among the least enjoyable either; (2) there is some support for the view that clergy respond to the elderly in an ageist manner; comparing activities involving different age groups, the clergy prefer the young and adults to the aged; (3) those clergy who share with the elderly an interest in expressive activities are more likely to enjoy ministering to the aged.

THIS paper examines three stereotypical views of clergymen's willingness to work with their older parishioners. While a number of empirical studies have appeared in the past two decades on the religious life of older people (for reviews see Blazer & Palmore, 1976; Riley & Foner, 1968) there has been remarkably little systematic research on how the clergy perceive pastoral work with the elderly. Further, as Moberg (1975) indicates, available reports provide little generalizability to the parish clergy as a whole. This gap in the research literature is especially interesting in light of the extent of reported pastoral contact parish clergy have with the aged (Moberg, 1970).

Research vacuums are often filled with stereotypical views which gain credibility through repetition, giving a cloak of respectability to untested popular conceptions. For instance, despite the extensive contacts ministers have with their older parishioners, it is often felt that this work is an unpleasant duty. It is likewise assumed that the clergy prefer to work with the young rather than the old and in this sense are prejudiced against older people and denigrate them and the expressive values they emphasize. The purpose of this paper is to test hypotheses derived from these views concerning the relative satisfaction ministers derive from their pastoral work with older persons, reanalyzing data from a national study of American Baptist clergymen.

THE STEREOTYPES TO BE EXAMINED

The first view to be examined is that parish clergy find pastoral contacts with the aged unpleasant. Moberg (1975) asserts that "cultural stereotypes, folklore and myths about aging and the aged bias [clergy] perceptions and actions. Various socio-psychological problems intrude to hamper their effectiveness." For many persons contacts with the elderly are psychologically troublesome, especially when the aged are sick and impaired. The old are a painful reminder of one's probable future. Ministers experience these personal insecurities no less than others. Thus, in spite of the fact that they are called upon to shepherd the elderly in their flocks, it is assumed to be a joyless duty. As a result, ministers should report receiving little pleasure from work with older persons.

The second stereotype is that parish clergy find ministering to the aged unpleasant because

[1]The survey from which the data reported here are derived was under the direction of the late Kenneth Underwood and Jeffrey K. Hadden, Professor of Sociology, University of Virginia; it was sponsored by the Danforth Foundation and is described in Hadden (1965). We are grateful to Professor Hadden for the opportunity to use these data. We also wish to thank David O. Moberg, Professor of Sociology, Marquette Univ., and William Arnold, Professor of Sociology, Univ. of Kansas, for their helpful comments and criticisms.
[2]Dept. of Sociology, Univ. of Kansas, Lawrence 66044 and the Midwest Council for Social Research in Aging, Kansas City, MO 64111.
[3]Institute on the Family and the Bureaucratic Society, Dept. of Sociology, Case Western Reserve Univ., Cleveland 44106.

of ageism. Ageism is a form of prejudice in which negative stereotypes of the aged are expressed and preference, purely on the basis of age, given to the young in the distribution of rewards and services (Butler, 1969; Butler & Lewis, 1973). In this vein Hammond (1970) speculates that

in a society where youth and young adulthood are exalted, clergymen, too, may prefer to be in touch with the young, the active, the vital. Ministering to parishioners who are old, then, might be regarded as an unpleasant necessity.

It is assumed, therefore, that parish clergy enjoy their contacts with older persons *less* than those with persons in other age categories, especially the young.

A social-psychological explanation introduced by Hammond (1970), states that many clergy find work with older persons incongruent with their own definitions of parish work and as a result find such work unsatisfactory. In brief, the argument is that if clergy generally find ministering to the aged unpleasant, some with an instrumental orientation to their parish duties will find it especially so because their definition of the role of the minister differs from that of most older parishioners. Thie incongruity in expectations occurs because over time the aged tend to disengage from instrumental, task-oriented activities and to place more emphasis upon expressive, socio-emotional activities (Clark & Anderson, 1967).

As a result of this shift in their orientation, the argument continues, the aged are more likely to appreciate the church as a surrogate family which furnishes them with opportunities for being wanted more than being useful, for having diffuse and affective personal contacts rather than performing instrumental activities, a place for being comforted rather than challenged. This perspective is reinforced by data indicating that pastoral calls from clergy and church friends are extremely important to older persons, relative to other church activities (Glock, Ringer, & Babbie, 1967; McCann, 1955).

It is therefore assumed that ministers with an instrumental orientation to their parish duties will be impatient with older parishioners who want to pass the time of day and to express themselves, this expression being an end in itself rather than a means to other ends. On the other hand, parish clergy who derive greater satisfaction from those role activities which call for an expressive orientation should find

ministering to the aged both enjoyable and rewarding; being more congruent with the aged in their ways of relating to the church, they should thus find greater satisfaction in ministering to older people.

THE HYPOTHESES

Four hypotheses have been developed to address the issues raised above.

Hypothesis 1: Clergymen as a whole will tend not to enjoy ministering to the aged.

Hypothesis 2: Parish clergy will enjoy ministering to the aged *less* than they enjoy most other role activities.

Hypothesis 3: Relative to other age groups in the church, the parish clergyman will enjoy ministering to the aged the least and enjoy ministering to youth the most.

Hypothesis 4: Ministers who derive greater satisfaction from those parish duties optimizing an expressive role orientation will be more likely to find satisfaction in ministering to the aged.

METHODOLOGY

Subjects. — To test these hypotheses concerning the relative satisfaction parish clergy derive from ministering to the aged, a secondary analysis of data gathered in a national survey of American Baptist parish clergy will be presented. The data were obtained in 1965 by a mailed questionnaire to a probability sample of a quarter of the full-time American Baptist parish clergy listed in the denominational directory. The 654 ministers who completed questionnaires represent a return rate of 68%. With greater visibility to the concerns of the elderly since 1965, it is possible that clergy attitudes may have changed and in fact become more positive. Nevertheless, the issue of whether or not clergy, some or all of them, share in culture-wide stereotypes about the aged can be examined with these data.

Measures used. — The dependent variable of this study is the clergy role of "ministering to the aged." Using the work of Blizzard (1956, 1958) and Kling (1959) on ministerial roles as a basis, Underwood and Hadden developed a composite list of ministerial roles which they tested on clergy attending church conferences and then further refined. The result was a set of 52 items which tap — usually with several items — a wide variety of clergy role activities. These activities include those of teacher, counselor, ritual leader and preacher, administrator, planner and promoter of church programs as well as spiritual and intellectual leader, and participant in both denominational and community organizations. Ministers were asked to respond to each item on a six-point scale "in terms of the enjoyment or personal satisfaction you gain from the activity, independent of time you may devote to it." The scale ranged from "definitely do not enjoy" (1) to "definitely enjoy" (6).

FINDINGS

Hypothesis 1. — If ministering to the aged is considered an unpleasant necessity by most parish clergy then it should receive a low satisfaction rating. This did not occur, however. The median rating of the item was 4.77 on the six-point scale. Indeed, when the scale is collapsed into thirds, 61% of the respondents fall into the upper third, indicating positive satisfaction, 34% in the middle third, and only 5% in the lower third. If 3.5 is the true midpoint of the role satisfaction scale, it is difficult to escape the conclusion that a majority of Baptist pastors enjoy contacts with their older parishioners. If these ministers are at all typical of parish clergy in general, then the idea that ministering to the aged is unpleasant and unsatisfying should be viewed with suspicion.

Hypothesis 2. — How does ministering to the aged compare with other parish role activities? Even though a majority indicates that such a ministry is enjoyable, it may be *less* so than most other role activities. In order to test this hypothesis, the median scores on the 52 role items were ranked. Twenty items rank above and 31 below ministering to the aged. The data do not support Hypothesis 2. While pastoral contact with the elderly is not among the most enjoyable of the minister's tasks, neither is it among the least.

Hypothesis 3. — The assumption of ageism among parish clergy would render the above ranking irrelevant. From this perspective, it is not the relative enjoyment of clergy role activities which is at issue but the relative satisfaction derived from ministering to parishioners in differing age groups. Four specific age categories, other than the aged, were identified in role items. References to the other age groups focused on "teaching" rather than the broader concept of "ministering." This obviously produces an unknown amount of con-

Table 1. Relative Role Satisfaction by Parishioner Age Category.

Role Items	Role Satisfaction	
	% with High Rating	Median Score
Teaching young people (i.e., junior high and high school)	78.5%	5.09
Teaching and working directly with adults	76.6	5.05
Ministering to the aged	60.7	4.77
Teaching undergraduate and graduate students	54.3	4.63
Teaching children	53.7	4.60

ceptual distortion. With this caution in mind, however, it is possible to test the third hypothesis. The percentage rating positive satisfaction and the median scores on these items are presented in Table 1. While the Baptist clergy registered relatively high satisfaction with reference to all of the age groups, a range does exist. The clergymen ranked teaching young people and adults higher and teaching children and students lower than they did ministering to the aged. Contact with young people received the highest satisfaction score, as hypothesized. While contact with the aged did not receive the lowest satisfaction rating, or median score, it did approach the lower end of the range, lending partial but incomplete support to the hypothesis.

Hypothesis 4. — In Hypothesis 4 the focus shifts from clergy, as a whole, to those who most enjoy ministering to the aged. If older persons tend to emphasize an expressive rather than an instrumental relationship with the church, a point we take to be sufficiently well documented, then those ministers who most enjoy expressive role activities should also derive greater satisfaction from pastoral care of the elderly.

As a test of this hypothesis, the clergy role items were factor analyzed. Six interpretable factors emerged and the items most clearly defining them are arrayed in Table 2. The factors may be construed as clergy role specialties, if one keeps in mind that individuals may derive satisfaction from more than one specialty. In fact, due to the practical necessities of their work, they may engage in most or all of them. The term specialty, thus, does not imply exclusiveness. Each, rather, is a cluster of highly intercorrelated role activities which satellite around the major role dimensions of the parish clergy.

Table 2. Six-Factor Varimax Loadings of Clergy Role Items for American Baptist Parish Clergy.

Items Loading Most Highly on Factor I — *Community Activism*	Factor Loadings					
	I	II	III	IV	V	VI
Influencing the policies of major organizations or institutions in my community	.78	-.01	.14	.06	-.04	-.04
Participating in creating plans for improvements of city life	.67	-.04	.12	.11	-.03	.06
Influencing the policies of organizations in my denomination	.67	.17	.26	.04	-.03	-.02
Organizing and helping groups who are victims of social neglect or injustice	.58	.01	-.01	.10	-.01	.04
Factor II — *Personal Evangelism*						
Participating in evangelistic meetings	-.15	.73	.18	-.09	.03	.05
Winning a lost soul to Christ	-.15	.72	.05	.08	.06	.02
Privately encountering God through prayer	.05	.70	.08	.11	.14	.08
Teaching people to use their Bibles in special meditation	.06	.67	.08	.06	.10	.21
Factor III — *Church Administration*						
Helping manage church finances	.12	.07	.74	.02	-.02	-.05
Managing the church office — records, correspondence, information center	.15	.05	.62	-.01	.08	.04
Raising money for special church projects	.18	.20	.06	-.06	.02	.07
Working with congregational boards and committees	.23	.08	.57	.14	.12	.17
Factor IV — *Counseling*						
Counseling with people facing the major decisions of life, e.g., marriage, vocation	.14	.07	.06	.73	.14	.03
Counseling with people about their moral and personal problems	.22	.10	-.01	.72	.04	.04
Helping a person or family resolve a serious problem, whether it be spiritual, social, psychological, or economic	.28	.18	-.01	.53	-.02	.04
Ministering to the sick, dying, and bereaved	.03	.19	.12	.50	.23	.10
Factor V — *Preaching*						
Preaching sermons	.03	.22	.03	.04	.67	-.01
Leading public worship	.09	.17	.06	.16	.60	.14
Preparing sermons	.05	.17	.03	.06	.51	.01
Factor VI — *Church Education*						
Teaching young people	.12	.19	.03	.09	.09	.53
Teaching children	.04	.28	.07	-.03	.04	.50
Recruiting, training, and assisting lay leaders and teachers	.20	.22	.35	.12	-.01	.42

Table 3. Correlations of Factor Scales with Ministering to the Aged.

Parish Clergy Role Specialties	Correlations
Personal evangelism	.38
Teaching	.33
Counseling	.28
Church administration	.25
Preaching	.21
Community activism	.05*

*This correlation is not statistically significant; all others are significant beyond the .001 level.

The items most clearly defining the six factors were combined to create additive scales and correlated with satisfaction with ministering to the aged. These correlations, in descending order of strength, are displayed in Table 3. Role specialties emphasizing personal contact with parishioners and involving a high degree of expressive activity, such as personal evangelism, teaching and counseling, correlate the most strongly with ministering to the aged. On the other hand, more instrumental role specialties such as organizational planning and management which involve less one-to-one personal contact with parishioners correlate less strongly with ministering to the aged. The correlation with community activism, a highly instrumental activity, is not statistically significant. These data support Hypothesis 4.

DISCUSSION

A beginning has been made at weeding out some of the less from the more tenuous views concerning parish clergy's contacts with aged parishioners. Some of the hypotheses were supported; others were not.

First, the idea that parish clergy do not enjoy ministering to the older people in their congregations seems to be incorrect, assuming, of course, that the American Baptist ministers surveyed here are typical of parish clergy in other denominations; that their attitudes toward the elderly have not become more negative since 1965; and that the measures used are valid indicators of role satisfaction. The majority reported that they enjoy contacts with their older church members. Nor does ministering to the aged fair badly when compared with other role activities. While it is not the most enjoyable of their tasks, it is not among the least enjoyable either.

We should not argue on the basis of these findings that all ministers are free of the effects of ageism. That issue is beyond the scope of our data. Clergy may, however, be less negative in their views than others while still not completely at ease with the aged. It may be recalled that ministers who derive the greatest satisfaction from the role specialty we called "personal evangelism" enjoy ministering to the elderly more than others ($r = .38$). In discussing the clergy who attended her seminars on death and dying, Kubler-Ross (1969) notes that while they were more at ease than many others in the helping professions, "What amazed me, however, was the number of clergy who felt quite comfortable using a prayer book or a chapter out of the Bible as the sole communication between them and the patients, thus avoiding listening to their needs and being exposed to questions they might be unable or unwilling to answer." This aspect of clergy-parishioner relationships needs further examination.

Second, the clergy seem to share to some extent the ageist perspective prevalent in our society. Compared to contacts with the more active youth and adults, clergy find ministering to the aged a less pleasurable activity. As Cowgill (1974) has argued, modernization, for all its benefits, has lowered the status of the aged. As the population of a society ages, the young are better-educated and trained for newer occupations, the aged lose by comparison. Youth is valued as a source of future leaders and pandered to in the market place, the media, and in public taste. The aged become defined as obsolete, unproductive, and expendable. The result is ageism, a lowered preference and priority for the aged. One interpretation of the data in Table 1 is that clergy do not escape ageism. They do rate pastoral contacts with the young higher in satisfaction than those with the old. Churches, like the culture around them, are youth-oriented.

This emphasis in the church may be motivated in part by considerations of institutional survival. Additonally, it may reflect the felt needs of the most influential age category in the church, the adults. They provide the major share of financial and lay leadership support for the organization. Their concerns, therefore, would more easily become the concerns of the organization. The young people of the parish are their children. Adolescents normally experience moral quandaries and must deal with important life decisions; these realities make parenthood vexing if not excruciating. If the church is youth-oriented, therefore, it may be, in part, by the insistence of parents who want all the help they can receive in guiding their children through the turbulent waters of pre-adulthood.

Why then are the aged not ranked even lower relative to the other age groups in ministerial role satisfaction? One explanation, consistent with organizational theory, is that the aged are less peripheral to the church than children and students. They are likely to exercise more influence and to contribute more leadership and financial support. Yet they run a poor second, in these areas, to the middle-aged. To the extent that the elderly place less emphasis upon instrumental involvement with increasing age, their leadership wanes and with it their organizational influence. This lack or loss of influence (Riley, Johnson, & Foner, 1972), makes the elderly vulnerable to ageism.

Third, the most unambiguous finding is support for the hypothesis of role congruence. Clergy with a more expressive orientation to their occupational roles derive greater satisfaction from ministering to the aged, who, themselves, tend to relate to the church in an expressive mode. It is not necessarily a concern for the problems of aging, as a social and moral issue, which affects clergy satisfaction in this area. Hammond (1970) suggests that while older people are concerned with legislation affecting their health and well-being, they are less interested in such issues than other age groups. Clergy who enjoy ministering to the aged seem to share this perspective. One item from another section of the questionnaire asked respondents to agree or disagree with the following statement: "Adequate medical care for the aged through some kind of governmental program is badly needed." This item is negatively correlated with satisfaction with ministering to the aged ($r = -.07$). It is not the aged in abstraction, therefore, that make the difference for expressive clergy but the aged as persons. Glock et al. (1967) demonstrated that older persons tend to seek comfort, not challenge, from their relationship to the church. Those ministers who are more comfort-oriented, not the community activists, enjoy meeting their needs. As in so many areas of social relationships, role congruence is associated with satisfaction.

SUMMARY

There are a number of matters to which parish ministers attend in the performance of their occupational role. One of these is ministering to their elderly parishioners. In the absence of generalizable data on this pastoral duty, it has been commonly understood to be an unpleasant, time-consuming task, which is less enjoyable than most other ministerial concerns. Further, there is a popular view that clergymen prefer pastoral contacts with the young and middle-aged adult members, instead of the elderly and in this sense reflect the ageist preferences of the American culture. A prevalent but untested explanation of these stereotypic expectations is that pastors actively involved in the many instrumentalities of church and community leadership find the expressive demands of the elderly burdensome, unproductive, and generally unsatisfying. A secondary analysis of data derived from a national probability sample of American Baptist parish ministers suggests that clergy do enjoy ministering to the elderly, but enjoy teaching adults and young people more. Although the pastoral care of the aged was not found to be unsatisfying, those who emphasize instrumental over expressive role activities tend to enjoy their contacts with the elderly less.

REFERENCES

Blazer, D. G., & Palmore, E. Religion and aging in a longitudinal panel. *Gerontologist*, 1976, *16*, (1:1), 82-85.

Blizzard, S. W. Role conflicts of the urban protestant parish minister. *The City Church*, 1956, *7*, 13-15.

Blizzard, S. W. The protestant parish minister's integrative roles. *Religious Education*, 1958, *53*, 374-380.

Butler, R. N. Ageism, another form of bigotry. *Gerontologist*, 1969, *9*, 243-246.

Butler, R. N., & Lewis, M. S. *Aging and mental health: Positive psycho-social approaches*. C. V. Mosby, St. Louis, 1973.

Clark, M., & Anderson, B. *Culture and aging*. Charles C Thomas, Springfield, 1967.

Cowgill, D. O. The aging of population and societies. *Annals of the American Academy of Political & Social Sciences*, 1974, *415*, 1-18.

Glock, C. Y., Ringer, B. B., & Babbie, E. R. *To comfort and to challenge*. Univ. California Press, Berkeley, 1967.

Hadden, J. K. A study of the protestant ministry in America. *Journal for the Scientific Study of Religion*, 1965, *5*, 10-23.

Hammond, P. E. Aging and the ministry. In M. W. Riley & A. E. Foner (Eds.), *Aging and society*, Vol. 2: *Aging and the professions*. Russell Sage Foundation, New York, 1970.

Kling, F. R. Role of the parish minister. Educational Testing Service, Princeton, NJ, 1959.

Kubler-Ross, E. *On death and dying*. Macmillan Paperback, New York, 1969.

McCann, C. W. *Long beach senior citizen survey*. Long Beach Community Welfare Council, Long Beach, 1955.

Moberg, D. O. Aging and its implications for theological education, *Journal of Pastoral Care*, 1970, *24*, 127-134.

Moberg, D. O. Needs felt by the clergy for ministries to the aging. *Gerontologist*, 1975. *15*, 170-175.

Riley, M. W., & Foner, A. *Aging and society*, Vol. 1: *An inventory of research findings*. Russell Sage Foundation, New York, 1968.

Riley, M. W., Johnson, M. & Foner, A. *Aging and society*, Vol. 3: *A sociology of age stratification*. Russell Sage Foundation, New York, 1972.

Analysis of religious activities and attitudes in a longitudinal panel of 272 community residents
produced the following main findings: positive religious attitudes remained stable despite general
declines in religious activities; there were several significant and substantial correlations between
religion and happiness, feelings of usefulness, and adjustment; these correlations also tended to
be stronger for older persons and tended to increase over time.

Religion and Aging in a Longitudinal Panel[1]   17

Dan Blazer, MD,[2] and Erdman Palmore, PhD[3]

Religion is thought to become increasingly important with the onset of late life and the inevitable approach of death. For instance, a conversation was overheard between two children. The first asked, "Why is Grandma spending so much time reading the Bible these days?" "I guess she is cramming for final exams," the second replies. This exemplifies the stereotyped view that the primary concern of the elderly in our society is religion and preparation for death. Mathiasen (1955) has asserted that religion is "the key to a happy life in old age. A sense of the all-encompassing love of God is the basic emotional security and firm spiritual foundation for people who face the end of life."

Investigators who have studied religious activity and attitudes of the elderly have been limited to cross-sectional analysis (Havighurst, 1953; Orbach, 1961) with the exception of two limited longitudinal studies (Streib, 1965; Wingrove, 1971). The general impression from the existing literature is that church attendance is generally at a high level among men and women in their 60s, but it becomes less regular in advanced old age (Riley & Foner, 1968). On the other hand, Orbach (1961) found no consistent age trends in church attendance when he controlled for other related factors. Private religious activities (devotional practices) have been shown to be greater in older age categories in one denomination (Fukuyama, 1961), and, again in cross-sectional analysis, such activities as Bible reading and prayer are reported in a greater percentage of the elderly

than in younger age groups (Erskine, 1965). One study indicates that these private activities increase with advancing age (Cavan, Burgess, Havighurst, & Goldhamer, 1949). There have been no longitudinal studies over an extended period of time to substantiate these conclusions. The cross-sectional differences by age groups may be due to waning religious activities in younger cohorts, rather than increasing activities with older age.

The general hypothesis that church-going and religious interests are significantly correlated with old age adjustment is stated by many authors (Barron, 1958; Mathiasen, 1955; Moberg, 1970). Edwards and Klemmach (1973), Scott (1955), Shanas (1962), and Spreitzer and Snyder (1974) have shown a significant correlation between life satisfaction and church attendance and church related activities. On the other hand, Havighurst and Albrecht (1953) found little relationship between professed attitudes toward religion and personal adjustment.

The Duke Longitudinal Study of Aging provides the first opportunity to examine the amount and patterns of decline or increase in religious activities and attitudes over time. The purpose of this paper is to analyze these patterns and to examine the correlates of religion with happiness, usefulness, personal adjustment, and longevity.

Longitudinal Study of Aging

The data examined in this study were collected as a part of the first longitudinal study of aging at Duke University (Palmore, 1970, 1974). The original sample was composed of 272 volunteers from the Durham area. The age range was 60 to 94 years with a median age of 70.8, at the first round of interviews (1955-1959). The sample contained both white and blacks, male and female participants in proportions that approximated

1. This study was supported by grant HD-00668, NICHD, USPHS, and by grant 5-T01-MH13112-03, NIMH, USPHS. Computer programming was done by Jennifer Buzun.
2. Resident and Teaching Fellow, Dept. of Psychiatry, Box 3880, Duke Medical Center, Durham, 27710.
3. Professor of Medical Sociology and Scientific Associate of the Center for the Study of Aging and Human Development, Box 3003, Duke Medical Center, Durham, 27710.

the race and sex distribution of the community from which the sample was drawn (67% white and 33% black; 48% male and 52% female). Socioeconomic class was determined on the basis of manual (45%) versus nonmanual occupations (55%). Survivors have been followed for nine rounds of examinations over the past 20 years. Ninety percent were protestant and 94% said they were church members. This is a somewhat higher proportion than the 78% of all persons in the United States over age 50 who reported that they are members of a church (Erskine, 1964).

The Chicago Inventory of Activities and Attitudes was administered in each of the nine rounds to date (Burgess, Cavan, & Havighurst, 1948). The religion subscale of the Activity Inventory, which includes measures of church attendance, listening to church services on radio and TV, and reading the Bible and/or devotional books, was used as an indicator of religious activity at a given point in time. Data was coded on a 0 - 10 scale (10 indicating the highest level of religious activity). The religion subscale of the Attitude Inventory, which is based on agreement or disagreement with such statements as "religion is a great comfort," and "religion is the most important thing to me," was used as a rating of positive religious attitudes at a given point in time and was coded on a 0 - 6 scale (6 indicating the most positive religious attitude).

The "happiness" and "usefulness" subscales of the Attitude Inventory were examined for correlations with the religion subscales. The Cavan Adjustment Scale, a rating of social and emotional adjustment by the interviewing social worker, was used as a measure of personal adjustment (Cavan et al., 1949). A longevity quotient was also tabulated for each panelist, which controls for the effects of age, race, and sex (Palmore, 1974). The LQ is the observed number of years survived after initial examination, divided by the actuarilly expected number of years to be survived after examination based on the person's age, sex, and race. For those who were still living (about one-fifth of the panel), an estimate was made of how many years they will have lived since initial testing by adding the present number of years survived since initial testing to the expected number of years now remaining according to acturial tables.

Religious activity and religious attitude were then correlated with happiness, usefulness, personal adjustment, and longevity. Controls were also introduced for sex, age, and occupation. These correlations were computed for both Round 1 and Round 7 to see if the relationships changed as the panel aged.

Some questions that were asked only in Round 1 were also analyzed. These included questions concerning religious activity at age 12, amount and type of prayer life, frequency of church attendance, frequency of listening to religious programs on radio and TV, and frequency of Bible and devotional reading.

Frequency

Religious activities were relatively frequent in this sample compared to national samples of persons over 65. For example, 61% of our sample reported in Round 1 that they attended church at least once a week compared to only 37% of a national sample (*Catholic Digest*, 1953). In addition, 59% listened to religious programs on radio or TV at least once a week, and 79% read the Bible or a devotional book at least once a week. Also, 43% reported that they prayed at a regular time during the day and 31% said that they "prayed continuously during the day," whereas only 3% said they did not pray at all.

Background Factors

The women were significantly more religious than men in activities (about .7 higher on the religious activity subscale, t-test significant at .02 level), and in attitudes (about .3 higher on the religious attitudes subscale, t-test significant at .05 level). This supports the general finding that women tend to be more religious than men (Orbach, 1961; Riley & Foner, 1968).

Persons from nonmanual occupations also tended to be more active in religion than those from manual occupations. The nonmanual group had a mean religious activity score of 7.2 compared to 6.1 for the manual group (t-test significant at .01 level). The mean religious attitude score for nonmanual group was 5.7 compared to 5.1 for the manual group (t-test significant at the .001 level).

However, church attendance at age 12 had no significant relationship to present church attendance. This is contrary to the idea that childhood training determines religious practices for the rest of life. Substantial proportions of those who attended church regularly as a child now attend rarely. There was a general decline in church attendance from age 12; 80% attended once a week or more at age 12 compared to 61% at Round 1.

Change

In order to analyze change over time in religious activities and attitudes, we plotted the differences in mean scores between each round and the initial round for the survivors to that round. Thus, these differences represent true longitudinal changes and cannot be attributed to attrition in the sample, because each comparison between the initial and later round is based on the scores of the same persons in the initial and later round. These analyses were also controlled for sex, socioeconomic status, and age. Religious activity did show a gradual but definite decrease over time (Fig. 1). This decrease from Round 1 was significant at the .02 level in Rounds 3, 5, 6, 7, 8, and 9. The decrease became steadily greater after Round 5 (about 10 years after Round 1). Religious activity among females remained significantly higher than that for males over time but declined in a similar manner. There was a greater decrease in religious activities among persons from nonmanual occupations than those from manual occupations, perhaps because those from nonmanual occupations started from a higher level of religious activity. There was also more decline among those over age 70 at Round 1, probably because of a greater decline in health, vision , and hearing.

In contrast, average religious attitudes remained quite stable over time, with almost identical levels at the early and the last rounds (Fig. 1). There was a slight, but temporary, increase in positive religious attitudes during the middle rounds (1964-1968). When separated for age, sex, and manual versus

nonmanual, no significant variation from this stable pattern was noted. Thus it appears that, when measured longitudinally, religious activities tend to gradually decline in late old age, but religious attitudes and satisfactions tend to remain fairly level, neither increasing nor decreasing substantially.

Correlates

Because our earlier analysis of longevity (Palmore, 1971) had found significant correlations between total activity and the longevity quotient (r = .15) as well as between total attitudes and the longevity quotient (r = .26), we expected that there would be substantial correlations of religious activities and attitudes with the longevity quotient. These expectations were contradicted by the data. There was almost no correlation between religious activities and the longevity quotient (r = -.01), nor between religious attitudes and longevity (r = -.06). Thus, in this sample, religion was clearly unrelated to a longer life.

On the other hand, many of the correlations of religious attitudes and activities with happiness, feelings of usefulness, and personal adjustment were significant (.01 level) and moderately strong, as expected. Religious attitudes were not significantly related to happiness, but they were significantly related to feelings of usefulness (r = .16),[4] especially among those from manual occupations (r = .24). Religious attitudes also had a small correlation with adjustment (r = .13) which reached significance among those from nonmanual occupations (r = .24).

Religious activities generally had even stronger relationships to happiness, usefulness, and adjustment. Religious activities were significantly related to happiness (r = .16), especially among men (r = .26), and persons over age 70 at Round 1 (r = .25). Religious activities were most strongly related to feelings of usefulness (r = .25), especially among those from manual occupations (r = .34), and those over age 70 (r = .32). Similarly, religious activities were significantly related to personal adjustment (r = .16), especially among those from manual occupations (r = .33) and among males (r = .28). These stronger correlations between religious activities and various measures of adjustment, compared to religious attitudes and ad-

Figure I. RELIGIOUS ATTITUDES AND ACTIVITY OVER TIME

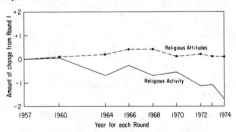

Fig. 1. Religious attitudes and activity over time.

---

4. All the correlations in this section come from Round 1. Correlations for Round 7 were similar unless noted otherwise.

justment, suggest that religious behavior was more important than attitudes in influencing adjustment.

The fact that these correlations were generally higher among the older persons is similar to the fact that the correlations tended to increase between Rounds 1 and 7. These facts support the theory that religion tends to become increasingly important in the adjustment of older persons as they age, despite the decline in religious activities such as church attendance.

Importance of Religion

In this "Bible Belt" community, most of the elderly studied reported relatively high levels of religious activity and positive attitudes toward religion. Women and persons from nonmanual occupations tended to be more religious in activity and attitudes. There was a general shift from more church attendance in childhood to less in old age. Part of this shift may reflect the general shift toward less church attendance in our society over the past half century.

Longitudinal analysis over 18 years showed that positive religious attitudes remained stable despite a general decline in religious activities. This supports the cross-sectional findings of decline in religious activities in old age but contradicts the theory of increasing interest in religion among aging persons.

There was no correlation of religious activity or attitude with longevity, but they were correlated with happiness, feelings of usefulness, and personal adjustment, especially among men, those from manual occupations, and those over 70. It was also observed that these correlations tended to increase over time. The greater correlations at older ages and in later rounds support the theory that religion becomes increasingly important for personal adjustment in the later years.

The stronger correlations between religious *activities* and various measures of adjustment, compared to the correlations between religious *attitudes* and adjustment, suggest that religious *behavior* was more important than attitudes. When interpreting these results several cautions should be borne in mind: the sample was composed of volunteers from a limited area, those who respond positively on one item tend to respond positively on others, correlation does not prove causation, etc. Nevertheless, limited as

they are, these findings do support the theory that despite declines in religious activities, religion plays a significant and increasingly important role in the personal adjustment of many older persons. One implication would be that churches need to give special attention to their elderly members in order to compensate for their generally declining religious activities and to maximize the benefits of their religious experience.

References

Barron, M. L. The role of religion and religious institutions in creating the milieu of older people. In D. Scudder (Ed.), *Organized religion and the older person*. Univ. of Florida Press, Gainesville, 1958.

Burgess, E. W., Cavan, R. S., & Havighurst, R. J. *Your attitudes and activities*. Science Research Associates, Chicago, 1948.

Catholic Digest. How important religion is to Americans. 1953, *17*, 7-12.

Cavan, R. S., Burgess, E. W., Havighurst, R. J., & Goldhamer, H. *Personal adjustment in old age*. Science Research Associates, Chicago, 1949.

Edwards, J. N., & Klemmach, D. L. Correlates of life satisfaction: A reexamination. *Journal of Gerontology*, 1973, *28*, 497-502.

Erskine, H. G. The polls. *Public Opinion Quarterly*, 1964, *29*, 679; 1965, *29*, 154.

Fukuyama, Y. The major dimensions of church membership. *Review of Religious Research*, 1961, *2*, 154-161.

Havighurst, R. J., & Albrecht, R. *Older people*. Longmans, New York, 1953.

Mathiasen, G. The role of religion in the lives of older people. *New York State Governor's Conference on Problems of the Aging*. New York, 1955.

Moberg, D. O. Religion in the later years. In A. M. Hoffman (Ed.), *The daily needs and interests of older persons*. Charles C Thomas, Springfield, 1970.

Orbach, H. L. Age and religion: A study of church attendance in the Detroit Metropolitan area. *Geriatrics*, 1961, *16*, 530-540.

Palmore, E. *Normal aging*. Duke Univ. Press, Durham, 1970.

Palmore, E. The relative importance of social factors in predicting longevity. In E. Palmore & F. Jeffers (Eds.), *Prediction of life-span*, Heath, Lexington, 1971.

Palmore, E. *Normal aging. II*. Duke Univ. Press, Durham, 1974.

Riley, M. W., & Foner, A. *Aging and society*. Russell Sage Foundation, New York, 1968.

Scott, F. G. Factors in the personal adjustment of institutionalized and noninstitutionalized aged. *American Sociologist Review*, 1955, *20*, 538-540.

Shanas, E. The personal adjustment of recipients of old age assistance. In R. M. Gray & D. O. Moberg (eds.), *The church and the older person*. Erdmans, Grand Rapids, 1962.

Spreitzer, E., & Snyder, E. E. Correlates of life satisfaction among the aged. *Journal of Gerontology*, 1974, *29*, 454-458.

Streib, G. *Longitudinal study of retirement*. Final Report of the Social Security Administration, 1965.

Wingrove, C. R., & Alston, J. P. Age, aging and church attendance. *Gerontologist*, 1971, *11*, 356-358.

A Multidimensional Approach to Religiosity and Disengagement[1]

18

Charles H. Mindel, PhD,[2] and C. Edwin Vaughan, PhD[3]

This study of 106 elderly Central Missourians examines religious behavior as an indication of "disengagement." It is argued that religiosity must be measured in both organizational forms such as attending religious services and the more subjective nonorganizational forms including prayer and listening to religious services and music on radio and television before an assessment of "disengagement" is made. Following Hochschild (1975) it is argued that from the perspective of researchers and others it may appear that an older person is "disengaged" but from the perspective of the individual he/she may be fully "engaged." Data support the thesis that elderly may be disengaged organizationally but engaged nonorganizationally.

IN the most thorough critique to date of social disengagement theory in gerontology (see, Cumming & Henry, 1961) Hochschild (1975) analyzes several dimensions of this theory. She notes that many researchers have been concerned with isolation rather than disengagement and that researchers have too often ignored the fact that one dimension of any relationship is the actor's own conscious feelings about it. She analyzes this "subjective dimension" in terms of interpersonal relationships, but we suggest that this concept also applies to the individual's relationship to organizations.

For example, the individual may continue to informally interact with former fellow workers, follow the progress of the former employer, and support politically or otherwise the interests of his former occupational grouping. To some researchers the retired worker may be "disengaged," but we would agree with Hochschild that there is an important "meaning" in this activity for this individual who may, from his own point of view, be fully "engaged." The symbolism, social relationships, and self-identity, although not necessarily reflected in formal organizational activity, remain a salient and integrative aspect of the individual's life.

Research on the religious behavior of the elderly provide an appropriate case in point. With notable exceptions (i.e., Gray & Moberg, 1962; Moberg, 1971), distinctions have seldom been made between religious preference, religious identity, religious identification, organizational participation, and religious behavior of a nonorganizational type.

For example, Morgan (1937) gave several "reasons" why older people are less religious. Studying 381 recipients of old age assistance in New York state, she found that, though 93% indicated that they had earlier in their lives attended church, only 43% continued to attend. Fifty-seven percent no longer attended; 52% of those indicated that they were *physically* unable to attend; 39% more indicated a loss of interest or a loss of belief.

Literally scores of articles have, at a relatively simple level of analysis, studied the relationship between church attendance and the aging process. (Maves, 1960, provides an excellent summary of early research in this area. A more recent survey of the literature in this field may be found in Heenan, 1972.) Bahr (1970) analyzed the previous research on this topic in terms of four models of religion and aging. One of his models the "progressive disengagement" model, which predicts a mutual severing of ties occurring between the aging person and others in his social system, is supported by his data. It is also consistent with the findings of earlier studies that religious attendance and participation parallel the decline in other forms of participation in voluntary organizations.

Bahr's conclusion indicates the kind of reasoning which often results from such data.

[1]This report is part of a larger project investigating the alternative living arrangements of the elderly. This larger project, entitled "Housing and Health Care Paths of Dependent Elderly," is supported by the U.S. Dept. of Health, Education and Welfare's Administration on Aging (Grant No. 93-P-57616) Dr. Ellen Horgan Biddle, principal investigator and Dr. Robert W. Habenstein and Dr. Charles H. Mindel as co-principal investigators. The assistance, criticism and advice of Drs. Biddle, Habenstein, and Richard Gorsuch gratefully acknowledged.
[2]Graduate School of Social Work, Univ. of Texas at Arlington, Arlington 76019.

[3]Univ. of Missouri-Columbia.

He states, "The evidence reviewed in this paper suggests the older the metropolitan male becomes the less likely he is to turn to the church" (Bahr, 1970). He concedes that there may be a change in the quality of religiosity with age which takes "psychological forms," although these are not specified (see also Moberg, 1965a & b, 1971).

Thus research on the religious behavior of the aged has frequently concluded that there is a decline in the religiousness of older people. These conclusions, we argue, result because researchers have too narrowly conceptualized religion in terms of participation in formal religious organizations. For the aged person the form or level of participation in the formal organizations of religion may change while leaving a strong psychological (subjective-meaningful) relationship within the life of the individual.

It will be one of the purposes of this paper to examine religious disaffiliation as an expression of disengagement. However, religiosity will be analyzed in *two* ways: (1) in the sense that most researchers often use it, namely, as organized religious behavior, and (2) in a more subjective and nonorganizational sense. By so defining religiosity the definition of "disengagement" is expanded to include both the conventional notion of disengagement from organizational membership as well as subjective disengagement from religion, i.e., personal, nonorganizational behavior. Disengagement is not seen as merely giving up membership in formal organizations but the surrendering of one's societal roles. One's role as "religious person" encompasses more than participation in religious organizations, it also includes private religious behavior and the feeling that religion has "meaning" for one's life (c.f., Gray & Moberg, 1962). The concept "role" is most commonly used to describe the way a person's behavior is organized relative to the behavior of another person or in terms of the expectations of a position which a person occupies in a social organization. In addition, the concept may be used, as we are in this instance, to explain how a person's behavior may be informed, organized, even directed by behavioral expectations (roles) which a person experiences vicariously through literature, memory of former role relationships - significant or important "others" whether contemporaneously present or not.

The importance of informal, nonorganizational religious expression for the aged as church attendance declines has been recognized. Moberg (1971), for example, echoing the earlier words of Burgess (1952) asserted that "activities like Bible reading, praying, and meditation increases steadily with age, [and that] as church attendance among the religiously oriented decreases use of the mass media increases." In this paper we will be exploring these facets of religious disengagement. It is our contention that, if an elderly person is truly disengaged from his/her religious role, this will be reflected in low levels of both organizational and nonorganizational religious expression. If low levels of organizational religious behavior are not matched by low levels of nonorganizational religiosity, then criticism of the narrow view of disengagement suggested above and by Hochschild appears relevant.

It has also been suggested by others (e.g., Morgan, 1937; Heenan, 1972) that the disengagement process originates in part because of a decline in the health of an older person. An older person's increasing infirmity forces him/her to give up active roles for a less active and less socially involved life. However, by defining disengagement in terms other than associational membership, it should be quite possible for an elderly person to be religiously "engaged" in a nonorganizational sense while being "disengaged" in an organized sense. If a low level of organizational religious behavior is not matched by a low level of nonorganizational religiosity for the elderly person in poor health, then declining health is not necessarily causing "disengagement" but possibly a transformation in the way religiosity and one's religious role is enacted.

The narrow view of disengagement as merely a reduction of associational memberships can be further revealed if we were to compare the level of activity in religious areas with the level of activity in other associational arrangements of the elderly. We should expect that low levels of social activity in general will be matched by low levels of organizational religious behavior. However, if the elderly individual was truly "disengaged" he/she should also maintain a low level of nonorganizational religiosity as well. If this is not the case, then what we have is a disengagement from organizational aspects of religion but continuation of or perhaps a transformation in the way in which a person enacts his/her role as a religious person.

METHODS

Sample. — This sample of 106 elderly living in central Missouri was selected as part of a larger study of extended family living arrangements for the elderly (Mindel, 1975). In particular these elderly lived with relatives, about half with siblings (52) and the other half (54) with children or grandchildren. Apart from a somewhat higher educational level (see below), this sample appears comparable by other demographic measures to the general population of elderly in central Missouri. Due to the requirements of the larger study, this sample was a purposive one gathered by a variety of sampling strategies (e.g., using the city directory, consulting ministers, consulting voluntary associations, etc.). Although not randomly selected, the sample seems appropriate for a preliminary analysis into the issues raised by this paper. Before generalizing the findings of this paper, this study should be replicated on a randomly selected, not regionally restricted, population of elderly.

In many ways this sample of elderly resemble the older population of the region studied. For example, approximately 11% were black; 82% were females; the median age was 77 years of age (ages ranged from 62 to 98, sd = 8.6 years). They appear to be somewhat better educated than the general elderly population with 44% having a grade school education only, 29% with a high school education, and a relatively high 27% with some college education. The relatively high number of college educated elderly may reflect the fact that this study took place in a fairly small (60,000 population) university town.

RELIGIOSITY

Religious attendance was measured by asking subjects to respond to the question "How often do you attend religious services?" They were given six choices: (a) at least twice weekly, (b) once a week, (c) twice a month, (d) 3-4 times a year, (e) only weddings and funerals, (f) never. In addition two scales, one to measure *organizational* religiosity and the other to measure *nonorganizational* religiosity were developed. These scales were first used in a study of religiosity among low income

families in Kansas City, Missouri (Cromwell, Vaughan, & Mindel, 1975). These items were selected from a pool of items on religious behavior. A principal axis factor analysis with a varimax rotation was performed on the items in both the Kansas City study (Cromwell et al., 1975) and the present study. In the Kansas City study the items formed two factors which we identified as organizational and nonorganizational religiosity. In the study presented here three factors emerged: Factor One was identical with factor one in the Kansas City study, namely, "organizational religiosity." Factors Two and Three were identified as "nonorganizational religiosity" and "personal religious feeling." In the Kansas City study these latter two factors emerged as Factor Two. In the present analysis we have combined Factors Two and Three and labeled them "nonorganizational religiosity." Organizational religious activity consisted of the following types of activities: attending religious revivals, attending and taking part in religious services, contributing money to religious activities. Responses were made on a scale of 0-2 with 0 = rarely or never, 1 = now and then, 2 = very often. Nonorganizational activities consisted of: listening to religious services on radio and television, praying alone or with family, listening to religious music, and whether or not religious ideas have helped in understanding one's life. The responses to these questions were scaled the same as the organizational set. The means for both of these scales were calculated, each item having equal weight, resulting in two scores, one for organizational religiosity, the other for non-organizational religiosity.

FINDINGS

Our first question contended that if an elderly person was truly disengaged from his or her religious role, this would be reflected in low levels of organizational and nonorganizational religious behavior and feelings. In Table 1 below the sample of 106 elderly are presented according to church attendance and average number participating in four types of nonorganizational religious activity. Several points need to be made. First, approximately 55% of the sample do not attend religious services at all frequently. Data such as this, while cross-sectional and incomplete insofar as being able to measure change, nonetheless, have served for other researchers (e.g., Bahr, 1970; Morgan, 1937) as a basis for earlier conclusions that older persons disengage from religious activities. Second, and more important, we can see that while a majority of the elderly in this sample do not attend services regularly, a majority of them are nonorganizationally religious "very often." Furthermore, the largest category are those who attend church irregularly but engage in nonorganizational activities very often. Disengagement from both organizational and nonorganizational religious behavior should have resulted in a high Yule's Q value. However the Q value, which measures the degree to which the cases fall on the diagonal, is very low (.17).

Table 1. Frequency of Religious Attendance by Participation in Non-Organizational Forms of Religiosity.

Frequency of Religious Attendance	Participation in Nonorganizational Religiosity			
	Very Often		Now & Then or Never	
	N	%(of total)	N	%(of total)
High (twice a week to twice a month)	32	30.2	16	15.1
Low (3 or 4 times a year or less)	34	32.1	24	22.6

Yule's Q = .17

To look more closely at the types of organizational and nonorganizational behavior, we analyzed the two patterns of religiosity by religious attendance. Table 2 presents the results of this analysis. As one might expect, those who attend church frequently are clearly higher on the organizational items and all differences between the two groups on these four items were statistically significant. However, when we examine the patterns of religiosity of the low attenders relative to the four-item nonorganizational religiosity scale, some interesting patterns emerge.

On all of the items the nonattenders show a relatively high rate of nonorganizational religious activity and feeling. On only one item, prayer, did the high attenders have a statistically significantly higher rate, and this difference might well reflect prayer activity in the context of religious services rather than

Table 2. Frequency of Religious Attendance by Participation in Organizational and Non-Organizational Forms of Religiosity.[a]

	Religious Attendance			
	High	Low		
Forms of Religiosity	$\overline{X}$	$\overline{X}$	t	p
	(N=47)	(N=58)		
Organizational				
Attends revival meetings	.51	.14	3.27	.01
Attends religious services	1.83	.22	19.20	.001
Contribute money to religious organizations	1.77	.95	6.15	.001
Regularly take part in religious activities	1.25	.19	7.81	.001
Organizational religiosity (Summary)	1.34	.37	12.45	.001
Nonorganizational				
Listens to religious services on radio and television	1.23	1.33	.60	.50
Sometimes pray, either alone or with family	1.68	1.38	2.12	.05>p>.02
Listen to religious music	1.47	1.26	1.38	.20>p>.10
Ideas I have learned from my religion sometimes help me understand my own life	1.77	1.52	1.96	.10>p>.05
Nonorganizational religiosity (Summary)	1.54	1.38	.42	.50

[a]Religiosity scores are scaled as follows: rarely/never = 0, Now and then = 1; Very often = 2

prayer at home. In fact, on the factor analysis of this scale on two different samples this item loaded highly on Factor One, the organizational religious activity as well as on the other factor, nonorganizational religious activity. On one item, listening to religious services on radio and television, the nonattenders show a slightly higher rate of activity. In general, differences were slight. However, from the perspective of this paper, the level of non-organizational religious activity of those who do not attend church is considerable and an important finding to those who argue that religion ought to be analyzed and studied apart from the context of formal organizational activity.

The elderly in this sample clearly engage in personal forms of religion which may well be as significant in their lives as the organizational activity is to those who attend church. Frequently those interested in the sociology of religion have focused either on the dogma or belief structure of people or on religiosity determined by patterns of church attendance

(Lenski, 1961). Nonorganizational and non-dogma dimensions of religiosity are frequently discussed (Glock & Stark, 1965) but seldom operationalized in research — and almost never in relationship to religious behavior of the elderly. Clearly those who no longer attend church have not abandoned their religious life so far as they understand it.

Table 3. Participation in Organizational and Nonorganizational Forms of Religiosity by Level of Health Impairment of Elderly and Involvement in Social Activities. [a]

	N	Organizational Religiosity			Nonorganizational Religiosity		
		$\overline{X}$	t	p	$\overline{X}$	t	p
Level of health impairment							
High	41	0.79			1.55		
			.15	ns		1.75	.10>p>.05
Low	65	0.81			1.37		
Involvement in social activities							
High	20	1.25			1.49		
			3.79	.001		.42	ns
Low	86	0.70			1.43		

[a]Religiosity scores are scaled as follows:
Rarely/never = 0; Now and then = 1; Very often = 2

Health and Religious Behavior

By dividing the sample of elderly into two groups based on their level of physical impairment several points emerge (Table 3).

First, it is apparent that impairment has no relationship to level of organizational activity. This is in itself a somewhat surprising finding since poor health or mobility limitations have long been used to explain why the elderly manifest declining levels of church attendance. This finding may be an artifact of the sample, which consists mainly of elderly who live with relatives and who may be more likely to provide transportation services to their elderly relative, including transportation to religious activities.

More importantly relevant to the concern of this paper is the level of nonorganizational religiosity. Our findings indicate that the relatively low level of organizational religious behavior exhibited by the high impairment group is not matched by low levels of non-organizational religious expression. Indeed, the highly impaired group are more religiously involved than the low impaired group. Apparently being ill does not draw one away from religion but perhaps draws one to it in a more subjective, personal way.

Activity and Religious Behavior

In our third hypothesis we suggested that organized religious activity is like many other social activities, and low levels of participation in social activities would be matched by low levels of participation in organizational religious behavior. However, a truly "disengaged" individual should also maintain a low level of nonorganizational religious expression as well. Dividing the sample of elderly into two groups, highly active and low in activity, we find that most of these older persons are relatively inactive (81%). This overall level of activity correlates well with organizational religious behavior. Those who are active in general are also active religiously in an organizational sense. However, the differences disappear almost entirely when we examine religiosity in the more subjective, nonorganization sense. These data again seem to be saying that we must separate religiosity as a community activity from religiosity as a personal subjective experience. Our data indicate that the elderly in this sample might have disengaged from religion in the community activity sense but they have continued to maintain or perhaps transformed the way in which they experience religion.

SUMMARY

This paper suggests several implications for those interested in theory and program opportunities for religious behavior for the elderly. Disengagement theory as frequently untilized in previous research has exaggerated the isolation or separation of the elderly from significant aspects of their pre-retirement lives — that despite disengagement from formal organizational activity they frequently retain significant meaningful relationships with these institutions or organizations. The subjective dimensions of one's relationships with organizations has largely been ignored in research.

Second, it is also suggested that approaches to measuring religion among the elderly, and perhaps among other low income or ethnic groups, have too long ignored the nonorganizational and the nonbelief dimensions of religious behavior. By the standards of previous research in religion among the elderly more than half of our subjects would appear to be non-religious or "withdrawn from religion." This study suggests that religion is still a salient factor in their lives as they understand it despite their lack of participation in its formally organized forms.

REFERENCES

Bahr, H. Aging and religious disaffiliation. *Social Forces,* 1970, *49,* 59-71.

Burgess, E. Family living in the later decades. *Annals of American Academy of Political & Social Science,* 1952, *279,* 107-115.

Cromwell, R., Vaughan, C. W., & Mindel, C. H. Ethnic minority family research in an urban setting: A process of exchange. *American Sociologist* 1975, *10,* 141-150.

Cumming, E., & Henry, W. *Growing old: The process of disengagement.* Basic Books, New York, 1961.

Glock, C. Y., & Stark, R. Religion and society in tension. Rand McNally, Chicago, 1965.

Gray, R. M., & Moberg, D. O. *The church and the older person.* Eerdmans, Grand Rapids, 1962.

Heenan, E. Sociology of religion and the aged: The empirical lacunae. *Journal for the Scientific Study of Religion,* 1972, *2,* 171-176.

Hochschild, A. Disengagement theory: A critique and proposal. *American Sociological Review,* 1975, *40,* 553-569.

Lenski, G. *The religious factor.* Doubleday, New York, 1961.

Maves, P. B. Aging, religion and the church. In C. Tibbitts (Ed.), *Handbook of social gerontology: The social aspects of aging.* Univ. Chicago Press, Chicago, 1960.

Mindel, C. H. Multigenerational family living: A viable alternative for the aged in industrial society, paper presented at the 10th International Congress of Gerontology, Jerusalem, 1975.

Moberg, D. O. Church participation and adjustment in old age. In A. M. Rose & W. A. Peterson (Eds.), *Older people and their social world: The subculture of the aging.* Davis, Philadelphia, 1965. (a)

Moberg, D. O. Religiosity and old age. *Gerontologist,* 1965, *5,* 78-87. (b)

Moberg, D. O. *Spiritual well-being: Background and issues.* White House Conference on Aging, Washington, 1971.

Morgan, C. H. Attitudes and adjustments of old age recipients in State and Metropolitan New York. *Archives of Psychology,* 1937, *214,* 1-131.

19

Religious Motivation in Middle Age: Correlates and Implications[1]

Vira R. Kivett, PhD[2]

The purpose of this study was to determine the relative relationship of self-rated health, age, sex, race, three measures of self-concept (actual, appearance, and ideal), education, occupation, and locus of control to religious motivation in middle age. The subjects were 301 men and women between the ages of 45 and 65 years from 22 randomly selected United Methodist churches. The results of the study show that factors reflective of the process of acculturation such as sex, ideal self-concept, and locus of control maintain the strongest relationship with religious motivation. Women, persons who have high idealized self-concepts, and adults who believe that what happens to them is under their personal control are less likely than others to be extrinsically motivated or to show a "self-centered" dependence upon religion. Consequently, the findings suggest that an important relationship may exist between the "comfort" or "challenge" functions of religion and spiritual well-being in later life for middle-aged groups.

THERE is convincing evidence that several dimensions of religiosity are inextricably bound to measures of adjustment in middle and later life (Blazer & Palmore, 1976; Edwards & Klemmack, 1973; Moberg, 1970; Spreitzer & Snyder, 1974). Research generally shows that indices of mental well-being such as happiness, feelings of usefulness, and personal adjustment increase with religious activity and interests.

The importance of religion to personality structure appears to lie in its function in life rather than in its historical or institutional substance (Allport, 1958; Luckmann, 1967; Pruyser, 1968; Yinger, 1969). Allport and Ross (1967) strongly argue that social scientists who employ the variable "religion" or "religiosity" should keep in mind the crucial distinction between religious attitudes that are intrinsic and extrinsic in order to determine the role religion plays in the individual's life.

Studies have shown that the extrinsic-intrinsic phenomenon constitutes a bipolar continuum of "motivation" that is associated with religious belief and practices (Hunt & King, 1971). Most individuals who profess some degree of religious conviction are thought to fall upon a continuum between two extremes, one of which is extrinsic motivation and the other intrinsic motivation (Hunt & King, 1971). Individuals who fall near the extrinsic pole are persons for whom religion is a self-serving, utilitarian, and self-protective commitment. Religion for these persons assumes a "comfort" function. It provides feelings of group participation at the expense of out groups. Brown (1964) described the extrinsic stance as promoting a dual support system, the components of which he referred to as "inner" and "outer" types. The "inner" type involves the use of religion as a personality support or a "crutch" in crises while the "outer" type is concerned with social gain. Allport and Ross (1967) also noted these two types of extrinsic motivation. Intrinsically motivated individuals internalize the total creed of their faith without reservation and, as a result, religion transcends other primary needs. This type of orientation is viewed as flooding the individual's total life with motivation and meaning. In contrast to these findings, Batson et al. (1978), in a study investigating the relationship between social desirability and religious orientation in adults, concluded that intrinsic religion is closely associated with desire to present a self-righteous image.

Research has shown that adults can be categorized as being intrinsically or extrinsically motivated according to a number of characteristics. Intrinsic-extrinsic qualities have been

[1]This research was supported in part by Grant No. 90-A-512/01 from the AoA, USDHEW.

[2]Asst. Prof. Dept. of Child Development and Family Relations, School of Home Economics, Univ. of North Carolina, Greensboro, NC 27412; and North Carolina Agricultural Experiment Station, Raleigh, NC 27607.

found to be associated with sex, age, education, church attendance, prejudice, and locus of control (Allport & Ross, 1967; Shrauger & Silverman, 1971; Strickland & Shaffer, 1971). Persons who were intrinsically, rather than extrinsically, motivated tended to be female, older, better educated, frequent church attenders, and less prejudiced. Intrinsically motivated individuals were found to possess greater feelings of power over their environment than extrinsically motivated persons (i.e., to perceive that they, not others, had direct control over their life situation).

Religious motivation appears to be a salient force in the successful resolution of life crises in middle and later adulthood. The ability to "transcend," as afforded by an intrinsic religious stance, or to rise above self-centered needs associated with role loss, health, death anxiety, and other circumstances associated with decline or privation is thought to fulfill an important developmental need associated with the aging process (Hunt & King, 1971; Kubler-Ross, 1975; McClusky, no date given, ca 1974).

Research in the area of religious motivation has been limited (Dittes, 1969; Hoge, 1972; Hunt & King, 1971; Strickland & Shaffer, 1971; Willits et al., 1977). Furthermore, a general weakness in the available studies has been a lack of research that shows the interrelationships between physical, psychological, and social variables and religious motivation. The incorporation of the intrinsic-extrinsic concept in multivariate studies can provide important information on the factors influencing differences in religious motivation. Middle adulthood, a period during which several major life crises typically occur, is an especially appropriate focus for studies in motivational concepts (Kuhlen, 1968). Findings from this research area can provide useful information for clinicians, practitioners, and others concerned with the problems of middle age. Of particular value is the identification of adults for whom religion may serve a superficial function and, subsequently, fail to serve an integrative and adjustive function in mid and later life. It was the purpose of the present study to determine the relative importance of several dispositional and situational factors to religious motivation in middle age.

PROCEDURES

Subjects

This study was a secondary analysis of data from earlier research by the author that focused on the antecedents of locus of control in middle age (Kivett, 1976; Kivett et al., 1977). The sample for the study consisted of 337 men and women between the ages of 45 and 65 years who attended church school classes of United Methodist Churches located in a southeastern "Bible Belt" state. All United Methodist Churches within a given geographical district were stratified into one of four categories based upon the size of church membership. Random procedures utilizing a sampling ratio were used to select 22 churches from the 50 available churches that represented a population of approximately 26,000 members. Within the selected churches, adults 45 to 65 years of age who attended church school classes were surveyed. United Methodist church school classes were chosen because of the expressed interest of district clergy leaders in middle age phenomena and in order to reach groups of middle-aged adults with known religious identification.

Five trained interviewers administered questionnaires to all persons attending the church school classes included in the sample. Because of some mixed age groupings, the questionnaires of 217 individuals whose ages fell outside of the desired age span were deleted from the total of 554 respondents, whose ages ranged from 28 to 96 years. Of the remaining eligible adults ($N = 337$), 36 were dropped because of incomplete questionnaires. Most of this fallout was related to respondents leaving the session early in order to fulfill other church responsibilities.

The mean age for the group ($N = 301$) was 53.6 years and the mean educational level was 12.7 years. Approximately equal percentages of males and females were represented in the sample, 47.8 and 52.2, respectively. White adults composed 88.4% of the sample with the remaining 11.6% being Black. The majority of both males (98.0%) and females (83.0%) were married.

Measures

The self-administering questionnaire consisted of four parts: (a) a face sheet for the recording of demographic data and self-rated health; (b) Rotter's Internal-External Scale (Rotter, 1972); (c) Hoge's Intrinsic Religious Motivation Scale (Hoge, 1972); and (d) a semantic differential self-concept instrument (Breytspraak, 1974).

Religious motivation, the dependent variable, was measured by the Intrinsic Religious Motivation Scale. This was a 10-item instrument in Likert form that assessed the dimension ultimate (intrinsic) vs instrumental (extrinsic) religious motivation. Low scores on the scale characterized intrinsically motivated individuals, or those whose master motive was religion and in whom other needs were of secondary significance. In contrast, high scores represented persons who used religion in instrumental ways and subsequently embraced their religious creed lightly, or selectively shaped it to fit more primary needs. The scale's reliability as measured by the Kuder-Richardson Formula 20 has been reported as .90. Item to scale correlations have been found to range from .55 to .80 (Hoge, 1972).

Self-rated health was determined by asking the subjects how they would rate their overall health in comparison to other persons their age — poor, fair, good, or excellent. Responses were coded one through four, respectively. The group mean for self-rated health was 1.9. Males were coded a one and females were assigned a two. Similarly, whites and Blacks were assigned a one and a two, respectively. The actual age at the time of the interview was used.

The three components of self-concept were measured by a semantic differential instrument that consisted of a list of seven bipolar scales, each scored from one to seven. The instrument provided a total score for each of the three concepts: "What I really am" (actual); "What I would like to be" (ideal); and "How I appear to others" (appearance). Positive self-concepts on the scales reflected high levels of activity, optimism, and autonomy and were observed through high scores. In contrast, negative self-concepts produced low scores. A rather high degree of time lapse and sample stability has been found for the semantic differential for young adults, $r = .97$ (Norman, 1969).

The actual number of years of school attended determined the education level. Work type at the time of the interview was recorded as the occupation. Occupational groups followed those utilized by the U. S. Bureau of the Census (1973) and included professional, technical, and kindred workers ($N = 53$); managers and administrators ($N = 50$); sales workers ($N = 27$); clerical and kindred workers ($N = 57$); craftsmen and kindred workers ($N = 31$); operatives ($N = 11$); laborers except farm ($N = 7$); and service workers ($N = 22$). An additional category was added that contained retired persons and housewives ($N = 79$). Service workers were regrouped with laborers for statistical purposes, and farm laborers were dropped because none were included in the sample.

The Rotter Scale was used to measure internal-external locus of control. A belief in external control, or the generalized expectancy that environmental rewards are determined by forces outside one's control, was indicated by high scores on the Rotter Scale. A belief in internal control, or that one has control over one's rewards through one's actions, was indicated by low scores. Test data on the Rotter Scale have shown that internal consistency estimates have been relatively stable, ranging from .65 (split-half techniques) to .79 (Spearman-Brown formula) (Rotter, 1972). Reliability coefficients using the Kuder-Richardson formula have ranged from .70 to .76.

Research Design

A general regression model was used to determine the relative importance of 10 independent variables to the dependent measure, religious motivation. The independent variables were categorized according to type: physical, psychological, or social; and their entry was controlled according to dispositional or situational characteristics. The selection of the independent variables was based upon support from the literature. They included: *Physical* — self-rated health (Maddox & Douglass, 1974); race (Cameron, 1969; Rosen, 1972); sex (Campbell & Fukuyama, 1970; Salisbury, 1964; Strickland & Shaffer, 1971); age (Strickland & Shaffer, 1971); *Psychological* — self-concepts actual, appearance, and desired (Bieri & Lobeck, 1961); *Social* — education, occupation (Strickland & Shaffer, 1971); locus of control (Kivett, 1976; Kivett et al., 1977; Shrauger & Silverman, 1971; Strickland & Shaffer, 1971).

Dichotomous (dummy) variables were created for the classification variables of sex, race, and occupation. Work categories included: professional, administrative, sales workers, clerical, retired/housewives, craftsmen, operatives, and laborers/service workers. The laborers/service workers group was selected as the reference group against which all other occupational groups were compared because of its distinctive characteristics (i.e., a general lack of educational requirements or skills).

MAJOR FINDINGS

Descriptive statistics for the continuous independent variables and religious motivation are found in Table 1.

Table 1. Mean, Range, and Standard Deviations for Continuous Independent Variables and Religious Motivation.

Variable (N = 301)	Mean	Range (Possible)	SD
Age	53.6	45-65	5.5
Education	12.7	0+	2.6
Self-concept (actual)	39.9	1-49	6.2
Self-concept (ideal)	43.6	1-49	5.7
Self-concept (appearance)	39.5	1-49	6.3
Locus of control	8.4	0-50	4.1
Religious motivation	18.9	1-50	4.5

A significant proportion of the variation in religious motivation scores was accounted for by the 10 independent variables under investigation, $r = .37$ ($r^2 = .13$) $p < .001$ (Table 2). Three variables, one representing each of the three categories of factors (physical, psychological, and social), accounted for almost all of the variance explained. These variables included: sex, ideal self-concept, and locus of control (Table 3).

As observed from the significant standardized betas in Table 3, sex differences accounted for more variation in religious motivation scores than other differences. Second in importance to religious motivation was ideal self-concept, and locus of control was third in importance. Females had internalized their religious beliefs more than males. Adults who perceived having control over their environmental rewards (internals) were more intrinsically motivated in their religious behavior than externally perceiving adults. Individuals who had high idealized self-concepts reflected low religious motivation scores (intrinsic motivation).

None of the independent variables showed spurious relationships with the criterion variable, religious motivation, despite some multicollinearity (Table 3). Pearson product moment correlations performed on the continuous independent variables showed several important relationships. Age was related to education, and health and education were

Table 2. Analysis of Variance of the Sources in Variation in Religious Motivation Scores Comprising Regression.

Source	df	Sequential SS	F Value (Unadjusted)	Partial SS	F Value (Adjusted)
Self-rated health	1	.01	.00	1.46	.08
Race	1	51.74	2.75	35.59	1.89
Sex	1	260.49	13.83***	160.62	8.53**
Age	1	44.11	2.34	45.07	2.39
Self-concept (actual)	1	18.98	1.01	16.06	.85
Self-concept (appearance)	1	21.49	1.14	58.89	3.13
Self-concept (ideal)	1	80.57	4.28*	76.73	4.08*
Education	1	58.99	3.13	1.96	.10
Occupation	7	205.46	1.56	212.07	1.61
Locus of control	1	84.78	4.50*	84.78	4.50*

$r = .37$ $r^2 = .13$ $df = 16,284$ $F = 2.74***$

Note: N = 301
  *$p < .05$
  **$p < .01$
  ***$p < .001$

Table 3. Beta Weights and Level of Significance of Independent Variables in Religious Motivation Analysis.

Variables	b Values	B (standardized)	t
Physical			
Self-rated health	.11	.02	.28
White vs Black	−.59	−.08	−1.38
Male vs female	.93	.20	2.92**
Age	−.08	−.09	−1.55
Psychological			
Self-concept (actual)	−.06	−.08	−.92
Self-concept (appearance)	.11	.15	1.77
Self-concept (ideal)	−.11	−.14	−2.02*
Social			
Education	−.04	−.02	−.32
Occupation[a]			
Professional vs Laborers	−1.26	−.13	−1.60
Administrators vs Laborers	−.25	−.03	−.37
Salesworkers vs Laborers	.65	.06	.77
Clerical vs Laborers	−1.26	−.14	−1.95
Retired Housewives vs Laborers	−.83	−.08	−1.01
Craftsmen vs Laborers	3.34	.24	2.46
Operatives vs Laborers	−.00	−.00	−.00
Locus of control	.14	.13	2.12*

[a]The occupational category "laborers" also contained service workers.

*$p < .05$

**$p < .01$

associated with actual self-concept. All three measures of self-concept were interrelated and locus of control was correlated with health and appearance self-concept. Older middle-aged adults were characterized by less education and poorer self-ratings of health. Positive actual self-concept increased with educational level, positive appearance self-concept and high idealized self-concept. Internal locus of control was observed more frequently among persons with good self-ratings of health and positive appearance self-concepts than among others. These examples of multicollinearity reduced the amount of unique variance explained by the factors, and served to lower the total amount of variance explained by the model.

DISCUSSION AND IMPLICATIONS

Considerable emphasis has been given in the literature to the important correspondence between various dimensions of "religiosity" and adjustment in middle and late adulthood. Self-concept, locus of control, and other variables such as sex, race, and age have been independently linked to some aspect of the religion variable. Few studies, however, have sought to investigate the relative importance of these variables to religious factors, and in particular to religious motivation.

The present study shows that the variables, sex, ideal self-concept, and locus of control, are important to religious motivation regardless of the influence of health, age, education, occupation, and actual and appearance self-concepts. Sex of the adult is paramount to type of motivation, followed by ideal self-concept, and locus of control (perceived control). Although the correlates of religious motivation represent physical, psychological, as well as social phenomena, they show considerable commonality in that each factor is highly reflective of the acculturation process.

Compatibility with Other Research

The observation of sex differences in religious motivation (i.e., that females are more intrinsic or internalize their religious beliefs to a greater extent than males) supports a general notion in the sociological literature. An example is found in the writing of Salisbury (1964) who pointed out that women are more "religious" than men in terms of several indices that include belief, attendance at church services, personal meditation practices, and religious activities. Most churches, according to Salisbury, have more women than men communicants. Campbell and Fukuyama (1970), conducted a study on more than 8,000 members of a single denomination, and found that females had higher scores than males on three church participation indices that included: belief orientation, religious knowledge, and devotional orientation. Results from the study also showed that women were less critical of the church and stronger "believers" than men. Strickland and Shaffer (1971) studied religious motivation in three age groups of adults 17 to 60 years of age. They found that religiously intrinsic subjects were more likely to be females than males. The analysis that generated this finding, however, utilized combined data from both young and old age groups.

The finding from the present study regarding the importance of ideal self-concept to religious motivation supports a premise by Thompson (1972) that self-concept appears to be an index of numerous aspects of personality and behavior. Similarly, Bieri and Lobeck (1961) stated that self-concept is a product primarily of the social learning of the individual, and as a result, it should be possible to demonstrate systematic differences in the self-concepts of persons whose social experiences have differed in fundamental ways (e.g., religious experiences).

A number of religious doctrines appear to have implications for the development of attitudes about the individual's potential for control over what happens to him. However, it has been found that across both liberal and conservative church groups, individuals assessed as intrinsic in religious belief professed an expectancy of internal control of reinforcement, or perceived that they, not others, were responsible for their rewards and punishments (Strickland & Shaffer, 1971). The importance of the religious variable to perceived control was documented further by Shrauger and Silverman (1971) who reported that among college students, persons who were more involved in religious activities perceived themselves as having more control over what happens to them. This observation was mediated by sex.

The intrinsic-internal relationship was also observed by Kivett (1976) and Kivett et al. (1977) in an earlier primary analysis of the data base reported here. Results of the study showed that persons who perceived that they had control over the rewards and punishments from their environment, internalized their religious creed and did not use their religion in instrumental ways. In contrast to the present study, the earlier study, which utilized the same regression model, looked at the antecedent importance of the religious variable to locus of control. In this context, religious motivation as an antecedent of locus of control contributed to more total variance explained in the equation ($r^2 = .19$ vs $r^2 = .13$) than when this process was reversed (i.e., when locus of control was treated as an antecedent of religious motivation [present study]). Locus of control was found to have more univariate relationships with the other antecedents than did religious motivation. As a result, when incorporated as an antecedent, the amount of unique variance contributed by the independent variables was reduced, more so than in the model utilizing locus of control as the dependent measure. This observation may have implications for the antecedent importance of one of these variables over another, but this is not clear.

The observation in the present study of the relative unimportance of education, occupation, and age variables to religious motivation in adulthood is not compatible with the findings of Strickland and Shaffer (1971). They observed older age and upper-socioeconomic status as predictive of an intrinsic religious stance. It should be noted, however, that the Strickland and Shaffer study employed a much wider age group than the study reported here. This discrepancy, as well as the effects of multicollinearity, could have contributed to the differences in findings between the two studies with regard to age, education, and occupation.

Little, if any, research has considered the relationship between health, per se, and religious motivation. The social deprivation theory as described by Glock (1972) and Glock and Stark (1965) advanced the notion of the "consoling" or "comfort" function of the church among persons experiencing certain social, physical, or psychological deprivations. Based upon this theory, it might be expected that persons experiencing privation, such as poor health, minority group membership, and low educational and occupational levels, would turn to religion in ways that would characterize them as either intrinsically or extrinsically motivated (e.g., persons who use religion to transcend self-centered needs or those who use religion instrumentally to serve personal needs). The lack of a significant association between health, race, education, and occupation and the religious variable in the present study, does not lend support to the deprivation theory. Support for the theory, however, is supplied through the finding relative to locus of control.

Implications of the Study

A major implication of this study is that men and women in middle-age can be expected to manifest different levels of commitment to their religious belief because of basic sex differences in religious motives. Shrauger and Silverman (1971) explained these differences through the suggestion that males and females attend to different aspects of religious teachings or they have different motives for being involved in religious activities. Because religious behavior may be viewed as more appropriate and desirable for females than males, women may have focused more on those aspects of religious training which emphasize injunctions to behave desirably so they may achieve favorable ends or avoid punishment. This explanation relied heavily upon the behavioristic view of the importance of positive reinforcement in the perpetuation of desirable behavior (e.g., the social recognition that may come to females who "live" their religious creed to the fullest extent). Batson et al. (1978), for example, pointed out an important relationship between an intrinsic religious stance and social desirability (i.e., that an intrinsic religious orientation relates to a desire to present oneself as more righteous than one actually is). Since the norms regarding religious involvement in our society are not as strong for males as for females, the value of "religious behaviors" in achieving positive reinforcement may be less salient for men.

The more extrinsic religious stance among males appears to be an example of the "outer" type of extrinsic motivation as described by Brown (1964). The pressures to achieve up-ward social mobility through occupational advancement may encourage males to use church membership and participation for the purposes of meeting the right people, making important business contacts, or for acceptance in the community. Such force is not generally exerted upon the majority of middle-aged females.

Another possible explanation of the male-female differential in religious motivation may also lie, in part, in the "social deprivation" theory (Glock, 1972; Glock & Stark, 1965). Since females still suffer relative social deprivation, especially those currently in middle age, they may use religion to transcend personal concerns of inadequacy of education, sex status, etc., by regarding religion as the master motive in life. In this perspective, religion performs a "challenge" function. Females' low scores on the religious motivation scale indicate that women tend to choose the intrinsic "challenge" function rather than the extrinsic "comfort" function although both functions are an alternative to them under the social deprivation theory.

A second implication of the present study is the apparent importance of the intrinsic-extrinsic notion of religious motivation to self-perception (i.e., self-concept and perceived control). The measure of "ideal" self-concept used in the study suggests the kind of individual the adult would "like to be" as pertains to activity level, extent of optimism or pessimism, and autonomy. The observation that high idealized self-concepts are more characteristic of intrinsically than extrinsically motivated adults, relates to the work of Gorlow and Schroeder (1972). They found that members of selected Protestant denominations could be classified according to eight major "factors" with respect to motives for participating in the religious experience. "Self-improvers," their second most important factor, clustered adults together who valued the religious experience for the purposes of increasing self-understanding, finding a way to deal with their limitations, and heightening goals. Given this perspective, it should be expected that individuals who strongly adhere to religious prescriptions (intrinsic motivation) would also reflect high "idealized" self-concepts.

The internalization of religion also characterizes adults with feelings of control over their lives. For example, Strickland and Shaffer (1971), following their study of religious motivation and perceived control, stated that individuals who see themselves as having control over what happens to them (internals) are likely to be persons who do not feel buffeted by outside demands and do not use religion as a self-serving and manipulative device to support themselves.

It might appear that external perception suggests that no control over one's fate includes God or powers beyond the individual's control. A close theoretical examination, however, shows that persons who internalize their religious beliefs and use them as a basis for making decisions in their daily lives are, in effect, exercising personal control over their environmental rewards (Strickland & Shaffer, 1971). Strickland and Shaffer suggest that persons with an intrinsic religious orientation, because of their perceptions of control over their environment, might be expected in religious activities (as in social movements, including social action) to seek understanding and to move more actively to accomplish their set goals with a belief that their actions are influential and can lead to change. This religious stance appears to be important in the processes necessary for successful adaptation in middle and later life. Similarly, there is considerable evidence that individuals who have a strong belief that their own behavior determines their life course are likely to: (1) be more alert to those aspects of the environment which provide useful information for their future behavior; (2) take steps to improve their environmental condition; (3) place greater value on skill or achievement reinforcements and be generally more concerned with their ability, and particularly their failure; and (4) be resistive to subtle attempts to influence them (Rotter, 1972). It should be noted that these characteristics of internally perceiving adults also closely parallel two of the eight motives for participating in the religious experience as seen by Gorlow and Schroeder (1972) (e.g., self-improvement, and guidance).

The cross-sectional nature of the present study does not allow for developmental implications. It is observed that the middle-aged do not differ in religious motivation according to age group. This finding is probably related to the short age span characteristics of the sample. Several investigators have spoken

to the stability of the intrinsic-extrinsic phenomenon and have suggested that it may be a basic, pervasive personality variable which manifests itself as a consistent cognitive style (Allen & Spilka, 1967; Allport & Ross, 1967; Hunt & King, 1971). If this concept is supported in future research, the intrinsic-extrinsic variable could be used to understand and predict numerous facets of secular behavior and not just that behavior described as "religious." Hunt and King's (1971) studies in religious motivation strongly support the antecedent importance of the religious variable. As a result, they suggest that religion is probably involved in the personality structure at its deepest levels and probably in multiple ways.

Although several variables in the present study were found to be important to religious motivation in the middle years, it must be recognized that the majority of the difference found in motivation was unexplained. The relative homogeneity of the group studied in reference to education, health, and occupation contributed in part to this occurrence. Other possible contributors to the small amount of variance explained in religious motivation may have been weaknesses in the measurement instruments or in the selection of multicollinear independent variables. Care should be taken in generalizing the results of this study to other religious affiliated groups and to other geographical areas.

SUMMARY

Data were collected on 301 men and women between the ages of 45 and 65 years from 22 randomly selected United Methodist churches within a given geographical district. The overall purpose of the study was to determine the relative relationship of self-rated health, age, sex, race, three measures of self-concept (actual, appearance, and ideal), education, occupation, and locus of control to religious motivation in middle age.

The results of the study show that factors reflective of the process of acculturation such as sex, ideal self-concept, and locus of control maintain the strongest relationships with religious motivation. These variables suggest those middle-aged groups for whom an important relationship may exist between the "comfort" or "challenge" function of religion and spiritual well-being in later life. Persons who are intrinsically motivated (i.e., those who internalize their religious creed more strongly) and seek religion for its "challenge" function (transcendence of self-interests and needs) are more likely to: (1) be female; (2) perceive that they, not others, have power over their environment; and (3) have high "idealized" self-concepts. Adults representing extrinsically motivated individuals appear to be attracted to religion because of either its "inner" or "outer" function in their lives. Males who are extrinsically motivated appear to be drawn to religion for its "outer" function, or for the social gain that religious membership might afford them. The "inner" type of extrinsic motivation, or the attraction of religion as a "crutch" or a help in crisis, without total commitment of the religious creed, is more common among adults who perceive relatively little power over their lives or who show indications of low "idealized" self-concepts.

In terms of the implications for spiritual well-being, the study points out those middle-aged groups for whom religion may function in rather superficial ways, and, subsequently, fail to effectively meet the spiritual needs of middle and later life. On the other hand, the data also show those groups who internalize their religious creed in a manner that will assist them in the transcendence of personal interests and needs that, reportedly, become more manifest with the passing years.

REFERENCES

Allen, R. O., & Spilka, B. Committed and consensual religion: A specification of religion-prejudice relationship. *Journal for the Scientific Study of Religion*, 1967, 6, 191-206.

Allport, G. W. *The nature of prejudice*. Doubleday, New York, 1958.

Allport, G. W., & Ross, J. M. Personal religious orientation and prejudice. *Journal of Personality and Social Psychology*, 1967, 5, 432-443.

Batson, C. D., Naifeh, S. V., & Pate, S. Social desirability, religious orientation, and racial prejudice. *Journal for the Scientific Study of Religion*, 1978, 17, 31-41.

Bieri, J., & Lobeck, R. Self-concept differences in relation to identification, religion and social class. *Journal of Abnormal and Social Psychology*, 1961, 62, 94-98.

Blazer, D., & Palmore, E. Religion and aging in a longitudinal panel. *Gerontologist*, 1976, 16, 82-85.

Breytspraak, L. M. Achievement and the self-concept in middle age. In E. Palmore (Ed.), *Normal aging II*. Duke Univ. Press, Durham, NC, 1974.

Brown, L. B. Classifications of religious orientation. *Journal for the Scientific Study of Religion*, 1964, 4, 91-99.

Cameron, P. Valued aspects of religion to Negroes and whites. *Proceedings of the 77th Annual Convention of the American Psychological Association*, 1969, 4 (Pt. 2), 741-742.

Campbell, T. C., & Fukuyama, Y. *The fragmented layman*. Pilgram Press, Philadelphia, 1970.

Dittes, J. E. Psychology of religion. In G. Lindzey & E. Aronson (Eds.), *The handbook of social psychology*. (2nd Ed.) (Vol. 5) Addison-Wesley, Reading, MA, 1969.

Edwards, J. N., & Klemmack, D. L. Correlates of life satisfaction: A reexamination. *Journal of Gerontology*, 1973, 28, 497-502.

Glock, C. Y. On the study of religious commitment. In J. E. Faulkner (Ed.), *Religion's influence in contemporary society*. Charles Merrill, Columbus, OH, 1972.

Glock, C. Y., & Stark, R. *Religion and society in tension*. Rand McNally, Chicago, 1965.

Gorlow, L., & Schroeder, H. E. Motives for participating in the religious experience. In J. E. Faulkner (Ed.), *Religion's influence in contemporary society*. Charles Merrill, Columbus, OH, 1972.

Hoge, D. R. A validated intrinsic religious motivation scale. *Journal for the Scientific Study of Religion*, 1972, 11, 369-376.

Hunt, R., & King, M. The intrinsic-extrinsic concept: A review and evaluation. *Journal for the Scientific Study of Religion*, 1971, 10, 339-356.

Kivett, V. R. Physical, psychological and social predictors of locus of control among middle-aged adults (Doctoral dissertation, Univ. of North Carolina at Greensboro, 1976). *Dissertation Abstracts International*, 1976, 37, 2481-B. (Univ. Microfilms No. 76-24,944, 153.)

Kivett, V. R., Watson, J. A., & Busch, J. C. The relative importance of physical, psychological, and social variables to locus of control orientation in middle age. *Journal of Gerontology*, 1977, 32, 203-210.

Kübler-Ross, E. *Death: The final stage of growth*. Prentice-Hall, Englewood Cliffs, NJ, 1975.

Kuhlen, R. G. Developmental changes in motivation during the adult years. In B. L. Neugarten (Ed.), *Middle age and aging*. Univ. of Chicago Press, Chicago, 1968.

Luckmann, T. *The invisible religion: The problem of religion in modern society*. Macmillan, New York, 1967.

Maddox, G. L., & Douglass, E. B. Self-assessment of health. In E. Palmore (Ed.), *Normal aging II*. Duke Univ. Press, Durham, NC, 1974.

McClusky, H. Y. Education for aging: The scope of the field and perspectives for the future. In S. Grabowski & W. D. Mason (Eds.), *Learning for aging*, Washington, DC. Adult Education Assoc. of the U.S., no date given, ca 1974.

Moberg, D. O. Religion in the later years. In A. M. Hoffman (Ed.), *The daily needs and interests of older persons*. Charles C Thomas, Springfield, IL, 1970.

Norman, W. T. Stability characteristics of the semantic differential. In J. G. Snider & C. E. Osgood (Eds.), *Semantic differential technique: A sourcebook*. Aldine, Chicago, 1969.

Pruyser, P. *A dynamic psychology of religion.* Harper and Row, New York, 1968.

Rosen, B. C. Race, ethnicity and the achievement syndrome. In S. S. Guterman (Ed.), *Black psyche: The modal personality patterns of Black Americans.* Glendessary Press, Berkeley, CA, 1972.

Rotter, J. C. Some implications of a social learning theory for the prediction of goal directed behavior from testing procedures. In J. B. Rotter, J. E. Chance, & E. J. Phares (Eds.), *Applications of a social learning theory of personality.* Holt, Rinehart, & Winston, New York, 1972.

Salisbury, W. S. *Religion in American culture,* Dorsey Press, Homewood, IL, 1964.

Shrauger, J. S., & Silverman, R. E. The relationship of religious background and participation to locus of control. *Journal for the Scientific Study of Religion,* 1971, *10,* 11-16.

Spreitzer, E., & Snyder, E. E. Correlates of life satisfaction among the aged. *Journal of Gerontology,* 1974, *29,* 454-458.

Strickland, B. R., & Shaffer, S. I-E, I-E, & F. *Journal for the Scientific Study of Religion,* 1971, *10,* 366-369.

Thompson, W. *Correlates of the self concept: Studies on the self concept and rehabilitation.* Dede Wallace Ctr., Nashville, TN, 1972.

U. S. Bureau of the Census. *Census of population: 1970 subject reports, Final report, Occupational characteristics,* (PC (2) - 7A). USGPO, Washington, DC, 1973.

Willits, F. K., Bealer, R. C., & Crider, D. M. Changes in individual attitudes toward traditional morality: A 24-year follow-up study. *Journal of Gerontology,* 1977, *32,* 681-688.

Yinger, J. M. A structural examination of religion. *Journal of the Scientific Study of Religion,* 1969, *8,* 88-99.

Life Changes and Perceptions of Life and Death Among Older Men and Women[1]

20

Pat M. Keith, PhD[2]

Although social scientists have suggested that feelings about life and death may be related, for the most part, theories of social gerontology have developed independently of conceptions of death and finitude. This study examines whether life changes are associated with concurrent life and death attitude types among older men and women. Data were analyzed from structured interviews conducted with 214 men and 354 women during the second phase of a longitudinal study of the aged in small towns.[3] Individuals were identified as positivists, negativists, activists, and passivists. Controlling for sex and income, changes in four life areas were examined in relation to these perceptions of life and death. Some of the patterns varied by sex, suggesting that the same changes have different implications for the well-being of men and women in late life. In general, those who had experienced discontinuity were more frequently negativists or passivists, while continuity tended to characterize positivists and activists.

T HIS study examines whether life changes that are assumed to contribute to independent assessments of life and death also influence concurrent life and death attitude types among older men and women. A fourfold typology is used to assist in the identification of factors associated with perceptions of life and death.

Development of a typology of life-death attitudes. — Theories of social gerontology, for the most part, have developed independently of conceptions of death and finitude (Marshall, 1975). Indeed, successful aging has been defined as the maintenance of activities or even expansiveness in life interests. Perhaps the exclusion of death in some theories of aging is most evident in the preoccupation with evaluations of life.

In fact, much of the theorizing has centered around prediction and explanation of various assessments of life. Empirically this approach is reflected in measures of satisfaction, morale,

adjustment, or other indices of adaptation. The neglect of death in some of the major theories of aging led Marshall (1975) to observe that "A reviewer of the social-psychological literature of gerontology might well conclude that death is not considered the inevitable termination of the life span."

Yet, the salience of death for the aged is well-documented. Cumming and Henry (1961) observed that it is reasonable that those who are approaching death will give some thought to it as well as to how their death will affect persons with whom they are close. In general, the aged do talk and think more about death but they also fear it less than those in other age groups (Kalish, 1976). As they age, people are socialized to their own death. Not only is their death more imminent but they have worked through the deaths of age mates, family, and friends, and have a greater repertoire of death experiences.

Two meanings of death for the aged that seem to have significance for evaluations of life were suggested by Kalish (1976). First, death as an organizer of time: old people are known to have limited time. Second, death as loss: old people are known to have suffered many death-imposed losses, as well as other

[1] Revised version of a paper presented at the annual meeting of the Society for the Study of Social Problems, 1978. This research was supported by the AoA, Office of Human Development, HEW, and with assistance from the Research Council of the Graduate School and the Univ. Extension Div., Univ. of Missouri-Columbia. I wish to thank the late Prof. Terence Pihlblad and Dr. Harold Freshley for their help and encouragement.

[2] Dept. of Sociology & Anthropology, 104 East Hall, Ames, IA 50011.

[3] C. T. Pihlblad, R. Hessler, H. Freshley, *The Rural Elderly Eight Years Later*, Univ. of Missouri, Columbia, MO, 1976.

losses that are often associated with the dying process (Kalish, 1976). This research focuses on the relationship between change, including losses, and perceptions of life and death.

Social scientists have suggested that feelings about life and death may be related (Erikson, 1963; Parsons, 1963). It has been theorized, for example, that fear of death develops in large part because it precludes the attainment of valued goals (Dumont & Foss, 1972). In fact, some evidence indicates that persons who have attained most of their life goals are less likely to fear death (Diggory & Rothman, 1961). These individuals would be apt to reflect positively on both their present activities and death as an aspect of the future. Persons holding this attitude pattern will be referred to as positivists.

Erikson noted that a loss of ego integration would be represented by a fear of death. And reminders of impending death may lead to despair which "expresses the feeling that time is now short, too short for the attempt to start another life and to try out alternate roads to integrity" (Erikson, 1963). Various losses occurring with old age have been identified as sources of despair that are reflected in death concerns (Rhudick & Dibner, 1961). Thus, a second type of response to life and death may be to devalue and feel negatively toward both (described here as negativists).

There is also the contingency that even though valued goals have been achieved, the attainments will not be sufficient to offset a fear of death. In fact, death may be perceived as diminishing the opportunity for continued fulfillment of goals. A reinforcement perspective suggests that those who are continuing to achieve their expectations will express greater anxiety about death in that death will end the pleasure they obtain from life (Nelson, 1974). Indeed, death as a foreclosing of ambition has been found to be a more distasteful prospect than loss of life (Diggory & Rothman, 1961). Individuals with these attitudes will be described as activists.

Finally, a fourth potential response pattern suggests that death will not be viewed with fear or concern, but rather as a respite from the disappointments of life because attempts to attain life goals may have been so overshadowed by failure. The awareness that life, which has been unpleasant, will soon end is combined with a forward-looking attitude toward death. Indeed, death may be accepted as a positive adjustment to life. Persons exhibiting this pattern will be referred to as passivists.

Life changes and perceptions of life and death. — Old age is frequently accompanied by a series of life changes, many of which are interrelated and involuntary. For the most part, they are decremental and represent reductions in capabilities that would otherwise facilitate morale and well-being. Considerable research has suggested that psychological well-being is diminished by personal and role losses. Lemon et al. (1972) have observed that a role change may involve a disturbance in interaction patterns and social rewards so that when a role support is altered, it may have lasting consequences for adjustment. Continuity in activities, however, is associated with a more favorable future time perspective of which conceptions of death may be a part (Chappell, 1975).

Thus, the literature suggests that role losses in old age will be reflected in perceptions of both life and death. Although data are not available to predict the characteristics of each of the attitude types, information derived from separate investigations of life satisfaction and death may be used to indicate some of the more salient transitions in late life.

Current levels of contact with friends and family (Edwards & Klemmack, 1973; Lemon et al., 1972; Martin, 1973; Pihlblad & Adams, 1972), membership in formal organizations (Palmore & Luikart, 1972), health status (Adams, 1971; Bull & Aucoin, 1975; Edwards & Klemmack, 1973; Smith & Lipman, 1972), and marital status (Berardo, 1970; Harvey & Bahr, 1974; Hutchison, 1975) are differentially associated with life satisfaction. Presumably changes in some of these areas may reflect a loss of role supports that are important for perceived well-being (Lemon et al., 1972).

In this research, changes in four life areas were examined in relation to perceptions of life and death: change in marital status, health, church involvement, and informal family and friend contacts. Although they do not include all of the changes taking place in late life, they represent some of the more important personal and role transitions that may occur. Further, the changes vary somewhat in the extent to which they may be involuntary, unanticipated, and highly central to an individual's life style, all factors that may be associated with the disruptiveness of change (Seltzer, 1976). Finally, as suggested by Lemon et al. (1972) the life areas encompass opportunities for both intimacy and somewhat more formal interaction.

METHODOLOGY

Sample. — Data were analyzed from structured interviews conducted with 214 men and 354 women during the second phase of a longitudinal study of the aged in small towns. Respondents resided in towns of 250 to 5,000 in a midwestern state. In the initial study respondents were randomly selected from a sample of towns drawn to be representative of small towns in the state (Adams, 1971; Pihlblad & Adams, 1972).

The respondents ranged in age from 72 to 99 with a median age of 79. The sample was Caucasian and was predominantly Protestant. Over one-half of the men and women had eight years or less of education. The median income for men was $3386 and $2041 for women.

Life change measures. — Except where noted, measures of change referred to perceived change during the eight-year interval between interviews. Following Gubrium (1974), current marital status was categorized to reflect change in social support. The widowed, divorced, or separated had experienced discontinuity while the married and never married had continuous social support.

Health was evaluated as better, about the same, or worse than eight years before. Since the number of respondents who had improved health was too small for separate analysis, they were categorized with those who had remained the same, thus representing persons who had not experienced decremental change.

Respondents reported the extent to which their contacts with friends and church activities were more, about the same, or less than they were eight years previously. Because of cell size those who had not experienced decremental change were placed in the same category. Change in church involvement was used as the measure of formal participation. Church activity is a dominant form of activity among the aged (Cutler, 1976) and remains one of the salient activities after bereavement (Heyman & Gianturco, 1974).

---

[4]In a longitudinal study, perceived change was found to be a better predictor of life satisfaction than actual change (Keith, 1977).

Fig. 1. Orientations toward life and death.

Measurements of attitudes toward life and death. — Life satisfaction was assessed by ten items (Wood et al., 1969). Response categories were agree, disagree, and do not know. Scores were obtained by summing across the ten items with higher scores indicating greater life satisfaction. The coefficient of reliability was .67 (Alpha). To form the typology, scores were divided by the mean ($\overline{X}= 12$, sd= 4.15). Types I and II (positivists and activists) had life satisfaction scores above the mean while Types III and IV (passivists and negativists) had life satisfaction scores below the mean (Fig. 1).

Attitudes toward death were examined by 12 Likert-type items reflecting the extent to which death was evaluated positively or negatively. A panel of three judges categorized the items as to whether they reflected "positive" or "negative" attitudes toward death; they revealed consensus on 11 of the 12 items (Table 1). Response categories were strongly agree to strongly disagree (0-4). Scores were obtained by summing across the items with higher scores indicating more positive feelings about death. The coefficient of reliability was .71 (Alpha). To form the typology, the scores were divided at the mean ($\overline{X} = 32$., sd = 6.94). Respondents who had more positive perceptions of death were located in Types I and III (positivists and passivists, Fig. 1). Persons with more negative attitudes toward death were classified in Types II and IV (activists and negativists).

Finally, although there is some contradictory evidence, sex, age, and income have been observed to impact perceptions of both life and death. Since the way in which life changes are

Table 1. Summary of Responses to Attitude Toward Death Items.

Items	Strongly Agree		Moderately Agree		Uncertain		Moderately Disagree		Strongly Disagree	
	N	%	N	%	N	%	N	%	N	%
(1) Do you agree or disagree that death is peaceful? (+)[a]	245	43.1	122	21.5	186	32.7	11	1.9	4	.7
(2) Do you agree or disagree that death is painful? (−)	50	8.8	56	9.9	277	48.8	54	9.5	131	23.1
(3) Do you agree or disagree that death is lonely? (−)	92	16.2	62	10.9	242	42.6	53	9.3	119	21.0
(4) Do you agree or disagree that death is something to fear? (−)	59	10.4	26	4.6	99	17.4	55	9.7	329	57.9
(5) Do you agree or disagree that death is part of a Divine Plan? (+)	442	77.8	26	4.6	87	15.3	4	.7	8	1.4
(6) Do you agree or disagree that to die is to lose everything? (−)	94	16.5	24	4.2	155	27.3	44	7.7	251	44.2
(7) Do you agree or disagree that death is something to look forward to? (+)	164	28.9	71	12.5	154	27.1	54	9.5	125	22.0
(8) Do you agree or disagree that death is the natural end to life? (+)	369	65.0	63	11.1	111	19.5	6	1.1	19	3.3
(9) Do you agree or disagree that the purpose of death is difficult to understand? (−)[b]	187	32.9	47	8.3	151	26.6	51	9.0	132	23.2
(10) Do you agree or disagree that death is something to ignore? (−)	38	6.7	19	3.3	159	28.0	44	7.7	308	54.2
(11) Do you agree or disagree that death leads to something better than life as we know it? (+)	10	1.8	2	.4	115	20.2	46	8.1	395	69.5
(12) Do you agree or disagree that death is abrupt and violent? (−)	29	5.1	21	3.7	268	47.2	80	14.1	170	29.9

[a](+) Denotes items judges rated as positive and (−) denotes items rated as negative. Scoring was reversed for positive items.

[b]There was consensus on all items except number 9. Two of the three judges rated it negative and one rated it positive.

experienced may vary with these factors, they were considered as control variables.

The differences in role supports accessible to men and women are of special interest. Not only may men and women undergo changes with varying frequency but how they confront the stress created by change may differ and be reflected in orientations toward life and death. Lowenthal et al. (1975), for example, suggested that women may be less able to deal with stress created by life changes. Other research, however, has indicated that women may adjust to certain changes (e.g., widowhood) better than men (Berardo, 1970).

RESULTS

Attitudes toward life and death. — Although one-third of the men and women were positivists, over one-quarter held negative attitudes toward life and death. The remaining 40% were about equally divided between activists and passivists (Fig. 1). Men and women differed somewhat in their perceptions of life and death in that women were more likely to be positivists and men had a greater tendency to be negativists (Table 2). Men were also more likely to be activists while slightly larger proportions of women tended to be passivists.

Level of income also influenced perceptions of life and death (Table 2) in that those with higher incomes were more likely to evaluate both life and death positively. Persons with lower incomes were more frequently passivists and negativists than their counterparts who were somewhat better off financially.

Age, however, was not associated with the attitude types. This may be due in part to the age homogeneity of the sample. Remaining analyses examine how sex and income relate

Table 2. Sex, Income and Attitude Type.[a]

Attitude Type		Sex						Income					
		Male		Female		Total		Low		High		Total	
Death	Life	N	%	N	%	N	%	N	%	N	%	N	%
(1) +	+	57	26.6	132	37.3	189	33.3	130	29.5	50	46.1	189	33.3
(2) −	+	54	25.2	69	19.5	123	21.7	93	21.1	30	23.4	123	21.7
(3) +	−	37	17.3	71	20.1	108	19.0	93	21.1	15	11.7	108	19.0
(4) −	−	66	30.8	82	23.2	148	26.1	124	28.2	24	18.8	148	26.1
Total		214	37.7	354	62.3	568	100.0	440	77.5	128	22.5	568	100.0

$X^2 = 10.85; df = 3; p < .01$ $\qquad$ $X^2 = 16.41; df = 3; p < .001$

[a]N's vary due to incomplete data.

Table 3. Change in Marital Status and Attitude Type by Sex and Income.

Attitude Type		Men				Women				High Income				Low Income			
		Continuity		Change		Continuity		Change		Continuity		Change		Continuity		Change	
Death	Life	N	%	N	%	N	%	N	%	N	%	N	%	N	%	N	%
(1) +	+	48	30.2	9	16.4	29	42.6	103	36.0	41	48.2	18	41.9	36	25.4	94	31.5
(2) −	+	45	28.3	9	16.4	18	26.5	51	17.8	22	25.9	8	18.6	41	28.9	52	17.4
(3) +	−	26	16.4	11	20.0	8	11.8	63	22.0	9	10.6	6	14.0	25	17.6	68	22.8
(4) −	−	40	25.2	26	47.3	13	19.1	69	24.1	13	15.3	11	25.6	40	28.2	84	28.2
Total			74.3		25.7		19.2		80.8		66.4		33.6		32.3		67.7
(N)			(159)		(55)		(68)		(286)		(85)		(43)		(142)		(298)

$X^2 = 12.04; df = 3;$ $\quad$ $X^2 = 6.23; df = 3;$ $\quad$ $X^2 = 2.78; df = 3;$ $\quad$ $X^2 = 8.42; df = 3;$
$p < .01$ $\qquad\quad$ $p < .10$ $\qquad\quad$ $p < .43$ $\qquad\quad$ $p < .05$

to life changes and orientations toward life and death.

LIFE CHANGES AND ATTITUDES

Marital status. — Sustained social support, as reflected in marital status, was more important in determining the attitudes of men than of women (Table 3). Men who had continuity in marital status were much more likely to hold attitudes that included a positive evaluation of life, and were described as either activists or positivists while almost one-half of those who had experienced change were negativists. Change in marital status was not associated with perceptions of life or death among women. When income was controlled, a change in marital status was associated with orientations toward life and death only among those with lower incomes. Among the low income aged, persons who had maintained continuity in marital status were more likely to be activists than those who had experienced change (Table 3). Yet, low income persons whose marital status had changed tended to hold somewhat more positive joint attitudes toward life and death than those with continuous marital relationships.

Health. — Men who had experienced a change in health tended to be negativists while men whose health had remained the same tended to be activitists or positivists. On the other hand, women whose health had deteriorated were just as likely to be positivists as negativists. Women who had experienced continuity in health, however, tended to be positivists. For the most part, within both of the income groups patterns of change and attitude types were comparable although low income persons whose health had remained the same were more likely to be activists than their peers who had suffered declining health (Table 4).

201

Table 4. Change in Health and Attitude Type by Sex and Income.

Attitude Type		Men Continuity		Men Change		Women Continuity		Women Change		High Income Continuity		High Income Change		Low Income Continuity		Low Income Change	
Death	Life	N	%	N	%	N	%	N	%	N	%	N	%	N	%	N	%
(1) +	+	41	34.5	16	17.0	78	48.8	54	28.6	47	58.8	12	25.0	72	36.2	58	24.7
(2) −	+	37	31.1	17	18.1	36	22.5	33	17.5	19	23.8	11	22.9	54	27.1	39	16.6
(3) +	−	16	13.4	21	22.3	20	12.5	50	26.5	5	6.3	10	20.8	31	15.6	61	26.0
(4) −	−	25	21.0	40	42.6	26	16.3	52	27.5	9	11.3	15	31.3	42	21.1	77	32.8
Total			55.9		44.1		45.8		54.2		62.5		37.5		45.9		54.1
(N)			(119)		(94)		(160)		(189)		(80)		(48)		(199)		(235)

$X^2 = 19.85$; $df = 3$; $p < .001$ $X^2 = 23.77$; $df = 3$; $p < .001$ $X^2 = 19.27$; $df = 3$; $p < .001$ $X^2 = 21.16$; $df = 3$; $p < .001$

Table 5. Change in Informal Activity and Attitude Type by Sex and Income.

Attitude Type		Men Continuity		Men Change		Women Continuity		Women Change		High Income Continuity		High Income Change		Low Income Continuity		Low Income Change	
Death	Life	N	%	N	%	N	%	N	%	N	%	N	%	N	%	N	%
(1) +	+	24	29.6	33	25.6	61	50.0	71	31.3	33	55.9	26	37.7	52	36.1	78	27.2
(2) −	+	31	38.3	23	17.8	31	25.4	38	16.7	18	30.5	12	17.4	44	30.6	49	17.1
(3) +	−	9	11.1	28	21.7	11	9.0	59	26.0	1	1.7	14	20.3	19	13.2	73	25.4
(4) −	−	17	21.0	45	34.9	19	15.6	59	26.0	7	11.9	17	24.6	29	20.1	87	30.3
Total			38.6		61.4		35.0		65.0		46.1		53.9		33.4		66.6
(N)			(81)		(129)		(122)		(227)		(59)		(69)		(144)		(287)

$X^2 = 14.81$; $df = 3$; $p < .002$ $X^2 = 25.62$; $df = 3$; $p < .001$ $X^2 = 16.79$; $df = 3$; $p < .001$ $X^2 = 21.03$; $df = 3$; $p < .001$

Table 6. Change in Formal Activity and Attitude Type by Sex and Income.

Attitude Type		Men Continuity		Men Change		Women Continuity		Women Change		High Income Continuity		High Income Change		Low Income Continuity		Low Income Change	
Death	Life	N	%	N	%	N	%	N	%	N	%	N	%	N	%	N	%
(1) +	+	18	24.0	26	27.7	69	52.3	58	30.5	28	46.7	25	44.6	59	40.1	59	25.9
(2) −	+	31	41.3	13	13.8	26	19.7	35	18.4	21	35.0	9	14.3	36	24.5	40	17.5
(3) +	−	10	13.3	20	21.3	16	12.1	47	24.7	3	5.0	10	17.9	23	15.6	57	25.0
(4) −	−	16	21.3	35	37.2	21	15.9	50	26.3	8	13.3	13	23.2	29	19.7	72	31.6
Total			44.4		55.6		41.0		59.0		51.7		48.3		39.2		60.8
(N)			(75)		(94)		(132)		(190)		(60)		(56)		(147)		(228)

$X^2 = 17.31$; $df = 3$; $p < .001$ $X^2 = 19.57$; $df = 3$; $p < .001$ $X^2 = 10.83$; $df = 3$; $p < .01$ $X^2 = 16.23$; $df = 3$; $p < .001$

Formal and informal activity. — Changes in formal and informal interaction have different implications for the well-being of men and women in late life. The relationship between change and outlooks on life and death, however, was comparable for both formal and informal interaction in that women whose participation had remained stable were likely to be positivists while men who had maintained levels of interaction were more often activists than positivists (Tables 5, 6). Thus, continuity in church involvement by men gave no assurance of fostering positive attitudes toward death. Indeed, 63% of those who maintained involvement held negative attitudes toward death (Table 6). Even so, persons who had continuous support from social participation more often had positive attitudes toward life.

Relationships between change in formal and informal associations and orientations toward life and death tended to be similar regardless of income. Among persons with higher incomes, however, stability and change in church involvement were about equally likely to foster joint evaluations of life and death that were positive.

SUMMARY AND DISCUSSION

Types of attitudes toward life and death. — Although little attention has been given to concurrent evaluations of life and death, the dominant hypothesis offered in the literature, and the one receiving the most support in this research posits that persons who have attained their goals and view life positively will have more accepting attitudes toward death. This hypothesis, however, is perhaps over-simplified in that a substantial proportion of the respondents exhibited different orientations toward life and death. Examination of the attitude patterns in relation to life changes also demonstrated the need for inclusion of the mixed types as well as the polar types. The analyses suggested the following conclusions and areas for future research.

Life changes and attitudes. In general, those who had experienced discontinuity were more frequently negativists or passivists than their counterparts who had undergone less change. Although continuity and sustained involvement in most life areas contributed to more

positive evaluations of life and death, in some instances, continuity in roles and relationships was also characteristic of activists. Among men in particular, continuity was more likely to be associated with positive attitudes toward life and less acceptance of death. Indeed, women more often expressed accepting feelings toward death although Templer & Ruff (1971) suggest that women exhibit more anxiety regarding death than do men.

A common pattern was for men who were experiencing life much as they had in middle age (i.e., health, participation) to view it favorably while they expressed concern about death. The tendency for continuity to characterize men who were activists may have had to do with differences in the perception of what death will be like. Men, for example, were more likely to think of death as an end while women saw it as another beginning (Vasser-Corbin & Troll, 1973).

The salience of change in marital status for men corroborated previous research in that men alone fare less well than women (Lowenthal & Robinson, 1976). In fact, men experience more difficulty establishing close relationships with persons other than their wives. This research also indicated that continuity in opportunities for intimacy derived from marriage was more important in determining the perceptions of life and death of men than of women.

Women are more likely to anticipate widowhood than are men, and the greater stability in friendships through the life cycle among women and the availability of age peers who are also widowed may help account for the seemingly greater ease with which women adapt to the loss of a spouse (Berardo, 1970; Blau, 1973; Lopata, 1973). Following widowhood, women are likely to seek intimacy from same-sex friends, and some literature suggests that friendships among women may come to replace family ties in late life (Lowenthal & Robinson, 1976). To the degree that male friendships are characterized by less intimacy and richness (Arth, 1962; Booth, 1972), they may be less likely to serve as a buffer against the potential desolation of widowhood (Lowenthal & Haven, 1968).

Activity theory suggests that sustained participation will foster psychological well-being. Lemon et al. (1972) extended this by posing that the loss of more intimate role supports would perhaps have more lasting consequences for adjustment than discontinuity in those providing less opportunity for closeness. In this research, however, change in both formal and informal roles was related to well-being.

Chappell (1975) has observed that church involvement, an indicator of formal activity, not only represents an area in which there is continuity in late life but it also extends to the future. This is interesting in light of the tendency for continuity in religious involvement to characterize men who were activists with a more positive orientation toward life than death. Men did not seem to derive comfort with respect to the future from religion to the same extent as women.

Isolation resulting from declining social interaction may foster the view that life is over and that the future is a time to wait for death (Kalish, 1976). Among both men and women, passivists had indeed lost informal contacts and had experienced diminished church involvement.

Insofar as income may represent some measure of success, there was only partial support for the view that fulfillment of life goals may be associated with less concern with death. Although persons with higher income tended to be positivists, those with lower incomes were more likely to be passivists with postive attitudes toward death as well.

Other research has shown that the relationship between social participation (Bull & Aucoin, 1975), marital status (Edwards & Klemmack, 1973), and well-being diminish when socioeconomic status is controlled. When income was held constant, however, change in both marital status and social participation was associated with joint evaluations of life and death. Although perceptions of life and death were associated with change in marital status only among the low income aged, change did not seem to foster negativism toward life and death concurrently. Among lower income groups in which care for a spouse who is ill may be undertaken primarily by the family, death may represent a release and may be reflected in observations about life and death to a greater degree than for their counterparts with higher incomes.

Clearly, we need to know more about the qualitative aspects of the impact of both incremental and decremental change on well-being.

Quite different meanings may be assigned to similar changes. For some, incremental change may be accompanied by negative evaluations while for others decremental change may not be perceived negatively (Campbell et al., 1976). Even after experiencing decremental change, women's perceptions of life and death, for example, were inclined to be more positive than were those of men. Additional data are also needed on the nature of the transitions in various life areas. Future measures of loss and change should take into account the characteristics of interpersonal relationships and the degree to which transitions are expected. Unanticipated changes, for example, are thought to cause greater disruption than those which are "on time" and expected (Seltzer, 1976). Thus, the extent to which the transition is anticipated, the degree to which the discontinuity can be "timed" by the individual (Seltzer, 1976), the importance assigned to the life area in which change occurs, the degree to which the change is limited or affects many other spheres of life, as well as recency, are factors that should be examined in future research on transitions in late life and well-being.

REFERENCES

Adams, D. Correlates of satisfaction among the elderly. *Gerontologist*, 1971, *11*, 64-68.
Arth, M. American Culture and the phenomenon of friendship in the aged. In C. Tibbitts & W. Donahue (Eds.), *Social and psychological aspects of aging*. Columbia Univ. Press, New York, 1962.
Berardo, R. Survivorship and social isolation: The case of the aged widower. *Family Coordinator*, 1970, *19*, 11-15.
Blau, Z. S. *Old age in a changing society*. New Viewpoints, New York, 1973.
Booth, A. Sex and social participation. *American Sociological Review*, 1972, *37*, 183-193.
Bull, C. N. & Aucoin, J. B. Voluntary association participation and life satisfaction: A replication note. *Journal of Gerontology*, 1975, *30*, 73-76.
Campbell, A., Converse, P., & Rodgers, W. *The quality of American life: perceptions, evaluations, and satisfactions*. Russell Sage Foundation, New York, 1976.
Chappell, N.L. Awareness of death in the disengagement theory: A conceptualization and an empirical investigation. *Omega*, 1975, *6*, 325-343.
Cumming, E., & Henry, W. E. *Growing old*. Basic Books, New York, 1961.
Cutler, S. J. Membership in different types of voluntary associations and psychological well-being. *Gerontologist*, 1976, *16*, 335-339.
Diggory, J. C., & Rothman, D. Z. Values destroyed by death. *Journal of Abnormal and Social Psychology*, 1961, *63*, 205-210.

Dumont, R. G., & Foss, D. C. *The American view of death: acceptance or denial?* Schenkman Pub., Cambridge, Ma., 1972.

Edwards, J. N., & Klemmack, D. L. Correlates of life satisfaction: A re-examination. *Journal of Gerontology*, 1973, *28*, 497-502.

Erikson, E. H. *Childhood and society*. W. W. Norton & Co., New York, 1963.

Gubrium, J. F. Marital desolation and the evaluation of everyday life in old age. *Journal of Marriage and the Family*, 1974, *36*, 107-113.

Harvey, C., & Bahr, H. M. Widowhood, morale and affiliation. *Journal of Marriage and the Family*, 1974, *36*, 97-106.

Hendricks, J., & Hendricks, C. D. *Aging in mass society*. Winthrop Publ., Cambridge, MA., 1977.

Heyman, D. K., & Gianturco, D. T. Long-term adaptation by the elderly to bereavement. In E. Palmore (Ed.), *Normal Aging II*. Duke Univ. Press, Durham, NC., 1974.

Hutchison, I. W. The significance of marital status for morale and life satisfaction among lower-income elderly. *Journal of Marriage and Family*, 1975, *37*, 287-293.

Kalish, R. A. Death and dying in a social context. In R. H. Binstock & E. Shanas (Eds.), *Handbook of aging and the social sciences*. Van Nostrand, New York, 1976.

Keith, P. M. Models of change, perceived change and life satisfaction. In E. Powers, P. Keith & W. Goudy (Eds.), Later life transitions: Older males in rural America. *Sociological Studies in Aging*, 1977, 134-159.

Kline, C. The socialization process of women. *Gerontologist*, 1973, *15*, 486-492.

Lemon, B., Bengtson, V. P., & Peterson, J. A. An exploration of the activity types and life satisfaction among in-movers to a retirement community. *Journal of Gerontology*, 1972, *27*, 511-523.

Lopata, H. Z. *Widowhood in an American city*. Schenkman, Cambridge, MA., 1973.

Lowenthal, M. F. & C. Haven. Interaction and adaptation: Intimacy as a critical variable. *American Sociological Review*, 1968, *33*, 20-30.

Lowenthal, M. F., & Robinson, B. Social networks and isolation. In R. H. Binstock & E. Shanas (Eds.), *Handbook of aging and the social sciences*. Van Nostrand, New York, 1976.

Lowenthal, M., Thurnher, M., & Chiriboga, D. *Four stages of life*. Jossey-Boss, San Francisco, 1975.

Marshall, V. Age and awareness of finitude in developmental gerontology. *Omega*, 1975, *6*, 113-129.

Martin, W. C. Activity and disengagement: Life satisfaction of in-movers into a retirement community. *Gerontologist*, 1973, 224-227.

Nelson, C. A study of life satisfaction and death anxiety. University Microfilm, Columbus, OH, 1974.

Palmore, E., & Luikart C. Health and social factors related to life satisfaction. *Journal of Health and Social Behavior*, 1972, *13*, 68-80.

Parsons, T. Death in American society: A brief working paper. *American Behavioral Scientist*, 1963, *6*, 61-65.

Pihlblad, C. T., & Adams, D. L. Widowhood, social participation and life satisfaction. *Aging and Human Development*, 1972, *3*, 323-330.

Rhudick, P. J., & Dibner, A. S. Age, personality and health correlates of death concerns in normal aged individuals. *Journal of Gerontology*, 1961, *16*, 44-49.

Seltzer, M. Suggestions for the examination of time-disordered relationships. In J. Gubrium (Ed.), *Time, roles and self in old age*. Human Sciences Press, New York, 1976.

Smith, K., & Lipman, A. Constraint and life satisfaction. *Journal of Gerontology*, 1972, *27*, 77-82.

Templer, D. & Ruff, C. Death anxiety: Age, sex, and parental resemblance in diverse populations. *Developmental Psychology*, 1971, *4*, 108.

Vasser-Corbin, L., & Troll, L. Age and sex differences in attitude toward death. Presented at Gerontological Society, Miami, Nov., 1973.

Wood, V., Wylie, M., & Sheafor, B. An analysis of a short self-report measure of life satisfaction: Correlation with rater judgments. *Journal of Gerontology*, 1969, *24*, 465-469.

Alienation and Age: A Context-Specific Approach*

WILLIAM C. MARTIN, *California State University, Chico*
VERN L. BENGTSON, *University of Southern California*
ALAN C. ACOCK, *University of Southern California*

21

ABSTRACT

A context-specific conceptualization of alienation is used to describe age-group differences. Traditionally, alienation has been treated in terms of specific modes (e.g., powerlessness, meaninglessness, normlessness, social isolation, self-estrangement). This research adds to each of these modes social structural contexts (e.g., polity, economy, education, religion, family) to produce a matrix of context-specific alienation. Age-group differentials on specific components of alienation are examined in a three-generation sample. The postulate that alienation is related to position in the social structure leads to the hypothesis that there is a curvilinear relation between alienation and age, the youth most alienated, the middle-aged least, and the elderly in between. The hypothesis is generally supported.

In the past two decades, there has been much social and psychological research on the concept of alienation. The concept is useful as it points to an important interface between the individual and his social system where feelings of estrangement (powerlessness, normlessness, meaninglessness) are correlates of marginal social status (loss of control over means of directing one's life, disaffection with goals of the broader society).

Past research has tended to investigate psychological modes of alienation while leaving unexamined, for the most part, issues concerning the social context. Hence there are some important sociological implications which have been little explored. To what extent is alienation differently related to the various sectors of the individual's social world? How is it related to the broader dimensions of social structure? Which groups in society manifest higher or lower alienation, and what are the underlying forces which cause such differences?

The literature treating problems specific to age-strata seems to justify a context-specific approach to alienation. Most young people in contemporary industrial societies must wait until they are well into their twenties before they enter adult systems of power and reward. Youth constitute a social group which has often been characterized as markedly alienated (see

Keniston, 1965; Whittaker and Watts, 1969). This estrangement is often manifest in political and educational disaffection (Friedenberg, 1969), which is related to broader social change (Bengtson, 1970). For example, the "alienated youth" of the 1950s have given rise to the "young radicals" of the 1960s; and if current seers of campus commitment are correct, the mood of the 1970s is apathy—an alienation born of a realistic assessment of powerlessness (e.g., Hitch, 1972). At the other end of the life cycle, those elderly who have "disengaged" from participation in many of the significant roles of mid-life have also been characterized as higher in alienation than their middle-aged counterparts (Cumming and Henry, 1961; Lowenthal, 1964). In short, age, as an index of participation in the central institutions of society, should be a significant predictor of levels of alienation.

This research has two aims. The first is to study alienation across various institutional contexts. The second is to test the proposition that differences in age (reflected in three generations) predict differences in alienation. We see age as an important correlate of type and extent of societal participation.

A CONTEXT-SPECIFIC MODEL: MULTIPLE MODES AND CONTEXTS

Alienation has been a recurrent theme in the media of contemporary society. It has emerged in popular art forms (e.g., *Easy Rider, Hair, I Am A Rock*). The refrain of one pop song says: "I am, I said, to no one there; and no one heard at all, not even the chair; I am, I

* This research was supported by the National Institutes of Mental Health (Grant #18158). We wish to acknowledge the assistance of Marijo Walsh for assistance in data analysis; and to Ted Jensen, Ingrid McClendon, and Archie MacDonald for assistance in producing this report.

cried, I am, said I, and I am lost and I don't even know why . . . leaving me lonely still." Alienation is often cited in scholarly literature as a cause or correlate of social problems: crime, delinquency, prostitution, and student unrest (see Etzioni, 1968).

Much thought and research has gone into examining the conceptualization, measurement, and operation of alienation. A bibliography compiled in 1969 by the National Institute of Mental Health cites 225 articles. Most of that research has focused on what may be called the *mode* of alienation: feelings of estrangement in reaction to the global sociocultural system (see Keniston, 1965).

Multiple Modes

In his classic review, Seeman (1959) noted five recurring components (or modes) of alienation. These are:

1. *Powerlessness:* the expectancy or probability held by the individual that his own behavior cannot determine the outcomes or reinforcements he seeks

2. *Meaninglessness:* the individual is unclear as to what he ought to believe; when minimal standards for clarity in decision-making are not met . . . a low expectancy that satisfactory predictions about future outcomes can be made

3. *Normlessness:* a high expectancy that socially unapproved behaviors are required to achieve given goals

4. *Isolation:* assignment of low reward value to goals or beliefs that are typically highly valued in the given society

5. *Self-estrangement:* a disjuncture between the degree of dependence of the given behavior upon anticipated future rewards.[1]

Examples are plentiful of the diverse ways in which social philosophers and sociologists have viewed these modes of alienation. For example, Karl Marx saw the worker in industrial societies as alienated because access to the means of production or economic decision-making was dominated by the ruling entrepreneurs. Alienation for Marx was primarily a characteristic of the economic sphere of society. Bottomore (1956:170–1) quotes Marx as follows:

> The more the worker expends himself in work, the more powerful becomes the world of objects which he creates in face of himself, and the poorer he himself becomes in his inner life, the less he belongs to himself. The alienation of the worker in his product means not only that his labour becomes an object, takes on its own existence, but that it exists outside him, independently, and alien to him, and that it stands opposed to him as an autonomous power. The life which he has given to the object sets itself against him as an alien and hostile force.
> The performance of work is at the same time its objectification. This performance of work appears in the sphere of political economy, as a vitiation of the worker, objectification as a loss and as servitude to the object, and appropriation as alienation.

This classical conceptualization of alienation emphasizes the worker as part of a whole category subject to similar alienating elements of a social structure (Kon, 1967). But the contemporary social-psychological conceptualization tends to fix on the individual's response to the total cultural system (Keniston, 1965; Schact, 1970). Cultural rejection may partly result from common age-category experiences, but it is basically an individual response (see Fromm, 1955).

Multiple Social Contexts

But to fix on the mode of alienation leaves unanswered an important question: Alienated from what? How may one characterize the several settings in which the above modes of alienation are experienced?

A statement of the context of alienation should be both inclusive and specific at the same time. Alienation has usually been thought of as a characteristic of masses, e.g., the proletariat, or minority groups or contemporary youth. Yet it is the individual who responds to alienating aspects of a society. Hence, we invoke the concept of social institutions which provides a compromise between breadth and specificity. The social system as a whole is seen as a complex of institutions—political, economic, educational, religious, and familial —in which people play socially prescribed roles. If such social interaction entails lack of power, or of values worth identifying with, or self-integration, then alienation may result.

Given an institutional perspective, it is possible to describe more specifically the perceived object of an individual's alienation. The model in Chart 1 represents an attempt to do

---

[1] More recently Seeman (1971) has redefined estrangement as a social isolation (loneliness) and added cultural (or value) estrangement to accompany self-estrangement (either a discrepancy between the ideal self and the real self, failure to live up to one's perceived potential, or doing unfulfilling or uncreative work). The five definitions in Seeman's 1959 paper were used as the basis for the operationalization of alienation in the present research.

POLITY	ECONOMY	EDUCATION	RELIGION	FAMILY	Σ
political power-lessness	economic power-lessness	educational power-lessness	religious power-lessness	familial power-lessness	POWER-LESSNESS
political meaning-lessness	economic meaning-lessness	educational meaning-lessness	religious meaning-lessness	familial meaning-lessness	MEANING-LESSNESS
political norm-lessness	economic norm-lessness	educational norm-lessness	religious norm-lessness	familial norm-lessness	NORM-LESSNESS
political social isolation	economic social isolation	educational social isolation	religious social isolation	familial social isolation	SOCIAL ISOLATION
political self-estrange-ment	economic self-estrange-ment	educational self-estrange-ment	religious self-estrange-ment	familial self-estrange-ment	SELF-ESTRANGE-MENT

	POLITY	ECONOMY	EDUCATION	RELIGION	FAMILY	Σ
Σ	political alien-ation	economic alien-ation	educational alien-ation	religious alien-ation	familial alien-ation	CONTEXT-SPECIFIC ALIENATION

Chart 1. A Model for Assessing the Perception of Context-Specific Alienation

just this, for it locates the specific social institutional context and modal expression of an individual's perceived alienation. (For another attempt at establishing a context-specific model of alienation, see Burbach, 1972.)

Each mode of alienation can be examined across institutions, and each institution can be examined across modes. Total alienation is represented in the lower right-hand corner. From this formulation, several different perspectives on alienation can be explored. For example, there are context-specific components of alienation, such as political powerlessness.[2]

The principal task of the following analyses involves between-age category comparisons of specific cell scores and scores summed across modes or across institutions. The total alienation score will also be examined.

HYPOTHESES FOR APPLICATION OF THE
PARADIGM TO GENERATIONAL GROUPS

The basic postulate of this research is that a sense of alienation varies with the extent of participation in the social structure. This argument is evaluated by examining levels of alienation in three groups, each representing differential involvement in the social structure. Hypotheses for testing will be stated on three levels of generality.

Level I Hypothesis

Differential involvement of age-strata leads to a general hypothesis: the middle generation (G2) is most involved in the social structure and will be lowest in feelings of alienation; the youth generation (G3) is least involved in the total social structure and will be most alienated; the old (G1), in the process of disengaging from the social system, will be in between. Thus, a curvilinear relation between the total alienation score and age is hypothesized.

Level II Hypotheses

Seven curvilinear hypotheses have been generated for the five specific modes and two of the specific contexts. These are derived from age-specific contrasts in social participation. In the case of religious alienation, it is predicted that G3 will be highest and both G1 and G2 will be lower. The religious experiences of the present cohort of young people deemphasize the institutional church, while the experiences of the middle and older generation do not. This represents an exception to the general curvilinear hypothesis. It is difficult to make a clear prediction for the ·educational institutions. Keniston's (1965) analysis would predict that value isolation and self-estrangement will be highest for G3 in all contexts, but the youth are much more involved in the educational process than the aged and the aged are still burdened by the taxes supporting education. It is also difficult to make a prediction for the family. Perhaps the dominance of primary re-

---

[2] Originally there were 75 items in the alienation scale, 3 for each cell. Pretesting and questionnaire size limitations resulted in the reduction of the scale to 25 items. See Dean (1961) for a discussion on the measurement of alienation.

lationships within the family will produce a lower level of alienation in all three generations than in the other contexts (Acock *et al.*, 1974).

Level III Hypotheses

It would be possible to generate 25 hypotheses (one for each cell of Chart I), but this would be highly speculative. However, for most of the 25 cells the curvilinear prediction is appropriate. Rather than pose specific hypotheses, we will do an *a posteriori* analysis of the data in Table 3.

MEASUREMENT, SAMPLING, AND STATISTICAL PROCEDURES

Measurement

Alienation was operationalized by applying each of Seeman's definitions of alienation modes to each institutional context. A 25-item questionnaire was designed, one question for each of the cells in the context-specific paradigm.[3] Responses to each question were scaled from *1* (little alienation) to *6* (high alienation). The key elements of Seeman's definitions were incorporated in each of the 25 items. Response options were alternatively reversed to minimize response-set.

Reliability and validity of a scale must be demonstrated in attempting to measure such a complex social-psychological construct as alienation. Pretesting of the 25-item scale demonstrated its verbal adequacy, reliability, and validity. The scale was administered to over 300 different individuals prior to the research. Each time feedback was requested as to the intent and understandability of the questions. Reliability (tested on an *n* of 40) was indicated by a test–retest *r* of *.64* (two-week interval). This is comparable to measures reported on other social-psychological concepts. Rotter (1966) reported similar test–retest *r*s for his locus of control instrument. Though feelings of

---

[3] Following are three examples of the items used:

1. (political powerlessness) How much influence do you feel you have over the policies and decisions the government (federal and state) makes?
2. (economic meaninglessness) Are the things that happen in the American economy often confusing to you?
3. (familial self-estrangement) Is your own family life or activity personally enjoyable to you in and of itself?

(The complete scale and its scoring will be sent upon request made to the first author.)

alienation may vary with the daily news, present job or marital satisfaction, etc., the reliability level indicates considerable continuity. Tests for internal consistency (item to item and item to scale) resulted in *r*s in the *.40* to *.70* range, indicating neither complete unidimensionality nor complete orthogonality of the items.

Pretesting with "known groups" was carried out to estimate the predictive validity of the items. The questions were administered to a group of incarcerated juvenile delinquents (*n*= 40), college students (*n=38*), and suburban, middle-aged service organization members (*n*= 28). The mean total alienation scores and the mean individual item scores varied in the predicted direction, the delinquents being highest and the service organization members being lowest. A *t*-test on the difference of the means indicated statistical significance at the *.05* level for *19* of the 26 comparisons (the 25 individual items, plus the total alienation scores). Only one comparison (educational meaninglessness) was not in the predicted direction. There was a *.67* point biserial *r* between delinquents—service organization members and alienation score.[4]

Research Sample

These data are from a larger study exploring the nature and extent of intergenerational continuity (see Bengtson and Lovejoy, 1973). The present analysis used *182* males who were members of three-generational lineages. We began by attempting to find grandfathers who had living children and grandchildren (age 15–26). This was done by getting in touch with male subscribers to a Southern California medical plan. Of the *840,000* members, *58,328* fit this category. From these a systematic sample (every eighth case) was drawn, yielding *7,112* men. These were sent a one-page questionnaire to determine if they had three-generation families as specified by the research design (i.e., with a grandchild age 15–26). There were only *585* who reported having such families based on a *70* percent return from the *7,112*.

Of these *585* families, *84* had direct linkage between (and supplied addresses for) three male members. That is, they were related along the male line, grandfathers, one father, and one grandson. Thus, *84* individuals from each generation received a questionnaire, making a total of *252* potential respondents in the male

---

[4] More complete data on reliability and validity are available upon request.

three-generation family sample. Of these, *182* returned completed, usable instruments (a *72* percent return rate).

The *182* males comprising the sample had an age range of 15–81; the average age for the three generations was 76, 44, and 18, respectively. As to current marital status, over *90* percent of the middle and older generations were currently married; over *90* percent of the youth generation were not. The sample was *95* percent white. Thus, nonwhites and unmarried adults are underrepresented in the sample. There was heterogeneity on the variables of education, occupation, income, and religion. (See Martin, 1971.)

Statistical Procedures

Several statistical procedures were used in the analysis of these data. The first approach was to examine means for each generation. Means were computed on total alienation (summing means over all cells), on the five modes of alienation, and on the five institutional contexts. These are reported in Table 1 and will be used in testing Level I and Level II hypotheses.

A second approach used in testing Level II hypotheses involved dichotomizing each of the *25* items into "alienated" or "not alienated." If an individual checked scale point *1, 2,* or *3* in response to an item he was considered to have given a not alienated response (in contrast to responses at scale points *4, 5,* and *6*). The dichotomizing was done to determine how *generalized* alienation is for each *generation* within each mode and within each institution. For ex-

ample, toward how many institutions does the average G1 feel alienation within the mode of powerlessness? Is this level of generalization greater or less than it is for the G2s? The data appear in Table 2.

Level III hypotheses were explored by comparing subcell means. Table 3 presents means for each generation within each cell.

DATA ANALYSIS AND INTERPRETATION

The general hypothesis that the most alienated would be the youth followed by the elderly and that the middle-aged would be the lowest was strongly supported by their total alienation score means. Table I shows that the average total alienation score for G3 was *82.8* followed closely by the mean for G1 of *76.3*. By contrast, the G2s had a significantly lower mean of *69.4* ($p < .05$). The most general alienation score (produced by summing over modes and contexts) does vary by generation in the manner predicted from the general postulate. The Level I hypothesis was supported—there was a curvilinear relation between alienation and age.

A major purpose of this study was to go beyond the general hypothesis and determine context-specific variations in alienation and see if these are predictable on the basis of age-related position in the social structure. The curvilinear predictions in the Level II hypotheses received clear support in five out of the seven cases (see Table 1). The exceptions in terms of *modes* of alienation were social isolation and self-estrangement, where the oldest generation was less alienated than expected. Even with these exceptions, however, the youth were higher than the middle-aged in all five modes of alienation. The data supported the predictions for *contexts* of alienation as well. In addition, as Table 1 indicates, the educational context followed the curvilinear relation with the qualification that the aged are the highest. For the family context we found a relatively low level of alienation for all three generations. The aged are surprisingly low.

The second approach to analyzing Level II hypotheses was to ask how generalized alienation is across modes within each context and across contexts within each mode. The appropriate data appear in Table 2. The results are similar to those shown in Table 1. However, it is interesting to observe the considerable variation in how generalized alienation is. For example, the average number of contexts of powerlessness for the aged was *3.4*. In contrast

Table 1. Mean Alienation Scores for Each Generation

	G1	G2	G3
a. Total alienation	76.3*†	69.4*	82.8†
b. Modes of alienation			
powerlessness	22.6*†	18.4*‡	21.0†‡
meaninglessness	20.3*†	17.5*	17.9†
normlessness	12.2*	9.6*‡	12.6‡
social isolation	10.9†	11.7‡	16.3†‡
self-estrangement	10.3*†	12.2*‡	15.1†‡
c. Contexts of alienation			
polity	19.2*	17.2*‡	19.8‡
economy	17.1*	15.2*‡	18.2‡
education	15.0†	13.3*	14.5
religion	15.8†	15.4‡	17.8†‡
family	8.6†	8.4‡	12.4†‡

* G1 and G2 means statistically significant in their difference ($p \leq .05$).

† G1 and G3 means statistically significant in their difference ($p \leq .05$).

‡ G2 and G3 means statistically significant in their difference ($p \leq .05$).

Table 2. Mean Number of Categories of Alienation for Each Mode and Context by Generation

Mode	Mean Number of Contexts		
	G1 (Old)	G2 (Middle)	G3 (Young)
Powerlessless	3.4*	2.6	3.1
Meaninglessness	3.2	2.6	2.5
Normlessness	1.4	0.9	1.4
Social isolation	0.9	0.8	1.9
Self-estrangement	0.9	1.1	1.6

Context	Mean Number of Modes		
Polity	2.8	2.4	3.0
Economy	2.4	1.9	2.4
Education	2.0	1.4	1.6
Religion	2.1	1.9	2.4
Family	0.4	0.4	1.1

* Values are for the mean number of contexts and modes in which members of each generation gave an alienated response. For example, a 3.4 for G1 on powerlessness means that the average G1 gave a response indicating alienation in 3.4 contexts of powerlessness.

the aged expressed social isolation and self-estrangement in an average of less than one context.

Inspection of Table 2 indicates that powerlessness and meaninglessness were much more generalized across contexts for all three generations than the other modes. It is also clear that the young had much more generalized social isolation and self-estrangement than either the middle or oldest category.

The data for the very specific hypotheses (Level III) are presented in Table 3. Only 9 of the 25 means exactly follow the curvilinear pattern. However, in 16 of the 25 cells, the mean of youth alienation was highest, as predicted. Also, in 15 of the 25 cells, the middle-aged mean was lowest, as predicted. In the

educational context, the elderly expressed greatest alienation in terms of power (control) and meaninglessness; but youth expressed greatest value isolation and self-estrangement.

DISCUSSION

The data presented above suggest two general conclusions. First, when one examines the total alienation scores (summed over all items, representing the five modes and five institutional contexts) the prediction of a curvilinear relationship between age and alienation was confirmed. This suggests support for the general postulate of an inverse relationship between an individual's integration into the social structure and the level of alienation he exhibits. Second, when one explores the more specific

Table 3. Mean Context-Specific Alienation Scores for Each Generation

		Polity	Economy	Education	Religion	Family
Powerlessness	G1	4.86*	5.10*	4.71*	5.46*	2.26*
	G2	4.17†	4.44	3.62	4.63	1.60†
	G3	5.05	4.75	3.65‡	4.98‡	2.61‡
Meaninglessness	G1	4.60*	4.73*	4.98*	3.87	1.97
	G2	3.90	4.00	4.00†	3.86	1.90†
	G3	4.12‡	3.91‡	3.30‡	3.85	2.61‡
Normlessness	G1	3.65*	3.30*	1.73	2.25*	1.19
	G2	3.15†	2.65†	1.46†	1.40†	1.14†
	G3	3.79	3.07	1.95	2.18	1.56‡
Social isolation	G1	2.95*	2.52	1.48*	2.03*	1.80
	G2	2.45†	2.43†	2.28†	2.50†	2.08†
	G3	3.44‡	3.25‡	2.80‡	3.55‡	3.26‡
Self-estrangement	G1	3.16*	1.48*	1.97	2.33*	1.35
	G2	3.71	2.02†	2.04†	2.90	1.48†
	G3	3.51	3.23‡	2.81‡	3.28‡	2.33‡

* G1 and G2 means statistically significant in their difference ($p \leq .05$).
† G2 and G3 means statistically significant in their difference ($p \leq .05$).
‡ G1 and G3 means statistically significant in their difference ($p \leq .05$).

manifestations of alienation—examining scores in the five modes and five institutional contexts —some exceptions to this overall pattern emerge. Hence the importance of a context-specific approach to alienation.

For example, the grandparents (G1) exhibited the highest total alienation scores of the three age groups with respect to powerlessness and meaninglessness (see Table 1). This is apparent in the economic, educational, and religious institutional contexts (Table 3). Moreover, the highest alienation levels for the youth (G3) can be seen in powerlessness in the political and familial settings, in their social isolation, and self-estrangement.

Age and Alienation. These specific findings provide additional support for the general theme that there are age differences in levels of alienation. There are two explanations that can be advanced for such age-group differences (Riley *et al.,* 1972). The first is a *maturational* explanation: alienation is a correlate of contrasting levels of psychological or social age. Age-grading represents an institutionalized progression through various positions in the social structure. In most spheres of social activity, the middle-aged are the "command" generation, in control of many of the resources of the social system. That they exhibit less feeling of alienation as a function of greater participation in and control over various systems within society is consistent with these data. One implication, then, is that as youth move into positions of the adult social structure, their level of alienation may decrease. Indeed, alienation may be an example of the developmental stake each generation has in the social system (Bengtson and Kuypers, 1973). The stake of the middle-aged in the future involves continuing the established order and transmitting its best features to the young. Implied is a lower level of skepticism, less alienation from social systems, than among youth. By contrast, the developmental tasks of youth center on the establishment of identities: by questioning, experimenting, and exploring, they seek to establish viable alternatives to the established institutions of the older cohort (see Mannheim, 1952; Ryder, 1965). This suggests a second implication: that the psychological consequences of high levels of alienation may vary by age. For youth, alienation from the present political order, for example, may be a constructive force in the forging of a new and more humane political ideology (see Keniston, 1968). For the

alienated middle-aged, it may take on the form of despair and stagnation the obverse of ego-integrity and generativity (see Erikson, 1964).

But there is a second interpretation of the age-group difference in alienation exhibited in these data: a *cohort-historical* perspective (Ryder, 1965). The contrasts observed between generations may be due to sets of different life experiences as they relate to the institutions involved. Mannheim (1952) observed that cohorts are uniquely shaped by the historical events impinging on members as they achieve adulthood. Heberle (1951) has suggested that these are particularly evident in political orientations, a view substantiated in recent research by Cutler (in press). The middle generation in the present research has been characterized by Reich (1970) as a cohort with consistent faith in rational contracts, organizational processes, and privacy; while the emerging generation evidences much less reliance on established institutions. One implication, then, is that the youthful cohort may maintain their higher alienation scores into adulthood, despite increasing involvement in the social structure.

Viewed from either a maturational (age-grade) or cohort (historical) interpretation, the research supports two more specific observations in the literature concerning alienation, age and social structure. The first is Keniston's (1965) argument that youthful alienation is a rejection of the values and goals that presently prevail in the social structure. The social (value) isolation scores of G3 were consistently higher in all contexts than those of G1 or G2 (Table 3). Extrapolating to the future, either youth will accept the dominant value-goal structure when they inherit the means of control (a maturational explanation) or they will make selective changes in it based on their unique cohort experiences (see Bengtson, 1970). This suggestion can only be tested by cohort-sequential studies on social change and generational continuity.

The second age-related postulate supported is the Cumming and Henry (1961) statement that the elderly disengage from the social structure. The G1 respondents expressed highest powerlessness and meaninglessness of the three generations. The elderly relinquish positions of influence to the middle generation (which had the lowest powerlessness and meaninglessness scores). In all five institutional contexts, the old scored higher in alienation than the middle generation; in three of the five alienation modes they are higher. Again, longitudinal designs are necessary to test for the expected increase in alienation scores between middle age and old age, as individuals move from the functional positions of adult life to the less "productive" positions of retiree, widower, grandparent, or retirement community occupant.

Multiple Modes and Contexts. The second major implication of these data is that alienation manifests itself in a variety of modes. As suggested by Seeman and others, alienation must not be considered unidimensional. In general, powerlessness and meaninglessness were the modes of alienation expressed most frequently by the sample. Not only did total alienation scores vary by generation (e.g., youth uniquely high in social isolation and self-estrangement), but the modal patterns of alienation were differentially manifest. Similarly, as implied in the conceptualization of this research, alienation manifests itself in a variety of social structural contexts. Political and economic alienation were most pervasive in the sample, but each generation had a different contextual pattern of alienation. The youth were noticeably high in familial and religious alienation. Alienation is a multidimensional concept: two individuals may have equal total alienation scores but vary dramatically in both mode and context of their alienation.

Primary relationships within an institutional context may have the net effect of reducing (or limiting the development of) alienation. In these data, scores on familial alienation were consistently low for the three generations. Although G3 had a significantly higher familial alienation mean than G1 or G2, this context was still G3s lowest mean. Of the five institutional contexts, the family is the one with the highest probability of primary relationships. The implication is that pervasive primary relationships in the other institutional contexts would reduce alienation.

SUMMARY

This research, using a multiple mode and multiple institutional context approach to alienation, focused on the variable of age-generation membership as an indicator of involvement in the social structure. The basic theoretical rationale was that alienation varies by the degree of structural integration of individuals, and that age is an indicator of such structural involvement.

Two findings emerged from the data. First,

there were consistent age differences in alienation, many following the postulated curvilinear relation. That is, it was consistently found that youth were most alienated, the middle generation least alienated, and the older generation in between.

Second, the exceptions as well as the manifestations of this pattern highlight the multidimensional nature of alienation. This underscores the importance of conceptually separating the multiple modes and institutional contexts of alienation. Thus, the concept of context-specific alienation proved, on the whole, to be theoretically relevant and empirically discriminating.

REFERENCES

Acock, Alan C., J. Dowd, and W. Roberts. 1974. *The Primary Group Concept.* Morristown, N.J.: General Learning Press.

Bengtson, V. 1970. "The Generation Gap: A Review and Typology of Social Psychological Perspectives." *Youth and Society* 2:7–31.

Bengtson, V., and J. Kuypers. 1973. "Competence, Social Breakdown, and Humanism: A Social Psychological Perspective of Aging." *Human Development* 16:181–201.

Bengtson, V., and M. Lovejoy. 1973. "Values, Personality, and Social Structure." *American Behavioral Scientist* 16:880–912.

Bottomore, Tom 1956. *Selected Writings in Sociology and Social Philosophy.* New York: McGraw-Hill.

Burbach, H. 1972. "The Development of a Contextual Measure of Alienation." *Pacific Sociological Review* 15:225–34.

Cumming, E., and W. Henry. 1961. *Growing Old: The Process of Disengagement.* New York: Basic Books.

Cutler, N. In press. "Generation and Political Orientation: Maturational vs. Cohort Experiences." *Public Opinion Quarterly.*

Dean, D. 1961. "Alienation: Its Meaning and Measurement." *American Sociological Review* 26(October):5:753–58.

Erikson, E. 1964. *Insight and Responsibility.* New York: Norton.

Etzioni, A. 1968. "Basic Human Needs, Alienation and Inauthenticity." *American Sociological Review* 33(December):870–85.

Friedenberg, E. 1969. "Current Patterns of Generational Conflict." *Journal of Social Issues* 25: 21–38.

Fromm, Erich. 1955. *The Sane Society.* New York: Holt, Rinehart & Winston.

Heberle, Rudolf. 1951. *Social Movements.* New York: Appleton-Century-Crofts.

Hitch, C. 1972. Report on Berkeley Students, reported in *San Francisco Chronicle*, January 24, 1972.

Keniston, Kenneth. 1965. *The Uncommitted.* New York: Dell.

————. 1968. *Young Radicals.* New York: Harcourt, Brace & World.

Kon, I. 1967. "The Concept of Alienation in

Modern Society." *Social Research* 34:507–28.

Lowenthal, M. 1964. "Social Isolation and Mental Illness in Old Age." *American Sociological Review* 29(February):54–70.

Mannheim, K. 1952. *Essays on the Sociology of Knowledge*. London: Routledge & Kegan Paul.

Martin, W. 1971. *Alienation and Age: A Study of Three Generations*. Unpublished Ph.D. dissertation, University of Southern California.

National Institute of Mental Health. 1969. *Social Aspects of Alienation*. Washington: Government Printing Office.

Reich, Charles. 1970. *The Greening of America*. New York: Random House.

Riley, Matilda *et al.* 1972. *Aging and Society*, Vol. 3. New York: Russell Sage Foundation.

Rotter, J. 1966. "Generalized Expectancies for Internal Versus External Locus of Control of Reinforcement." *Psychological Monographs* 80:1–28.

Ryder, N. 1965. "The Cohort as a Concept in the Study of Social Change." *American Sociological Review* 30(February):843–61.

Schact, Richard. 1970. *Alienation*. New York: Doubleday.

Seeman, M. 1959. "On the Meaning of Alienation." *American Sociological Review* 24(December):783–91.

————. 1971. "Alienation: A Map." *Psychology Today* 10:84–7.

Whittaker, D., and W. Watts. 1969. "Personality Characteristics of a Nonconformist Youth Sub-Culture: A Study of the Berkeley Non-Student." *Journal of Social Issues* 25:65–89.

V

Policy and Program

Probably no part of the field of religion and aging is as familiar to the leaders and members of our churches and synagogues as that having to do with the services to the elderly which are or ought to be provided by government, social agencies, and religious institutions. In recent years these issues have been widely addressed. In the following selection of papers we have included first the policy statements and recommendations of the 1961 and 1971 White House Conferences as representative texts. The remaining papers report some of the more creative reflections on programming to meet the needs of the elderly. We have included two brief accounts of programs which, while not sponsored by religious institutions, may be stimulating to those concerned with what churches and synagogues can do. These are the papers on SAGE (Senior Actualization and Growth Exploration) and Project Find which conclude the section.

The White House Conference policy statements and recommendations might be said to represent the wide agreement among the religious communities concerning the needs of the elderly with respect to the traditional religious services offered by the churches and synagogues. They go further, emphasizing the need to change social attitudes toward aging, to work toward new ways of ministering to the spiritual well-being of the elderly and of enabling the elderly to live and die with dignity. Dieter Hessel's wide-ranging interview with Maggie Kuhn, founder of the Gray Panthers, makes many suggestions for the church's work with the aging and the enlistment of the leadership of lay members and of the elderly themselves. One of her proposals involves intergenerational education, an example of which is described in the paper by Marie Malveaux and Eleanor Guilford. Robert Mc-Clellan's chapter from his book, *Claiming a Frontier: Ministry and Older People*, offers practical suggestions for helping a church or synagogue get started in developing programs to meet the needs of the elderly. Finally, the paper by Arthur Flemming, chairman of the 1971 White House Conference, describes a project which, if adapted to the life of a local congregation, might do much to increase awareness and transform attitudes toward the elderly and their needs, while the account of the SAGE project describes ways in which self-help groups using the techniques of contemporary humanistic psychology may help older people grow and transcend the negative expectations of our culture with respect to the post-retirement years.

WHITE HOUSE CONFERENCE 1961
POLICY STATEMENT AND RECOMMENDATIONS *22*

THE MEANING OF LIFE is to be found solely in man's relationship to God. It is this relationship which gives meaning to all human values. In the light of it, every period of life, including that of old age, is possessed of intrinsic value and sublime potential. Viewed in the light of an eternal destiny, old age is seen to have an importance as great as that of youth or the middle years. To young and old, the divine imperative is addressed: "Thou shalt love the Lord thy God . . . and thy neighbor as thyself."

Role of Religion in the Life of the Older Person

Religion's concern with human dignity at every state in the span of life derives from the fact that each individual is created in the image of God. As a consequence, religion seeks to build a living fellowship of believers in which the aging find and share the true benefits of being a part of the household of God. It is this conviction which likewise demands a concern for such matters as the maintenance of social welfare institutions by religious bodies and the proper conduct of those sponsored by Government or voluntary agencies in a manner consonant with the nature of man and the sanctity of existence. Similarly, it is the basis of a concern for the right of every individual to a burial befitting human dignity.

It has been suggested that "man's potential for change and growth is much greater than we are willing to admit and that old age be regarded not as the age of stagnation but as the age of opportunities for inner growth." In light of this, congregations should recognize that their elder members are often specially endowed with gifts of wisdom, serenity, and understanding. To the aging person, religion extends an invitation to see the later years of his life as "rich in possibilities to unlearn the follies of a lifetime, to see through inbred self-deceptions, to deepen understanding and compassion, to widen the horizon of honesty, to refine the sense of fairness." The religious community assists the older person to deepen his relationship to God and to accept the assurance of eternal life.

Recommendations

So that religion may play its full and proper part in the life of the aging, it is recommended that care be exercised to provide suitable transportation and facilities for participation in worship and services with congregations. In order to reach the shut-ins, greater use should be made of religious radio, TV, and recordings, as well as the personal ministries of members and leaders. It is urged, also, that State, county and municipal governments recognize the need for more chaplaincy services in public institutions caring for the aging. Ways of providing such services should be studied on local, State and national levels by religious bodies and public agencies.

The Role of the Older Person in the Congregation

Within the life of the congregation each older person should be treated as an individual. Each is entitled to responsible membership within the religious fellowship. Any attitude on the part of the congregation which hinders the exercise of this right must be regarded as a contradiction of religious teaching. It should rather be its concern to foster relationships calculated to imbue in the elderly a sense of belonging, of being needed and useful in a vital way. This will go far to promote a richer religious experience for the aging and will likewise provide a salutary example to be followed in the family circle and in the outer rings of society.

Specifically, responsible membership should involve all or some of the following roles: that of worshipper, learner, teacher, counselor, leader or elder, volunteer aide, and member in congregational organizations. When congregations overemphasize some of these roles and under-emphasize others, older persons often are placed at a disadvantage. We affirm that these roles are all significant.

It is recommended that the congregation study the age and sex composition of its membership with a view to determining whether the prevaling distribution of roles and the available congregational organizations allow adequate outlet for the abilities, experience and needs of older members.

Role of the Congregation in Affecting Attitudes Toward Older People

We underline the obligation of religious groups to instill, as an essential of sound family life, an attitude of respect for the individuality and intrinsic importance of each aging member. Thus, while both the family and the congregation will feel direct responsibility to provide special services, educational materials, and programs for the aging, every effort should be made to see that these do not involve an unnecessary separation from the main stream of familial or congregational life. It is urged, also, that all congregations make their services available to nonmembers.

Recommendations

Our society, by reason of its preoccupation with frontier development and economic advance, has tended to glorify youth and denigrate old age. The time has come to recognize that the "cult of eternal youth is idolatry." The congregations must reaffirm by teaching, by the example of their own practice and by preparation for aging, the religious conviction of the beauty and worth of old age. We further urge that religious bodies make a greater use of radio, TV, drama, and other media in affecting changes of attitudes toward older persons.

To the end that our congregations may better instill proper attitudes toward the aging, greater provision should be made for specialized training of the clergy and of lay workers in understanding and serving the needs and potentialities of old age. This means workshops, seminars and refresher programs for those in active service as well as expanded programs of instruction in colleges, theological schools and seminaries.

The approach to society at large should be made by establishing dynamic and cooperative associations with every segment of the community: business, labor, education, government, the professions, and voluntary citizen groups. The effort here should be to insure that all necessary facilities and services are available to help individuals to adjust to the new circumstances in which they find themselves with the approach of old age. In addition, religious congregations should work for legislation and industrial practices which contribute to the orderly transition from active employment to retirement and a useful old age. Churches and synagogues, having expressed their concern for counseling and psychotherapeutic services for the aged, should work likewise for such services where needed.

Conclusion

Religion, in its teaching, ritual and organization, is uniquely equipped to guide and aid men in making the closing years of life a time of deepening fulfillment. To this end, it must remind itself and the entire community that the goal is not to keep the aging busy but to help them find in every moment an opportunity for greatness. At the same time, it must always insist that "the test of a people is how it behaves toward the old," remembering with gratitude the contributions that have been made as well as the problems inherited.

Religion can assist the aging in finding within themselves and in the fellowship of faith the resources to meet those problems and fears which seem inevitably to accompany one's latter years. In illness, trouble, and infirmity as well as in hours of joy and exultation, the community of faith offers strength, comfort and benediction in many forms. Religion binds a man to creation and the Creator, and enables him to face the future with hope. This group summons, then, the great religious bodies of the Nation, their congregations, seminaries, organizations, and related agencies, and all Americans who share their concern for the aged, to join in expanded efforts toward seeing that each of our senior citizens receives the benefits, spiritual and material, he richly deserves.

NOTE: Quotations in the body of this statement are taken from a paper, "The Older Person and the Family in the Perspective of Jewish Tradition," presented by Professor Abraham J. Heschel at the White House Conference on Aging.

WHITE HOUSE CONFERENCE 1971

SECTION ON SPIRITUAL WELL-BEING

Introduction

The Section on the Spiritual Well-Being of the elderly involved over 200 Delegates. Although many of the participants in the Section were religious leaders, a number of other professional and technical occupations were represented. Among them were educators, legislators, social workers, business people, consultants, volunteer workers, service agency administrators, and young people.

The work of the Section was guided in part by the thought and experience of many of the group who were themselves elderly. Of the Delegates named to the Section, one-fifth listed themselves as retired. The breadth and depth of discussion was also enhanced by the participation of a substantial group of minority persons (18 percent were Black, Asian American, American Indian, or Spanish American).

The recommendations of this Section encompass some of the most significant trends of the day among religious bodies. Changes in attitudes are reflected in recommendations stressing ecumenism and interfaith responsibilities. New relationships between government and religious organizations are envisaged, with the religious community having a much greater role in community service to the elderly. And finally, the Section Delegates had the courage to take up a problem that is becoming one of the most controversial of the day. That is, the prolongation of life entirely by artificial means as opposed to legalization and sanctioning of the right of old people to choose to die naturally and in dignity.

Preamble

Spiritual Well-Being relates to all areas of human activity. In referring to man's spiritual well-being, we consider those aspects of life ". . . pertaining to man's inner resources, especially his ultimate concern, the basic value around which all other values are focused, the central philosophy of life—whether religious, anti-religious, or non-religious—which guides a person's conduct, the supernatural and non-material dimensions of human nature."[1]

Whether rich or poor, advantaged or disadvantaged, every person has a right to achieve a sense of spiritual well-being. "We believe that something is wrong with any society in which every age level is not clearly of meaning and of value to that society. The spiritual needs of the aging really are those of every person, writ large: the need for identity, meaning, love, and wisdom."[2]

As Delegates to the White House Conference on Aging in the Section concerned with spiritual well-being, we call attention to this fact of life: to ignore, or to attempt to separate the need to fulfill the spiritual well-being of man from attempts to satisfy his physical, material, and social needs is to fail to understand both the meaning of God and the meaning of man.

Whether it be the concerns for education, employment, health, housing, income, nutrition, retirement roles, or transportation, a proper solution involves personal identification, social acceptance, and human dignity. These come fully only when man has wholesome relationships with both fellowman and God.

The concerns apply to all ages. Basic needs do not necessarily change with age, but they often are intensified.

Therefore, the White House Conference on Aging states that all policies, programs, and activities recommended in a national policy on aging should be so developed that the spiritual well-being of all citizens should be fulfilled.

In this context, the Section on Spiritual Well-Being of the White House Conference on Aging makes the following policy recommendations.

RECOMMENDATIONS

Recommendation I
Religious and Governmental Cooperation

The government should cooperate with religious bodies and private agencies to help meet the spiritual needs of the elderly, but in doing so should observe the principle of separation of Church and State.

Recommendation II
Training in Spiritual Well-Being

The government should cooperate with religious organizations and concerned social and educational agencies to provide research and professional training in matters of spiritual well-being to those who deliver services to the aging.

Recommendation III
Funding Professional Training

It is recommended that the government provide financial assistance for the training of clergy, professional workers, and volunteers to develop special understanding and competency in satisfying the spiritual needs of the aging.

Recommendation IV
Chaplaincy Services

It is recommended that all licensing agencies in the State require that institutions caring for the aged must provide adequate chaplaincy services. In certain instances in which cooperating church organizations cannot obtain financial support for such service, government should be empowered to supply it upon the recommendations of the State commision of aging or other appropriate agencies.

Recommendation V
Evaluating Programs for the Elderly

It is recommended that the Federal Government should establish a continuing system of evaluation of present and proposed government-funded programs serving the elderly. One of the functions of such a system would be a determination of a program's effect upon the spiritual well-being of the elderly.

Recommendation VI
Acquainting the Elderly with Services

It is recommended that a much greater, more diverse information flow is necessary to acquaint the elderly with all the services which are available to them. Social Security Administration should be required to disseminate adequately the information necessary to acquaint the elderly with all the services which are available to them, such as by enclosing information with Social Security checks.

Recommendation VII
Elderly in Age-Integrated Programs

Efforts should be made to meet the spiritual needs of the aging by ministering to them in conjunction with people of all ages, as well as in groups with special needs. It is noted that special attention should be given to allowing older persons to share in the planning and implementations of all programs related to them.

Recommendation VIII
Home Delivery of Spiritual Consultation

As a part of total programming for older persons, communities should make available religious or other spiritual consultation to the aged in their own homes, using the clergy and other trained persons. Special emphasis shall be given to assist and utilize personnel of those religious bodies lacking financial resources often available to larger groups.

Recommendation IX
Concern for Man as a Whole Being

Since man is a whole being with interrelated and interdependent needs, religious organizations should be actively concerned with spiritual, personal and social needs.

Recommendation X
Religious Bodies as Referral Agencies

Religious organizations must be aware of agencies and services, other than their own, which can provide a complete ministry to older persons. Other organizations designed for the benefit of older persons should develop, as a part of their services, channels to persons and agencies who can help in spiritual problems.

Recommendation XI
Religious Bodies as Advocates

Religious bodies should exercise a strong advocacy role in meeting the needs of the elderly, working for programs, both public and private, that contribute to the well-being of the elderly and protecting them from those who would victimize or demean them.

Recommendation XII

Protecting the Rights of the Elderly

Religious bodies have traditionally and properly developed their own philosophies. We recommend that they work together with the elderly and coordinate their efforts with other groups to develop and declare an affirmation of rights for the elderly. These rights should include the basic values of all while insuring the basic right of freedom of religion.

Recommendation XIII

Inter-Faith Community Programs

It should be the national policy that religious bodies and other private agencies make it their concern to bring together the services of the entire community to provide opportunity for interfaith broad-based community programs for the aged through multipurpose community centers.

Recommendation XIV

The Right to Die With Dignity

Religious bodies and government should affirm the right to, and reverence for life and recognize the individual's right to die with dignity.

References

1. Moberg, David O., *Background and Issues Paper on Spiritual Well-Being,* 1971 White House Conference on Aging, p. 3.
2. Bollinger, Thomas E., "Spiritual Needs of the Aging," *The Need for a Specific Ministry to the Aged,* Southern Pines, N.C.: Bishop Edwin A. Penick Memorial Home, 1969, pp. 50-51.

CHURCHES AND OLDER PEOPLE

23

Phillip E. Hammond

What, then, is the view churches have of old people? How do they minister to the elderly? Since billboards urging Americans to "worship this week" so frequently picture young married couples and their children, it might be assumed that old people are not very visible to churchmen. That assumption, however, would not be accurate; the range of services performed by churches for the aged is enormous.[25] It has even been estimated that as much as one-third of a minister's counseling and pastoral calling time is spent with old people.[26] If clergymen continue to feel special responsibility for the sick and the dying, and if illness and death continue their trend toward localization in the elderly, the estimate of one-third can probably be pushed upward.

Unfortunately, no systematic data are known to this writer which indicate how clergymen feel about the elderly, and inference yields contradictory answers. On the one hand, clergy probably are more comfortable with parishioners their own age and those younger, especially in a counseling situation.[27] By this reasoning, only "old" ministers may enjoy their contacts with the aged. Correlatively, in a society where youth and young adulthood are exalted, clergymen, too, may prefer to be in touch with the young, the active, the vital. Ministering to parishioners who are old, then, might be regarded as an unpleasant necessity.

On the other hand, it is quite clear from a number of investigations that ministers enjoy personal calling and counseling, and research indicates that the least amount of minister-parishioner conflict arises from such contexts.[28] If most ministerial contact with the elderly *is* personal calling and counseling, then it could well be that such contact is, in fact, enjoyable. Actually, this conclusion has some basis in theory when one considers the defining characteristics of most minister-parishioner interaction. From the clergyman's point of

[25] Good recent descriptions of these services are found in E. T. Culver, *New Church Programs with the Aging* (New York: Association Press, 1961); White House Conference on Aging, 1961, *Background Paper on Services of Religious Groups for the Aging* (Washington, D.C.: Government Printing Office, November, 1960); Paul B. Maves, "Aging, Religion, and the Church," in Clark Tibbitts (ed.), *Handbook of Social Gerontology* (Chicago: University of Chicago Press, 1960), 714–720; Margaret Frakes, "The Church and Older People," *Christian Century*, 72 (1955), series beginning 1201–1204. A portrait of a local parish's services is found in H. Lee Jacobs, *Churches and Their Senior Citizens* (Iowa City: University of Iowa Press, 1957).

[26] P. B. Maves and J. L. Cedarleaf, *Older People and the Church* (Nashville: Abingdon Press, 1949).

[27] See Robert E. Mitchell, *Minister-Parishioner Relations* (Report of the Bureau of Applied Social Research, Columbia University, New York, 1962), esp. Chap. IX.

[28] For the second of these points, evidence is available for Protestants only. See *ibid.*, IV–7, IX–7.

view, there is generally "business" to transact: persuading a person to take on a committee assignment, or to increase his financial pledge, or to alter his civil rights opinion, for example. But where such business may burden many parish calls, those with elderly parishioners are not as likely to be so burdened. The sense of being involved with people over crucial issues may be missing from contacts with the elderly, it is true, and that absence may take away from the enjoyment of the contact. But the disadvantage brings an advantage also; without business to transact, there is less chance of failure and more room for pleasure.[29]

The fact is, of course, no one knows which of these two contradictory views is the more accurate portrayal of contemporary clergy's orientation toward old people. Parishioners might be assumed to have attitudes toward old people which are roughly parallel with the attitudes of all adults—in or out of the church—but their attitudes are distilled from relationships in economic, neighborhood, and family spheres as well as in the religious sphere. The minister, too, may have one set of attitudes toward the old persons in his own family, but toward the elderly in his congregation, with whom he interacts as clergyman, he very likely has a different set. Without question, the range of ministerial attitudes extends from great dislike of old people and their problems to great affection for and delight in contacts with the elderly. What is not known is the distribution of attitudes along this range.

To some significant degree, however, attitudes of the clergy are only minimally important to churches' programs for the aged. Given their value premises, churches are committed to helping the elderly, and what they do is but a matter of awareness and resources. No doubt a minister whose personal view of the aged is negative will do less for them in his ministry than will his colleague whose personal view is positive. But sociological analysis would argue that factors other than personal orientation are probably far more important. Thus, churches with more resources will do more for older people than will churches with fewer resources. And churches in the inner city with older congregations will do more than suburban churches serving mainly young families. From an array of possible programs, a church will choose those ministries to old people which reflect its level of awareness, amount of resources, and the priority given to the aged relative to other groupings. What are some of those programs, and on what basis will choices be made?

[29] Suppose, for example, that churches regularly counted on bequests from most or all dying parishioners. The *nature* of ministerial contacts with older people, we are saying, would be different. In a fascinating, though inadequately documented, paper, Luke M. Smith argues a similar point—that Congregational clergymen are less likely than Episcopal clergymen to have close friendships with parishioners. Episcopalian theology defines a clergyman's priestly, sacramental duties as paramount, whereas the Congregational minister must regard *all* of his contacts with parishioners as "utilitarian." See Luke M. Smith, "The Clergy: Authority Structure, Ideology, Migration," *American Sociological Review*, 18 (1953), 242–248.

As variegated a list as will be found is contained in the Background Paper, "Services of Religious Groups for the Aging," White House Conference on Aging, 1961. Classified by the type of problem they confront, these programs are cited here in part:

Income and Employment
1. Use of old people for paid part-time jobs in the church.
2. Formal contacts with state employment services.
3. Retirement counseling.
4. Counseling on investment, taxes, wills, budgets, applications for assistance.

Health, Medical Care, Rehabilitation
1. "Library" of sickroom equipment to lend.
2. Counseling on choice of hospitals, doctors, nursing homes, funeral arrangements.
3. Visiting of the elderly ill.
4. Sponsorship of hospitals and nursing homes.
5. Chaplaincy services within hospitals.

Housing
1. Sponsorship of homes for the aged.

Education
1. Library of books relevant to aging.
2. Preretirement classes or forums on aging.
3. Bible classes for the elderly.

Free Time, Recreation
1. "Golden Age Clubs."
2. Care of church gardens.
3. Sale and exhibition of handwork and hobbies.

Religion
1. Pastoral counseling.
2. Facilitating participation in religious services by, for example, earphones, transportation service, and tape recordings.

Confronted by this or a similar list, a church will of course choose not at random but only after asking some questions.[30] Since the effect will be to eliminate some programs, such question-asking amounts to a placing of value on each alternative. The questions, therefore, might be as follows:

1. Is this program commensurate with a church's tradition and theology? Some denominations, for example, do not regard the church building as an appropriate place for "recreation." Golden Age Clubs, therefore, might rank so far down on the list as to be not considered at all. Similarly, counseling on investments may be prohibited among those for whom the stock market is a sinful use of money. Less precise, but no less binding

---

[30] Perhaps the logical first question is whether the list exhausts the possibilities, whether other programs might be added for consideration. We shall assume here, however, that the realistic alternatives could be fully listed.

perhaps, is the tradition that places such emphasis on familism that any attempt by the church to usurp the family's responsibility for caring for its elderly would be proscribed. Quite probably in contemporary America, however, strict *theological* prohibitions on any of the above activities would be relatively rare. More likely, some programs would be eliminated on remaining grounds.

2. How effectively can the church conduct a given program? Most churches, for example, have job openings for very few persons other than the full-time clergyman. As worthy as the part-time employment of old people may be, many churches may decide that their resources can better be spent in bringing more old people into contact with jobs *outside* the church. Correlatively, maintenance of an adequate supply of sickroom articles for loan may unduly tax the budget of an average church, especially as it includes more than crutches and bedpans. Clearly, an orthopedic bed is a more important item from the standpoint of the old person needing one, yet the capital outlay and storage facilities necessary probably make such an item unfeasible as part of a *church* program. But this example suggests the importance of the third question.

3. How effective is the church relative to other agencies in conducting a given program? Presumably any program for the aged can be ranked along a continuum from those activities which *only* churches do to those activities which *other* agencies do also. The *effectiveness* or, to use an economic term, the "marginal utility" of a particular church program for the elderly will thus be assessed in the context of the church's peculiarity in pursuing it. For example, only the church can supply tape recordings of its worship services to shut-ins; regardless of the quality of the recording or the availability of other tape recordings, therefore, the church is likely to place high value on this activity. Bible classes or pastoral counseling are other programs that might be regarded as "peculiarly" religious and therefore not undertaken except by churches. Contrarily, sponsorship of hospitals, nursing homes, or homes for the aged, though in some instances pioneered by churches, is not uniquely a church activity in the present day.

These three questions would seem to underlie Maves' recommendation that the church's task vis-à-vis older people is twofold: (1) doing those things which it is "uniquely fitted to do," and (2) doing those things which need doing because no one else is or because it is in a better position to do them.[31] Few problems are likely to arise over the "uniquely religious" activities; the marginal utility of installing hearing aids in pews or railings on front steps, of providing radio broadcasts of worship services or rides to church for those who do not drive, and of offering worship and pastoral calling to the elderly is no doubt such that they will readily be done if resources are available. Similarly, at the other end of the continuum there are probably few difficulties, once the church has evaluated its relative effective-

---

[31] P. B. Maves, "The Church in Community Planning for the Aged," *Pastoral Psychology*, 5 (1954), 13.

ness. Marginal utility for the church declines for those activities which nonchurch agencies do as well or better. Thus, fewer than one-fourth of all older persons living in institutions live in church-sponsored homes [see Vol. 1, Chap. 6.B.7, pp. 141–142], and in the years since World War II the proportion of institutions for the aged which are religiously sponsored has been declining.[32] Max Feder cites the National Directory of Housing for Older People for his statement that, "As of January, 1965, 292 church-sponsored housing projects have been completed, with 53 more such developments in the blueprint stage."[33] But even though this number seems large, it is easily surpassed by secular developments.

It is the area between the extremes where policy decision-making agonizingly arises, especially in local parishes. Shall churches give over their resources to Golden Age Clubs? Should another clergyman be hired so that more pastoral counseling can be provided? And to what extent should the church serve as therapeutic counselor for anxious old people, as provider of welfare services, as mediator between older people and secular community agencies? These are not questions easily answered, for, though the values implicit are ones the church readily acknowledges, to allocate resources in these directions is to forgo other values toward which resources might be directed.

One major resource to be included in churches' consideration of their ministry to the elderly is their location and physical plant. With the exception of elementary schools, no other agency in society has followed the neighborhood ecological pattern as closely as have churches. It is a rare community where one or more church buildings are not in the immediate vicinity of every resident. Built generally to include meeting rooms, office space, cooking facilities, and so forth, churches are peculiarly situated to focus on neighborhoods, as well as on congregations of like believers or fellow worshipers.

But despite a neighborhood location and a set of values that clearly support a ministry to the aged, churches have not received notably helpful directives and recommendations. Goals have been clarified,[34] and sources such as those mentioned above have *exemplified* programs that might be carried out. But no particular rationale

---

[33] Cf. the 1939 figures cited in Maves and Cedarleaf, *op. cit.*, 251, with those in Samuel W. Blizzard, "Expanding the Role of Organized Religion to the Aged," in D. L. Scudder (ed.), *Organized Religion and the Older Person* (Gainesville, Fla.: University of Florida Press, 1958), 95.

[33] Max Feder, *The Senior Citizens Program in Our Temples*, Synagogue Research, Survey No. 8 (New York: Union of American Hebrew Congregations, 1966), 14. The housing here refers to low- and middle-income retirement communities and apartments.

[34] For example, in the White House Conference on Aging, *Background Paper on Religion and Aging* (Washington, D.C.: Government Printing Office, March, 1960) 13; Barron, *op. cit.*, 166; Maves and Cedarleaf, *op. cit.*, 75–80; Culver, *op. cit.*, 7–20.

or organizational philosophy justifies an unambiguous allocation of a church's resources, especially for choosing among alternatives between the extremes. The consequence, as Maves points out, is that "Local churches generally assume that their regular religious services of worship are open to persons of all ages. . . . In this sense they would feel that they are ministering to the aged. . . . [But] it is doubtful if many local churches have gone very far in adapting their programs to the needs of older people."[35]

This is not to deny that change in churches has occurred. The training in counseling which seminaries now give is a significant change with ramifications for ministering to the aged.[36] And something of a norm seems to have emerged to the effect that "oldsters should not be singled out" but should instead be integrated as much as possible into the parish body comprised of all ages.[37] Maves and Cedarleaf recommend a two-step diagnosis in developing a ministry to the elderly: discovering first the constituency (for example, how many aged in the parish, where, and whether members of a church), and second, determining their patterns of association, their interests, and so forth.[38] Jacobs, moreover, urges that "every congregation" institute a religious education for older persons *beginning with the fortieth year*.[39]

What is missing in such recommendations, of course, is a precise rationale. *What* patterns of association and interests are to be learned, and what is to be done with such knowledge? What is to be the *content* of a religious education that anticipates old age? Persons making the suggestions are not unaware of the gap, but until a rationale is forthcoming, probably any church program for the aged remains "experimental" or, at least, qualifying as a "good thing," unassailable in the abstract but perhaps not the best expenditure of time, effort, and money.

The problem, however, is not unique to the church's stance vis-à-vis older persons; it pervades ecclesiastical strategy. The remaining pages of this essay, therefore, are an attempt both to explicate the general problems of strategy and to suggest how a rationale for "aging and the ministry" may emerge.

---

[35] Maves, "Aging, Religion, and the Church," 721.

[36] H. Richard Niebuhr, D. D. Williams, and J. Gustafson, *The Advancement of Theological Education* (New York: Harper & Row, Publishers, 1957), 122, refer to this change as "one of the most influential movements in theological education." A cursory look at a random selection of Protestant seminary catalogues reveals that virtually all now include clinical training in hospitals or other institutional settings. Over 40 per cent offer courses in personality development and 25 per cent offer either a course on aging or include aging as one focus in a course on developmental problems.

[37] Jacobs, *op. cit.*, 6; Feder, *op. cit.*, 12; E. B. Jackson, "Religion, Psychiatry, and the Geriatric Patient," *Mental Hospitals*, 11 (1960), 15.

[38] *Op. cit.*, 164–165.

[39] *Op. cit.*, 17–18.

An analysis of ecclesiastical strategy

In 1844, Theodore Parker preached "A Sermon of Old Age" at the Music Hall, Boston. He was only 34 at the time but already a renowned preacher and author. What he said—and did not say—about old age is instructive today.[40]

Life is likened to an apple that ripens, sweetens, and then reddens without getting bigger.

Such is the natural process . . . the same divine law is appropriate for every kind of animal. [The old person] thinks the old is better. [He] loves to recall the old times, to revive his favorite old men. . . . The pleasure of hope is smaller; that of memory greater. . . . His affections now are greater than before; yet it is not the mere power of instinctive affection— the connubial instinct which loves a mate, or the parental instinct which loves a child; but a general human, reflective, volitional love, not sharpened by animal desire, not narrowed by affiliated bounds, but coming of his freedom, not his bondage. . . . His religion is deeper, more inward than before. It is not doctrine alone, nor mere form. There is little rapture. . . . His religion is love of God; faith and trust in Him; rest, tranquility, peace for his soul.

[However] the man reaps in his old age as he sowed in his youth and manhood. He ripens what he grew. . . . Here is an old man who loved nothing but money. . . . There is no want so squalid, no misery of poverty so desperate, as the consciousness of an old miser in his old age of covetousness. Pass him by. . . . Here is a woman who has sought chiefly the admiration of the world, the praise of men. . . . Now the audience is tired of her, and laughs at the hollow voice, the bleary eye, the spindle limbs. The curtain falls; the farce is at an end. Poor old butterfly!

The sermon combines, then, a rather sophisticated developmental view of life, an awareness of socially structured differences among people, an almost cavalier disregard for the woes of old age, and, by default, the assumption that the church can preach, can admonish, but need not look out for the welfare of those who lived unwisely. "They ripen what they grew." A disengagement theory—the view that old people selectively withdraw from social life, leaving their instrumental activities but retaining, indeed sharpening, their emotional connections with others—that theory, one surmises, would be very congenial to Theodore Parker. But beyond warning people that "such is the natural process," the church has no obligation. There is no conception of the church as a multifaceted agency, doing some things uniquely and some things that other agencies also do. There is no implicit model of the ministry as existing at national and regional levels and in specialized forms as well as in local parish structures.

Now much of this conception has changed. When the church's ministry to the aged (or to any "problem") is discussed, there is im-

---

[40] The quotations and paraphrase to follow are from a pamphlet published by The Fraternity, Boston (1859), and sold by H. W. Swett and Co.

228

plicit at least the idea that the ministry is more than local parishes. Church bodies at regional and national levels issue statements, carry out research, invest huge sums of money, exert political pressure, and conduct information campaigns. Specialized ministries, with no connection to local parishes other than a financial one, are found in higher education, city slums, hospitals, developing nations, and, of course, in old people's homes. Church strategy for dealing with the aging, therefore, must be set in a context quite different from the context in which Parker preached his sermon.

For example, given the demographic, ecological, and cultural trends whereby older people became increasingly delimited socially, specialized ministries to retirement communities, inner-city parishes, and geriatric hospitals may well increase. Such ministries, however, will reflect the "ministry" of usual parish churches only in the sense that overseas missions do now. Similarly, when the "church" undertakes support of a medical-aid-for-the-aged bill or tries to expand the coverage of social security, local congregations are involved more as aggregations of individual citizens than as corporate bodies.[41]

Therefore, although the "social issue" of aging is far less controversial for churches than, say, war, poverty, civil rights, or criminal rehabilitation, questions remain. Despite the frequency with which they are given lists of goals with respect to aging, ministers do not have to be urged to "help old people confront loss as loss," to "help maintain dignity in our senior citizens," or to "make the latter years of earthly life a time of fulfillment." The questions are *how* to achieve those goals, through *what* social structures, and by *whom*.

An answer, with some logical connection to the preceding pages, begins to emerge with consideration of the following chart:

IMPLIED ORIENTATION TOWARD ACTIVITY:

[41] See, for example, Phillip E. Hammond and Robert E. Mitchell, "The Segmentation of Radicalism—The Case of the Protestant Campus Minister." *American Journal of Sociology*, 71 (1965), 133–143, for a discussion of how one specialized ministry, apart from its success in achieving stated goals, influences the larger church organization. The general point is discussed in N. J. Demerath, III, and Phillip E. Hammond, *Religion in Social Context: Tradition and Transition* (New York: Random House, Inc., 1969), Chap. 6.

Across the top of the chart are listed examples of programs for older persons which churches have undertaken or might undertake. As the additional designation indicates, these activities differ in terms of the implied orientation, ranging from the segmented, specific, affectively neutral, instrumental orientations required for legislation to the more diffuse, integrative, socio-emotional, expressive orientations implied in the worship service. To use other examples, when churches build retirement homes (or old people's homes, or geriatric hospitals) the accumulation of capital, arrangements for financing, construction, and managing, and decisions on admission and maintenance require calculation, criteria of success, and a general "hard headedness." But a program of "friendly visitation" or pastoral calling requires almost the opposite orientation——the noncalculating, accepting warmth connoted by the term "expressive."[42]

The chart contains one other assertion which needs to be added: The more instrumental the orientations required by the activity, the more effectively can it be carried out by a regional, national, or specialized ministry; but the more expressive the orientations required, the more effectively can the activity be carried out by a local parish ministry.

Consider now the following statement in the context of the theory implied in the chart:

It is the prophetic business of the church to stand up for human rights. . . . The present concern about aging offers the church one more opportunity to stand in the community as a witness to one basic tenet of both Christianity and democracy——the essential worth of every individual, as a *person*.[43]

It would be difficult to argue *against* such a view, but it can be maintained that to the extent the church effectively "stands up" for human rights, it does so with instrumental methods which do not treat individuals as "persons" but as political objects. Insofar as the church treats individuals as persons it does so locally, in face to face contact, through the parish.

A hypothesis presented earlier should now be recalled——that older people selectively disengage, retaining their involvement in the church

---

[42] It is important once again to realize that the distinction between "instrumental" and "expressive" is an analytic one, that is, there is always the assumption of instrumental for *what* or expressive of *what*. Thus, the clergyman *conducting* worship may view his role as instrumental for the achievement of ecstacy by worshipers, while *their* orientation is expressive of the desire to be in touch with the divine. Similarly, the erstwhile instrumental act of building a hospital, with criteria of success, progress, and final operation, could "express" one's motivation to create monuments. The choirmaster obviously plays an instrumental role in providing music which enhances the expressive worship, just as the ribbon-cutting ceremony "expresses" celebration that a building project is completed. Nevertheless, most activities can be classified by the degree of instrumental-expressive balance that is expected of most participants, and it is this classification that is implied here.

[43] Culver, *op. cit.*, 92. Italics in the original.

as an expressive agency but withdrawing their involvement in it as an instrumental agency. Old people, we said, expect the church especially to comfort, not to challenge.

Assuming the correctness of the statements illustrated by the chart, and of the assertion regarding older people's selective disengagement, we can conclude that, as seen by the aged themselves, *the ministry is largely a ministry of the local parish.* Such a conclusion does not deny older people's interest in legislation regarding their welfare or their concern for retirement housing, but it does assert that such concerns are less than the comparable concerns of persons not yet old. And it does assert that the aged, even though churches provide them with "instrumentalities," will nevertheless regard the church as failing unless it also provides them with "moral support." The conclusion suggests, as another example, that older people will more readily participate in Golden Age Clubs than they will organize them or arrange for their location, staffing, and financing. And the conclusion certainly suggests that, when asked "What is the church?", older people will more likely answer that it is the agency where they worship and which visits them at home.

The report from St. Philip Neri Roman Catholic parish in St. Louis conveys this orientation:

> What stands out more clearly than anything else [during periods of illness in elderly parishioners] is the support they received from their children, their relatives, their church, and their neighbors. We are not stressing solely the question of financial support. The support that they looked for mostly was moral support.
>
> This service . . . called for no machinery, no reports, no statistics. Many people have asked us what can be done to extend this personal service without institutionalizing [sic; read "bureaucratizing"] it. This is the eternal question. . . . One thing is sure, they cannot promote it by some of our present highly specialized and mechanized methods.[44]

The fact is, of course, the church's ministry has *had* to bureaucratize or use "specialized and mechanized methods" in order to achieve many of its goals—both instrumental and expressive—including goals furthering the welfare of the aged.[45] But as far as the elderly are concerned, the church chiefly provides "moral support," an expressive act of local parishes. The distinction, though analytically clear, is frequently obscured in empirical reality. Sudnow describes the activity of a Catholic chaplain in "County" hospital:

---

[44] Catholic Charities of St. Louis, *op. cit.*, 4, 8. See also H. J. Wershow, "The Older Jews of Albany Park," *The Gerontologist*, 4 (1964), 198–202.

[45] For example, of nearly a hundred news releases from the Housing and Urban Development Agency announcing church-sponsored retirement homes, fewer than one-third indicated sponsorship by a local church, and most of those created separate administrative corporations. The majority were sponsored by regional or interdenominational groups.

His main responsibility, it seems, is administering last rites. Each morning . . . at each ward, he consults a master schedule . . . containing patient's names, religion, sex, and diagnosis. All patients who have been posted [to die] are identified with a red plastic border . . . placed on their cards. The chaplain . . . enters these patients' rooms and administers extreme unction. After completing his round on each ward, he stamps the index card of the patient. . . . His stamp serves to prevent him from performing the rites twice on the same patient.[46]

The impersonality of such action is no doubt shocking to the behind-the-scenes observer. At the same time, the chaplain-specialist's task *is* facilitated. The critical question in assessing his effectiveness is how the activity is presented to and interpreted by the aged individual.

The "social gospel" or welfare orientation of ministers has had its critics and defenders from the beginning. In this day, Fichter suggests that all the nonsacerdotal things the parish priest does may cause him to wonder if his "spiritual" function is being neglected.[47] Contrarily, Fairchild and Wynn ask:

Is it possible . . . that the constriction of the pastor's interest to family living in the parish has led to an overdevelopment of his "priestly" and "pastoral" roles, wherein he becomes a "father" instead of a "prophet" in his ministry?[48]

But what is not seen, and therefore not questioned, is whether the church might do both these things though segmentally, some at regional or national (and perhaps ecumenical) levels, others at local parish levels. Some, being instrumental tasks, require the impersonality of formal association; others, being expressive tasks, require instead the informal, personal contact.

It is not difficult, if the foregoing analysis is correct, to locate the desires of older people on this question: They want and "need" the personal contact. Presbyterian parishioners ranked as most helpful about their churches the "sermons and congregational worship" and next the "personal friendships within the congregation." But all together, the investigators conclude, the chief desire is for the church to provide "meaningful relationships, especially involving the whole family."[49] Psychiatrist E. B. Jackson warns clergymen that "the older people become, the more they need explanation, support, encouragement and appreciation."[50] And Newman Biller asserts, "First and foremost, the Synagogue can become a concrete symbol of the idea that

[46] David Sudnow, *Passing On* (Englewood Cliffs, N.J.: Prentice-Hall, Inc., 1967), 73.

[47] Joseph H. Fichter, *Religion as an Occupation* (Notre Dame, Ind.: University of Notre Dame Press, 1961), 142–145.

[48] R. W. Fairchild and J. C. Wynn, *Families in the Church: A Protestant Survey* (New York: Association Press, 1961), 17.

[49] *Ibid.*, 198, but see all of Chap. 6.

[50] *Op. cit.*, 14–15.

life is a continuity; it is a symbol that has existed in the hearts and souls of Jewish people for thousands of years."[51] For all parishioners, perhaps, but certainly for older people, the church is a symbol of "community," of intimacy. It is, in their view, an expressive, not an instrumental, agency.

Should such a point of view not be obvious? One would expect the ministry, say Gray and Moberg, "to emphasize primarily spiritual needs of senior citizens, yet [in] most official publications of major Protestant denominations . . . a 'social-service orientation' is more pronounced than the 'personal religious-experience orientation.' "[52] The church, understandably, finds training and admonishing its ministers to *do* things easier than helping them *be* things. Clearly it is erroneous to assume from this discussion that the older person has *no* interest in what has been termed instrumental activity. Obviously matters of housing, income, and health are major concerns. The question we are raising, then, is not *whether society* need attend to such concerns but *how* the *church* can reasonably share in those concerns. And, more importantly, we are raising the correlative issue of which agencies of the church can best meet which needs of the aged.

It would appear that churches, through their supra-parochial channels, are addressing many of the instrumental needs of America's elderly. They sponsor hospitals and build retirement communities; they support appropriate national legislation and initiate information campaigns. *But the strategic question is a question of its aims for the local parish*—whether the local parish should continue to be the major channel through which the church's programs (instrumental and expressive alike) flow, or whether regional, national, and specialized channels will increasingly be given the instrumental tasks, leaving the parish structure chiefly to discharge the expressive tasks. It might accurately be said that regional, national, and specialized channels *are* on the increase.[53] But it is by no means clear that local parishes are performing their role as intimate centers of "community." Moreover, in the context of a differentiating society, it is not clear just how local church organizations can do so. One thing might be pointed out, however, as an Episcopal report perceptively notes:

Mass living, with its resultant loss of personal relationships, is one of the most important factors which the churches face. . . . The growth of multiple organizations and units within the congregation has been a response to these needs. *There is a dichotomy, however, between the growth of these organizations which are usually based on age or sex groupings and the drive to minister to the whole family in its new consciousness of unity.*[54]

[51] Newman M. Biller, "The Role of the Synagogue in Work with Old People," *Jewish Social Science Quarterly*, 28 (1952), 287–288.

[52] *Op. cit.*, 48.

[53] As one example, see Donald B. Meyer, *The Protestant Search for Political Realism, 1919–1941* (Berkeley: University of California Press, 1960).

[54] National Council of the Episcopal Church, "The Family in the United States" (Report prepared for the Lambeth Conference Deliberations on the Family in Contemporary Society, 1958), 14. Italics added.

Granting the viability of a strategy which calls for local parishes to maximize their "community" function, then,[55] certain implications for the church and ministry become clearer. The day is no doubt passed when the parish can be the office of vital statistics for its neighborhood, but some of the following may be functional equivalents.[56]

Implementing the strategy

It was pointed out above that most local parishes share with elementary schools the pattern of following *neighborhood* lines. This fact might, therefore, underlie most local churches' ministry to the aged. They already exist as buildings, for example, and frequently they have a sizable clientele of old people already available. Moreover, churches, however new their physical plants, are established agencies in society; most people know of them, trust them, and are aware of how to behave in them. Timidity and confusion, which may characterize the feelings of the elderly about new agencies, are less likely to arise around churches.

Perhaps the first step a local church should take, therefore, is to determine the number and location of old people in its purview. Not only will the parish then know better how *it* can operate, but also information on housing and health needs can be transmitted to regional, ecumenical, or specialized church agencies.[57] On the basis of such knowledge, a number of "community" or expressive functions might be deemed worthwhile.

For example, given their locations, churches are logical places for hosting Golden Age or Senior Citizens Clubs. [*See the description supplied by Madge, Chap. 8 in this volume.*] To maximize the expressive function for the neighborhood, however, membership in the club cannot be contingent on membership in a specific church; "religious" activities (narrowly defined) must take place at other times.[58] Much self-direction of such clubs by the elderly themselves probably cannot be expected since their aim in participating is largely sociability, not some goal (such as economic gain) for which the club is a

---

[55] Lest there be misunderstanding, we repeat what has been implicit before: This is not a conservative call for the church to "stick to religion and keep out of politics." It is rather an acknowledgment that religio-political affairs are most effectively conducted by church agencies other than local parishes, and a further acknowledgment that: (a) people in fractionated society need centers of community, and (b) local parishes may provide such centers. Moreover, if this is true of people in general, it is truer yet of old people.

[56] No claim is made for the originality of these suggestions. Rather, given the rationale, these suggestions seem to follow. See n. 25, above, for sources describing many church activities for old people.

[57] For local parishes to accent an expressive ministry, in other words, does not absolve them from involvement in the instrumental activity of other church agencies.

[58] Frakes, *op. cit.*, 1329.

means. The church should recognize, therefore, that the instrumental tasks of leadership may have to be met by others.

An analogous program to which local churches can commit themselves is that of hosting adult education courses. Many church buildings are utilized throughout the week, but many are not. As discussed elsewhere in this volume, continuing education through city school systems and university extension divisions is an expanding endeavor. [*See Eklund, Chap. 11, pp. 342–343 in this volume, and Chap. 5, pp. 111–120 in Vol. 1.*] For the older person to benefit maximally, neighborhood sites must be available, and churches can usefully minister in this way.

Whether through a club organization, or more likely through the ministerial office, the church is often nicely situated to direct old people to welfare agencies and services available to them. There would seem to be no excuse for a minister's failing to know the range and limits of such agencies; an important part of his ministry to the elderly can be a referral system. [*See the discussions by Morris and by Schwartz, Chaps. 2 and 4 in this volume.*]

Separation of the elderly in the church, many observers agree, can go too far. Parishes large enough to sustain religious education or study classes for older persons are put in a dilemma, therefore, because large size calls for dissection, and age-grading is a standard dissecting technique used in churches as well as elsewhere. The use of "family nights," or potluck suppers, and family observance of holidays in the church have been suggested as multigenerational devices, but it is significant that these activities, too, are socio-emotional. In activities where educational background, occupational interrelationships, or other instrumental characteristics intrude, age-grading appears to remain important.

The minister can play a role of intermediary between generations, however. "The filial responsibility for the care of parents has become so ingrained in Jewish family life," says Newman Biller, "that even today many Jews have a sense of guilt, if not shame, when they are compelled to place a parent in a home for the aged."[59] And though Jews, Catholics, and Protestants are known to differ with respect to this norm of "filial responsibility,"[60] nevertheless the process of aging in modern society may well bring emotional strains between generations for which the ministry can be a help.

Certainly programs of "friendly visiting,"[61] whereby members of a congregation regularly call on the homes of older persons, are commensurate with the strategy identified here. So too, of course, is the

---

[59] Biller, *op. cit.*, 285.
[60] Robert M. Dinkel, "Attitudes of Children Toward Supporting Aged Parents," *American Sociological Review*, 9 (1944), 71–83.
[61] Frakes, *op. cit.*, 1234.

increasing conception of the minister as a counselor, a trend which not only is seen in seminary education but also conforms to elderly parishioners' wants. [*See Vol. 1, Chap. 14.3.b and 14.6.e, pp. 327, 337.*] The titles of "father," "rabbi," and "pastor" connote guidance and advice; old people especially would have the ministry maximize this aspect of its work.

One area of gerontological counseling, the increase of which shows no signs of leveling off, is that of dying patients in hospitals. [*Cf. the discussions by Lasagna and by Schwartz, Chaps. 3 and 4 in this volume.*] We observed earlier that death is becoming increasingly "age-specific," occurring more and more among the aged, and more such deaths occur in hospitals. Thus, the ministerial time with death preparation increases as more individual deaths can be anticipated and as they take place under medical supervision. Glaser and Strauss imply, from their research into the matter, that ministers, chaplains, nuns, etc., are not only very evident in "terminal" cases, but also their presence is very useful for doctors and nurses as well as for patients and their families.

A chaplain whom we observed derived great satisfaction . . . from his ability to converse with dying patients about their oncoming deaths as well as about their postdeath affairs. His satisfaction is highly instructive for two reasons. He could respond to patients' invitations to talk and, indeed, draw them into conversation better than could the nursing and medical personnel. And he was wonderfully able to wed his professional standards, with their emphasis on giving spiritual and psychological comfort rather than medical care, with his sense of the humane—of what was a proper human death.[62]

Related to the counseling of the dying person is the changed task of ministering to the survivors. Blauner estimates that, unlike citizens of yesterday, Americans today attend only one or two funerals a decade through their middle-age.[63] Death, then, though less wrenching for society, since it more often occurs among the elderly, can be more wrenching for the "inexperienced" survivors; the clergyman ministers to the aged by ministering to his family.

And finally in this brief list of recommendations which seem to flow from the strategy as elaborated in this essay, why should churches not own and operate funeral homes? Not only is the cost of dying inordinately high when operated by a profit-making enterprise, but also death remains the example *par excellence* of a religious event. Yet the religious overtones of funerals conducted by secular businesses are not automatic but must be planned. If churches can buy bakeries,

---

[62] Barney G. Glaser and Anselm L. Strauss, *Awareness of Dying* (Chicago: Aldine Publishing Company, 1965), 98–99.

[63] Robert Blauner, "Death and Social Structure: A Functional Analysis," *Psychiatry*, 29 (1966), n. 43.

hotels, even girdle factories, which have no "intrinsic" religious meaning, why can they not buy mortuaries, which do? To maximize the community function, funeral homes in neighborhoods might even be mutually owned by the various churches in those neighborhoods.[64]

Conclusion

Readers might be surprised that more or different recommendations
were not forthcoming in this essay. It is this writer's belief, however,
that ministers and others interested in church practices do not need
additional specific suggestions. Numerous sources, including a number cited above, provide a rich assortment of ideas and programs for
ministering to the aged. What is needed, rather, is a rationale and a
specification of organizational ideology, which permits choices to be
made in a nonrandom way. Sociology, of course, is only one source of
help in this regard; theology is an obvious other source of help, but so
also might cost accounting, psychiatry, or political science have relevant theory for advancing the church's understanding of its posture
toward the aging.

So it is that we have been speaking more about church strategy
than about ministerial behavior. And so it is that many important considerations—whether the ministry is conducted in a rural or urban
setting, for example, or whether a congregation is liberal or conservative in economic outlook—are ignored. Exclusion of these considerations should not be taken to mean their unimportance, any more than
theology is unimportant in a ministry to the aging, but each of these
factors permits refinements, or sets limitations, on the operation of the
others. The social scientific limitations have been the focus here. It
may well be one of history's greater ironies, we said near the outset of
this essay, that, at the same time society becomes more differentiated,
it produces larger proportions of aged persons whose needs appear to
be for less differentiation. The gerontological strategy of the church
should, it would seem, be directed toward easing the strains of that
differentiation.

---

[64] Many of the "funeral insurance" clubs are sponsored by churches, it is true, but
these are not necessarily neighborhood based, a fact that would seem to be of considerable significance if the analysis here is correct.

THE CHURCH'S CONTINUING ROLE WITH THE AGING

24

Maggie Kuhn

The ethical possibilities of life are broader than any philosopher has guessed, stronger than any psychologist has suspected.—David Hackett Fischer, *Growing Old in America*

M: Churches and synagogues have a tremendous opportunity in the last years of this century for creative new ministries, if they take seriously the experiences, skills, and human resources represented in the older members of their congregations. The churches are acculturated like other institutions in Western society and still remain youth-oriented. I believe that this is a detriment to their ministry. It deprives the young of a holistic approach to life as a continuum; and if the churches are still oriented to the youth, they are either neglectful or highly paternalistic in their attitudes toward older people. But agism works both ways. It's very cruel for the young, people in their late teens and early twenties; it's very oppressive for people in their later years. There are many commonalities that the old and the young share, only society has kept us apart so we seldom have an opportunity to discuss or even consider how much we have in common.

How shall we deal with aging in our present society? What are appropriate responses by the church? There are ten points which I'll briefly describe. Together they comprise the continuing role of the church.

1. *The educational-nurturing role.* Churches transmit the tenets of our Christian faith to the young, the middle-aged, and the elderly. Christian education and nurture ought to be a continuum, just as life itself is. Christian nurture, as I see it, ought to deal in a very substantive way with attitudinal change so that people in their middle and later years understand themselves and have built into their own self-images a sturdy approach to the kind of demeaning, diminishing attitude that society takes toward the human aging process.

The church has not paid enough attention to spiritual-intellectual nurture of older people. To begin, the church library should have pertinent books and periodicals for older persons as suggested in the Bibliography.

At the same time we need to plan more significant educational experiences with older persons. Our children and young people are presumably in church school classes or on retreats, so they are participating in a formal program of Christian education. Christian nurture is supposed to be an ongoing task of the church, one of its unique characteristics and vocations. It may be that the insights we're getting about age today, because we're confronted with the new statistics and the facts of longevity, may help us to refine and extend the whole process of education to enhance the quality of life in the community.

E: I'm aware of a tremendous tendency in most churches to single out the elderly—in Christian education and in most social services.

M: Church education is age-segregated. Education in the churches and in public schools is age-graded education. Educational materials are written for children of various ages, young people, and adults. It really separates people by age. Perhaps this approach to Christian education should be questioned and serious consideration given to integenerational learning. A few churches have been experimenting with education which is not entirely age-segregated, which enables old people to contribute to the nurture of the young, and which enables young people to prepare themselves for new roles. The old should be interpreting their experience as a part of the educational process. Would it be feasible to institute special Sundays or church family nights when there could be some intergenerational or cross-generational teaching and learning? I can imagine some younger teen-agers spending an hour or so Sunday morning or evening with the oldest members of the congregation, recording their conversations on portable tape recorders and playing back the tapes for more general discussion/education (e.g., using life-review procedures described in Chapter II). The Christian education committee could work out some good lively questions for starters.

I saw some fascinating experiments in a Lutheran congregation in Philadelphia where most of the members were old and white. They were scared to death of the big black teen-agers who had moved into their old neighborhood. There had been some purse-snatching too. The young pastor teamed up with the social studies teacher in the high school where the teen-agers were enrolled and designed the interviews as a class project. Gray Panthers assisted in bringing teen-agers and old people together. It was great all around. Fears and tensions lessened. Trust was built. New aspects of the gospel were clearly shown. They established interaction and built some trust. I don't know how far any follow-up went.

E: What might they have done to make this learning more action-oriented?

M: They might have worked out some kind of escort service whereby the black teen-agers would take the elderly shopping and be their protectors, instead of their attackers. The Black Panthers, in their early stages in many of the large metropolitan areas where there were Black Panther activities, included a very successful escort service. The young black men would offer "safe passage" to older people in the ghetto. I understand that a group now beginning to work in Philadelphia has money from the Law Enforcement Assistance Administration to fight crime on the streets. They're doing it with a rather thorough community organization effort, pairing up people who need protection with the people who might otherwise have been their attackers, giving young people who need money some small remuneration, and also training people to have more pride in their community.

2. *The counseling role.* Many pastors have had clinical training in pastoral counseling. They have been extremely helpful in dealing with the problems and crises of their parishioners. Their counsel is trusted and appreciated. But we see that the counselor's role needs to be augmented by the counseling that educated, concerned, and informed lay people can do, particularly in training and counseling for the retirement years.

E: Have you seen any efforts by churches to train their own people to do this?

M: I haven't to date, and this is probably because I haven't been traveling as widely as I should and observing as many churches. I would hope that for the near future this would be a goal. Even though people have worked hard and have looked forward to their retirement, when their retirement day comes, following the "gold watch" ceremony, there is a great trauma—and some people never recover from that shock. There is anxiety and fear and a very great loss of self-esteem.

E: It would be refreshing to imagine a congregation actually dealing with these fears, letting people talk about them. I suppose it's much easier to gloss over the problems and assume that retirement is "wonderful."

M: That's a very good comment. This is how most congregations probably would treat it, despite the fact that people go through more psychological changes in the last twenty years of their life than they do in the first sixty. Older persons experience the traumas of retirement; death of friends, spouse, children; lack of income, health, mobility.

E: Is there a special reluctance on the part of old people to seek pastoral counseling on this subject, or any other?

M: Some of the people whom we've been in touch with, who have called us, or whom I've met in my travels have said that they are pretty sure that their ministers would not understand. They're loath to bring those problems to the attention of their pastors, and this is sad. They probably feel somehow that the ministers are too busy or too preoccupied with other administrative matters to take the time to talk with them.

E: How are pastors going to obtain this special sensitivity, since they have not experienced retirement?

M: The pastors could indeed enlist the help of lay people in the congregation who are going through the shock and are quite upset by it.

E: One technique a pastor might use is to gather recent retirees to talk about what they've been through in order to educate him or her. In the process the minister might convince them that they ought to do something with other people who are retiring.

M: Yes. They themselves could serve as a resource for counseling and all kinds of very practical advice for people who are preparing for retirement. The preparation should begin in middle life. Church members in middle life don't want to think about getting old. They are too preoccupied with getting ahead and keeping ahead in the rat race. But when there is a crisis in their lives, or with their aging parents, they look to the church to help in some way. When they are compelled to retire from their jobs, they often retire from life. I think we have to lay that all out in front of our congregations and do what we can to help them to see other options.

I think that the church has another task in its counseling role—education in human sexuality. Sometimes that doesn't come into the counseling setting, or there are questions about it that members of congregations hesitate to ask; but ministers should feel comfortable enough with that whole field of human life to bring up the question if it isn't brought up by the counselee. There's some technical information which needs to be sought by the laity and ministers about social security benefits and some of the complications that exist in getting those benefits and pension rights worked out. Sometimes employers will give you that advice, but they may not; and the church ought then to be counseling people to what they really can expect.

E: Do you picture this as including primarily the members, or some kind of community service? Oftentimes the church is surrounded by older people, especially in transitional neighborhoods, who do not necessarily belong to that congregation.

M: I would hope that the counseling role of the church would be extended to the community and that the pastor and other people in the congregation would seek out, in a changing community, some of the isolated old people, because they are really shut out from the usual services that are available.

3. *The congregation as an extended caring family.* We think of the church as ministering to and involving in its membership the conjugal, or nuclear, family—fathers, mothers, and children—but in the church family there are people who don't particularly fit that formula. I'd like to think of the congregation itself as being an extended family, including people of different ages.

A few years ago, Hoekendijk, the Dutch theologian, was talking about "the pantomime of the gospel"—the acting out of the gospel message of love of neighbor. The church's own life-style could indeed be made to demonstrate ways to order and reorder the structures of society. The church can provide some models for society. For example, the church has structured much of its own life and worship in terms of the family—the conjugal, nuclear family consisting of father (the breadwinner), mother (the homemaker), and young children needing the care and protection of parents.

Increasing numbers of church members don't fit that family mold. They are quite apt to be widows, divorced parents, adult children living far away from parents, etc. Our mobile postindustrial society has put great strain on nuclear families and practically destroyed the old extended family. I'd like to see congregations become extended families, providing mutual assistance and emotional support for their members— extended families not based on kinship but on common concern. Children who seldom see their grandparents would have associations with old people. In turn, lonely old people would have some young ones to look after. The congregation, as an extended family, has an opportunity on a continuing basis to care for its members and to provide the kind of support that families usually provide. There could be shared tasks. There could be care of members who become ill or disabled, or face the crisis of death or accident.

I'm wondering whether the deacons, or a similar group, could be given major responsibility. In the Presbyterian church deacons have a duty to visit the shut-ins and care for "the poor" of the parish. It seems to me that the deacons could take on concern and advocacy for older members who are lonely, infirm, and homebound. Many of these people may indeed be poor and living on shockingly low incomes. Social service agencies employ outreach workers to do what deacons and other lay people in the churches should consider as a mandate of the gospel. Deacons should make it their business to find out what services are available and see that necessary services are provided. Meals On Wheels and homemaking and nursing services are available in many communities. Deacons should be monitoring such services and pressing for their improvement. Church leaders have clout that we often fail to use. Compassion is not enough. Friendly visits are obviously the first steps in establishing and maintaining contact and finding out what the homebound really need. Some of the deacons might take training and then function as counselors.

E: How do you reach that stage where people really care for each other in congregations?

M: It's probably an advanced stage of congregational life. Maybe it's wishful thinking at this point. I think, though, that a congregation could begin to try it in particular neighborhoods. Some churches have divided their membership into parish units. There is an effort being made to bring together people who live within geographical proximity of one another. Those people might look at who they are, what their particular interests and needs are, and begin to act like an extended family and move toward some substantial effort, rather than just a romantic notion. One kind of sharing which has become very popular is between older members of the congregation and young children of young families who haven't older relatives to help out. That could be extended. People have helped each other in times of bereavement. They've taken over the business of providing food for the bereaved family, for the relatives that may come. They house the relatives.

E: What do they pay the pastor to do then?

M: That's a tricky question. The pastor is the enabler, the organizer, the energizer for the new life-style; and that keeps him or her quite busy.

4. *Preaching the gospel. Proclaiming the word.* The teaching elder shares this task with lay people who also preach and speak. I think of preaching as extending into

something like a speakers' bureau, which could include pastors and lay people who go out to a variety of community groups and talk about the facts of growing old in a new, affirming way. Certainly what the minister says from the pulpit on Sunday morning sets the prevailing ethos of the congregation.

E: One practice that I've noticed in some congregations is that for a particular Sunday the preacher arranges some sort of preliminary study with a few people. They will actually look at the text or pick a text together and talk about its meaning. Maybe that would work especially well with some of the concerns that older people face. Why not study texts that pertain to those concerns and build a sermon together? (E.g., Ex. 20:12; Job 12:12; Ps. 71:9, 18; Prov. 21:29; Isa. 40:28–31; II Cor. 4:16; I Tim. 5:1–2.)

M: I like that. That's great. Another variation would be to have the minister announce this and then have some follow-up discussion in a coffee hour after the service to relate it to their particular living situation. The interaction of the congregation with the task of preaching is a great idea. I think of preaching as being informed by a thorough understanding of the Bible and also of the ethical-moral issues involved and the judgment that could be proclaimed in the Word. I think of preaching as not accommodating members to the faith, but of challenging the members to continue to contribute, to be socially responsible adults.

E: We don't realize how much we influence people by what we say. They can pick up on the tiniest point we make in a sermon. If we imply that somebody, because they're getting older, isn't quite as sharp, they will pick up on that, even though we're saying just the opposite in our little study group.

M: It seems to me that the effectiveness of preaching is dependent upon the whole life of the congregation. The church teaches by what it does. Preaching that is congruent with the whole life of the congregation does have a central role; but where real participation, goal-setting, and decision-making are lacking in the life of the congregation, where there is a lack of genuine affirmation of life and of each other in the life of the congregation, preaching itself won't make much difference. Preaching is effective within the context of a caring community.

5. *The social witness role.* This is another continuing responsibility of the congregation. The church can help to change the agist attitudes and policies of our country. Social criticism and analysis of our sick society ought to be a very important aspect of social witness and action. If churches took seriously the predicament of the young and the old in our age-segregated society and used their own channels of interpretation, communication, and interaction to discover the particular problems of the members of the congregation, the social witness of the church as a whole could be addressed to today's problems and the resolution of these problems.

Many people are very anxious about their elderly relatives who may become confused, or fall and have an accident, or develop some disorder or chronic disease with which they cannot cope. The housing needs of older people are very complicated; and I would hope that the church, which has met housing needs by building retirement homes, would look beyond that institution to the plight of old people in declining neighborhoods and would motivate its members to think of sharing housing space. Many widows who live in big, old houses all by themselves—and the majority of older women are widows—should be encouraged to share that housing space with people of other ages. This could be a beneficial experience for everyone involved. Since 96 percent of older persons live in the community, rather than in institutions, attention must be focused on noninstitutional housing and related needs.

The need for continuing citizen action to reform nursing homes and other extended-care facilities ought to be heavily laid on the conscience of the church. The United Presbyterian Women gave the Gray Panthers a grant to develop an action guide for citizens' groups (Elma Griesel and Linda Horn, *Citizens' Action Guide: Nursing Home Reform)*; and we hope that many congregations will be using that material, investigating the nursing homes in their community, and working with nursing home administrators, staff, and patients to reform the system.

E: One of the frustrations that people probably feel regarding social witness, in terms of the issues facing older persons, is to get a picture of the key organizations and legislation. Do you have any advice to local church task forces on aging? How do they keep track of what's happening? Are there certain agencies at the city or county level that they ought to be particularly alert to, and what legislative handles do they have? Are there certain organizations that help them keep track of new legislation?

M: The field is burgeoning. There are state and area-wide agencies established by the Older Americans Act of 1965 and its various amendments. The Older Americans Act provides funds for state programs on aging and area planning agencies to coordinate services in the larger metropolitan areas and in the counties. The church should be familiar with staff persons in those agencies. From your State Commission on Aging or Office on Aging can be secured the names and addresses of the area offices on aging. The area offices do general planning and coordinating of what is being done for old people within a particular geographical area. The focus is on services. The church should be aware at every point of existing services—what they provide, what they don't provide, and how they can be secured.

There are three very large national organizations which have been organized with many local groups. One of these, the American Association of Retired Persons (AARP), and its sister organization, the American Association of Retired Teachers (AART), have more than 10,000,000 members across the United States and 2,000 to 3,000 local chapters.

E: Do they lobby?

M: They lobby on the national level very successfully for services and programs that will benefit the elderly. They're primarily concerned with "direct services" for old people. They're not too much into basic social change. The local groups tend to be social and recreational. The AARP provides an insurance program which Colonial Penn underwrites. It's a large and very lucrative insurance program. It provides different kinds of health policies that supplement Medicare and Medicaid and give reimbursements for extended hospital visits. There is a drug service, where people can secure pharmaceuticals and prescription drugs at reduced prices. There is also a travel agency that many people use which provides interesting tours. AARP publishes a magazine, *Modern Maturity,* and monthly newsletters.

E: If those large organizations spend most of their energy on practical needs of retired people (probably those with a reasonable amount of money who can afford insurance and travel), who is monitoring what the agencies do at the county level?

M: This monitoring role is something that the Gray Panthers have taken on. As you know, the Gray Panthers are a coalition of old and young people working for social change.

E: Do the Gray Panthers exist all over the country?

M: No, we have a limited number of affiliates: approximately forty across the country. We're stronger on the West Coast (especially California) and in the Northeast than we are in other sections. Or national office is in Philadelphia. There's a second structure, called the National Council on Aging, that has been working, in training and research, providing bibliographical materials and program resources. It has local councils. The third big group organized on a national basis is the National Council of Senior Citizens (NCSC). This, too, has local councils. It's closely affiliated with the labor movement, and the local groups frequently include retired union members who come into local councils for social activities. The NCSC provides health insurance coverage for its members and newsletters carrying legislative information at local, state, and federal levels.

E: Are they lobbying hard on certain issues like mandatory retirement, etc.?

M: They're lobbying hard for equitable and increased social security benefits. They've been highly critical of Medicare and Medicaid. They have not, until very recently, done anything about mandatory retirement. The unions have held the line on mandatory retirement. They have, by and large, encouraged early retirement and have negotiated union contracts on that basis. We feel that the time has come to challenge that, and Chapter V on mandatory retirement suggests why. All those groups are doing some good things, and the church should know about their general goals. In addition to knowing about the government agencies and these private, large agencies, it's important for churches to be on the mailing lists of state offices on aging so that they can be aware of state and local legislation that needs to be supported. They should also be on the mailing lists of the Senate Special Committee on Aging in Washington and the House of Representatives Select Committee on Aging. Those committees have been doing investigative reporting, have conducted hearings in Washington and across the country, and have been pressing the Federal Government and its executive branches and Administration on Aging for the kinds of services that old people need and want. Another very important resource for churches is the weekly newsletter of the National Senior Citizens Law Center in Los Angeles. This center is staffed by lawyers who are working in the public interest. They are the backup legal council for community legal aid societies and legal services across the country. They're very cognizant about all kinds of legislative matters. pensions, social security, health rights, guardianship, and a variety of other issues that concern the elderly.

Our overall aim in the church's social witness is to affirm the contribution of older persons to our society and to draw upon their accumulated experience, skills, and wisdom in working for a society with more just access to its goods and services.

6. *The church and the dying.* As a part of ministry, the church should be educating its members about death with dignity and the right to die with dignity. Many congregations are encouraging their members to sign the Living Will and to discuss as a congregation its several provisions. It's a very important document directed to the family, physician, lawyer, and clergy. The Living Will can be found on page 111.

E: What's the legal status of that document?

M: It's not a probate document, except in the State of California. In the summer of 1976, Governor Brown signed into law an instrument that makes it possible for people to decide in advance to sign a document instructing those who survive that there should be no artificial or extraordinary means used to extend or prolong life when it is reasonably clear that death is imminent. The mandate is to absolve the survivors of any feelings of guilt. This is a free and responsible decision on the part of the person about his or her demise. It seems to me that this is a very important instrument to discuss in the congregation in appropriate ways and to have as many people as possible in the congregation sign it, and also to work with the courts and with bar associations to get this kind of document legally binding in all fifty states.

E: Besides the Living Will, what other practices ought the church to favor and develop regarding the terminally ill? For example, I'm convinced that a lot of people who visit the terminally ill on behalf of the deacons, or some other group, are really not prepared to carry out a constructive role.

M: It's often a shock to people who visit someone who shows great weakness, physical deterioration, and mental confusion. This is a task that needs some preparation and some understanding of the finitude of everyone. We all have to die and we should accept this as a part of life.

E: It seems to me that there should be as much special training for that role as there is for the counseling role, if we envision lay people doing that.

M: I would hope that this would be very much on the church's agenda. A final aspect of this very important and critical subject is the support that increasing numbers of churches are giving to the organizing of memorial societies, investigating the practices of local funeral directors and pressing for disclosure of their fees. There ought to be some agreement on the part of funeral directors as to limitation on costs. The emphasis ought to be on memorial services rather than glorification of the corpse. There ought to be encouragement to have very simple burials in plain pine boxes or cremation, as well as arranging for certain parts of the body to be donated for medical research. A memorial society is a democratic nonprofit association of people formed to obtain dignity, simplicity, and economy in funeral arrangements. Experience has taught us that simplicity can reduce both suffering and expense at time of death. Grief is not measured by the size of the funeral or the expense of the casket!

Memorial societies have been formed in forty-one states, often through the leadership of church members. Information may be secured from the Continental Association of Funeral and Memorial Societies, Suite 1100, 1828 L Street, N.W., Washington, DC 20036.

E: I believe that Jessica Mitford pointed out a few years ago that the funeral industry had successfully lobbied to require embalming in some states, even when there is cre-

A LIVING WILL

To My Family, My Physician, My Lawyer, My Clergyman

To Any Medical Facility in Whose Care I Happen to Be

To Any Individual Who May Become Responsible for My Health, Welfare, or Affairs

Death is as much a reality as birth, growth, maturity and old age —it is the one certainty of life. If the time comes when I,_____ _____ can no longer take part in decisions for my own future, let this statement stand as an expression of my wishes, while I am still of sound mind.

If the situation should arise in which there is no reasonable expectation of my recovery from physical or mental disability, I request that I be allowed to die and not be kept alive by artificial means or "heroic measures." I do not fear death itself as much as the indignities of deterioration, dependence, and hopeless pain. I, therefore, ask that medication be mercifully administered to me to alleviate suffering even though this may hasten the moment of death.

This request is made after careful consideration. I hope you who care for me will feel morally bound to follow its mandate. I recognize that this appears to place a heavy responsibility upon you, but it is with the intention of relieving you of such responsibility and of placing it upon myself in accordance with my strong convictions that this statement is made.

Signed_____

Date_____
Witness_____
Witness_____
Copies of this request
have been given to_____
_____

Prepared by the Euthanasia Educational Council,
250 West 57th Street, New York, NY 10019

mation. What do you think should be the church's position?

M: The Gray Panthers joined in a series of hearings that the Federal Trade Commission had on funeral practices. Not too many people testified. The Gray Panthers presented some evidence of the expense of funerals, the way in which the grief of the survivors is exploited, etc. Since then, some funeral practices have been investigated; many funeral directors now offer the option of inexpensive funerals and simple burials. The churches should be lobbying for this and insisting that the funerals which they have a part in arranging meet these new and human standards.

7. *The church's position toward retirement and nursing homes.* Church members are often admitted to nursing homes when their families can no longer care for them. Some of the nursing homes are church-related. The nursing home scene has not been a pleasant one. Newspapers have exposed all kinds of abuses and neglect of patients, along with the exorbitant prices and profits that the nursing home industry has been able to realize. We believe that the nursing home industry (with some marked exceptions) will not appreciably change without vigilance on the part of churches and community groups; and we would hope that the church would take some initiative in organizing not just friendly visitors who will go on a one-to-one basis to see residents, but who will really organize the residents and families of residents for their own welfare and act as advocates.

Many local churches, as well as judicatories, are administratively responsible for retirement and nursing homes. The church needs to be aware of the rights of the residents and to take steps to ensure their well-being. Many churches will form groups of officers and members, including young and old, to work on task forces on aging so that there can be some continuing interaction with the residents of retirement and nursing homes. I often wonder why it took Ralph Nader and two young college students to blow the whistle on the nursing home scene, when for decades ministers and lay people have been visiting extended-care facilities as a part of their pastoral ministry.

E: Apparently it must have something to do with a limited definition of "ministry" as primarily being one-on-one, person-to-person, without concern for the structural issues involved.

M: It's hard to believe that a consistent visitor in a particular facility wouldn't be aware of the quality of care and what was needed to secure it and to affirm good care when it was apparent.

8. *The use of church facilities for clinics, multipurpose centers, nutrition sites, etc.* We would like to get some books and magazines made available in those places where old people come for hot lunches, but that's hard to do, because the guidelines don't call for that. The primary business is to get the food hot, get it served on time, get people in and get them out. If you have a nutrition site in your church, you could introduce people to books and new ideas. I have a feeling it might lift the level of interest and morale of the constituents and the staff.

E: A production-line mentality can become habitual. An acquaintance tells me that a lot of retired folks come to the local church family night supper; but if the church doesn't have a specific program that begins right when the dishes are cleared, they're ready to leave. Generally they're not going anyplace. But to get them just to lean back in their chairs and talk to one another requires some intervention techniques.

M: Another thing that's interesting is that some people go the rounds of the nutrition sites. They know that they have good food at a certain place on Monday and at another place on Tuesday. The nutrition sites have a large educational task in addition to providing food. Moreover, they should be helping to organize food co-ops and community gardens.

E: To me one of the more insidious developments is the legalization of bingo. Playing bingo has gone beyond the realm of occupying time.

M: You're absolutely right. There are a lot of multipurpose centers that are more than food distribution sites, where people come for the day and the principal activity is bingo. It's very easy to get a big, warm-body count where you have bingo games going on—nothing interferes with the bingo game. We're perpetuating the mindlessness.

E: This becomes a challenge to the church. One church I know of takes its turn a week at a time serving the food in the soup line. Instead of sending a group down just to feed them, they have an intergenerational committee that presents a program as well.

M: One of the things that works quite well, especially if there's a turnover, is introducing yourself to some of the people in the line—just interviewing with such questions as: Where are you from? What did you do? They then start talking with one another, and the motivation to get involved (at least in this way) builds. You just have to get them started.

9. *Setting up a task force on aging.* A task force on aging ought to have some ongoing responsibilities recognized by the pastor and officers of the church, and there ought to be a small working budget assigned for its work. It should be action-oriented as well as concerned for adequate services. Much of its work and strategy should be directed to changing some of the corporate structures of our society and the church. Congregations have much more clout and influence than they sometimes recognize.

The pastor(s) and officers of the church have a specific role as formal leaders—to enable, energize, and motivate emerging natural leaders from the group and give them full opportunity to develop, grow, and exercise leadership.

E: What are some of the areas of work for such a task force?

M: The local task force on aging could obviously begin with an age study of the congregation. It would be interesting for the congregation to know the age span of their members—who are the youngest and who are the oldest, and where they live. Usually the older members live closer to the church and are not too apt to be fully involved in the life of the church. They're isolated, even from the church. The government offices—the area offices on aging—and community services of various kinds have outreach workers who are supposed to find the isolated elderly, people who have locked themselves in one-room apartments and who are afraid to come out; but the church often has these people on their membership rolls and ought to be seeking them if they don't come out themselves.

E: So we do this particular age profile, which I imagine most congregations have. What then?

M: A lot of people are very discouraged that the age pyramid shows relatively few members who are young and a growing group of people who are old. They're despairing about the church's future, and feel that they're losing ground. If the survey could also include some assessment of the experience of people in their later years, the task force on aging could build a skill bank, begin to identify the skills that are needed by the congregation and the community, and encourage older members to be very much a part of community change and community action.

E: Have you noticed that very few people over sixty-five teach Sunday school, except the adult Bible classes?

M: Yes. And it would be marvelous if older people were teaching the very young ones. Many children in our congregations today live far away from their grandparents. There are a variety of new "foster grandparent" roles that the older members of congregations could play in relation to the younger members, particularly teen-agers who are often isolated and alienated from their families. People of their grandparents' age might be able to be more understanding and have more time.

E: Would the task force on aging have an issue focus primarily, or would it try to think in terms of training people to take on certain roles?

M: Both. Some of the issues are poverty, income maintenance, unavailability and expense of quality health care, housing; all of those very practical issues have to be dealt with in social action strategy. Beyond that, there is the enabling role to help retired people to move to new kinds of jobs which begin to use the experience and accumulated skills of older Americans and deploy them in a variety of new jobs that our society really needs. Possible jobs are in hospitals and nursing homes. We've defined the patient advocate as someone who could be very helpful in emergency wards and clinics, by being at the side of the patient and identifying his or her needs and seeing that care is given. There is a great deal to be done to reform the courts and our penal system. People who have time and experience ought to devote some time during every week to watch the courts, learn all they possibly can about criminal justice and injustice, visit correctional facilities, and provide some continuing friendship and counsel to the people who are released offenders.

We'd like to see many people, particularly those who are homebound or physically immobile, be media watchers. We have a Gray Panthers "media watch" priority, which is developing criteria for viewing prime-time television—local stations as well as the network programs—commending programming that is not agist or sexist or violent, complaining about the way in which much of the media programming depicts age and also about the commercials which are pretty demoralizing and demeaning. We were able, as Gray Panthers, to get the Good Broadcasting Code of the National Association of Broadcasters amended to include a restraint on programming that is objectionable from an age point of view. Now it remains to be seen whether or not that code is followed.

We'd like to see retired clergy prepare themselves to be

ethical counselors in stockholders' meetings and to corporate management. The great corporations, particularly national ones, have a large debt to society and lots of practices that pollute the earth and the waters, that make unbridled profits, and that oppress workers. Those practices ought to be known to the stockholders, and stockholders ought to be pressing for corporate accountability.

E: Why do you single out clergy for this role?

M: Well, it's something that shouldn't be restricted to the clergy, but it just seems like an appropriate thing that ministers might want to do. For one thing, they have certain recognized credentials to raise the moral issues, to keep ethical issues on the agenda, and to be aware themselves, as students of ethics and moral values in society, of constructive ways corporate power can be used. The churches have had some success, through the National Council of Churches, in monitoring the way in which church investments are made. We've made some very important points on that score and more of it should be done.

10. *Pressing for change in seminary education.* The local church ought to be pressing for changes in seminary education. Theological education in general gives very little attention to pastoral ministries, or the role of ministers with regard to aging members of their congregation. Ministers could avoid the discouragement and lack of competence that many of them have felt if there were some preparation for these kinds of ministries in seminary education. There should be dialogue between the churches and seminary faculty who are concerned about ethics, particularly social ethics. We should be pressing in churches for some good

theological undergirding of these new ministries. Biblical-theological awareness ought to be part of seminary theological education today.

E: That's a helpful summary of the task of the church. But very few local churches would feel that they have enough expertise by themselves to do those ten things. If they utilize the resources of a larger judicatory—whether it be a district, a presbytery, a diocese, a conference, or an association—maybe it would be easier to think about developing a program. What would be the special contribution of a presbytery, or similar judicatory in other denominations, in helping congregations develop this kind of ministry?

M: Presbyteries ought to be providing ongoing training. There ought to be a series of workshops, at least annually, for ministers and lay people of the churches. There could be deployment of roles. Certain churches, with their own geographical basis and membership, could give special attention to one or several of the roles. Within the judicatory's oversight and coordinating role, all of these ten, plus other functions, could probably be developed. I would hope that the judicatory would be working on an ecumenical basis too. Much more could be done on an interfaith basis if congregations and judicatories were committed to serious ministries. Meanwhile, don't overlook the resources already in the congregation and the community.

The laity ought to play a major role in all of the various tasks of the church. They know the anxiety of retirement. The women know how difficult it is to live with a husband who is going through the trauma of separating from a lifetime career. And who knows better how to deal with the death of a spouse than does a widow or widower. From an empathetic point of view, lay people have something very special to give. The church's task in dealing with the anxieties, the fears, and the myths that have grown up in our society about growing old and being old could be described as countercultural—going against the societal stream which declares that old people are surplus, wastefolk, not useful anymore in producing profit or goods. They have a sense of history. They have demonstrated, in their own survivorship, what it takes to cope and survive in the face of change; and the church has a unique role in identifying the kinds of ministry that seem to me to be clearly needed.

E: One of the problems I see in this area of ministry is that the church is tempted to hire people to do the work or to leave it to the full-time church staff. What is your view of that pattern?

M: If the church falls into this trap, the church is merely mirroring society's assumption that old people have nothing to give and that only somebody who's professionally trained in ministries has anything to offer. I'd like to think that the older members of congregations, in their own existential situation, have a great deal to give and that they should be the ones who define the goals and work out the kinds of ministries to be done by the church. Maybe people who have retired from their jobs, and who are themselves in their later years, might be the ones who would carry out these new tasks. They certainly should be intimately involved in determining the work of the congregation. If we're honest and serious about the makeup of the local congregation, there are many kinds of human resources available to us.

The church must launch a massive attack on agism in all its oppressive and constraining forms. Congregations and judicatories have perpetuated age-segregated housing ghettos. Church boards and agencies have continued the wasteful policies of society in requiring mandatory retirement of their staff members. Theological education itself must change to equip students in various fields with the knowledge and skill they need to reach older persons in the worshiping community.

We need to enlist the help of liberation theologians, Bible scholars, Christian ethicists, and church educators in sensitizing both church and society to the damage that agism does to people and groups. Biblical and theological perspectives are essential to support the changes that must come to congregational life and outreach.

A second Reformation waits in the wings!

WORKING AT THE GRASS ROOTS 25

Robert McClellan

This chapter offers specific guidelines to enable leaders to work at the grass roots in developing and evaluating ministries among older persons. The reader is invited to consider the "How To" material presented which is the result of experiences gained in the Action/Investigation project of the Chatsworth Adult Center, Point Loma Community Presbyterian Church, San Diego, California. It is hoped that the step-by-step suggestions will stimulate action for beginning a ministry to, for, with, and of older persons in local congregations.

1. Begin Where You Are!
   The initiator may be a pastor, priest, rabbi, or lay person(s).

   Stop — Take time (it will probably be from some other priority).

   Look — Pay attention — look at older persons as if you have never seen them. Look with them at some common concern or need.

   Listen — Go where they are — homes, centers, parks,

gathering places, meetings, hospitals, nursing homes.

Aim — Try to see a bit of life as older persons see it.

2. Include Older Persons in your Life Space

Read — Newspapers, magazines, books that focus on older persons. Subscribe to *Dynamic Maturity* (AIM), *Modern Maturity* (AARP), or *The Gerontologist.*

Attend plays, watch television specials, movies; attend lectures related to aging and the aged.

Trust them — They have coped. They are for you. They can help. They have wisdom and experience.

Affirm them — Encourage them. Support them. Give them responsibility.

Touch them — Touching is talking. Sharing experiences, ideas, concerns is good therapy for all.

Respect them — Let them feel they are important to:

You	Church or Synagogue
Themselves	Community
God	Life

3. Ask yourself:

"What am I, what is our church or synagogue doing about older persons?"

Time spent: _____

_____

Activities: _____

_____

_____

What is good? _____

_____

What is poor? _____

_____

What am I (are we) feeling? _____

_____

4. Find Someone to Share your Concern
   A person   A committee
   A couple   A group
   A family

5. Involve a Committee or Official Board
   Report your concern. Suggest study of the matter. Seek concern and approval of the board. Indicate resources available, handbooks, etc. See "Tools for the Task" (Appendix).

6. Call Two Special Meetings of Interested People — One Week Apart
   a. First Meeting
      Get acquainted.
      Share common interests and concerns.
      Receive input from specialist(s), i.e., Area Agency on Aging, college professor, social worker, other community resource persons.
      Distribute *Claiming A Frontier: Ministry and Older People* for further study and action.
      Select chairperson, and two to eight other persons, mostly older, to form Steering Committee to choose Task Force on Older Adults.
      Let pastor, priest, rabbi, or his/her appointee serve as Advisor.
      Steering Committee should meet during the week before the next group meeting.
   b. Second Meeting
      Steering Committee reports recommendations for Task Force membership.
      Group selects Task Force on Older Adults.
      Show *The Second Spring of Samantha Muffin* (use *Study Guide for a Single Showing*).
      Review the congregation's present programs for older persons in light of Samantha Muffin's experience.
      Assign responsibility for developing ministries among older persons to Task Force.
      Task Force report to Official Board.

7. Work With the Task Force

Meet regularly: Weekly, bi-weekly, monthly, (More frequent meetings provide more input, stimulus, progress).

Materials: Continue use of *Claiming A Frontier: Ministry and Older People* and other books, handbooks, and manuals recommended in "resources."

The Second Spring of Samantha Muffin: Review one segment at each meeting (Use *Study Guide for Series of Programs.)*

Visit programs in community — ministries to, for, with, of older people. Evaluate.

Group sharing — at each meeting, share experiences, concerns, insights, information, feelings.

Records — Keep records of actions and progress.

8. Gather Information on Unmet Needs and Resources

Process includes:

Discovery — exploring and analyzing needs of the constituency.

Guiding — formation and integration of groups.

Helping — groups define and achieve goals.

Evaluating and Consolidating — group experience is put together through sharing.

Reference: *Older People and the Church,* Maves and Cedarleaf (1949).

Resources:

a. *Instructional Manual for the Older Adult Church Survey Project,* David L. Batzka (1974). This manual is designed to enable a local congregation Task Force to make important surveys:

Survey of members of congregation 55 years and older — questionnaire composed of 62 questions.

Community Social Service Survey containing 12 questions and guidelines.

Church Program Survey, including guidelines for conducting survey.

b. *Mission Action Group Guide: The Aging,* published by Woman's Missionary Union, Southern Baptist Church (1972).

Manual includes:

Personal preparation actions
Orientation actions
Survey actions
Planning actions
Process
Activities
In-service training action
Sharing actions
Resource list

c. *Senior Adult Utilization and Ministry Handbook* by Raymond A. Kader (1974).
Manual includes:
Perspective.
Utilizing the many talents of senior adults; survey forms most useful.
Ministering to active senior adults.
Ministering to shut-ins and nursing home senior adults.
Organizing small, middle size and large churches.

d. *Six Steps to Develop a Program for Older People,* compiled by Bella Jacobs (1972).
Manual includes:
Step One: Rationale for Program
Step Two: Form a Steering Committee
Step Three: Find a Sponsoring or Advisory Committee
Step Four: Group Structure
Step Five: First and Second open meetings
Step Six: Project in Operation

9. Consider Models of Programs
Resources: Use *Claiming A Frontier: Ministry and Older People,* also, *Aging Persons in the Community of Faith: A Guidebook for Churches and Synagogues on Ministry To, For and With the Aging,* by Donald F. Clingan (1975).
Review each model.
Consider which elements seem to meet apparent needs of your people in your situation.
List possible elements which you might include in a program for your congregation/community.
Dream of your potentials.

List names of persons who might help among your constituency.

Contact source of model(s) for further information.

10. Plan Your Program

Keep in mind that *you* are creating, revising programs for *your* situation. What works in another place *may* or *may not* be useful in yours. *Everyone* in this work is a *learner*. There is no right or wrong way.

Essential ingredients:

Needs and input of older persons themselves

Goal of *renewal* and *fulfillment* of older persons; not amusement, diversion, or killing of time.

Ministry *to, for, with,* and *of* older persons. Try for aspects of each of these in your program.

Be sure you know *why* you are doing *what* you are doing.

Evaluate results as you proceed (a mini-evaluation after each meeting in the early stages is often helpful).

Early course corrections may save grave mistakes. They also help in motivation and direction. They insure a valuable sense of "ownership" which is basic for long-range effectiveness.

Choose One Area of Focus

Pick the most urgent need discovered, or a genuine need you feel you can handle: i.e., Meals on Wheels, transportation, telephone reassurance, handyman service, educational classes, arts and crafts, Fellowship Programs, etc.

Involve Older People

Let it be theirs from the beginning. Use Senior Power.

Remember your situation is unique.

Build Program in Increments.

Add emphasis as you go, as needs and resources in persons and facilities emerge.

Consult specialists for direction.

Undergird your effort with personal and group prayer.

GENERAL CONSIDERATIONS

1. **Remember Relationships**

   Older people are a gold mine of experience, skills, and possibilities.

   Help them feel they belong to one another and to the group.

   Keep channels of participation open.

2. **Everybody Grow!**

   Look for signs of growth and involvement.

   Check "Twelve Rejuvenating Techniques" for guidelines of emphasis (Chapter 4).

   Be persistent and expectant.

   Progress will probably be like the growth of a snowball — slow at first, gaining in momentum, size, and effectiveness.

   Keep in mind the "signs of renewal and fulfillment" (Chapter 3).

   Enlarge scope to meet more needs of more people, and with more involvement.

3. **Key Factors**

   Spiritual concern for older persons as persons.

   Understanding.

   Patience.

   Flexibility.

   Involve older persons *always*.

   Support and encourage.

   Multiply leadership through participation and responsible delegation.

   Balance — There must be input if there is to be output.

   Motivate unceasingly.

   Feedback regularly to official board.

   Interpret program through word of mouth, and written communication in congregation and community.

   Do not let models scare you, especially if you are a beginner or in a small congregation.

   Programs of great usefulness can be in any size or type of congregation or community if wisely developed.

   Consider joining with another church or synagogue in your ministry among older persons.

   Use community resources.

SUMMARY

Begin where you are. Do your thing. Older people can experience renewal and fulfillment. They are able to help themselves with support from others. Stay with it. You will grow in effectiveness and do more. Show appreciation through recognition. The need is big. No one can do it all. Your contribution will help others. What you find and do may become more effective than anything any person or group has yet found and done.

There is no magic in this book. It calls for genuine interest and hard work. There are many resources in persons and material. Older people are the most important resource. Nobody can do for you and your church or synagogue what you and your congregation need to do.

BEGIN NOW!
CLAIM YOUR SHARE OF THE FRONTIER!!

REFERENCES

Aging Persons in the Community of Faith. A Congregational Guidebook for Churches and Synagogues on Ministry To, For, and With the Aging. Published for the Institute on Religion and Aging by the Indiana Commission on Aging and Aged, 1975.

Batzka, David L. *Instruction Manual for the Older Adult Church Survey Project.* The National Benevolent Association, the Division of Social and Health Services of the Christian Church (Disciples of Christ), Department of Service to Congregations, 1974.

Jacobs, Bella. "Six Steps to Develop a Program for Older People." The National Council on the Aging, Inc., Washington, D.C. 1972.

Kader, Raymond A. *Senior Adult Utilization and Ministry Handbook.* Clearwater, Florida: Kader Specialties, 1974.

Maves, Paul B. *Older People and the Church.* New York: Abingdon-Cokesbury Press, 1949.

Mission Action Group Guide: The Aging. Published by Woman's Missionary Union, Southern Baptist Church, 600 North 20th Street, Birmingham, Alabama 35203, 1972.

THE SAGE PROJECT ...
A NEW IMAGE OF AGE *26*

KEN DYCHTWALD. PhD. at the age of twenty-seven is already a well known figure in the human potential movement. He is Codirector of the Sage Project and President of the National Association for Humanistic Gerontology. In addition to lecturing and leading workshops nationally on bodymind awareness. personal growth, and holistic health, he serves as a consultant and adjunct instructor at several universities. He is the author of *Bodymind* (Pantheon. 1977). *The Sage Papers* (forthcoming) and numerous articles on issues of health and growth.

For the past four years, the staff and clientele of the *Sage Project* in Berkeley, California have been attempting to generate positive images of aging by demonstrating that people over sixty can grow and transcend the negative expectations of our culture. Through the creation of a humanistically focused self-development program for men and women over sixty years of age, they have been exploring the many ways in which the later years of life can be a time for health, vitality, expanded awareness. and the realization of self that comes from having lived a long and full life.

The Sage approach to personal growth with older adults is eclectic in technique, drawing from a wide range of Western therapeutic and self-awareness methods such as biofeedback, relaxation training, sensory awareness, gestalt. encounter, psychodrama, art and music therapy. massage and journal writing. as well as a variety of Eastern self-developmental disciplines and processes such as meditation, yoga, tai chi, kum nye. chanting, and pranayama breathing exercises. In addition, the Sage approach to group work and individual counseling is holistic in practice since it focuses on the individual as a whole person working simultaneously with the mind, body. and spirit.

Sage was formed in early 1974 by Gay Luce. Eugenia Gerrard, and Ken Dychtwald. At present, the Sage staff is composed of twenty psychologists, physicians. breathing, movement, and art therapists, and specialists with extensive training in a wide variety of human arts. The Sage Project is unique in that it is the first highly successful program to merge effectively a humanistic clinical approach to self-development and personal growth with a much needed demand for creative and positively oriented gerontological programs and services.

Sage is supported primarily by grants from the National Institute of Mental Health, the San Francisco Foundation, other private foundations and private donations. National acclaim and recognition have been accorded Sage for its innovative programming, high quality clinical work, and most importantly, for the surprising results that have emerged from the first three and one half years of experimentation and research. In many instances, the Sage methods and approach have proved to be successful in increasing the physical health, emotional stability, and self-esteem of its elderly participants.

According to Sage participant, 75 year-old Herb Pillars:

I came here afraid of dying and even more afraid of being a burden in my old age. Now I'm not nearly so afraid. . . . As for the changes, I came here with arthritis in my hands, terrible backaches, and a stiff neck. I still have a little trouble with the arthritis, but the backache is gone, and I can now twist my head and see the traffic behind me on the road when I'm driving. Also, I used to smoke. You can't smoke and deep breathe at the same time!

Another Sage member, Ellie Karbach, 73, described herself as "an old post-cancer case with high blood pressure." Says Ellie:

At Sage I have been learning how to be alive and vital again. For example, I was recently at a party and ate some of the wrong things. When I went home, I suffered from a tachycardia [rapid heartbeat] attack. I immediately put myself into a state of deep relaxation and practiced yogic breathing and the attack quickly passed. . . . In addition to becoming more aware of myself in a physical way, I have also been learning quite a bit about my mind and my feelings. In my Sage group I had a chance to work through some of my long-repressed grief about losing six people including my brother within a short period of time. One day I was doing my deep breathing exercises when emotions started coming up and I began to cry. . . . I wept bitterly for two hours, and I wept away a score of sorrows. And, finally, I started to laugh, thinking of all the people who have loved me all my life and still love me. . . . Thanks to Sage, I'll never be the same. No one ever had a chance at age 73 to live a new life as I have.

According to Frances Burch, 68:

I've seen people in this group change their physical and mental outlook. They're more open and responsive, their lives are more exciting, and they have more possibilities and choices. I feel much better myself. I've seen things go on here that are amazing . . . self-healing. Here we're learning to tap new personal power sources through our spiritual growth. I'm finding energy that I haven't had in years.

At present, the Sage Project has four primary programs: (*a*) Core group programs; (*b*) Institutional programs; (*c*) Professional training and research; and (*d*) National development and national networking.

CORE GROUP PROGRAM

The Sage core group program was the first of the various Sage experiments to gain national recognition for the way in which it was able to revitalize the minds, bodies, and spirits of its older participants. By so doing, it suggests new and more positively oriented images of aging to all of those involved in the process of growing older. Sage core groups begin each fall and meet weekly for nine months at Sage headquarters in Berkeley, California. Composed of about twelve relatively healthy older people and two staff members, each core group becomes the medium in which staff and participants share their skills and themselves as a means of personal exploration focusing on improving physical and psychological functioning. To date, Sage has graduated four core groups and is presently working with different program designs with the four new core groups that began this year.

Graduates of Sage core groups are welcome to join the Sage community which is an action-oriented, ongoing self-help group run and coordinated entirely by core group members. In addition, core group graduates may continue for a second year of intensive leadership training under the careful guidance of Sage staff. If qualified, core graduates may become Sage co-leaders and program coordinators in one of the various Sage service facilities. Presently, many of the core graduates have become actively involved in Sage group leadership and, in fact, two of the new core groups this year are being designed and led entirely by core graduates.

INSTITUTIONAL PROGRAM

In 1975, Sage extended its range of clinical services and investigation when it began its institutional program. Since then, Sage staff have been conducting groups in various institutional settings around the San Francisco Bay Area including homes for the aged, nursing homes, rest homes, and convalescent hospitals. Many of the residents of these institutions are severely limited in their physical and psychosocial functioning due to sickness, intense depression, and senility.

Sage institutional groups meet twice each week throughout the year and are composed of ten to twenty participants and two or more staff leaders. The program has been attempting to explore a variety of methods and techniques for body/mind development and revitalization in order to discover what methods and practices effectively generate the most worthwhile changes in the lives of the residents in these institutions. Drawing upon a wide range of techniques, activities, and human communication skills, Sage staff have been met with a great deal of success as many of the participants seem to experience heightened awareness, improved mental acuity, improved social and psychophysical skills, and an enhanced appreciation for their own self-responsibility as a result of their Sage experience. Because of the depressing conditions that prevail in many institutions of this type, the Sage institutional program has received a great deal of attention and support from senior residences, institutions, and hospitals throughout the country.

PROFESSIONAL TRAINING AND RESEARCH

Since the work that is being carried out by Sage suggests a variety of ways in which a humanistic self-development program can be effectively utilized to remedy the depression and body/mind decline of the later years, it is important that the techniques, instruments, and outcomes of this work be disseminated to the professional community at large. Preliminary research being carried out jointly by Morton Lieberman of the University of Chicago's Committee on Human Development and Dean Manheimer of the Institute for Research in Social Behavior in Berkeley, California has shown that the Sage approach and methodology in the core groups have been significantly successful at lowering stress, heightening self-esteem, increasing coping skills, and several other key psychosocial variables.

In addition, Sage offers professional training programs, workshops, seminars, and institutes. Ranging from one-day intensive workshops and six-day residential training seminars to year-long apprenticeships in the various Sage ongoing groups, Sage training programs are executed under the carefully supervised professional guidance of Sage staff. Sage staff also teach and design courses in self-development, body/mind awareness, and humanistic gerontology at colleges and universities nationwide.

NATIONAL DEVELOPMENT

Because of the significant success of the Sage approach and because of the need for humanistic and creative programs for older people Sage staff have become involved in a great number of lectures, presentations, and consultations at universities, growth centers, community centers, medical facilities, and mental health clinics throughout the country. Over twenty-thousand people have attended Sage presentations.

Through these presentations and specially designed consulting activities, Sage staff have aided in the development of several hundred similar programs nationwide. Sage has also produced three award winning video-documentaries about the various aspects of its work (available to rent or purchase) and is presently working on several training manuals and relevant resource catalogs for professionals looking to expand their knowledge of Sage-type methods and techniques.

In this way, Sage has been reaching out into the national community in an attempt to generate new activities and programs that will support positive images about the possibilities for growth, health, and self-fulfillment in the later years of life. Out of this national outreach and development program has grown a new organization, the National Association for Humanistic Gerontology, which has been founded by Ken Dychtwald, one of the Sage codirectors.

THE NATIONAL ASSOCIATION FOR HUMANISTIC GERONTOLOGY

When Sage began its work in January 1974, its founders knew of few people who were attempting to incorporate personal growth and holistic health methods and beliefs into their work with older people. Those who were experimenting with humanistically focused health, education, and recreation methods were doing so alone, usually with very little financial or psychological support and with minimal contact with others throughout the country who were involved with similar activities.

However, through outreach, training, and national development programs, Sage has been discovering that there are thousands of people and institutions who are committed to many of the same innovative visions and practices. Although there has been a growing body of people and information that support a humanistic approach to gerontological services, programs, and research, there has not been a formal organization or network established to act as a clearinghouse and central resource agency for all of the shared ideas, techniques, materials, and experiences. As a result, many people and projects have lacked support, stimulation, and relevant information-sharing.

In response to this situation, Sage has given birth to the National

Association for Humanistic Gerontology. This new organization was designed specifically to aid in the creation of a national network of people, institutions, and programs for the purposes of resource sharing, mutual support and stimulation, and the advancement of ideas, methods, and visions related to a humanistic approach to gerontology.

In the early stages of its development, the NAHG is being supported and sponsored by the staff and resources of the Sage Project. Membership in NAHG is open to professionals and nonprofessionals alike. During the next three years, the NAHG will be developing a national resource listing which will be a "people and programs" resource network that will allow NAHG members to know who is doing what, where, and with what results. Several "whole earth" type catalogs of relevant and worthwhile information will also be assembled. NAHG members receive a quarterly newsletter and reduced rates at NAHG conferences and symposia and on all NAHG catalogs and publications.

27

Old and Young
Can Learn Together:
The Youth-Aging
Project

Marie Malveaux, M.S.W.
and
Eleanor Guilford, A.C.S.W.

"Yuck! I'd rather die young than grow old and lonely."

The above statement was a response by a Catholic high school senior to a query, "What is your general attitude about growing old?" Except for her reference to dying, the student's response was typical of most of the statements made by her peers. The younger generation's expression, "Yuck!," is of itself, intended to convey a feeling identifiable with another set of Three R's: Repudiation, Repugnance, and Repulsion. The stark fact is that such statements do reflect to a large degree the general attitude held by many youths and young adults toward growing old.

What were the reasons that led our staff to propose and our Board of Directors to approve the project described in the title? To all of our staff and Committee members, the litany of problems facing the elderly was painfully well-known—poverty, inadequate health care, sub-standard housing, lack of transportation, social isolation, insufficient opportunity for employment and meaningful roles following upon mandatory retirement, and, of special concern to us, the loss of status within our youth-oriented society. But if the dignity of the person proclaimed by all major religions was to be a reality for all ages, as well as all races, colors, and creeds, was there not a need for young people to know older people better and thereby to come to love and honor them?

The idea of including the subject of Aging in the curriculum of Catho-

Mesdames Malveaux and Guilford are on the staff of the Catholic Committee for the Aging of Catholic Charities of San Francisco, and are, respectively, Director and Supervisor of the project described in their article.

lic schools seemed to us consonant with the goals of both Catholic Charities agencies and Catholic educational institutions. "Catholic Charities, as an organized institution, has the basic knowledge and expertise to create that positive other-awareness, and it must constantly seek new opportunities to build the bridges that bring people together in understanding, acceptance, and love." [1] The goals of our Catholic educational institutions include the development in students of a recognition of their personal worth by permeating the learning process with a Christian spirit. Moreover, there was the consideration that the majority of youth we attempt to help today will live to grow old themselves. Could we begin to help them now to develop a better image of the older persons that they themselves would, in time, become?

With this conviction, we developed the goals of the Youth-Aging Project: (1) to facilitate a more positive view toward aging as a natural stage of human development; (2) to develop a curriculum which would be directed toward increasing the awareness of young persons toward older persons in our society; (3) to accomplish both these ends by stimulating the involvement and relationships of older persons with youth; and (4) to suggest that the project become a model which could be used in other schools.

We felt that such a project had the potential for breaking down barriers to communication and understanding of various age groups. We recognized the potential of younger persons to be in a position soon to help bring about

effective changes to meet the needs of older persons. We hoped that they would be able to enjoy for themselves some of the benefits of the changes.

Method

To develop such a project required the assistance and participation of school administrators, teachers, older persons, students, and community persons in planning areas of interest and activities which could be included in curriculum content. Basically, the curriculum would include the aging process—the biological, psychological, and social aspects of aging.

From the parish-based Senior Centers, several older persons volunteered to be Senior Resource Leaders. These were the people who would participate in and lead discussion in the classroom.

Most of the students favored the novelty of the proposal, and expressed their interest by relating their own personal experiences with their grandparents or other significant older persons. These young people *were* concerned about their relationships with older people.

Community persons were enthusiastic in their support of the project and made themselves available for consultation when needed. One hospital administrator was so favorably disposed toward the need for the project that she offered not only to participate but also to contribute space in the hospital's community room for classes.

Developing a Curriculum Model

Pertinent resource material, in addition to the collection of facts, ideas, and suggestions offered by the various groups, were included in the development of a working draft for the suggested curriculum model. Guidance

---

[1] *Toward a Renewed Catholic Charities Movement*—A Study of the National Conference of Catholic Charities, Preliminary Report, Phase I, September 11, 1971, pg. 5.

was offered by a learning specialist and a retired school supervisor to help develop an outline. The finished draft included these areas: (1) Objectives; (2) Activities; (3) Class Content; (4) Implications. We developed objectives for six classes:

First Class

(a) To examine what the attitudes of high school students are in relation to old age.

(b) To determine the interests of high school students in the various aspects of aging (a ten-point questionnaire was used for this purpose).

Second Class

(a) To continue and/or complete the objectives of the First Class.

Third Class

(a) To recognize the status of elderly persons in the United States in relation to our (society's) attitudes and values.

Fourth Class

(a) To present aging as a natural developmental stage in life.

(b) To consider some of the psychological aspects of growing old.

Fifth Class

(a) To discover and become aware of the physical aspects of aging and aging persons.

Sixth Class

(a) To understand some of the social aspects of aging in relation to the individual's social changes and in relation to his changing environment.

We also devised an evaluation sheet which was to be used several weeks after the completion of the course. The suggested curriculum model had been designed so that it could be utilized by any existing class—that is, there was sufficient flexibility to permit its adaptation to classes in Religion, History, English, Art, Drama, etc.

Although our Project was designed for high school classrooms, we suggest that the curriculum can be adjusted to almost any grade level while retaining the basic goal of helping students to know older people.

Since the participation of the Senior Resource Leaders proved to be a most valuable resource to the success of the Project, we believe that it is pertinent to highlight the background of these older persons.

Backgrounds of Senior Group Resource Leaders

All were retired persons who were still active. The ages of our Group Resource Leaders ranged from forty-four to seventy-seven. All were, or had been, involved in giving service both to young and older people in various ways. Their experiences spanned the fields of public health, nursing, education, music, art, and social work. They possessed a wealth of wisdom which they shared with students during classroom discussions. Their backgrounds and experiences were vital to the idea of including persons who did not consider chronological age to be a barrier to personal growth and who were engaged in self-fulfilling activities. Moreover, they had not lost their interest in and affection for young people.

Implementing the Project

The Project was implemented in three Catholic high schools. Each school and each classroom presented a unique and challenging learning experience. The dialogues between young and old created a lively atmosphere and an understanding and awareness of others.

Immaculate Conception Academy: Senior Religion Class

On the first day, two senior high schools devoted their Religion classes to discussion on aspects of aging and the problems of growing old. Classes were conducted without Senior Group Resource Leaders.

The questionnaire was used for the purpose of ascertaining student interest for future use and for getting some idea as to current gaps in knowledge, even though it would have been impossible to meet the needs within one class period.

These students were studying a unit on Marriage, so we transposed our curriculum plan to adapt itself to their current studies. Using this method, we were able to include the subject of aging within the flow of the Marriage class. Many of the students, thinking seriously about marriage, had not thought about such facts as that they might possibly outlive their spouses and that they might be alone. A review of current statistical information about aging in relation to marriage led to discussion about Social Security payments, remarriage, family finances, etc. One point of discussion flowed easily into another as the natural curiosity of the students facilitated their interest in the various aspects of aging in relation to marriage.

During the second day, our Senior Group Resource Leaders joined the class. Students continued discussing marriage, but in relation to aging vis a vis leisure, second careers, and the role of senior centers. It was helpful to have a retired secretary who was engaged in the "Women for Peace Movement" (students were highly interested in her role), as well as the President of our Senior Center Council.

We found that the Principal-Teacher was concerned about the student's need to know about and become aware of the various legislative policies affecting older persons. While we were unable to have a particular seventy-two-year-old Senior Group Resource Leader present, we distributed her well-written letter to Senator Frank Church questioning his stand on HR-1. The discussion resulting from the use of the letter served to expose students to a current issue and gave them a chance to react to their own stereotypes about the mental inactivity they often attributed to older persons. Our two-day session ended with the Principal-Teacher making a brief recapitulation of the highlights of our discussions. She expressed the thought that student interest and enthusiasm in the subject of aging was a good indicator that they would welcome an extended session.

Convent of the Sacred Heart: Community Service Class

We were able to completely implement the project at this school by having six classes, once weekly, with a group of junior and senior students. The Director of Studies and the Principal graciously received our Senior Group Resource Leaders, making them feel very welcome.

The students were surprised to note that the Senior Group Resource Leaders were as interested in as many of their everyday problems as they themselves were, and this provided a common bond for understanding and concern. This led to expressions of mutual feelings of dignity and recognition on the part of both groups. The Resource Leaders had well-learned, diversified backgrounds and were able to communicate skillfully with these highly knowledgeable but curious students.

One of the rewarding by-products of this particular class was the fact that our older persons, on two occasions, remained after class for discussion with the classroom teacher, expressing their own curiosity about the methods of teaching religion to students today. They were so impressed by her explanations that they expressed a desire "to return to school," but compromised by requesting that the teacher be a guest leader for a series of discussions at their Senior Center.

Presentation High School: I—Ninth Grade Personal Growth and Development Class

In this class, we covered the aspects of aging, using student responses to two items on the questionnaire: (1) "What is your general attitude about growing old?" and (2) "How long would you like to live?" This also gave us a chance to explore with the class some of their reactions to their own responses, while we emphasized the aspects of aging relevant to their responses.

These students showed not only a high degree of sophistication in their responses but also enthusiasm about exploring some of their personal experiences and myths about aging, and were able to consciously explain their insights about aging in line with their current studies of personal growth and development. Discussion stimulated their interest in identifying some of the aspects of aging that were closely akin to some aspects of adolescence, and enable them to see the difference while articulating their personal experiences of "old age" which pointed to their understanding of changes in human growth.

This class was highly stimulated to look into some of the social aspects of aging in relation to older persons as consumers. We raised the question as to why older persons are never represented among department store mannequins. This opened up a Pandora's Box of excitement, with students undertaking the questioning of department store sales ladies and managers on the subject. This simple activity provided much food for thought and reflection as the students gained some insights into the psychological deprivation of aged persons by society. One student reported that a large department store manager took her for a "crack" merely because of her inquiry. The class was faced with looking at some of the practical, everyday experiences which some of the elderly face and to question the impact of such experiences.

Presentation High School: II—Senior Class—Child Development

With the cooperation of the classroom teacher, we were able to distribute questionnaires several days prior to the beginning of the project. This allowed time for us to assess specific student interests beforehand, planning to use these as a take-off point for the first day of classes. Actually, this method proved more fascinating than we had anticipated, as it revealed the students' concerns and gave, at the same time, an indirect view of how they perceived older persons.

A large number chose the emotional aspects of aging, death and dying, institutional care, and the physical and social aspects of aging. Few noted an interest in topics which would touch upon older persons as consumers, in social and community action, in transportation, or in older persons' organizations. None noted an interest in the White House Conference On Aging. (These selections, we noted, closely approximated those made by students at two other schools.)

Our second day of classes were led by three Senior Group Resource Leaders, with the classroom teacher acting as another resource leader, for each of the four groups into which the class was divided. Each group discussed a selected topic of interest while wearing a simulated form of the Emphathic Model Equipment· Students wore dark plastic glasses (mydriatics), plugged their ears with cotton, and wore two layers of masking tape on their fingertips to provide insights into the effects of visual, auditory, and tactile deprivation. The idea was also to try to stimulate student thinking about ways in which society could provide the necessary stimuli for increasing an individual's ability to live safely in and maintain his orientation to his surroundings.

During these two days of classes, students displayed a surprising interest in learning and discovering more about their capacities to think about their feelings and observations about older people. They verbalized, rather cogently, their need to have more classroom time to communicate more fully with older persons, and to explore, in depth, some of the topical interests which they had selected.

We felt a definite advantage in having a classroom teacher whose enthusiasm and sensitivity about the subject of aging was reflected in most of the attitudes of her students in this class, as in her Physiology class.

On Getting Old

We found that students did not hesitate to "tell it like it is." The themes running through the free form verses that follow were those commonly expressed by most students.

I don't really want—
to get old . . . but—
I hope when I do . . .
I don't look
as old as—
I am.

It really doesn't
bother me—as long as—
my mind stays straight—
and . . .
my body isn't falling apart.

Growing old is getting wrinkles and not
being able to do the things we do now—
like playing football, acrobats and swimming (not just floating around).

Makes me feel—
I have to . . . . .
. . . organize more things—
—in my schedule . . . because time—
is running out. . . . .

Major Consideration in Implementing the Project

We found that there are so many ways of bringing young and old together to share in learning from each other.

One of the main priorities, in our experience, was to locate "key persons." These were the people who were sensitive to and had some understanding of the multiplicity of problems faced by older people. These were the persons who had a keen awareness of the distorted effects of massive denial of old age. They had deep convictions that it was unfair to deprive young persons of the social, physical, and spiritual realities surrounding older people and the aging process. They were aware of the loss of roles faced by older persons. They had maintained positive relationships with their own parents and grandparents, as well as with many young people. They believed in the use of the potentialities of older persons. They believed that the experience and wisdom of older people should be shared with youth.

Summary

In view of the rapidly growing elderly population, the development of positive attitudes toward aging and older persons must be nurtured if we are to stimulate the growth of effective public and private policies toward the aged.

The present day needs of our culture call for positive engagements between young and older persons. These goals fall within the province of Catholic Charities philosophy.

The Youth-Aging Project reported upon in this paper represents the cooperative efforts of a Catholic Charities agency and Catholic educational institutions to engage the young and the old in dialogue.

The Project brought about real enrichment in learning on both sides as well as honest communication and respect for people both old and young. We noted that the students were astonished at the liveliness, intelligence, knowledge and talents of the older people. And the surprising number of common denominators shared by old and young presents us with a challenge to use divine and human values to provide depth and ultimate meaning to all of life. This challenge which lies before us was well expressed by one of the ninth-grade students, who wrote: "Growing old is a part of your life, different from the rest. Your surroundings are different, your reactions and everything you do is different. It is a new way of living. You might be more comfortable and happy, or you are likely to dislike being old. But whether or not you like it you can find ways to cope with it."

In view of our experience with the Youth-Aging Project, we believe that Catholic Charities agencies can lead the way in joining hands with Catholic School Departments in helping to support a morality which respects the dignity of older people. This dimension of the helping process begs for awakening in both the young and the old.

SUBSTITUTE ACTION FOR RHETORIC 28

by Arthur S. Flemming

During the last twenty months it has been my privilege to meet with thousands of older persons in all parts of the nation. As I have listened to their comments and their questions the following three messages have been repeated many times:

•We want to be in a position where we can make decisions relative to our lives; we don't want other persons to be making these decisions for us.

• We want to continue to be involved in life; we don't want to be put on the shelf.

•We want to be treated with dignity.

Our society has been responding to these messages in many different ways. There have been significant increases in the annual income of older persons as a result of major changes in our Social Security laws. Additional resources have been made available to support service programs for older persons—especially those programs that are designed to help the aged remain in their own homes or other places of residence. The opportunities are increasing for older persons to choose from among various types of housing accommodations. There is a growing recognition of the importance of transportation in their lives.

The conscience of the nation has been aroused to the point where some action is being taken to correct conditions in substandard nursing homes. Significant steps have been taken to deal with the issue of preventing and caring for illnesses—both mental and physical. New opportunities are being opened up for the continued involvement of older persons in life today. There is a growing recognition of the need for a ministry which will confront the spiritual concerns of older persons.

Opportunities Increase for Involvement

The forward momentum in all of these areas is attributable to increased activity on the part of government at all levels as well as on the part of individuals and organizations in the private sector.

In every one of these areas, however, both older persons and persons working with older persons can demonstrate the inadequacy of the responses that society has made the message of older persons. In some instances, they can demonstrate that those who are the beneficiaries of these reponses are still confronted with serious problems. In other instances, they can demonstrate that many older persons have not been reached by these responses.

This is due in large part of the fact that millions of our citizens do not know and understand the world of the older person. They do not know and understand this world because they avoid becoming acquainted with it.

Many older persons, for example, are lost to society—to the extent that they are unaware of the resources and services available to them. Wherever an older person is lost to society, there is a local congregation, parish or synagogue within two or three blocks, in our urban areas, and within two or three miles in our rural areas. The fact that the members of these congregations, parishes or synagogues have not "found" these older persons means that they are guilty of a sin of omission.

If, instead of passing by on the other side of the street, the members of these congregations, parishes and synagogues, decided to visit these older persons, they would begin to know and understand the world of the aging. Many of them would be moved to compassion. Then we would begin to experience the widespread change in attitudes toward the older person that we must have if the forward momentum in the field of aging is to be accelerated to the point where many of today's older persons will benefit from it.

Project FIND

We have been involved recently in a program which underlines what happens when the doors are opened to the world of the older person. Project FIND grew out of two considerations. The first consideration was that many older persons are lost to society. The second consideration was that in recent years there has been a sharp increase in benefits under the food assistance programs administered by the Department of Agriculture. In this fiscal year, for example, it is estimated that elderly participants in the Food Stamp program will receive benefits of approximately $44 million, compared with only $45 million in fiscal year 1969.

It was decided, therefore, to see what could be done to build bridges between older persons lost to society and the food assistance program. The Department of Agriculture was requested to prepare a leaflet which would describe the food assistance programs, spell out the eligibility requirements, and then indicate what steps could be taken to establish eligibility. The Social Security Administration was asked to include the leaflet with the Social Security checks that would be received by beneficiaries on August 3, 1972.

The mailing also included a prepaid postal card which persons were invited to fill out if they felt they needed some personal help in the area of food assistance programs. A similar opportunity was afforded persons who receive benefits under the Federal Retirement System. As a result of these mailings, approximately 1,400,000 older persons returned the cards.

The federal government entered into a contract with the American Red Cross under which that organization agreed to enlist the cooperation of their local chapters in recruiting and training volunteers who would personally contact every person who sent in a card. At the time this article was written, 35,000 volunteers have contacted over 1,000,000 of the persons sending in the cards. The work will continue until all have been contacted.

Needs of Elderly Emerge

It is inspiring to look at the results of Project FIND to date through the eyes of the persons associated with the American Red Cross who have been living with the project morning, noon and night over a period of six months. The following conclusions are included, among others, in the official report by the Red Cross to the federal government.

1. "An upsurge in the number of elderly found eligible for food assistance even in those areas where the more affluent were of the opinion that the elderly poor did not exist."

It is far too easy for our society to put older persons out of sight and out of mind. If we are willing to go and visit we make discoveries that cannot be made in any other manner.

2. "Many new people at the community level became aware of the needs of the

Dr. Arthur S. Flemming was Chairman of the 1971 White House Conference on Aging and is presently Chairman of the Post Conference Board of the White House Conference on Aging.

elderly. There are indications that "grass roots" actions are being planned to try and meet the needs of the elderly."

No one can become involved in programs for visiting older persons and ever be the same again. Some will confront their needs and turn aside. If they do, they will forever after live with troubled consciences. Many will confront their needs and, because of their commitment to a compassionate approach to the needs of their fellow human beings, will become involved in "grass roots' ' actions designed to meet the needs of the elderly.

3. "Perhaps the greatest indentifiable needs for the elderly are two—medical and transportation. Volunteers reported that many of the elderly who sent in cards were either not interested in food assistance or were on food assistance programs but were concerned about their medical needs. The costs of drugs were high on their list of concerns. Some persons who were contacted were helped to get information on Medicare and Medicaid."

This conclusion points up how volunteers who visit older persons move from vague rhetoric relative to the plight of the elderly in our nation to an identification of specific issues that call for constructive solutions. This particular conclusion, growing out of the experience of more than 35,000 volunteers, is consistent with the findings and recommendations of many of the 3500 delegates to the White House Conference on Aging. Strong grass roots support for the recommendations of the White House Conference in this and other areas will be forthcoming only as many other persons have experiences comparable to the experiences of the volunteers who participated in Project FIND.

4. "For many of the elderly who were phoned or visited, it was the first contact in many days with a friendly person. Word came to headquarters, "it was nice that someone cares."

Millions Confront Loneliness

This conclusion points up the fact that millions of older persons are called upon, day in and day out, to confront loneliness. Local congregations, parishes and synagogues have it within their power to deal with this issue. They can do it by identifying the lonely elderly with in their neighborhood and working out plans which will assure that regular visitations will take place. Why do so many local groups within our religious community turn aside from this opportunity for service?

In brief, many persons in our nation need to change their attitude toward older persons from indifference to concern. If they do, we will obtain vigorous grass roots support for many of the recommendations of the White House Conference on Aging. This in turn will mean an acceleration of action in the field of aging that will help older persons today—not tomorrow when for many it will be too late. This change in attitude will take place if persons who have placed at the center of their lives the commandment "Thou shall love thy neighbor as thyself" decide to dedicate a portion of their time to visiting the elderly. Then and only then will they develop an understanding of the world of the elderly which will motivate them to substitute action for rhetoric.

VI

Ministry to the Aged

The papers in the earlier sections of this book have searched our religious heritage to see what it has to offer concerning growing old, developed some of the theological meanings of aging, and made varied suggestions for church programs for old people. In other articles some social scientists have presented and critically examined widely-held myths concerning the older population, while others have analyzed social science conceptions or presented the findings of research on the religious attitudes and practices of the elderly. Having garnered all of this wisdom, thinking, and information, the important question of what the minister actually does in his or her personal ministry to the aging remains. How can ministers incarnate the essential meanings of the religious message in their daily interactions with older persons? How might concepts such as care, dignity, and the creation of meaning inform one's work with the old? The authors in this section focus their attention on these concerns and give the testimony of their own experience.

The first two articles explore the dimensions and implications of several concepts. Nouwen makes an important distinction between care and cure. The old, he argues, can teach us much about care, the participation in another's joy and pain, while the desire to cure, which too often serves our own egotistical needs, may lead us to avoid the sufferer when cure is not possible. The dimensions of dignity as a quality of life are explored by Christiansen who develops several principles which could guide action supporting the dignity of the aged even in the face of the many losses of later life.

The remaining three articles describe the conceptualization and application of particular patterns of ministry. In his theory of personality development Erik Erikson has suggested that the central task of the latter part of life is the development of integrity, of coming to terms with the value of the life one has lived. Ross describes her way of relating to older persons as "a ministry of helping form meanings out of events and experiences" through sharing and reflecting together upon daily occurrences and memories of the past. The same basic approach is used by McMahill in creating funeral services which celebrate the deceased person's life in the context of the ultimate, of a particular historical period, and of the immediate daily lives of family and friends. In the final article Novick discusses the role the specific practices of traditional Judaism can play in filling important psychological and social needs in the later years.

CARE AND THE ELDERLY 29

Rev. Henri J. J. Nouwen

Introduction

A minister is called to care, to care for his people, to care for his people in the name of the Lord. This sounds rather obvious, quite acceptable and clearly biblical. But still . . . everytime we try to give care its central place in our lives as ministers, the obvious proves less acceptable, the acceptable less biblical and the biblical less obvious than we had thought.

I am very glad for the opportunity to speak about care and the elderly because of my conviction that it is exactly in our care for the elderly that the real nature of care reveals itself to us. For, although care for the elderly is in no way different from care of children, adolescents, young adults and middle-aged people, it has the unique potential to unmask the illusion of the obvious and acceptable and to criticize our often unconscious misconceptions about ministry.

Thus, ministry to the elderly starts by allowing the elderly to minister to us and care for the elderly starts by creating in us the space where care can be recognized in its real nature. The millions of elderly, not only those whose physical and mental vitality allows them to articulate their needs, but also, and even more, those who have become silent by loneliness and isolation, carry with them a great treasure of collective wisdom, which needs to be continually discovered and held in esteem.

It is about the wisdom that I would like to speak. I will do this by asking your attention to two questions: (1) What do the elderly teach us about care? and (2) How do we offer care to the elderly? After having responded to these two questions, I hope to conclude with a remark about care and the Gospel.

I. What do the elderly teach us about care?

A. Care versus cure.

The elderly remind us, in many ways, that care is distinctly different from cure. In our contemporary society this is far from obvious and certainly not very acceptable. We live in a world in which people are more concerned with cure than with care. What we want is to bring about changes, to make a visible difference. To be a professional means to master the skills with which we can repair what is broken, put together what has fallen apart, reunite what is disjoined, restore what has decayed, and heal what is ill. In short, to be a professional is to be someone who cures. Doctors are considered to be good doctors when their patients who entered a hospital on stretchers can leave it on their own feet. Psychologists are called competent when their clients feel less confused after treatment than before. Social workers are seen as capable when their interventions make a difference for the life of the community. Also ministers are praised according to successes of their programs and projects. In all this the main question is: How much cure can we bring about? It is our accomplishments, our achievements, which count. They make us feel at home in this world and they give us a sense of being "with it."

But slowly, imperceptibly, maybe, we have made our sense of "self" dependent not on who we are, but on what we do, not on our inner strength, but on the results of our work, not on our personal integrity, but on the praise or blame of our milieu. Thus, without even realizing it, our altruistic concern to cure the ills of others has made us so much oriented toward success that we have become what others make us; in other words, we have sold our soul to the world. I am not suggesting that cure, as skillful professional work, is unimportant. I am only saying that, when the ability to bring about changes in the lives of others becomes the criterion of our sense of self and therefore of our vocation, we pervert the basis of our ministry and endanger our own spiritual health. This is the great message of the elderly, not so much by what they say as by who they are. The elderly do not offer to the professional who is primarily concerned with cure much chance of satisfaction. They confront the doctor with the limitations of his healing powers, the psychologist with the relativity of self-fulfillment, the social worker with the lasting ambiguities in human relations, and the minister with the undeniable reality of death. In short, they confront all who live with the illusion of any final cure. But it is exactly this confrontation that opens the way for a constant reawakening of our primary call which is not to cure but to care.

B. The nature of care.

What then is care? The word care finds its origin in the word "kara" which means: to lament, to mourn, to participate in suffering, to share in pain. To care is to cry out with those who are ill, confused, lonely, isolated and forgotten, and to recognize their pains in our own heart. To care is to enter into the world of those who are broken and powerless and to establish there a fellowship of the weak. To care is to embrace affectionately those who are only touched by hostile hands, to listen attentively to those whose words are only heard by greedy ears and to speak gently with those who are used to harsh orders and impatient requests. To care is to be present to those who suffer and to stay present even when nothing can be done to change their situation. To care is to be compassionate and so to form a community of people honestly facing the painful reality of our finite existence. To care is the most human of all human gestures, in which the courageous confession of our common brokenness does not lead to paralysis but to community.

The elderly with their unique place in their own and in our histories can show us the irreplaceable value of this ministry of care. Because in their midst lies hidden the great wisdom of old age.

This wisdom says not only that all human healers have to face death, the great mocker of all cures, but also that through the love of a caring friend we can come in touch with the deeper cravings of life. This wisdom makes us aware not only of the illusion of immortality, but also shows us new life whenever someone says with a word or gesture: "I see your pain, I cannot take it away, but I won't leave you alone." This wisdom not only makes us remember that there are many doctors, counselors, ministers, priests, who offered help, but also makes us grateful for those who by their kindness, personal interest and authentic concern offered care far beyond the limitations of their curing expertise. It is this great wisdom of old age, sadly enough hidden for many elderly themselves, which needs to be discovered over and over again in the midst of our blinding world so that the elderly can be our teachers, revealing to us the great human vocation of care.

When cure is not undergirded by care then doctor and patient, psychologist and client, minister and parishioner, are tempted to relate to each other as the powerful to the powerless, the knower to the ignorant, the have to the have-not. The false silence of a doctor, the pretentious distance of a psychologist, and the self-righteous snobbery of a minister often inflict pains which hurt more than heal the wounds they want to cure. Many people have returned from a clinic cured but depersonalized and not a few felt offended by the spiritual manipulations of those who preached them the good news. But when the humble confession of our basic human brokenness forms the ground from which all skillful healing comes forth, then cure can be welcomed not as a property to be claimed, but as a gift to be shared in gratitude. Thus, the great wisdom of old age is that cure without care is more harmful than helpful, but that for those who make care their primary concern, cure is no longer a property to be claimed, but a gift to be shared.

C. Resistance against care.

Are we willing and ready to hear this message of the elderly? It certainly is not an easy message. Who wants to hear that more important than to change the world is to become a real part of it? Who wants to confess that our good intentioned attempts to influence the life of others can make us violent and even destructive? And who wants to give up his or her claims on life, health, and happiness as properities to be conquered and is willing to receive them as gifts to be shared? To say it a little more traditionally: "Who wants to be converted?" And especially: "Who wants to be converted by the elderly?"

Let us at least realize that we carry in us a deep-seated resistance against care. This is not so strange. Because to cry out with those who suffer, to be present to their pains and to show compassion with their anxieties asks us to come in touch with our own sufferings, pains and anxieties. Is it not true that those who confront us with their many unanswered and unanswerable questions often raise deep apprehensions in us since they challenge us to raise the same questions in our own lives? When someone says: "I do not know if it is worth staying alive," the person may confront us with a question that we have not yet dealt with ourselves; and when someone else shows fear for death, he or she may ask us to become aware of our own hidden denial of mortality. I am not saying that we help people by confessing that we have the same problems and pains as they have. That is not caring, that simply is commiserating. But I definitely believe that we can only care to the degree that we are in touch with our own doubts and fears and can only listen to the story of others with our own story in heart and mind.

Those who ask for care invite us to listen to our own pains, to know our own wounds and face our own brokenness. And when those who ask for care are the elderly we are also invited to realize that all pains are acolytes of our unavoidable death. It is therefore not so surprising, certainly not in our pain and death-avoiding world, that we have a deep-seated resistance against care, a resistance against the recognition of our own wounds and our own need of healing. But it is exactly by breaking through this resistance that true liberation can take place, liberating the giver as well as the receiver of care. The great mystery of care is that it always involves the healing liberation, redemption and conversion, not only of the one who is cared for but also of the one who cares. When both come together in common vulnerability, then both experience a new community, both open themselves to conversion, and both experience new life as grace.

Thus, the elderly not only teach us what real care means, but they also show that care only becomes real in a mutuality in which those who care and those who are cared for are both aware of their wounds and open for the healing gifts to each other.

II. How do we offer care to the elderly?

We now can ask how concretely can we offer care to the elderly. I'd like to discuss in some detail three concrete ways of caring: Listening with care, playing with care, and working with care.

A. Listening with care.

To listen remains one of our most precious and rewarding forms of ministry. To listen is to become a student of your parishioner. Just as teachers learn their material best by preparing it for presentation to their students, so too troubled parishioners start understanding best their own story when they have to tell it to a receptive listener. If ministers were to think of themselves as eager students who want to learn the story of others, they probably would worry less about their techniques. Let us reflect for a moment on our own experience. Isn't the interested listener who really wants to know our story one of the greatest gifts of life? When we have a chance to tell our story to someone who cares, we are blessed. Because it is in the listener that we discover that we have a story to tell in the first place. When someone says: "Tell me more, I really want to know," then we begin to realize the uniqueness of our life and the "never-heard" quality of our story. Then we become aware of the connections between events and of the trends and patterns that have led us to this place and this time. Then we start to take ourselves seriously enough to believe that our story constitutes a unique part in the mosaic of human existence (a contribution to which we are responsible). In the eyes of the listening-receiver, we discover that we have a gift to be grateful for, even when that gift is a life full of distortions and conflicts.

Listening, however, is not a sympathetic nodding or a friendly repetition of hmm, hmm, hmm. No, it is a very active awareness of the coming together of two lives. When I listen, I listen not only *to* a story, but also *with* a story. It is exactly against the background of my own limited story that I discover the uniqueness of the story which I am privileged to hear. It is precisely with my own articulate awareness of the piece of living which I represent that I can be surprised, sadly or gladly, and can respond from the center of my own life. Thus, listening is a very active and extremely alert form of care. It might even be a listening with words, gestures, laughs, smiles, tears and touch. It all depends on who is telling the story and who is receiving it. The important thing is that two lives are coming together in a healing way. It is like weaving a new pattern with two different lifestories stretched out on the same loom. After a story is told and received with care, the lives of two people have become different. Two people have discovered their own unique stories and two people have become an integral part of a new fellowship.

It will be clear that careful listening to the elderly has a special quality because the elderly have such a full story to give. Careful listening to the elderly is revealing to them the uniqueness of their contribution to the experiment of living and to receive their story as a lasting gift which transcends the boundaries of birth and death. It has nothing to do with a patient hearing of the same old tales. Instead, it is a freeing of the human experience from the chains of the individual memory and a way of integrating this experience in the common human memory which remains available as a source of learning to all generations.

B. Playing with care.

To play is one of the most precious ways of being together and creating human fellowship. To play is the affirmation of the goodness of the here and now and the celebration of the moment. We play not because we want to accomplish something, but simply because we are alive. When we play we are most ourselves, because in play we realize that all we are and all we have is a free gift. When you watch children running behind a ball up and down the street, climbing in trees, jumping over fences, trying to catch each other, hiding in self-made huts and self-dug holes, clowning with Indian feathers, cowboy hats, fire helmets and Zorro suits, getting wet, dirty and bruised . . . when you watch all that, then you might suddenly sense, with a certain melancholy, that life is a playful dance in the presence of God.

It is no secret that in becoming adult we necessarily become more human. In fact, it seems that the wisdom of childhood is easily forgotten. Play is soon replaced by competition and celebration by rivalry. Even the games which often fill our weekends ask more attention for the records of a few super-athletes than for the creative interaction of many loving people.

Is it possible for the elderly to refind the wisdom of the child in a second playfulness? To care for the elderly means to play with the elderly in the hope that by playing together we will remind each other that dancing is more human than rushing, singing more human than shouting orders, poetry more human than *The Wall Street Journal*, and prayers more human than tactful conversations. To play with the elderly is to recapture the truth that what we are is more important than what we achieve. It is not a regression to a childish state, but a progression to a second innocence in which the acquired skills and insights of adulthood are fully integrated. This second innocence can lead us to the mature and critical realization that celebration is the most human response to life. This is of utmost importance in our worship. When worship is no longer play and when all gestures and words have become deadly serious, then we have made God into another demanding boss and have forgotten that he is a loving father who calls us children and not rivals, friends and not slaves.

To play with the elderly, therefore, does not require us to become part of a card or poker game—although that might be part of it—but it means to help in the development of a lifestyle in which life can be enjoyed and celebrated. This can include walks to rediscover nature, poetry to rediscover words, music to rediscover sounds, and prayer to rediscover God. It can include all that may bring us together in a common reverence for creation and open our hearts in gratitude.

C. Working with care.

The third form of care for the elderly is to assist in the development of a new sense of work. One of the great tragedies of our time is that in human creativity usefulness has been divorced from beauty. The dominant question in work has become: "How practical is it and what does it cost?" Whole cities have been built so exclusively useful that their sheer ugliness did visible harm to the physical and mental health of those who live there. The irony of usefulness, is that, when beauty is no longer part of it, it quickly becomes useless. In the days when the houses, churches and cities were built which now attract tourists from all over the world, beauty was not perceived as an added decoration of useful things, but as the quality to which all work was directed.

To work with care means to work for beauty as the context in which people can affirm each other's humanity. I am more and more convinced of the great damage which ugliness does to our inner sense of wholeness. Impersonal buildings evoke impersonal behavior, cold and gray housing complexes create cold and gray responses of those who live in them. Are we enough aware that the feelings of loneliness, isolation, rejection and despair are not only related to interpersonal situations but also to the simple absence of beauty? Many elderly starve from lack of beauty. They often live in rooms or houses so void of nature or art that there is nothing to talk with or about. You cannot talk to bare walls, but you can converse with a painting, a wallhanging, a flower, and even with a well made piece of pottery.

Our society makes the elderly think that after retirement, work is no longer important. Our society says to the elderly: "You have become useless since you can no longer perform useful work." To care for the elderly means to dispel this illusion and to work with them for beauty. Making something, not because someone needs it, nor because it can be sold, but simply because it is beautiful might, paradoxically, give birth to the most useful creations. The life and work of many artists prove the point.

A divinity school student who enjoyed "useless" needlepoint work once said: "God created the world with all the plants, trees and animals, with all the mountains, valleys, seas and rivers . . . but God did not do needlepoint work." That seems to express very well the great value of work with care. It indeed would be an invaluable service to our society when the elderly would ask new attention for the deep human desire to participate in God's creative work and would work together with those who care to make a more beautiful world.

Conclusion

We saw how the elderly teach us that care and not cure is the basis of ministry, that all changes in our concrete life situation can only be fruitful when they are gratefully received in the context of a mutual vulnerability. We also saw how listening, playing and working are three ways of careful presence to the elderly in which the basic values of life can be reclaimed and reaffirmed.

What does this mean for the Gospel of Jesus Christ? Everything, since to care is indeed to have the mind of Jesus Christ, who "did not cling to his equality with God, but emptied himself . . . and became as we are" (Philippians 2, 6-7). The great mystery of our salvation is that God came to us in Jesus Christ, not first of all to take our pains away but to share them. He did not cling to his power to cure but cared. He cried out with us by entering so deeply in our human situation that nothing human is alien to him. To care, therefore, is not only the most human of all human acts, but also divine in nature since by caring we participate intimately in God's redemptive work. When in careful listening we lift up the story of one person into the larger story of mankind, we also connect the human story with God's story. When by careful play we say that *being* is more important than *achieving*, we also reaffirm the divine revelation that we all are children of one God. And when by work with care we create beauty in which people can live joyfully, we also realize the common human vocation to give visibility to the Glory of God in the midst of our world.

Thus in caring for the elderly we are not just fulfilling one of our many human obligations, but we are witnesses to the love of God, Whose divine care became present to us in His Son Jesus Christ, our Brother and Lord.

DIGNITY IN AGING: NOTES ON GERIATRIC ETHICS[1] 30

DREW CHRISTIANSEN is a Jesuit priest and research associate at the Woodstock Theological Center at Georgetown
University, Washington, D.C. He is completing a doctoral
degree in social ethics in the Department of Religious Studies at
Yale University, where his dissertation concerns problems of
dependency in old age. He has written an extended treatment of
the ethical issues related to aging for the forthcoming *Encyclopedia of Bioethics* (Macmillan Free Press). At the Woodstock
Center, he is a member of an international Jesuit collaboration
on human rights his own work focusing on the link between
rights and basic human needs. He has worked as a student intern with the Institute of Society
Ethics and the Life Sciences, where he first began study of the moral issues related to aging.
In addition to academic study of aging, he hopes to develop a ministry for the aged in Washington. His leisure activities include vegetable gardening, hiking, reading (mostly nonfic-
tion), and conversation.

One of the extensive changes brought about by modern medicine has been
the increase in the percentage population of elderly people and their life
expectancy. Good health and longer life, however, have created a new
problem for old people and for their families: How is an old person to live
with dignity in an activist culture? Some of the tactics elderly people use to
sustain an honorable self-image, some way in which society deprives aging
people of dignity, and some suggestions for augmenting the dignity accorded old people in American society are discussed here. Together these
observations are intended to lay the foundations of an ethics of aging. Like
any ethics it suggests some rules for interacting with persons who happen
to be old. In that respect, it begins with the recognition of certain social
problems and aims at guiding behavior so as to alleviate those problems.
In short, it offers some ideals of conduct. But it also takes cues from how
people actually behave when they grow old and how others conduct
themselves toward the aged. It begins, therefore, from the existing ethos
and those styles of conduct toward old age which are found to be worthy of
praise or blame.

---

[1] This article is based on material which originally appeared in the *Hastings Center Report*
under the title "Dignity in Aging" (February 1974, Vol. 4, No. 1) and in *Soundings* under
the title "Ideal Old Age" (Spring 1974, Vol. LVII, No. 1, and is adapted here with permission.

DIGNITY: OUTSIDE AND IN

What is dignity? For the purpose of preliminary definition, I take a formulation from Erving Goffman (1967). Goffman talks about "face" as a self-image which is accepted, ignored or rejected by a social circle. In the course of maintaining face, a person attempts to make events conform to or affirm his or her self-image. Dignity is one of the functions of this process.

Dignity, according to Goffman (1967), is related to two other qualities, pride and honor. He writes:

> When a person manifests these compunctions (that events conform to his/her self-image) primarily from duty to oneself, one speaks in our society of pride; when he does so because of duty to wider social units, and receives support from these units in doing so, one speaks of honor. When these compunctions have to do with postural things, with expressive events derived from the way in which a person handles his body, his emotions and the things with which he has physical contact, one speaks of dignity, this being an aspect of expressive control that is always praised and never studied [pp. 9-10].

Goffman's definition is actually quite useful. First, it rightly focuses on the postural element, appearance and self-expression. The (Greek) linguistic root of the word dignity refers to a person's looks, that is, to how one appears. But there is none of the modern distinction between outward appearance and inner reality. The term refers equally to the appearance *one gives* and to how one looks to others. He *took* a dignified pose, we say; or, she *conducts* herself with dignity. But also, she *strikes one* as possessing dignity, or his dignity *shines through* everything he does. It is a translucent reality. It shows itself outwardly, but expresses something within. This is Goffman's (1967) second contribution. Outward poise is indicative of an inner strength. It is an "aspect of expressive control," a sovereign freedom toward the events which touch one's life.

There is a dynamic tension between the behavioral face of dignity and the personal reality. This tension has led to much conceptual confusion. In this article I am concerned with the former outward reality. I do not thereby intend to deny a substantive content to the notion of human dignity. But I do want to focus on the social matrix in which dignity is realized.

Goffman (1967) also points to the region of experience in which dignity is manifest. That is, to one's person and especially to one's body. A meeting or trial can be conducted with dignity; ceremonies of all sorts lend importance to the persons that carry them out. But for the most part, it is the rituals we enact for one another everyday at close range which help to create the sense of worth we call dignity. In greetings and invitations, through recognition and neglect, praise and blame, we contribute to each other's sense of worth. So, it is to the small and particularly the family relations of old people to which I turn attention.

From the point of view of ethics, Goffman's (1967) understanding of dignity and the person has some drawbacks. In particular, there is a problem with his paradigm of interaction, the performance. It assumes a model of the individual as an actor. Ethics and some forms of philosophical thought proceed from another paradigm: the person as agent (Arendt, 1958; Downie & Telfer, 1969; Hampshire, 1960; MacMurray, 1957, 1961; Niebuhr, 1963; Winter, 1966). It is this concept of persons which underlies the following comments.

I do not accept Goffman's (1959) understanding of the person as a repertoire of roles for an actor whose self is only a peg on which to fit a mask. Social life and moral life require that one forego the luxury of uninvolved observation for the sake of action and communion. For only in action and in the company of other persons does life acquire that intensity of meaning we call worth. Persons are agents, not performers. They *do* act, decide, suffer, and trust. So, in focusing on what follows on the outward social face of dignity, I do not deny that persons are valuable in themselves. But I do accept the phenomenological reading of Schutz (1967) that human beings find themselves paradoxically both dependent on and free toward one another. As a consequence, I take the task of ethics to be to understand and advance the free cooperation of persons in a society.

Outer recognition and inner worth are two aspects of one reality. When, however, we speak of aging with dignity, like dying with dignity, our attention is not so much on a given person's actualization of dignity, but on the conditions which either augment or diminish the capacity for living with dignity. We are talking about the habits of the moral community which affirm the worth of the person. In community terms, "the person is a way of treating others and treating oneself [Ricoeur, 1965]."

Ricoeur notes that this mutuality of opinion by which persons are regarded as persons is a fragile affair. That fragility is surpassed, he suggests, only when esteem appears in a relation of creative love. All ethics and especially geriatric ethics, which deal with persons in their weakness and vulnerability, ought to be referred to this caveat. Only love bestows the ontological security which overcomes the intrinsic instability of social relations. Thus, with respect to aging I shall be concerned with those minimal conditions which would permit a person to grow old with dignity, with that degree and type of social recognition required to provide ordinary men and women with the possibility of aging with grace.

This task of setting the outward conditions of a dignified life troubles modern society. Traditional groups were able to give their members a sense of worth through a clearly designated hierarchy of offices. One's honor came from one's station in life. With modernization, however, the concept of honor has grown obsolete (Berger, Berger, & Kellner, 1974). As a result the moral middle ground between legal coercion and a socially unsupported claim for recognition of human rights has virtually disappeared. Lacking the taste for metaphysics, we nonetheless cling to a sacred sense of the inviolability of the human person. But our culture allows us no recourse short of legislation to support that sense of common humanity. There is a paucity of ways for ratifying a person's worth aside from defiance on the one hand and statutory enactment on the other. The ethical test of our institutions, says Peter Berger (1974), is whether "they [will] succeed in embodying and stabilizing the discoveries of human dignity which are the principal achievements of modern man."

The social issue of dignified aging concerns the outer reality, the minimal conditions; its actualization is another matter. Once basic conditions are set, we cannot assure that everyone will live and age with dignity.

Following Kass (1974) we can say that the possibility of facing old age with dignity can be destroyed from without (and, of course, from within), "but the actualization of that possibility depends largely on the soul, the character, the bearing" of the aged person. Dignity, therefore, is a virtue, a distinguishing excellence of character. It is not something which can be given like an award, or suddenly withdrawn like a borrowed tool. Indeed, it becomes most apparent that dignity is a virtue when events turn against a person. Although originally created by social interaction, dignity is a personality characteristic which sustains the self even in the face of society's opposition.

There are, then, at least three distinct meanings of the term dignity. There is the normative concept by which we ground our judgments about the worth of human persons and by which we designate their sacredness. There is social behavior, on the one hand acting with dignity, and on the other fostering the capacity for dignity in others. There is also the virtue, the inner strength, the sovereign freedom toward the events that touch one's life. The three are connected, but it is the second which will concern us here.

Much of what I say about the dignity of old people can be applied to other deprived men and women in our society too. The unique problem facing the elderly, however, is that from the virile point of view of American culture, old age is a period of irretrievable loss and decline. Other disadvantaged groups (Blacks, women, young people) all have some chance to grow and prosper, to share in the American dream of power and affluence, or better, to invent a new way of life. Old people are just going to get older and die. Thus, old age confronts people with harsh existential challenges to dignity. The aging process assaults the illusion that dignity and independence are equivalent, and forces us to see that dignity is a fragile affair dependent on the support we extend toward one another.

CONDITION OF LOSS

Aging is a process of loss. The viability and adaptability of the body decrease. In addition to physical deterioration, there is also loss of responsibility and autonomy in American society (Goldfarb, 1965). There are losses, too, of old friends and cherished relationships.

One index of the social diminishment old people suffer is the kind of respect paid them in conversation. In her delightful book *Nobody Ever Died of Old Age*, Sharon Curtin (1972) reports the practice of a nurse on a ward of an old age home. This woman must have believed somehow that the patients had nothing important to say to one another, for when she was on the floor, she effectively denied them permission to speak. Whenever they spoke she would take the comment as addressed to herself.

Conversations of other adults with old people frequently take this domineering pattern. If some respect is shown an old person at the outset, younger people quickly turn to their peers for continued interchange. Others close to the old person take it upon themselves to speak for the aged, or to second their remarks as if they needed support and clarification. Young people insist on seeing a bright future. To avoid the harsh realities old people face, they turn talk to the gay and hopeful things which interest themselves.

Another manifestation of the low status of old people is the boredom their talk induces in the young. When we are bored by an expert with an established reputation, we may have twinges of self-doubt: Did I have the wrong expectations? Was I tired, preoccupied? When a speaker has social standing, we go to lengths to understand or criticize. If the speaker is in a position of power we become worried at his crass insensitivity, or outright stupidity. But when an old man or woman bores a young person with his or her talk, there is no anxiety. The younger person is simply bored. The old person is tuned out. There is no search for hidden wisdom; no self-doubt; no worry over subtle dangers of retaliation for lack of interest. At best, there is studied politeness. These implicit rules of conversation are an index of the older person's loss of power and dignity. The losses of physical decline are therefore compounded by a loss of recognition in society. Not only one's health, but one's standing in society too, declines as one grows old.

DIGNITY AND ITS DEVICES

Defiance and Self-Respect

The dignity of the aged comes largely from their own determined effort. In the face of society's indifference, they carry on in significant patterns of action. Deprived of public esteem, they lead their lives *as if* their autonomous conduct were socially significant.

One can think of dignity as self-respect. A "dignified" individual does not permit the lack of social recognition to impoverish his or her self-esteem. For a person to live or die with dignity, therefore, does not mean that he or she is rightly acknowledged by the community. The widow in *Zorba the Greek* suffers abuse from her neighbors. Finally she is murdered by them. Though she is scorned by her village, she lives and dies with dignity because she chooses the terms by which she will act.

Dignity is often identified with defiance, that is, with the maintenance of self-respect under pressure. Certainly defiance is one face of dignity. Denied access to the usual powers which bring recognition in our society, old people employ defiance as a tactic to gain confirmation of their worth from an unwilling world. I would like to share with you an incident of defiance by an old man: my own grandfather.

Grandfather Christiansen, an independent character, came to live with us when he was past seventy. Even when he moved in with us, he kept to himself in his attic apartment. One Sunday afternoon I returned home from college and stopped upstairs to chat with Grandfather. It was a warm talk and toward the end of the conversation we chatted a bit about his chronic complaints. Then he confessed he had some new troubles. He planned, he told me, to visit a doctor within the week.

In one of those unconscious conspiracies which the young and healthy make against the old and sick, I discreetly informed my parents of the old man's predicament. Half out of cautious sensitivity, half out of reluctant recognition of new realities, we talked in hushed tones about what would have to be done.

The next morning my mother received a telephone call. Grandpa was in the hospital. There was no emergency. He had simply walked the steep hill to the hospital and demanded that he be admitted. There had been no prior arrangements and no request from his physician. For his own sake, he had defied the system—and won.

Before he left the hospital, he once more boldly asserted his autonomy by signing himself into a city nursing home, before the family or medical people could gain any power over him through temporizing generosity. Grandfather represents for me the defiant dignity of the aged. By surprise, boldness, and a studied aloofness he was able to make decisions on the handling of his own decline. By making these decision for himself, even as he was failing in physical terms, he augmented his dignity. The movie *Kotch* provided a vivid portrayal of a similar character.

Interdependence

Extreme independence is one way in which dignity is maintained. It is sometimes assumed that self-assertion is the only way to be free of degrading dependence and domination by others. That can be the case only for a privileged few. There are some elderly people who live with an independent dignity because they have sufficient material resources. Others, like my grandfather, are blessed by sustained good health and the pluck to plunge on undaunted. Many more people, however, receive dignity from interdependent sharing of their lives with their families or friends.

Because the myths of individualism so dominate our society and even much sociological theory, the interdependence of old people with their natural or fictive families remains an almost invisible factor. Let me take an example first from young married life. There is an assumption on the part of most American couples that they should not expect financial assistance from their parents. The parents for their part do not feel any binding claim on them to help. Nonetheless, despite the assumption of independence on both sides, many young couples receive assistance from their parents in the form of gifts, interest-free loans, and services such as babysitting, sick care, and home repairs.

This exchange of services which both parties only partially recognize is an ingenious set of social relations. While providing for fundamental needs, both parties retain a significant margin of freedom. The exchange of support in a situation in which both parties retain their freedom is what I term interdependence. It is probably the most common way in which the dignity of old people is fostered.

Like young people starting families, pensioners and retired people receive aid from their middle-aged children. The basis of this help seems to be an exchange of services (Townsend, 1957). Insofar as the older generation can offer something in return for the help they have received, they are willing recipients. The gifts they give grandchildren, the rent they pay, the assistance they give in home repairs, the holiday festivities they provide, all establish an equality between them and the grown children on whom they rely. A symmetrical relationship exists between the donor and recipient.

When a threshold is reached beyond which the older person can no longer contribute to the exchange of goods and services, the system breaks down. The relation becomes assymetrical. The giving becomes one-sided. Under these conditions, a number of tactics are possible. Generally they are techniques of avoidance. By physical withdrawal, the old person asserts his or her independence. Withdrawal represents a bid to sustain autonomy in circumstances which would otherwise mean an undignified dependence.

As long as some semblance of equality and independence can be preserved through an exchange of services with families and fictive kin, old people have a way of living with dignity. They can accept assistance with honor, and remain independent without isolation.

Serenity

There are old people who maintain dignity in later years not so much by power, defiance, interdependence, or isolation, as by choosing for themselves some task to carry on with love and skill. Since the days of World War II victory gardens, for example, my maternal grandfather had cultivated a vegetable garden. It was one of the famous sites of the neighborhood. He could be seen working there every morning. In the warm growing months of summer, he would stop at half the kitchen doors on the block with gifts of lettuce, Swiss chard, tomatoes, and zucchini, as he went home for his midday meal. Grandpa Caccese retired at 67, and despite the pain of cancer and radiation therapy, he kept the garden until he died at 80. That last fateful spring, he cultivated, planted, weeded, and did everything leaning over a cane.

One July evening that year my father sighted Grandpa coming from the garden which was located in our backyard. He was moving slowly through the alley. He walked only a few steps at a time before stopping and propping himself against the house to support his pain. My father overheard him bidding farewell to his garden. "Goodbye Andy's backyard. Goodbye. I won't be back." He died two weeks later.

A few weeks after his death, my grandmother asked me to help her with a job. We had to go into the cellar to rack Grandpa's last batch of homemade wine to separate the wine from the dregs. Grandpa had left instructions even as to the week it had to be done. As I opened the wax seals on the bottles, I learned something else about my grandfather's great dignity. He had known in May he would be dead in August. He had insisted on it with painful certainty against my consoling objections. Ordinarily the shifting of bottles was done in late August or early September. That year he did the job in May, leaving the instructions that we should finish the correction in the fall. That kind of care and concern for a chosen task is what I call serenity. It involves no great power or wealth, it doesn't even demand superb health, but it shows a strength of spirit we call dignity. It is the kind of old age Simone de Beauvoir (1973) thinks impossible, but one that is lived by countless older people of unjaded sensitivity. They love life, and they show their love of it by careful execution of deeds they themselves have chosen.

The following similar example is from Howard Thurman's (1951) *Deep is the Hunger*:

I watched him for a long time. He was so busily engaged in his task that he did not notice my approach until he heard my voice. Then he raised himself erect with all the slow dignity of a man who had exhausted the cup of haste to the very dregs. He was an old man—as I discovered before our conversation was over, a full eighty-one years. Further talk between us revealed that he was planting a small grove of pecan trees. The little treelets were not more than two and a half or three feet in height. My curiosity was unbounded.

"Why did you not select larger trees so as to increase the possibility of your living to see them bear at least one cup of nuts?"

He fixed his eyes directly on my face, with no particular point of focus, but with a gaze that took in the totality of my features. Finally he said, "These small trees are cheaper and I have very little money."

"So you do not expect to live to see the trees reach sufficient maturity to bear fruit?"

"No, but is that important? All my life I have eaten fruit from trees that I did not plant, why should I not plant trees to bear fruit for those who may enjoy them long after I am gone?"

Importance of Recognition

Certainly old age brings a gradual diminishment of the areas over which a person exercises responsibility. But ordinarily the actual impairment of autonomy suffered by the aged is not as severe as society treats it as being. More responsibility is withdrawn from the aged than physical or intellectual decline requires. A crucial support for dignity with aging, therefore, is social recognition commensurate with the ability and powers the aging person retains.

Sharon Curtin (1972) makes this point with a cautionary tale she relates in *Nobody Ever Died of Old Age*.

It seems that Grandmother, with trembling hands, was guilty of occasionally breaking a dish. Her daughter angrily gave her a wooden bowl, and told her that she must eat out of it from now on. The young granddaughter, observing this, asked her mother why Grandmother must eat from a wooden bowl when the rest of the family was given china plates. "Because she is old!" answered her mother. The child thought for a moment and then told her mother, "You must save the wooden bowl when Grandma dies." Her mother asked why, and the child replied, "For when you are old [pp. 196-197].

Loss and Indignity

An assumption is frequently made that old people suffer indignity because of their waning resilience before the pressures of circumstance. That is not necessarily so. An ethic for aging must be based on the principle that the losses of age do not detract from a person's essential autonomy. Frailty and modest means do not entail humiliation. Even dependence is no reason for old people to bear indignity. The shame of aging comes in the uses other people make of old people's need. Dependence becomes a humiliation only when it is an occasion for a donor to exact more losses from the person in need than that person's ill health or poverty have already exacted. Indignity is the result of a loss of social recognition.

Abraham Maslow (1972) had a name for this kind of transaction. He called it a "low-synergy" situation. Loss means the loser's injuries will be compounded, and that someone else will gain. This is the humiliation of the aged: that their losses are compounded. Once defenseless, they are laid low. The first principles of an ethics of aging should be: *losses are not to be compounded (unnecessarily)*. Another formulation of this principle reads: *physical loss does not warrant inflicting social penalties on the aged.*

Submission

Another way in which the elderly, especially the elderly poor, are humiliated is that they are forced to wait in many offices and agencies. Waiting is only one form of bureaucratic submission required of the aged. They are continually asked to leave their affairs in the hands of others. The effect of submission is to reduce the agency of old people, to hand power over their lives and happiness to others.

A second principle of an ethics of aging should be: *Maximize the autonomy of older people over their own affairs.* Physical loss should be no warrant for others to make decisions for them. The conditions under which physical decline involves an irreversible transfer of power and responsibility have to be clarified and defined. Perhaps in the future some of those circumstances will be legally delimited. For the most part, however, such limitations will depend on the self-restraint and moral sensitivity of all those who deal with old people.

Health professionals and families regularly make medical and caretaking decisions for the aged infirm. Responsibility is apt to be unnecessarily denied old people. Accordingly, a third principle of geriatric ethics might read: *No one on account of age should be denied direction of those spheres of responsibility he or she chooses to assume.* This applies especially to medical care and maintenance in old age institutions.

In the area of responsibility and its diminishment, two observations may be helpful regarding the conditions under which declining strength is accompanied by a relinquishment of responsibility. First, old age is a gradual process involving a scale of loss. Old age comes by increments and families and helping professionals should respond accordingly. Since the exchange of goods and services is the principal way in which old people preserve equality with their adult children, all should be alert to those familial services the elderly still render. Tensions rise when families are conscious only of what they have already lost and of what they must now supply. The inevitability of geriatric decline creates social confusions which are costly to dignity. Unconscious rules which govern dealings with sick people get inappropriately applied to the crises of aging. As a result, even a single, early crisis can be an occasion for families to seize power and dignity from old people. There is usually no sudden need to take all responsibility from the elderly. At each point no more responsibility should be lifted from them than they themselves choose or the situation absolutely demands. At each stage a certain sphere of responsibility remains, and it should be fostered as long as possible. A margin of autonomy exists in very many, if not nearly all, the crises of aging. That liberty may only be the freedom to take an attitude toward illness, loss, and death. But adult children and health professionals should be aware that often even that elementary freedom is denied the old. At every stage, as much responsibility should be granted the old person as his or her condition permits.

Indifference

The last way in which old people are denied dignity is the general indifference of others to their interest and concerns. In many ways, this is a more difficult problem with which to deal than submission and diminishing responsibility, because it concerns countless daily encounters in informal settings. There are no crisis points to identify, no semipublic affairs to be settled at law, no transfer of funds to draw attention to the problem. Indifference is invisible and pervasive.

Overcoming indifference means reviving common interests between old and young. The crucial task facing those who seek to respect the dignity of the aged is to find something in the life experience of the aged which will create a field of interest between them and society at large. The dignity of the aged must be rooted in the condition of aging itself. The autonomy granted older people must be compatible with the loss which characterizes old age, and the respect given them must be sustained despite their diminishing powers. In the low synergy society in which we now live, this is a contradiction. It means giving power to the powerless. In a high synergy

307

society, the physical losses of old age would not entail social losses. As Abraham Maslow (1972) noted, "societies with high synergy have techniques for working off humiliation, and societies with low synergy do not." In the latter societies, he wrote, "life is humiliating. It must be." Low synergy societies, therefore, let the force of circumstances dictate the relations between people. In high synergy societies, on the other hand, the constrictions of nature are overcome by the bonds of men and women to one another. In a high synergy society, the physical losses of old age would not entail social losses. On the contrary, both old people and society would profit from the distinctive life experience of the elderly.

The Hindu Example

"As I spoke with old people," writes Sharon Curtin (1972),

> I became more and more aware of the fact that our culture does not have a concept of the whole of life. Instead life is divided into childhood, adulthood, and old age. Instead of a cycle, a vision of unity, we have a vision of stages, in which only one—adulthood—has the possibility of being lived productively, independently and vigorously [pp. 226–227].

One of the values of a dignified old age for society at large will be a renewed sense of the wholeness of human life (Buhler, 1968). This holistic appreciation of life would include the loss and diminishment which our society now excludes from its experience as well as the drive for achievement which has characterized it for so long.

In Hindu society we have an example of a culture in which the losses of old age are given special status. Older Brahmins were traditionally expected to retire from active family and social life. Their task was to attain spiritual self-realization through renunciation and contemplation. "When a householder sees his skin wrinkled and his hair gray and when he sees the son of his son, then he should resort to the forest," reads the *Manu Smitri* (du Bary, 1959). Alone or together with his wife, the Brahmin is to be a self-controlled and silent sage living on roots and fruit. He was expected to be "friendly toward all, spiritually composed, ever a liberal giver and never a receiver, and compassionate toward all beings. . . ." By becoming an ascetic, the Hindu elder appropriates the processes of loss which make up old age and spiritualizes them. His natural diminishment is freely transformed into spiritual insight. As a result the signs of old age are not marks of a slow decline but the starting point for a new life task.

If attention is to be paid, dignity and autonomy maintained, and an ideal of old age made possible in America, a basic reorientation of American culture will be necessary. Those latent aspects of life we all share and which are manifest in old age must be emphasized and developed. Particularly important is the need to develop an un-American consciousness of finitude and limitation. As we become more aware that we live on a small planet with precious few resources, we must confront the finitude of life. We become ecologically conscious. Saving, reusing, recycling, and a frugal use of energy become duties. This approach to reality is supremely appropriate to old age when human resources are declining and every scrap of power and ability must be cherished and used wisely. The old are experts in personal ecology. They have much to teach us about living with limitations and recognizing our finitude. Old people have to face up to the basic deception in the technological myth: the belief that there can be growth without limit. Just as old people are pioneers in the use of leisure, they can be pioneers too in the creative use of limits.

REFERENCES

ARENDT, H. *The human condition.* Chicago: The University of Chicago Press, 1958.

DU BARY, W. T. (Ed.) *Sources of Indian tradition.* New York, 1959.

DE BEAUVOIR, S. *The coming of age.* New York: Warner, 1973.

BERGER, P., BERGER, B., & KELLNER, H. *The homeless mind: Modernization and consciousness.* New York: Random House, 1974.

BUHLER, C., & MASSARIK, F. (Eds.) *The course of human life.* New York: Springer, 1968.

CURTIN, S. *Nobody ever died of old age.* Boston: Atlantic, 1972.

DOWNIE, R. S., & TELFER, E. *Respect for persons.* London: Allen and Unwin, 1969.

GOFFMAN, E. *The presentation of self in everyday life.* Garden City: Doubleday/ Anchor, 1959.

GOFFMAN, E. *Interaction ritual.* Garden City: Doubleday/Anchor, 1967.

GOLDFARB, A. I. The intimate relations of old people. In S. M. Farber (Ed.), *Man and Civilization: The family's search for survival,* New York: McGraw-Hill, 1965.

HAMPSHIRE, S. *Thought and action.* New York: Viking, 1967.

KASS, L. R. "Averting one's eyes, or facing the music?—On dignity in death." *The Hastings Center Studies,* 1976, 2(2), 65–80.

MACMURRAY, J. *The self as agent.* New York: Harper, 1957.

MACMURRAY, J. *Persons in relation.* New York: Harper, 1961.

MASLOW, A. *The farther reaches of human nature.* New York: Viking, 1972.

NIEBUHR, H. R. *The responsible self.* New York: Harper & Row, 1963.

RICOEUR, P. *Fallible man.* Chicago: Regnery, 1965.

SCHUTZ, A. *The phenomenology of the social world.* Evanston: Northwestern University Press, 1967.

TOWNSEND, P. *The family life of old people.* Baltimore: Penquin, 1957.

THURMAN, H. *Deep is the hunger.* New York: Harper & Row, 1951.

WINTER, G. *Elements for a social ethic: The role of social science in public policy.* New York: MacMillan, 1966.

Discovering the Spiritual Resources In Aging   31

a ministry of helping form meanings
out of events and experiences

By Patricia Ross

The spiritual resources of aging are not something we can print in a pamphlet and hand to an older person. They are instead the strengths and learnings gleaned from a lifetime of experiences. Ministry with the aging must, then, be a cooperative venture — a sharing, reflecting, building, clarifying task which has the potential of enriching both parties. In this paper I would like to share some of the insights, meanings, and belief two older women have shared with me. In addition some comments will be made about the theory behind this style of ministry and the methods which seem best suited to it.

Let me introduce the two women with whom this ministry was shared. First, Clara Parker. Last Spring at 87 years of age Mrs. Parker had plans for a very full summer — a trip with her children, plants to tend in her yard and patio picnics. Then early one morning she went to her utility room to investigate a noise, tripped and fell, breaking her hip. With determination and whispered prayers she managed to get to the telephone to summon help. Mrs. Parker has endured operations, hospital indignities, rest home frustrations now for a year. Presently she is home, and for her that's enough. She says,

> When I was in the rest home I said to the nurse 'All I want is to get home—
> I'd be willing to thumb a ride if I could just get home. And I wouldn't care
> if I ever went anyplace again.

With the help of friends and family Mrs. Parker still gets out to shop and to church, but most of her life is centered in the quiet routine of her little house. She takes comfort in the furniture and possessions which surround her there, and she takes pride in her ability to live alone. She says,

> When Mr. Parker was alive he said to me — 'Now if I die first you get yourself to a retirement home. Don't try to live alone.' Well I said to him — 'If I die first you get *yourself* to a retirement home. You can't live alone, but I can.' I eat decent. I always cook myself a good meal and I eat it on dishes. Mr. Parker told me that after his first wife died he used to cook something and eat it right out of the pan. I think that's terrible. I eat decent and I serve my food on dishes.

Eating for Mrs. Parker and many older persons is more than physical nourishment — it's a ceremony and a statement of independence. Mrs. Parker chooses her own food and serves it with dignity. Her displeasure during her stay in the rest home was most vividly expressed in complaints about food — not that it wasn't nutritious but that she had no choice in its selection, no voice in the way it was served. Mrs. Parker also indicated the importance of eating as a communal activity when she said,

> You know twice a month I go to the Senior Citizens group at the church. We all take a dish to share. We eat well at those meetings. The food tastes better when we eat together.

Eating alone and cooking for oneself lack the element of community that is so important in our culture, but Mrs. Parker and her friends have found a way to cope with this.

Mrs. Wilma Ross is twenty-three years younger than Mrs. Parker. Mrs. Ross' husband retired four years ago. They have enjoyed the added freedom of retirement and had opportunities to travel and spend extra time with grandchildren. The family — especially grandchildren — are an important source of meaning in Mrs. Ross' life. She said,

> It's nice to have someone to think about especially when you are older like I am. When I went home and Cindy grabbed me around the neck and started squeezing the breath out of me . . . It's things like that that make you feel you have a reason to go on living. That's one thing about a big bunch of grandchildren — they give a continuity to life. It's nice to know there is still somebody that thinks a little something about you. That means a lot to a person as you get older. There's so much less that you can do that it's nice to know that there's still somebody that thinks a little something about you. And you don't feel that your own children have forgotten you, but your own children are raising families . . . they are busy . . . and they can't be doing for you and being with you all the time.

Mrs. Ross is fortunate not only in having her family but also in being able to be close to them. This is not always the case in our society where "transfer" and "moving" are household words. Separation from family can make holidays especially trying to older persons. At such times solitary eating and separation from family can combine to make the day very lonely. Mrs. Parker described one solution to this problem.

> Last Easter we had dinner at the church with some of the younger ones. Some women in the church cooked a ham, and we brought salads and desserts. Then we were grandparents to some of the little children whose grandparents live a long way off.

I talked with both women about things that worry them. Mrs. Parker said:

> I'm so afraid of falling again — I just live with that fear. My son doesn't like me to be here alone. He's afraid I'll fall and no one will know. He wants me to move. I really don't want to move . . . the only place I'd really care to move to has a two year waiting list . . . And in two years I probably won't even be here. So I guess I'll just have to live day by day and hope that I don't fall.

Mrs. Ross said:

> Well, I just don't think I do too much worrying — If worrying means thinking about something and thinking something will happen to Lester. Put it this way, he's worth more to me alive than dead. And this idea of being left all alone . . . I just can't conceive of living by myself after so many years of being together . . . Women that go on living by themselves — I just marvel at them . . . I just don't think I'll be able to.

I also asked each of them about new frustrations in their lives. I said, "We all have some frustrations — do you have any new ones in your life right now?" Mrs. Ross said:

> The frustration that I have now is that my memory isn't what it used to be. I go to say something and the word is completely gone and I can't bring it to mind . . . That's the biggest frustration I have right now! And it's one I'm going to have the rest of my life. I am going to have to cope with it.

Do you feel any better able to handle frustrations now than when you were younger?

> Yes, yes. I don't shed any tears about this because this is just something that is gone and I have to accept it. Life is too short to worry about it. And I figure if people can't stand me when I can't remember they can just stay away from me.

Mrs. Parker said:

> Lately when I go to church I can't hear anything. I do wish they would turn up the speakers. Otherwise I'll just have to stay home. But my mind is still good. That's the main thing.

Assuming that a person's past experiences may hold spiritual resources for aging requires that we find ways to harvest past experiences. First of all we have to be convinced that a person's report of his own experiences has value to him and to us. Portland has a beautiful new forestry center. In it a visitor can touch and see wood from trees all over the United States. By pushing a button a tape recorded voice and moving pictures will tell how to plant trees, make plywood or paper, or how to fight a forest fire. But there is another way to experience the forestry center. Each day a retired forester is on duty. The day we visited the "Forester of the day" was a little man with fluffy white hair, a sheaf of dog-earred notes, and sparkling eyes. His tour of the center was slower paced as he added personal anecdotes to the canned information that was available on the tape recorders. Before long most of the people had drifted away from him, preferring the efficient technology to the complications of encountering a human being. But those who stayed carried away more than information — they carried with them an image of a lover of trees who had lived with them for many years and knew the trees as more than a crop to be harvested. My hunch is that the image of that man will have meaning long after the names of the trees and techniques of forestry seen in the center have been forgotten.

In addition to having the conviction that the sharing of human experiences is important for the fabric of human meaning one must cultivate skills of listening. First we must be able to suspend our own viewpoint long enought to receive the report of another. For an excellent discussion of this see the March 1971 issue of the *Register,* "Lived Moments into Meaning." In that article it is suggested further that we must learn to "receive with respect what has been going on behind their forehead as made articulate in their expression of it.[1] Sharing of this type requires further that we" . . . follow the other person through their developing transformation of concrete event into meanings. Perhaps also helping them to clarify, make more intense, say most beautifully and significantly what they want to say . . ."[2] All of this must be done without interrupting the process with reports of our own experiences or opinions. This is a time to receive. Michael Novak says it very well when he states,

> No man becomes himself in solitude. Men create one another; identity is a gift one man confers on another. One condition of becoming a person, then, is to be able to appreciate other persons. It is to be able to accept them as persons . . . It is to put others at the center of one's attention, to treat them as ends, and to marvel that they are what they are. It is to cease using people and to begin, perhaps for the first time, to notice them.[3]

Both Mrs. Parker and Mrs. Ross have faced difficulties and learned to cope — this ability to get through the tough times is one spiritual resource of older persons that is also needed by younger persons. Mrs. Parker has survived two husbands and a daughter in addition to the more recent hardship of a broken hip. I asked her what helps her get through hard times. She said,

[1] Snyder, Ross, "Lived Moments into Meaning," *Register,* March 1971. Volume LXI, Number 3, pp 18, 19.

[2] *Ibid.*

[3] Michael Novak.

Well, I cry — and if there is someone around to talk to I talk. I just get it all out. Then I pick up the pieces and go about my business day to day. When Mr. Parker died I cried for days. We had just three and one-half years—Good years. After I buried him I came home. I just got in the door and leaned back and cried. After a while I knew this had to stop so I was talking to a friend and I said, "You know I'm alright until I start to set the table or sit down to eat, but then it seems like I just start to cry again." She told me to turn on the radio at times like that. I did that for a while and it seemed to help.

I asked Mrs. Ross what helps her when there is something troubling her. She said,

Well, I talk — but I don't talk out loud — I have a conversation with God. I guess you wouldn't call it prayer —

Oh, how is it different?

Well, I imagine it's prayer, but not any formal or stylized prayer I feel. I say what I would say if I were saying it out loud to another person — it doesn't matter if I'm ironing or washing dishes, or what. Of course I don't get the answer back I would get from another person, but at times when I have gotten through I get the same feeling I would have if I had said something and talked out loud to somebody and they had reassured me. I have reassurance and a feeling that whatever has bothered me is not bothering me anymore . . . it is gone.

Praying like this really seems to help —

Oh definitely. It's not like talking to myself. I do that sometimes too — but I just go round and round. I really believe there is a power outside of me that takes hold of me. And of course I can't go to sleep without praying — even one night not too long ago I found myself praying "Now I lay me down to sleep . . ." and I thought to myself, "You're really getting old, lady, when you go back to childhood that far — but sometimes habit carries through. But that isn't my prayer anymore. Sometimes I pray for the women of the world — that carries over from my Women's Fellowship work. And I pray for my family, for people that are sick that I know, people who maybe have had a death of someone very close to them — and prayers like that. But so many times for myself it's sort of a feeling like I am having a conversation with somebody.

How did you learn to pray like that?

I just learned . . . it just came naturally. You know I was quite a kid to go to Sunday school and I wouldn't miss Sunday school ever unless I lived in a town where they didn't have a Sunday school — which happened several times when I was young. Maybe sometime or other I had a Sunday school teacher that said you didn't have to pray a stylized prayer. Maybe we could go back to my mother. When I was a youngster there was never a time passed that my mother didn't sit down on the bed beside us all and said our prayers. Of course, that prayer was just a child's prayer like all children pray—
I don't know when, but just someplace this other kind of praying started. When I got older — when I was a teenager I remember many a time when I had His help.

So you've always prayed this way —

Well no. There was a time when I couldn't pray at all. I remember this

Jehovah's Witness came to our town and he said no one should ever pray directly to God nor should we pray the Lord's Prayer. When I heard that, it was just like someone put a cold hand on my shoulder and I felt cold all over. And I started thinking the Churches are always fighting and bickering and maybe there is nothing to all of this religion. Then there was a time that if things weren't going well I would curse. And things seemed to straighten out. That really scared me. Then I told one of the minister's wives about what had happened to me and she said that if I was so weak willed I would let a silly statement like that wreck my faith I deserved to lose it. I thought that was a low blow but later as I thought about it I have come to feel she was right. I finally got over it and I feel I've struggled for it so that it means more by having done it myself.

My approach to a ministry with older persons is based on the assumption that the spiritual resources are there in the person. A person who has lived sixty, seventy, or eighty years of life with a bit of success has developed some strength, some know-how that will serve her or him in the last years of life. However, new problems arise, networks of peer relations begin to break down. There may be questions of worth with limited activity. The facing of death — one's own and that of loved ones may require renewed or added spiritual resources. Therefore, in addition to enabling a person to recognize and hold on to the spiritual resources which have arisen out of experiences all during his life it is important to encourage the person to accept his past life for what it was and of necessity had to be.

The idea of reflecting upon one's past life and coming to accept it as it was, comes from the personality theory of Erik Erikson. In this theory it is assumed that growth takes place in critical stages each having a task which the individual works at before moving on to another stage. Thus a baby must discover a sense of trust as opposed to mistrust, and a young persons establishes a sense of identity. Similarly in the later years of life a person gains a sense of integrity versus despair and disgust as he accepts his life as it was and as it had to be. None of this is done by the individual in isolation — society, history, significant persons influence the life and identity of a person, but the individual has the responsibility for his own life. There is self-confidence and satisfaction where a person has a sense of integrity. Erikson suggests that its absence results in

despair and an often unconscious fear of death: the one and only life cycle is not accepted as the ultimate of life. Despair expresses the feeling that the time is short, too short for the attempt to start another life and to try out alternate roads to integrity. Such despair is often hidden behind a show of disgust, a misanthropy or a chronic contemptuous displeasure which . . . only signify the individual's contempt of himself.[4]

4 Erickson, Erik., *Identity and the Life Cycle,* "Psychological Issues", Vol. 1, Number 1, New York: International University Press, Inc., 1959.

One of the first things Mrs. Parker shared with me when I visited was a picture album. In it she had arranged a carefully selected series of pictures. Houses in which she had lived, her family, other people she had known, vacation shots and finally a four generation picture in which she appeared with a great-granddaughter and her son. Mrs. Parker called her life story a love story and recalled a college romance that had ended but then had been rekindled forty-four years later after the death of her first husband. She remembered many things about her first marriage— her decision to go to work during the war, her children, her husband's long illness — but the real joy of her life was telling about Mr. Parker striding up to the bank of telephone directories in Chicago's Marshall Field Store, looking her number up in the Portland, Oregon directory and coming to find her.

> My marriage to Mr. Parker was nothing but a good time, she said. He told me I was his first love and he had never forgotten me.

Whereas Mrs. Parker has sorted through the experiences of a lifetime and fitted them together into a story, Mrs. Ross has a drawer full to the brim — ready to be rummaged through. As we talked, the work of selecting, sorting, discarding, and saving in a meaningful order was in progress. I asked her what she would say her greatest accomplishment had been. She said,

> You are going to laugh when you hear this — but my greatest accomplishment is my family. My four children and then on top of all that my grandchildren. There is nothing that really gets a person more than when a little grandson comes and pets you and say, "I love you." You know that's your accomplishment. And I have never done much else. I've done a lot of other things, but this is my biggest one, I think.

I asked her: From where you are now, how would you say being a woman has affected your life? She said,

> How can you know what it has done to your life? You've been a woman all your life . . . you just accept the fact that you are a woman . . . I accepted the fact that I was married. I was Mrs. Ross. I stayed home to raise the family. And on top of that, if women had just as much to do getting housework done, as I had . . . they wouldn't want more to do. I remember how just getting the laundry done — hanging it on the line — sometimes heating the water on the stove and finally folding the clean pieces fresh off the line and putting them in the basket. Women don't like to be idle. If they don't have a lot to do in their homes they are going to have to go somewhere else. And that's why women — and they should have — that's why they want equality — But for me — I knew who I was and what I was supposed to do.

I asked each woman: If you were just starting life, would you live it differently? Mrs. Ross said,

> I can't say that I would.

Could you tell me more about that?

> Well, you there's lots of times when you'll think "Oh, if I could just live

316

it over, I'd do a lot differently. And there are some things that you would like to live differently; but if I had to go back and start all over again, as I was when I first started, I imagine I would still do the same . . . the only thing, maybe I would try harder to get more education. I was a little bit lazy when I started out the time before.

Mrs. Parker said.

Oh no — I don't think I could. After all I did the best I could with what I had.

Persons who have gained a sense of integrity as opposed to despair and disgust demonstrate certain convictions and attitudes toward life. One important conviction is that individuals bear a responsibility to make something of their own lives. This conviction is held in connection with the belief that history and society play a part in the drama of our lives. History and society have an impact on our lives but they don't just sweep us along. We make choices and the choices matter. Mrs. Parker reflected this belief as she talked about her life. She said:

When the children were grown I went back to work. It was during the war when I read in the paper where it said to "Get a Job — do what you're good at." So I got a job — but then it wasn't too long until Mr. F. got sick. Well, I decided to keep my job. I hired a nurse to stay with him during the day. I took care of him at night. I'd come home from work and come into the house and it was just like being hit in the head. But at least I didn't have to be around sickness all day . . . That went on for eleven years. They were hard years but at least I didn't come out a tumbled down old woman.

In Erikson's theory one of the attributes of having accepted one's one and only life as it was is supposed to be a certain freedom from the fear of death — Life has been full and I did my part so when the time comes I'm ready. Both Mrs. Ross and Mrs. Parker expressed this kind of an attitude toward death. First Mrs. Ross:

Do you ever think about death — about your own death?

Yes, when you get to be 60 and over you begin to think about death, but I don't have any morbid thoughts about death. I sometimes wonder how it will come — but not to the point, you know, of getting all jittery and frightened inside about it. When I got to be 60, I had quite a spell of thinking about it a lot, wondering about it and sort of feeling that I would like to push it a long way off. And I would like to know how long I was going to live. But that has died down now and I don't seem to worry about it and think about it so much.

You mentioned earlier that you thought about being separated from your family —

Oh! yes . . . mostly the fact of dying is this idea of not being able to watch my family . . . see my grandchildren grow up, and see all the great grand-children that I might have. And then too there's always that feeling that I have . . . maybe everybody has it . . . I sometimes feel that I'm the only one that has the doubt . . . and I think "Is there anything more after we are gone or do we just completely stop right then . . . and then there's no more consciousness of any type . . . And sometimes I get just a little bit jittery in thinking about that.

Then I think that so many times when you go to bed at night so terribly tired, and you lie down on the bed and you are so happy to be able to go to sleep and you think, "This must be sort of what death is, only you just don't wake up." I really do wonder sometimes if this business of sleeping at night which sort of regenerates us isn't also a way of helping us to accept death — just go to sleep.

When you go to sleep, of course you wake up. But when you first go to sleep, when you are in that deep, deep sleep, it's hard to wake up from . . . well maybe that's what death is. And the point is we have to accept it . . . there's no way we can get out of it, and fighting about it, and worrying about it isn't going to stop it. You have to go about each day as it is without worrying about it. I had a friend with heart trouble. She used to say she tried to live each day without leaving any loose ends — And I guess I try to do that too.

Mrs. Parker said:

Every morning when I wake up I go out and get the paper. I read it in bed from cover to cover. I always read the obituaries — Ever so often I see someone that I know has died. I knew a great many people from my years of working at the store. Seems like I've outlived most every body. Just the other day I was so sorry to see that a woman I had known had died. And since my daughter died I've missed her so — I'm not a bit afraid to die — I'm more afraid of falling and going back to the hospital.

All of this talk of accepting past life and facing death sounds very final but it need not indicate a passive withdrawal from life — in fact, quite the opposite is frequently the case. As a person accepts this final stage of life and his own self worth he may be free to participate more fully in those activities which continue to meet his needs. For Mrs. Parker at 88 this past year has been one of letting go of some plans and accepting a quieter life, but within this context she continues to make her own plans and choices. Fortunately her children respect her desire to do this. One benefit of having accepted her life as it was is that she feels free to ask for help when she needs it. A ride to the beauty shop or the supermarket — help with lawn or housework are simple things but they can become real problems where older persons feel hesitant to ask. Feeling comfortable with one's own worth allows you to accept help while maintaining self respect.

Mrs. Ross may have 20 years to reach the stage Mrs. Parker is in — meanwhile she has plans to build a house on the basement foundation in which she and her husband have been living. She takes classes and participates in clubs and always has a sweater on her knitting needles for one of her grandchildren. But looking ahead she says,

When the house is finished they are going to find out that Mom is going to stay home a lot more . . . She's going to have something to stay home for . . . to be able to look out and see the sunshine and the people walking by.

At this point Mrs. Ross hasn't had too much need to ask for help and she hopes that time will never come,

Yes, it's important for me not to have to ask for help, I like to give help but I don't like to ask for it. And sometimes I have even felt sorry for myself because so and so didn't do something I thought they should do without my telling them to . . . I won't tell so they won't know. Maybe if I'd tell them they would really be helpful.

So a freedom to ask for and to receive help is balanced with the desire to do what you can for yourself. One spring day Mrs. Parker said,

You know I really feel thrifty today. I cleaned all my mirrors and windows — all but that one over the flower box. I'll get David to do that one when he comes to help with the yard.

The conversations with Mrs. Parker and Mrs. Ross are not finished with this writing. Mrs. Parker has accepted her life as it was and takes pride in it. She would like someone to write her "love story" — future sharing might involve collaboration with her in such a project. Mrs. Ross is about the business of accepting her past life and growing the meanings in it. Future conversations with her can continue that process and possibly strengthen her confidence in her ability to live alone and ask for help when she needs to. Such conversations take time and patience. They may seem suited to the days of leisurely pastoral calling rather than these days of super highways and three meetings a day. However, I would maintain that they have value for young and old alike. As Erikson says, "Healthy children will not fear life if their elders have enough integrity not to fear death."[5] This ministry rejects the idea that the experiences of the old have no relevance for us in changing technological times. For while the technology involved in riding a horse or changing clothes on the line has reduced importance in our times, the human value and the meaning involved in the individual's experience of such tasks — the caring, nurturing, aliveness, self-worth, industry does continue to have importance for our times. The fact is such conversations have been worked into programs of several kinds in our area. A youth group made visiting a rest home a regular part of their program for nine months. They went once a month in the late afternoon. They talked with older persons who wanted to talk and then sang songs with their guitars. Several of the young people felt this was a most meaningful part of their program. One minister in our area has older persons who meet to eat together and then spend part of the time together sharing their life stories. And finally through Portland's Northwest Pilot Project lay persons are helped to visit older persons regularly. The important thing is recognizing the value to both young and old in sharing these life experiences and life stories. Once the value is recognized the opportunities will be many.

5 Erikson, Erik, *Childhood and Society,* New York: W. W. Norton and Co., 1963. P. 269.

The Funeral Service As A Ministry Of Meanings 32

By Dave McMahill

One of the efforts rather well received around here from the McMahill co-pastorate has been the style of funeral services we have developed. It is a recurring surprise to us that this should be so, because neither of the Pastor McMahills ever had a trade course in funerals at Chicago Theological Seminary (it wasn't offered — and we wouldn't have taken it anyway).

When the first call came to lead a funeral service — about five days after starting on the job in Grand Island, our first full-time co-pastorate — my first impulse was to run out and buy the latest minister's handy guide to funeral services. Fortunately, I didn't, and was forced to reflect on what really ought to go into a funeral service.

I took the basic clue from a phrase we tossed around quite a lot in seminary days, "Ministry of Meanings." The funeral service, it seemed to me, ought to be a time of quietly celebrating some of the meanings of that person's life. It ought to be a time of making sense out of that person's life and death (as much as it is possible to make sense out of death . . .) in such a way that enables survivors to move ahead and live their own lives in spite of the pain and emptiness and regrets and loneliness that always are present. And it should in some way help people to make sense out of their own grief — not in order to deny grief, but in order to be in charge of it and not totally overcome by it.

Meanings always grow out of relationships — "there is no self in and of itself, but only self-in-world." So to celebrate some of the meanings of a person's life, it is necessary to lift up certain kinds of relationships in that person's life. I find it helpful, in fact, necessary, to set the person's life in three contexts: in the context of the "universe" (or "the ultimate"), in the context of his period of history, and in the context of his immediate, daily living.

A. *In the context of the "universe" or "the ultimate"*: no matter what actual words I use, I try to capture about each specific life some of what the Psalm writer expressed in Psalm 8. "When I look at thy heavens, the work of thy fingers, the moon and the stars which thou has established; what is man that thou art mindful of him and the son of man that thou shouldst care for him? Yet thou hast made him little less than God, and dost crown him with glory and honor." What a curious and mysterious mix each person is — so small and insignificant in the midst of the vast universe, and yet so unique and wonderful, almost as if all the forces of the whole universe somehow focus down to bring each person to life. It is important, I feel, to say in some way or another, that in the midst of the vastness of God's creating, which ha_ been going on for billions of years and still is, this one new person appeared, a new creation by God, a new miracle, unique, distinct, and ultimately valuable. Never before had there ever been such a person, and never again would there be one exactly the same.

B. *In the context of the person's period of history*: Few, if any, of the person's whose lives we have celebrated in a funeral run the risk of being mentioned by name in history books anywhere. But it is hard to find a person who did not participate in some private way in some of the great movements of history of his day. For example, a number of older persons in our church in Grand Island came to the United States in the early 1900s after living a short time in one of the several German communities in Russia. That massive migration clearly influenced the shape of American history, and significantly made its mark on local history here in central Nebraska. Or, again, many of our older men were railroad workers in the days when the railroad was perhaps the single most important communication and transportation link in our country. The private participation of these railroad workers in such a big chapter of history is an obvious and very important part of the meaning of their lives. Or, again, some persons seem to have made their place in history by standing against trends they considered to be wrong. One lady spent many years being a friend and counselor to young girls from broken and disrupted homes. She took her place in history as one who kept love and hope alive in a period when many people were experiencing the disintegration of families and a lack of love and hope.

C. *In the context of their immediate, daily lives*: What made this person memorable to those present at the funeral celebration? For one person, it was the huge garden she cultivated and harvested each year. For another, it was a courageous, life-long battle against muscular dystrophy. For another, it was her devotion to the church. For another, it was her artistry with flowers. Simply asking the family a day or two before the funeral, "How do you remember him (her), and then sharing some of those memories, has been greatly appreciated. Here is where the personal, unique life gets celebrated; here is when we can say "thanks" and know just what it is for which we are thankful. Here, too, is when I try to help make sense out of people's grief. As I finish some of what made this person's life memorable, I usually say something like, "Certainly you hurt and are sad. Certainly we all wish we could turn back the clock to a day when he was here and healthy. We hurt now because we cared so much. We grieve because his life meant so much to us. We do not lightly say good-bye to someone whom we have cherished so much. Our sorrow is not primarily a symbol to us of how awful life is, but rather how wonderful it is. For if it were not wonderful and beautiful, who would be sad at all when life on this earth is done?"

So often around the time of the funeral people are feeling terribly overwhelmed by their grief, and are feeling guilty about showing it. It appears to have been very important time and again to have made sense of the grief in this way — as opposed to denying the grief or chiding them and making them feel guilty for having grief. The theory is much the same as in a nursery school or in counseling: the more people can verbalize and clarify what is happening to them and what is going on in that vast ocean of pre-consciousness, the more they have power over their own lives. To make sense of grief does not mean that people stop crying. It means they are not defeated by it.

The three contexts in which we set a person's life are not just chosen at random. We celebrate a life in the context of the universe or ultimates because sooner or later a funeral needs to deal with the ultimate meanings and ultimate questions. Was this person's life just another stand of hay in the Cosmic Haystack with little or no ultimate meaning or value, or was this life ultimately valuable and meaningful and worthwhile? At the funeral for a person who had been hopelessly senile for fifteen years and who had no family and only a few remaining old friends, the friends were feeling very sad and dejected not so much because of her death but because of the lonely, confused way she had lived her last fifteen years. In the service I said, "Yes, she did live a long time in loneliness and died that way; nevertheless, her life in all its loneliness and confusion is still ultimately worthwhile and valuable; her life nevertheless is received by God as complete and acceptable." After the funeral, her friends reported how important it was to them to be reminded of that fact, which they knew down inside but which they had forgotten in their sorrow over the desolate life and death of their friend.

I try to set a life in the context of a person's period of history because virtually every person in some way or another lives in a stream of history. The person who traveled across the United States as a child in a covered wagon and who later as an elderly person watched Neil Armstrong on television step out on the moon, lived in an amazing flow of history and to a great extent was shaped by it. The person who worked two shifts back to back on the railroad for twenty years was related whole-heartedly to a great movement of history and received some of his meaning from it. We receive so much of who we are from the particular flow of history into which we are born and in which we participate.

The last context of every-day living is also very necessary, for not only are a person's meanings ultimate and historical, but also are private and personal — the kind of perfume she wore, the size of garden he planted, his life-long battle with accidents and illness, her stubborn dedication to her church, his habit of walking five miles a day, her enjoyment of her children and grandchildren. I once attended a funeral where this context was ignored and I felt cheated of the opportunity to remember the very specific and personal meanings of that unique life.

Although I (or Jane and I when we lead a funeral together) usually do all the speaking during a funeral (which we do because of the emotionally charged nature of it all), I do seek out input from the family, asking for their memories, and giving them the opportunity to request something special during the service, such as a favorite reading. The family also usually chooses the music, most of which I try to endure.

The order of service or "journey" is nothing out of the ordinary. Perhaps a jazz band provides great celebrative funeral music in New Orleans but not in Grand Island, Nebraska. Hopefully each step along the way contributes to the total ministry of meanings. Here are portions of one recent funeral celebration:

OPENING: For everything there is a season and a time for every matter under heaven. A time to plant and a time to pluck up what is planted. A time to weep and a time to laugh. A time to mourn and a time to dance. A time to be born and a time to die.
PRAYER: O Thou who art the very fountain of all life and the

beginning and ending of all that is, we gather here in reverent celebration of the life of M.S. How much we would like to turn back the time to a day when she was here and healthy. Yet we cannot, and we lift up to thee our grief and sorrow. How much we want to say "come back", yet in humbleness we admit before thee that none of us can escape the final limitation. Lord, receive our sorrow and may we feel thy pulsebeat of life even in our grief. Gather each one of us here that we may courageously give thanks for the beautiful and faithful life of M.S. Open us to thy grace and peace which is freely offered to each of us, that we may say YES to thy great gift of life, even in our sadness. Hold us close to thee. Amen.

A HYMN OR OTHER MUSIC

READINGS: Selections from Genesis 1.1-5, 26-28, 31; Psalm 8; selections from Psalm 23 and I Corinthians 13.

MUSIC

MEDITATION: "So faith, hope, and love abide, these three, but the greatest of these is love."

Billions and billions of years ago, long before any creatures roamed this planet, long before there even was a planet earth, a great and awesome heartbeat pulsed through the universe, and with power and care formed the massive stars and the planets, even this wondrous planet with all its life-giving resources, and in love the great and awesome Creator formed the greatest miracle of all— how or when we do not know — his miracle was a creature that stood erect, and spoke a language — a creature capable of receiving the Creator's love and passing it on. The Creator looked at what He had made and said, "That's good." And in love He continued to create, continued to surge up in new creatures, each one unique and special, each one no less a miracle than any other.

In the midst of the wild joy of God's creating throughout these billions of years, one child appeared on June 15, 1887, a new miracle, a new creation, and at the moment of her birth it was almost as if all the meaning and beauty of the universe had come to a focus. M.S. was brought into this world by her parents, Mr. and Mrs. W.S. on a farm west of Grand Island. She was born into a close knit family, and from her very beginnings the seeds of faith, hope, and love were planted in her.

She grew up with five sisters, — — — — —, and four brothers, — — — —, having also lost an infant brother.

In 1916, she began her work in the flower business, at a greenhouse in Grand Island. Incredibly, to you and I who live in a computerized, often impersonal world, one of her jobs with the greenhouse was to go out on foot all over Grand Island to collect payments, often after working late into the night to prepare an arrangement for someone's wedding or funeral. When the greenhouse closed down, she went into business for herself with her sister in their flower shop. Hard work? Yes, with hours lasting until past midnight many a day. A work of love and artistry? Yes, with elegant and careful designs done with great pride.

Far more memorable to us is her life of faith, hope, and love. Popular history of the last eighty-five years has not exactly been one marked by great devotion to church and the Christian faith. In direct contrast, M.S.'s devotions to the church and the faith stands as an inspiration to us all. About the only thing that would keep her away from worship was if she was so sick she couldn't get out of bed. An hour on Sundays was not enough for her. If there was a program on television with religious content, she watched it. If there was a special time of worship at her church, she was there. If she found a good devotional book, she read it. She lived a disciplined life of devotion and it gave her tremendous power for living.

Better than anyone else here she understood the power of hope. As a young woman when her back was broken she was told, "You'll never walk again." She ignored that prediction, and even though it came slowly, she did walk again. Over the years, time and again, her body was badly injured in accidents. By all rights, she might have given up years ago, and if she had, everyone would have understood that so many accidents are too much for a person to bear. But she came back again and again, as if to say, "In spite of this latest accident, I refuse to be a victim." Even in her last months, she closed out her life with dignity.

And the greatest was love. Yes, her heart did stop last Saturday morning, but there is a sense in which she gave her heart away. And what a miracle, the more she gave her heart away, the larger it grew!

She gave it to her mother, whom she cared for in her final years. She gave it to her sister, whom she cared for and worked with. She gave it to her brother as she kept a long vigil by his bedside as he lay dying. She gave it away to her friends in the church, supporting and helping whenever possible, in the big tasks and the small ones — making quilts, sponsoring young people who were raising money for Church World Service, taking time to be a friend to children. Remember how she said the only thing that ever made her mad was to see an older person mistreating a child. She gave money to efforts to help low-income people. She came to see you if you were in the hospital. After being moved by the need for private nursing care rooms, she and her sister arranged to donate a building for that purpose. When her church built a new sanctuary, she donated new pews. To friends who once quarreled, she encouraged them to seek peace.

Last Saturday, her life passed into eternity, like a mountain stream that finally reaches the vast ocean. She was the last member of her generation of her family, and she leaves behind her nieces and nephews and cousins, and many good friends.

Perhaps the most fitting memorial of her life would be for every child in the world to have enough to eat, for persons to be at peace with one another, for her church to grow and be faithful, for us all to be motivated by the same love that filled her life.

Now she is gone from this earth and is received by God's love in a way we simply do not understand. Even though her body could not go on anymore, it still hurts to say good-bye. Tears are appropriate now and in days to come, for we do not lightly let go of someone for whom we have cared so much. We feel sorrow not because we lack faith, but because God made us to care so much, and even our sorrow is a gift from God.

She takes her place in history now as one whose life was truly beautiful. But let us be reminded that above any accomplishments which were hers, her life finally receives its greatest worth from God Almighty, who called her into being, who sustained her, and who now receives her life as totally worthwhile, complete, and acceptable in His sight. His love gathers her up now in ways none of us knows fully.

May we, too, be opened to that vast ocean of love as we live and die.

PRAYER: O Thou who hast ever been and who shall ever be, even as all life flows from thy creative hands, even as did the life of M.S. flow from thy hands into this life, so now her life flows back into thy hands. How grateful we are for her life. How much we are inspired by all she was. We thank thee for all the great memories we hold. We thank thee for all that the Man of Nazereth meant to her and for her efforts to follow in His way. Now in this hour may her family and friends receive thy peace in a special way. Embrace them all. Comfort them, and when they need to weep, let them do so with no shame. We rejoice in the life she lived, and we are grateful that now her life is received by thee as complete and acceptable. May thy love for her and her family continue now and forever. Amen.

BENEDICTION

Often a brief graveside commital follows, which seems to be a necessary act of closure. I weave together some readings from Kahlil Gibran and from the Bible, something like this:

"If you would know the secret of death, how will you find it unless you find it in the heart of life? If you would indeed behold the spirit of death, open your heart wide unto the body of life, for life and death are one, even as the river and the sea are one. "I would call to your attention the symbols of God's gift of life that surrounds us even at this time — the flowers, the grass and trees, each other, drawn here by care. Where is death's victory? Even though we will all someday die from this life, God's gift of life has the final victory. 'I am the resurrection and the life,' said Jesus. The beauty, the meaning, the worth of God's creation cannot finally be destroyed by death. Thanks be to God!"

A prayer of commital, and time of silence, and a closing benediction finish the funeral celebration.

There are a number of trappings and a great deal of artificiality I would like to be able to change in the setting of the funeral celebration, but that's another subject. But even in the midst of a setting I would not have chosen had the choice been mine, it is still necessary to carry on a ministry of meanings, to the one now dead and to his family and friends, remembering that his meanings grew out of his special and unique mix of relationships with the universe, his period of history, and his day-to-day living.

How Traditional Judaism Helps The Aged Meet Their Psychological Needs

33

Louis J. Novick

Executive Director, Maimonides Hospital and Home for the Aged, Montreal, Canada

IT is the purpose of this paper to show that traditional Judaism is uniquely suited to meet some of the important psychological needs of the aged. By analyzing these needs and the elements of traditional Judaism, we will attempt to establish the relationship which exists between them.

Aged people in untold numbers are denied satisfaction of several extremely important psychological needs in modern industrial society. Among these needs are the following.

1. *The need to play a socially significant role and to enjoy the status associated with it.* While medical advances have resulted in a dramatically increased aged population, retirement robs old people of their role as producers of goods and services and the high status which attaches to this role. While women who are housewives do not have to face the ordeal of retirement from a job, they do have to grapple nevertheless with a significant alteration in their social role as their children mature, marry and leave the parental home. Finding significant social roles for old people to play remains a great unsolved problem of modern industrial society.

2. *The need for warm intimate relationships with others.* Industrial society is characterized by great physical mobility which is required if one is to avail himself of the best opportunities for economic advancement. People move to those areas where the most lucrative jobs are to be found.

Other factors too, create mobility. Continuous prosperity enables people to move to new neighbourhoods which confer on one a higher social status. Powerful forces operating within specific ethnic groups impel them to move into new areas. Because of the neighbourhood changes which result, the aged whose restricted economic circumstances and attachment to familiar surroundings make it difficult for them to move, become gradually aware that they are strangers in neighbourhoods which they have been inhabiting for years.

In addition, the longer one lives the more apt is one to lose relatives, friends and neighbours through death. Thus, aged people face increasing isolation as the availability of individuals who have great emotional meaning for them, continues to decrease.

3. *The need to utilize time in a socially acceptable manner.* How important a value society places on the proper use of time is reflected by the expressions, "wasting time", "spending time" and "losing time". Not to create a schedule of activities through which time is gainfully spent, is apt to fill one with a sense of anxiety and guilt. However, without adequate social roles to play and with few relatives and friends, it is difficult to create a meaningful daily schedule of activities.

Faced with a loss of significant social roles, greatly diminished social contacts and an inability to utilize time for socially constructive purposes, the aged person becomes oppressed by a sense of social isolation and uselessness. Feeling no challenge to achieve socially valuable goals, he may decide that life is no longer worth living. Why invest feeling in anything? He becomes apathetic.

It is in connection with the above mentioned needs that traditional Judaism has a great deal to offer the aged person. A prior analysis of some of the beliefs of traditional Judaism and the practices associated with them will help us understand why this is so. Let us first examine some of these beliefs.

Beliefs

1. *Beliefs pertaining to the role of God in the world.* God is the Creator of the Universe. All matter, animate and inanimate, owes its existence therefore to Him. All that man possesses, his very body and soul, he owes to God.

God, however, is not an impersonal power, disinterested in the welfare of His creatures. He is deeply concerned about what transpires in His universe. Thus He revealed himself to Abraham, Isaac and Jacob, the fathers of the Jewish people. He promised the land of Israel to their descendants. He rescued the Jewish people from Egyptian bondage. He revealed Himself to Moses on Mt. Sinai, giving to him and to the Jewish people the Torah and its "mitzvot", or commandments, which, as interpreted by the Talmud, constitute a way of life bringing great benefit to man. Because of His interest in man God both rewards and punishes him, though the processes of reward and punishment are not necessarily readily apparent. God is characterized by kindness, patience, understanding and a readiness to forgive man for his sins. He is the "braychah" or well-source of allgood which is given to man.

2. *Beliefs pertaining to the role of the Jewish people and the individual Jew.* It is the role of the Jewish people as a group, and therefore of every individual Jew, in accordance with a covenant made with God at Mt. Sinai, to live a holy life in order thus to emulate God who Himself is holy. The holiness of God is reflected, as already stated, by His characteristics which have been enumerated above. One lives a holy life therefore by imitating God with respect to these characteristics. One also hallows life by acknowledging the role of God in the world as the Creator and source of all that one possesses.

The *specific* ways through which Jews may hallow life in the manner just explained, are set down in the Torah which was revealed to Moses. These ways, called "mitzvot" or commandments, are divided into two categories (a) Mitzvot pertaining to man's relationship with God. (b) Mitzvot pertaining to man's relationship with his fellow man. Dealing properly with one's fellow man constitutes in fact, a way of serving God. One of the most important of all mitzvot is the study of Torah, which is God's word to man.

3. *Beliefs pertaining to the ancestors of the Jewish people.* Abraham, Isaac and Jacob are the fathers; and Sarah, Rebecca, Rachel and Leah are the mothers of the Jewish people. These ancestors are believed to be possessed of special merit or *z'chut,* in the eyes of God, which may be utilized to invoke God's favor on behalf of the Jewish people.

4. *Beliefs pertaining to the Land of Israel.* The Land of Israel was promised by God to Abraham, as the area which would belong to his descendants. In its earth, the fathers and mothers of the Jewish people are buried. God led the Jewish people to this land after their deliverance from bondage in Egypt. In this land, the great kings of Israel ruled, its prophets preached, and many of the great rabbis lived. The city of Jerusalem, site of the Temple, is located there. Many of the mitzvot can be performed only in the Land of Israel. It is the land to which generations of Jews, living in

the countries of the dispersion, longed passionately to return during the almost 2000 years, following the exile of the people, which came in the wake of the destruction of the Temple by Titus, Emperor of Rome in the year 70 C.E. It is the land of which the rabbis said, *Avirah d'Yisrael machkim,* i.e. "the environment of Israel induces wisdom". Israel with its significance as the land in which Judaism flowered, and with the opportunity it offers Jews, living in it as a sovereign people, to bring to highest fruition the national aim of serving God, inspires the individual to achieve greater clarity concerning the raison d'etre of the Jewish people and of one's own role as a member of that people.

Mitzvot

The beliefs just mentioned are reflected in the mitzvot which a Jew performs every day of his life. Because it is the purpose of the mitzvot to hallow life, they are related to the ordinary activities of daily living. Thus before any food is eaten, an appropriate sentence must be recited acknowledging God as the source of the food. The sentence begins always with the words, *Baruch atah.* The word *baruch* is an adjective related to the noun *braychah,* which means "a well". "You are as a well-source, oh God, our Lord King of the universe, who creates the fruit of the tree," is the acknowledgment one makes, for example, when eating all manner of fruit.

Not all food however may be eaten. The word "kosher", in Hebrew, means "suitable or appropriate for a specific purpose". Kosher food is thus food suitable, in the spiritual sense, for consumption. Meat and dairy products when mixed together are not kosher or suitable for eating. This prohibition stems from the injunction in the Torah against eating a kid cooked in the milk of its mother. It would seem that the Torah

wished to sharpen in man a sense of compassion for all living creatures thus encouraging him to imitate the Creator who is compassionate. It is sufficient for the goat that its kid has been slaughtered. Why cook its offspring in its own milk? To ensure that this prohibition would never be transgressed against in error, the rabbis forbade the consumption together of any meat and dairy products.

Certain creatures are suitable for consumption by man while others are not. The kosher animals, among mammals, are those that possess a cloven hoof and chew their cud. These are the herbivorous animals which are peaceful by nature as opposed to the carnivorous animals, not possessing the above characteristics, which must live by killing other animals. The pig, possesses behavioral traits which, in man, would be considered objectionable. It seems to be the purpose of the Torah to develop in man a respect for norms of behaviour which are peaceful and circumspect by insisting that only the flesh of animals whose behavior reflects these norms, be consumed by him.

When a person performs the biological function of elimination, he pronounces a sentence beginning with the characteristic phrase, *Baruch atah,* in which he acknowledges the fact that God is the creative source from whence man's body, so wondrously constructed, has emanated; and that were even one of the hollow parts found in the body either to burst or be clogged, it would be impossible for man to continue his physical existence. Such an acknowledgment would be best appreciated by a person who has suffered a stroke or an enlarged prostate or a gall bladder attack.

A Jew acknowledges the fact that his senses have been restored to him, when he arises in the morning, by saying an appropriate prayer. Three times each day, in the morning, towards sunset and when night has fallen, he prays to God. On his doorpost there is attached a metal or wooden box called a *mezuzah* in which is placed a piece of parchment, containing portions of the Torah [1] which state that the commandments of God shall be taught diligently to one's children and placed on the doorpost of one's home. As he leaves or enters his home, a Jew kisses the mezuzah, thus acknowledging that he fully accepts the commandments of the Torah as a guide to proper living. A Jew is not considered fully clothed unless he wears, throughout the entire day, a four cornered garment, from each corner of which are suspended fringes, called *tsitsis*. By its very oddity this garment catches one's attention. Its purposes, like the mezuzah, is to remind man of God's commandments. [2] He wears a head covering, usually a skull-cap, as a mark of respect for the omni-present Creator. In his relationships with people, the Jew is guided by commandments which direct him to be honest and compassionate. During his leisure hours, when he is not at work, a Jew will study the word of God, the Torah. Thus a Jew is literally immersed in the performance of mitzvot during all of his waking hours.

Having analyzed some of the important unmet psychological needs of the aged in modern industrial society and some of the important beliefs of Judaism; and having described briefly some of the mitzvot practiced daily which reflect these beliefs, let us now see how the mitzvot and the beliefs they reflect help the aged to meet their needs.

Role of Mitzvot and Beliefs in Status Achievement

As has already been stated, it is the group aim of the Jewish people to hallow life by following the mitzvot of the Torah. As expressed in the *Oleynu* prayer, it is also the group wish of Israel, that ultimately all mankind will accept the One God, so that the world will be perfected under His kingdom. Furthermore, to the extent that the Jewish people follows the mitzvot, it will be rewarded by God. [3]

An aged Jew who practices the mitzvot of the Torah therefore, plays an exalted role. By so doing he helps his people to achieve its aim; brings closer the possibility that mankind as a whole will emulate Israel in its worship of the One God; and adds to the merit of Israel in the eyes of God.

There can be little doubt concerning the sense of social status which the performance of mitzvot and knowledge of Torah confer on the aged person. A resident of Maimonides Hospital and Home for the Aged in Montreal, most deeply revered by both fellow residents and staff, was Mr. S., who consciously and persistently followed the mitzvah of instituting peace between residents whenever an altercation arose. He was as careful with respect to mitzvot which concerned interpersonal relationships as he was with respect to mitzvot which had nothing to do with such relationships. He was regarded as being a "complete Jew, good to God and to people."

Certain mitzvot cannot be performed unless a basic minimum number of people are present. Thus public prayer cannot take place unless ten people are in the group. Pronouncing certain prayers, in the grace which follows the eating of a meal, is not possible except in the presence of three people. Each person among the group of ten or three respectively is aware of his importance

[1] Deuteronomy 6: 4–9; 11: 13–21.
[2] Numbers 15: 37–41.

[3] Deuteronomy 11: 13–21.

to the others, since without him specific prayers could not be said at all and the opportunity for public prayer would not be available.

Similarly the pronouncing of the blessings on the occasion of being called to the Torah, requires that a congregation of Jews be present. Being thus called to the Torah constitutes a public honor which adds to the status of the individual.

A person who follows the mitzvot with devotion is rewarded with the title of *tsadik,* in the case of a man, or *tsadaykes,* in the case of a woman. Both terms represent the male and female forms of the noun, "righteous", and reflect the reverence in which the individual is held by the group. The person who possesses a good knowledge of the Torah has conconferred upon him the title of *talmud chacham* i.e. wise man. The *talmid chichim* enjoys enormous prestige in the group.

It is significant to note that the word for old man in Hebrew, *zakayn,* is synonymous with the word *chacham* i.e. wise. It was assumed by the Talmud that one who had achieved old age probably had the opportunity, through long experience, of achieving too, an understanding of the role played by God in the universe. Hence, the mitzvah of the Torah, "Thou shalt rise before old age and honor the presence of the aged",[4] is interpreted to mean that any old person, even one who does not possess a good formal knowledge of Torah, must also be respected. Thus the mere fact of having achieved old age confers great status upon the individual.

Satisfying the Need for Warm Relationships

All life is sacred to the traditional Jew. The prohibition against *tsa'ar*

ba'alay chayim i.e., "causing pain to living creatures", is a mitzvah which devolves also on non-Jews. An animal slaughtered with a knife having a nick in it, is rendered thereby unkosher or unsuitable for consumption because of the suspicion that the nick might have caused the animal undue suffering. Man, created in the image of God and possessed of an immortal soul, must certainly be treated with consideration. "And thou shalt love thy neighbour as thyself",[5] is a cardinal mitzvah in the Torah. The noun *rechem,* in Hebrew, means "womb". The verb *rachaym* is derived from the same root as *rechem.* It signifies having the same feeling for another that a mother has for the child whom she carries in her womb. Since there is no closer relationship possible than that which exists between a mother and the child she carries, the verb, *rachaym* means much more than "to sympathize". It means "to empathize", to put one's self literally into the skin of one's neighbour. Jews, in defining their attitudes towards others have referred to themselves as *rachmanim b'nay rachmanim,* i.e. people capable of empathy, descended from ancestors who were characterized by a sense of empathy for others. To feel love for and to deal kindly with one's neighbour constitutes the gateway through which God is served.

A traditional Jew therefore, relates himself to others through the values of love and consideration for people. Throughout the ages, he has encouraged the forlorn, healed and visited the sick, redeemed those who were imprisoned, clothed the naked, arranged marriages for orphaned girls, and adopted the orphaned. Towards people in general, he applied the criterion, "Let the honour of your acquaintance be as dear to you

---

[4] Leviticus 19:32.

[5] Leviticus 19:18.

332

as your own".[6] An aged Jew whose social relationships are guided by such ideals, not only feels love for others, but induces in others, by his actions, love towards himself.

The attitude of a Jew towards another Jew is determined not only by the latter's status as a human being but by his being too a member of the Jewish people whose aim it is to hallow life. Since the Jewish people, as a whole, are believed to be rewarded by God to the extent that individual Jews observe the mitzvot, each Jew is held to be a spiritual surety for his fellow Jew. *Kol Yisroel arayvim zeh ba'zeh.*[7] It becomes the duty of each Jew therefore to assume responsibility for the manner in which his fellow Jew conducts himself. Here then is the source from whence springs the deep concern Jews feel for each other. This source, reinforced by considerations of a common history and a common fate, has so influenced Jewish behaviour, that non-religious Jews too, feel a sense of deep distress whenever their brethren are mistreated. If a Jew in Russia or Aden is pinched, the pain is felt by his fellow Jews in North America. *Kol Yisroel chaverim* i.e. "All Jews are comrades."

The sense of comradeship among Jews is particularly present in groups which are engaged in performing a mitzvah, the consummation of which is conditional upon the presence of a specified minimum number of people. Aged Jews who attend synagogue services daily—morning and evening, or who sit down together to say grace after each meal, develop a tremendous feeling of comradery and togetherness.

Moreover, a traditional Jew is suffused with a sense of God's love for him and of his love for God. The Talmud states, "The Holy One, well-source of good, wanted to grace Israel. Therefore

He gave them the Torah and mitzvot in abundance".[8] The Torah and its mitzvot are the means through which the Jew is enabled to live in the most exalted manner possible. Hence he sees in every mitzvah which he is called upon to perform daily, an expression of God's love for him. The aged Jew, who performs the many mitzvot, feels himself therefore, surrounded by God's love. Were he to be the sole inhabitant of a desert island, he would not feel alone. "For my father and mother have forsaken me, but God will accept me."[9] "Can a woman forget her sucking child, or to have mercy on the child of her body? Yea should these even forget, yet I (God) would not forget you (Israel)."[10]

When Maimonides Hospital and Home for the Aged in Montreal, transferred its aged residents from its old building to a new building which had just been completed, it had been unable to arrange for affixing a mezuzah on the door of each resident's bedroom prior to the transfer. For several weeks, until the new mezuzot arrived, a great deal of unhappiness was expressed by the residents over the missing mezuzot. Something vital was missing from their lives. The very function of the mezuzah is to remind the Jew of the mitzvot, the expression of God's love for him. The absence of the mezuzot constituted a missing link in the chain binding the residents to God. When the mezuzot finally were affixed, their joy was great.

The Sabbath is a particularly important means of developing in the traditional Jew a sense of relationship with God. On the Sabbath, God terminated his creative labor. Thereafter he turned over to man, domination of the earth and all its products. It was necessary for man to realize however, that his

---

6 Pirke Avot, 2:15.
7 Sanhedrin, 27.
8 Makot, 23.
9 Psalms 27:10.
10 Isaiah 49:15.

power of domination came from the hands of God, and was to be exercised only in accordance with the laws of God as set down in the Torah. Since the exercise of this domination by man takes place through his *creative* labor, what better way is there to get him to express his willingness to subject himself to the will of God than to require that he desist from performing creative labor on the Sabbath day? By thus curbing his domination of the world about him, the Jew expresses symbolically his recognition that it is God who really dominates the world which He has created, and that the Jew recognizes and accepts this fact.

It was for the purpose of giving to the Jewish people the responsibility of testifying constantly to the role of God in the world and of living in accordance with His laws, that God delivered them from bondage in Eygpt. Therefore, the same sentence in the Torah which commands the Jewish people to observe the Sabbath, makes mention too of their deliverance from Egypt.[11]

The Sabbath, with its prohibition of creative labor; its kiddush, additional synagogue prayers, full Torah reading and Torah study, zmirot and havdalah; its emphasis on inviting guests to join in the festivities; its insistence that one clothe one's self in finery and prepare the best of food, creates in the Jew a keen sense of closeness to God and *Klal Yisroel*, the community of Israel. On the Sabbath, the Jew possesses a *n'shamah y'sayrah*, literally an enlarged soul i.e. a greater consciousness of relationship with God and with the people of Israel.

The following examples will suffice to illustrate the meaning of the Sabbath to the aged residents of Maimonides Hospital. Mrs. Z., a blind resident, following many months of living in the Hospital, was discovered, one Sabbath

day, climbing the steps to the fourth floor. Nobody had been aware of this practice on her part. Since a non-Jewish staff member operates the elevator on the Sabbath, Mrs. Z. could have avoided climbing stairs. When asked why she did not use the elevator, she answered that she simply *enjoyed* using the stairs. It gave her a *keener* sense that this was the Sabbath day. When Mrs. Z. climbed the stairs, she felt *a deep sense of God's presence and relationship with Him.*

A group of residents requested that during the summer, when because of the length of the day the supper meal is served before the Sabbath services commence at sundown on Friday evening, they be permitted to eat at the termination of the services in order that it would be possible for them to sing together the "zmirot" i.e. the special prayer songs associated with the Sabbath meals. Eating after the services and singing the zmirot would give them the opportunity to express their appreciation of the meaning of the Sabbath. It would bring them into closer relationship with God and with other Jews, celebrating the Sabbath all over the world. It would also bring them into renewed relationship with departed family members and with the countless thousands of Jews during the ages, who had celebrated the Sabbath in a similar fashion. Women who light the Sabbath candles, speak directly to God while the tears roll down their cheeks. Their relationship with Him is close and direct. First hand observation leaves no doubt concerning the closeness of this relationship.

The synagogue is another means through which a traditional Jew relates himself to God. "The synagogue is more a home to me than my own home". These were the words used by Mr. H., after he had brought a specially embroidered table cover as a gift for the synagogue table. Some residents will

---

11 Deuteronomy 5: 13–15.

sit in the synagogue alone when no services are in session. They feel a direct sense of relationship with God as they sit in the house dedicated to His worship. So keen is the sense of relationship which many Jews feel with God that they will preface any plans they may be making with the phrase, *Im Yirtseh hashem*, i.e. "If God so wills it"; or with the phrase, *B'ezras hashem*, i.e. "with the help of God."

The sense of relationship with God remains strong even among patients who have suffered severe brain damage which has rendered them confused. At Maimonides Hospital in Montreal, a brain-damaged confused patient, Mr. T., frequently quotes a sentence repeated often in the Torah, *Anee Hashem Elokaychem*, i.e. "I am the Lord your God". The central idea expressed here is the *personal interest* which God informs the Jewish people, He, as a distinct personality, has in them. The fact that Mr. T., even though in a general state of confusion, continues to refer to this sentence, would seem to indicate that he still retains an awareness of his relationship with God.

Through the mitzvot, Jews are related not only to God, to individual human beings and to the living Jewish people as a whole; they continue also to be related to those who have departed this world. For a period of almost one year following the death of a parent, sibling, or child the mitzvah is observed, through the recitation of the Kaddish prayer during each of the three daily services, of praising the name of God, who gives and takes away life, thus signifying one's acceptance of His will while concurrently honoring thereby the soul of the departed. In the *Yizkor* prayer, recited during each of the major holiday services, the souls of departed relatives and the souls of *all Jews* who died as the result of persecution, are mentioned in the deepest reverence. Indeed it is believed that the souls of the departed intercede with God in the interests of the living.

For the traditional Jew, the ancestors of the Jewish people are not merely ancient historical figures. They are believed to be involved in the everyday affairs of the people and deeply concerned about its fate. Jews believe that these ancestors intercede, on their behalf, with God. The names of Abraham, Isaac and Jacob are mentioned in all three daily services.

It is customary when mentioning the name of a departed relative to pronounce immediately thereafter, the phrase *alav hashalom*, i.e. "peace be upon him." Should the name of Moses, for example be mentioned, the phrase *alav hashalom*, is also used, as though Moses were a contemporary. Indeed the name of Moses is never mentioned without using, in conjunction with it, the appellation *rabaynu*, i.e. "our teacher". Moses, to the traditional Jew, is much more his teacher than any living person possibly could be. He is *the* teacher par excellence—the rabbi through whom the Torah was received from God.

During the holiday of Sukkot, a Jew upon entering the Sukkah invites Abraham, Isaac, Jacob, Joseph, Moses, Aaron and David to dine with him. At the Passover seder, a cup is set aside for the Prophet, Elijah. When the grave of Mother Rachel was recaptured in the six day war, Jewish newspapers throughout the world stated that Rachel no longer wept for *her sons* who now had returned to her. Jews will sing with great fervor that, "David, King of Israel *lives* and *exists!*"

The aged Jew who follows traditional Judaism enjoys a wealth of the warmest relationships with a veritable host of people no longer alive in the physical sense.

Finally the Jew feels himself related very powerfully to the Land of Israel, the "land of our fathers", the land promised by God to the Jewish people. The effect of this land on sick aged Jews depressed and burdened with many problems is remarkable. At Maimonides Hospital, a group of 160 residents successfully undertook the raising of $4,000 for the planting of trees by the Jewish National Fund. A movie about Eretz Yisroel or a speaker whose topic involves the Land of Israel, are certain to be accepted with great enthusiasm. Aged residents of Maimonides Hospital, at a meeting which took place during the first week of June, 1967, literally roared with youthful vigor that each one among them *must forget his own needs* and give money sacrificially in order that Israel be saved. Such involvement constituted the greatest form of therapy for many depressed patients who forgot their personal problems in their concern that the land and its people be saved. As news of the great victories was announced, they approached each other and members of the staff with the salutation, "Mazel Tov, Israel has been saved".

Utilizing Time in a Socially Acceptable Manner

Time is an extremely important factor in the performance of many of the mitzvot. The morning prayer, *shacharis,* which name is derived from the noun, *shachar,* i.e. "dawn", may be recited only from dawn to noon. The afternoon prayer, *minchah,* is recited usually just before sundown. The evening prayer, *maariv,* which name is derived from the noun, *erev,* i.e. "evening", may be recited only after the sun has set completely and stars are visible in the sky. The day of the traditional Jew is thus broadly organized by the regulations which determine when the different prayers may be recited. Since going to the synagogue to recite these prayers provides him with opportunities for conversation with friends and participation in Torah study sessions, particularly between the *minchah* and *maariv* services, he is engaged, during the significant portion of the day spent at the synagogue, in meaningful highly important activities which bring him into close relationship with God and people.

Breakfast may be eaten only after the morning service terminates. Between then and the *minchah* service, a traditional Jew may study Torah or take advantage of the many opportunities available to him for carrying out the mitzvah of giving help to others. This he may do through his activity as a member of a service group within the synagogue, as a member of a Zionist organization, as a volunteer in a social service agency, or by giving service to friends and acquaintances.

The regulations governing the Sabbath are particularly effective in helping the aged person organize his time. The Sabbath candles on Friday eve must be lit during a specific period, prior to sundown. One must prepare for the Sabbath by cleansing one's body properly and getting dressed in the finest clothing that one possesses. In homes for the sick aged, it is the general experience of staffs that the residents who follow traditional Judaism prefer to be bathed on Friday.

From all that has been said, it seems obvious that the mitzvot and the beliefs inherent in them constitute a powerful factor helping the aged Jew play a significant role in life, retain a sense of status, establish warm relations with God and people and organize his time properly during his years of retirement.

SOURCES AND ACKNOWLEDGMENTS *34*

The editors gratefully acknowledge the sources of the material reprinted in this reader and wish to thank the copyright holders or authors who have given permission to reprint their contributions.

1. "Judaism and Gerontology" by Benjamin Blech. Reprinted by permission of the author from *Tradition*, Summer, 1977.

2. "Respect for Age in Christianity" by Kenneth R. Knapp. Reprinted with permission from *Social Thought*, Spring, 1976, Copyright © 1976, National Conference of Catholic Charities, 1346 Connecticut Avenue, N.W., Washington, D.C.

3. "The Older Person and the Family in the Perspective of the Jewish Tradition" by Abraham J. Heschel. Reprinted from *Reports and Guidelines from the White House Conference on Aging*, 1961. Series Number: 1, U.S. Dept. of Health, Education, and Welfare.

4. "A Theology of Aging" by Seward Hiltner. Reprinted from *Organized Religion and the Older Person* by permission. Copyright © 1958, University of Florida.

5. "Religious Images of Aging" by Evelyn Eaton Whitehead from *Aging and the Elderly* by permission of Humanities Press, Inc. Copyright, © 1978, Case Western Reserve University.

6. "Aging: A Theological Perspective" by Charles E. Curran. Reprinted from *Social Thought*, Summer, 1979 by permission of the author and copyright owner.

7. "In the Aging Years: Spirit" by Ross Snyder. Reprinted by permission of the author. An earlier version appeared in *The Chicago Theological Seminary Register*, September, 1973.

8. "A Demographic Profile of the Over-65 Population" by Carol LeFevre was written especially for this reader.

9. "Exit and Existence" by Robert Kastenbaum is reprinted from *Aging, Death, and the Completion of Being*, edited by David D. Van Tassel (University of Pennsylvania Press, 1979). Reprinted by permission of the publisher.

10. "Who the Senior Citizens Really Are", a speech given by Louis Harris to the annual meeting of the National Council on Aging, October 2, 1974, is reprinted with the permission of Louis Harris and Associates, Inc.

11. "The New Ageism and the Failure Models" by R.A. Kalish. Reprinted by permission of *The Gerontologist*. Vol. 19, No. 4 (1979).

12. "Social Myth as Hypothesis: the Case of the Family Relations of Old People" by E. Shanas. Reprinted by permission of *The Gerontologist*, Vol. 19, No. 11 (1979).

13. "Sociology of Religion and the Aged: the Empirical Lacunae" by E. F. Heenan. Reprinted from *The Journal for the Scientific Study of Religion*, Vol. 2 (1972) by permission.

14. "Aging and the Ministry" by Phillip E. Hammond is the first part of an article reprinted by permission from Matilda White Riley, John W. Riley, Jr., and Marilyn E. Johnson, *Aging and Society*, Volume II: *Aging and the Professions*. The Russell Sage Foundation, 1968.

15. "The Phenomenological Approach to Images of Aging" by M. Philibert. Reprinted with permission from *Soundings*, Vol. LVII, No. 1. Copyright © 1974, The Society for Religion in Higher Education and Vanderbilt University.

16. "Parish Clergy and the Aged: Examining Stereotypes" by C. F. Longino and G.C. Kitson. Reprinted by permission of *The Journal of Gerontology*, Vol. 31, No. 3 (1976).

17. "Religion and Aging in a Longitudinal Panel" by D. Blazer and E. Palmore. Reprinted by permission of *The Gerontologist*, Vol. 16, No. 1 (1976).

18. "A Multidimensional Approach to Religiosity and Disengagement" by C. H. Mindel and C. E. Vaughan. Reprinted by permission of *The Journal of Gerontology*, Vol. 33, No. 6 (1978).

19. "Religious Motivations in Middle Age: Correlates and Implications" by V. R. Kivett. Reprinted by permission of *The Journal of Gerontology*, Vol. 34, No. 1 (1979).

20. "Life Changes and Perceptions of Life and Death Among Older Men and Women" by Pat M. Keith. Reprinted by permission of *The Journal of Gerontology*, Vol. 34, No. 6 (1979).

21. "Alienation and Age: A Context-Specific Approach" by W. C. Martin, V. L. Bengston, and A. C. Acock. Reprinted by permission of *Social Forces*, December, 1974.

22. The White House Conference Reports: *Religion and Aging*, Reports and Guidelines from the White House Conference on Aging, 1961, Series Number 7; and *Toward A National Policy on Aging*, Proceedings of the 1971 White House Conference on Aging, Volume II.

23. "Churches and Older People" by Philip E. Hammond, the second part of the article referred to above. Reprinted by permission.

24. "The Church's Continuing Role with the Aging" from *Maggie Kuhn on Aging: A Dialogue Edited by Dieter Hessel.* Copyright © 1977, The Westminster Press. Used by permission.

25. "Working at the Grassroots" by Robert McClellan. Reprinted by permission from Robert McClellan, *Claiming a Frontier: Ministry and Older People,* © 1977, The Ethel Percy Andrus Gerontology Center.

26. "The Sage Experiment" by Ken Dychtwald. Reprinted by permission from the Spring, 1978, issue of *The Journal of Humanistic Psychology.*

27. "Old and Young Can Learn Together" by Marie Malveaux and Eleanor Guilford. Reprinted with permission from the *Catholic Charities Review,* February, 1974, by permission of the National Conference of Catholic Charities, Washington, D.C.

28. "Substitute Action for Rhetoric" by Arthur S. Flemming. Reprinted by permission from the February, 1973, issue of *engage/social action.*

29. "Care and the Elderly" by Henri J. J. Nouwen. Reprinted from a speech given to the Ministers and Missionaries Benefit Board of the American Baptist Churches in 1975 by permission of the author.

30. "Dignity in Aging" by Drew Christiansen. Reprinted by permission from the Spring, 1978, issue of *The Journal of Humanistic Psychology.*

31. "Discovering the Spiritual Resources in Aging" by Patricia Ross. Reprinted by permission from *The Chicago Theological Seminary Register,* September, 1973.

32. "The Funeral as an Occasion of Interpretation" by David McMahill. Reprinted by permission from *The Chicago Theological Seminary Register,* September, 1973.

33. "How Traditional Judaism Helps the Aged Meet Their Psychological Needs" by L. J. Novick. Reprinted by permission from the *Journal of Jewish Communal Service,* Spring, 1972.